MODERN PLAYHOUSES

Modern Playhouses

An Architectural History of Britain's New Theatres, 1945–1985

ALISTAIR FAIR

OXFORD
UNIVERSITY PRESS

OXFORD
UNIVERSITY PRESS

Great Clarendon Street, Oxford, OX2 6DP,
United Kingdom

Oxford University Press is a department of the University of Oxford.
It furthers the University's objective of excellence in research, scholarship,
and education by publishing worldwide. Oxford is a registered trade mark of
Oxford University Press in the UK and in certain other countries

First Edition published in 2018

Impression: 1

Published in the United States of America by Oxford University Press
198 Madison Avenue, New York, NY 10016, United States of America

British Library Cataloguing in Publication Data
Data available

Library of Congress Control Number: 2017952710

ISBN 978–0–19–880747–6

Printed and bound by
CPI Group (UK) Ltd, Croydon, CR0 4YY

Preface

Thirteen years elapsed between the appointment of Denys Lasdun as architect of the new National Theatre and the completion of that building. This volume draws on research which has taken as long, although my experience has, I think, been happier than was Lasdun's. My earliest work on twentieth-century British theatre architecture was carried out as a graduate student between 2004 and 2007. Theatres cropped up in subsequent research and writing, but it was only in 2013 that I had an opportunity to return seriously to the subject, when I was appointed to a Chancellor's Fellowship and then a lectureship at the University of Edinburgh. This book is the result. Whereas my doctoral dissertation looked in detail at a limited selection of theatres from the period 1926–91, including purpose-built theatres, 'found spaces', and conversions, this study is simultaneously more expansive and more focused. Discussing some seventy examples, it takes as its subject the purpose-built civic, repertory, and university theatres constructed around Britain between the 1950s and the 1980s. It argues that these theatres are not only significant works in their own right but that they also shed light on the period's architectural, urban, and social histories.

My doctoral research was funded by an Arts and Humanities Research Council studentship as part of a collaborative project, 'Designing Dynamic Environments for the Performing Arts' ('DeDEPA'). More recently, grants to cover the costs of research trips and the purchase of images for publication have been made by the Carnegie Trust for the Universities of Scotland, the Royal Society of Edinburgh, and the Society of Architectural Historians of Great Britain.

Many people have contributed their time and knowledge to help the project come to fruition. I would like to thank the staff of the many local authority and university archives around Britain on whose collections I have drawn and without which this project could not have been completed. Many took considerable time to point me to relevant materials in their care, and my research has benefited immeasurably from their assistance. I am also particularly grateful to the ever-helpful staff of the Victoria and Albert Museum's Theatre Collections. The Association of British Theatre Technicians kindly opened its records, as did the Theatres Trust, where Fran Birch, Kate Carmichael, and Stephanie Rolt have been especially helpful over the years. It was a joy to be able to visit many of the theatres, and to be given access to (and permission to quote from) their own records. Valeria Carullo at the RIBA digitized a large number of photographs with efficiency.

I am indebted to colleagues for creating a congenial environment in which to work. Alan Short supervised my doctoral research with enthusiasm. I would also like to thank the DeDEPA team and 'Sounding Panel' for their interest, especially Peter Barrett, Rachel Cooper, Anne Dye, and Sebastian Macmillan. Tim Benton and Nick Bullock examined my doctoral dissertation and were generous in their encouragement. In Edinburgh, I have benefited from the insights of my colleagues, especially Richard Anderson, Alex Bremner, Ian Campbell, Miles Glendinning, and Ola Uduku.

I have been fortunate to be able to talk to many people who have had a hand in commissioning, funding, designing, or living with post-war theatre buildings, and would like to acknowledge helpful discussions with Brian Annable, Ian and Marjorie Appleton, David Beidas, Andrzej Blonski, the late Anthony Field, Mark Foley, Tim Foster, the late Martin Froy, the late Colin George, the late Roderick Ham, Michael Heard, Michael Holden, the late John Honer, the late Paul Iles, Iain Mackintosh, Michael Mellish, James Dunbar-Nasmith, Duncan Noel-Paton, the late John Partridge, the late Jack Phipps, Barry Pritchard, Donald Roy, Ric Russell, Mhora Samuel, David Staples, Christopher Stevens, Nick Thompson, Hazel Vincent Wallace, Jennifer Wilson, and Graham Winteringham. Peter Longman deserves special thanks for lengthy conversations about 'Housing the Arts' and for reading an early (and somewhat longer) version of Chapter 2.

Many other historians of post-war architecture and post-war Britain have shared their knowledge, and I would especially like to thank Barnabas Calder, Louise Campbell, Elizabeth Darling, Geraint Franklin, Miles Glendinning, John R. Gold, Elain Harwood, Jessica Holland, Iain Jackson, Judi Loach, Peter Mandler, Christine Hui Lan Manley, Alan Powers, Andrew Saint, Otto Saumarez Smith, Mark Swenarton, Florian Urban, Diane Watters, and William Whyte. Robert Proctor kindly read several draft chapters and made many helpful suggestions for their improvement.

I am extremely grateful to Oxford University Press for publishing this volume, and would like to acknowledge the work of Stephanie Ireland, Cathryn Steele, and their colleagues in overseeing its course through the Press. Manikandan Chandrasekaran kept the production process on track, Marilyn Inglis copy-edited the text with enthusiasm, and Jane Bainbridge was an attentive proofreader. I owe a particular debt to the Press's two anonymous readers who commented in detail on a draft of the complete manuscript.

My parents, Mandy and Malcolm Fair, have always encouraged my work. Other members of my family have not only taken an interest but have often also accommodated me on my travels. I am grateful to Judith and Ian Green, Hazel and Keith Hickman, Bernadette and Phil Catchpole, and Kathryn Gilmour and the late Alice Long. Ian and Mary Fair provided regular light relief with news of the antics of my nephews, John and Caleb. My grandmother was always keen to hear how the project was going and kept me well supplied with newspaper clippings, but sadly did not live to see the book in print. I hope that she would have enjoyed it. Last but not least, Anthony Catchpole has lived with this project for as long as I have. I am grateful to him for always being there.

Contents

List of Illustrations

List of Abbreviations

ABTT	Association of British Theatre Technicians
AITT	Association Internationale des Techniciens de Théâtre
AJ	*Architects' Journal*
BedA	Bedfordshire Archives, Bedford
BA&LS	Bromley Archives and Local Studies, Bromley
BLTA	British Library Theatre Archive [online]
BoA	Bolton Archives, Bolton Central Library, Bolton
Bodleian	Bodleian Library, Oxford
BRO	Berkshire Record Office, Reading
CAT	Cambridge Arts Theatre Archives, Cambridge
CEMA	Council for the Encouragement of Music and the Arts
CHC	Coventry History Centre, Coventry
CIAM	Congrès Internationaux d'Architecture Moderne
COID	Council of Industrial Design
CORT	Council of Repertory (later Regional) Theatres
CTA	Crucible Theatre Archive, Sheffield
CUA	Cardiff University Archives and Special Collections, Cardiff
DA	Dundee City Archives, Dundee
DES	Department of Education and Science
DLSL	Derbyshire Local Studies Library, Matlock
DRO	Derbyshire Record Office, Matlock
ERDF	European Regional Development Fund
ERO	Essex Record Office, Chelmsford
ESRO	East Sussex Record Office, The Keep, Brighton
FRO	Flintshire Record Office, Hawarden
GA	Glasgow Archives, Mitchell Library, Glasgow
GLC	Greater London Council
GLL	Guildhall Library, London
GSMD	Guildhall School of Music and Drama, London
HA	Highland Archives, Inverness
HES	Historic Environment Scotland Archive, Edinburgh
HHC	Hull History Centre, Hull
HKPA	Howell Killick Partidge and Amis
HTA	Housing the Arts
JRL	John Rylands Library, Manchester
LA	Leicester Archives, Leicester
LCC	London County Council
LoB	Library of Birmingham
MoC	Museum of Croydon, Croydon
MRC	Modern Records Centre, University of Warwick
NA	Nottinghamshire Archives, Nottingham
NRS	National Records of Scotland, Edinburgh
NUU	New University of Ulster
QTA	Questors Theatre Archive, Ealing, London

PFT	Pitlochry Festival Theatre Archive, Pitlochry
PRONI	Public Record Office of Northern Ireland, Belfast
RAKP	Rowand Anderson, Kininmonth and Paul
RCL	Reading Central Library, Local Studies Collection, Reading
RCS	Royal Conservatoire of Scotland Archive, Glasgow
RDC	Rambert Dance Company Archive, Waterloo, London
RHW	Renton Howard Wood
RIBA	Royal Institute of British Architects, London
RMJM	Robert Matthew, Johnson-Marshall
RSA	Richard Southern Archive, University of Bristol Theatre Collections
RSC	Royal Shakespeare Company
SBTA	Shakespeare's Birthplace Trust Archive, Stratford-upon-Avon
SCA	Sheffield City Archives, Sheffield
SHC	Surrey History Centre, Woking
SLSL	Sheffield Local Studies Library, Sheffield
SRO	Suffolk Record Office, Ipswich
STA	Scottish Theatre Archive, University of Glasgow Library
TA	Teesside Archives, Middlesbrough
TNA	The National Archives, Kew, London
TTT	The Theatres Trust, London
UGC	University Grants Committee
UoB	University of Bristol Theatre Collections, Bristol
UoDun	University of Dundee, Archive Services
UoEd	University of Edinburgh Library, Centre for Research Collections, Edinburgh
UoEx	University of Exeter Special Collections and Archives, Exeter
UoL	University of Leeds Special Collections, Brotherton Library, Leeds
UoLiv	University of Liverpool Special Collections and Archives, Liverpool
UoMan	University of Manchester Archives, Manchester
UoN	Newcastle University Archives and Special Collections, Robinson Library, Newcastle-upon-Tyne
UoSt	University of Stirling Archives and Special Collections, Stirling
UoSx	University of Sussex Archives, The Keep, Brighton
V&A	Victoria and Albert Museum, Theatre Collections Archive, London
W&SA	Wiltshire and Swindon Archives, Swindon
WSRO	West Sussex Record Office, Chichester
YSJU	York St John University, York

Write a letter to the Chairman of a theatre company:-

(i) *that will promise his company a cash grant of £100,000 in 1971/72*
(ii) *that he can show to his local authority and quote in the press*
(iii) *which will not be a commitment*
(iv) *which will not annoy the Department of Education and Science*
(v) *which will not be noticed by the auditor*

Assume that the commitment rations are committed until 1973/74.

(Question on a spoof 'Diploma in Housing the Arts Management [Intermediate Grade]' examination paper, *c.*1971, from the personal collection of Peter Longman. Edited slightly for grammatical sense.)

Introduction

'The Pattern Is Now Quite Different'

In 1971, the Arts Council of Great Britain marked the twenty-fifth anniversary of the award of its first charter. Writing in a celebratory report published the following year, its then secretary-general, Hugh Willatt, reflected on the previous quarter-century. Not surprisingly, his mood was upbeat. He described the situation in the 1930s, portraying the decade as one in which regional British theatre was increasingly run down. He then suggested that the 1950s and 1960s had witnessed a remarkable change in theatre's fortunes:

> The pattern is now quite different. The repertory theatre will have moved very much to the centre of things [. . .], rehoused in a modern building, with restaurants and bars open to the general public. Its young director will have seized the opportunities given by his building to say something to the worker in industry and to the young as well as to the middle-class and middle-aged, and not only in his performance of plays; to promote programmes and events outside the basic scheme of nightly performances; special children's performances, tours to outlying towns, jazz and poetry recitals, art exhibitions and concerts on Sunday evenings, participation in festivals, young people's clubs on Saturday mornings, visits to factories, film shows. A new purpose-designed building can be fully used during the day and not just for evening performances and rehearsals. This theatre will have been the creation of local effort and its audience will amount to 10,000 to 15,000 people for each production with several thousands more involved in fringe activities. The audience may still mainly come from those educated at grammar school and universities. For all that they will be younger and socially more widely drawn than they were a generation ago.[1]

Willatt's argument was that regional theatre had been reinvented. By extension, so had the buildings in which regional theatre was housed. The result was the modern playhouse.

Willatt could have named numerous examples from across Britain in support of his argument. The opening in March 1958 of the Belgrade Theatre, Coventry, inaugurated a wave of construction that continued until the early 1980s. The National Theatre in London was the grandest expression of this trend, but developments

[1] Arts Council of Great Britain [hereafter 'ACGB'], 'The Arts Council of Great Britain: the first twenty-five years' [report, 1972], p. 13.

outside London were just as significant, if not more so. The architectural critic Colin Amery wrote in 1972:

> New theatres have been springing up outside London like the proverbial mushrooms. But unlike mushrooms they haven't been growing silently in dark, damp corners—indeed they flourish on large sites in centres of towns and are often not single growths but 'arts complexes'. Colchester in Essex is the latest town to open a new theatre. Hot on its heels are new projects at Leicester, Derby, Manchester, Watford, Ipswich, Lincoln, Warwick, Salisbury, and elsewhere.[2]

Although the number of new theatres in Britain might seem to have lagged behind other nations, such as West Germany,[3] clearly something was afoot. The book *New Theatres in Britain* (1970) covered seventy-eight recent projects,[4] while in 1980, an Arts Council official reported that 'a complete list of theatres built, converted, or modernised since the war would total more than 100'.[5] As a result, the historian Dominic Shellard has concluded that 'perhaps *the* defining feature of post-war theatrical development in the regions has been the construction of new regional theatre buildings and the housing within them of new companies'.[6] *Modern Playhouses* provides the first history of these civic, repertory, and university theatres. These buildings are significant in their own right. They also shed light on the wider history of post-war British architecture, the history of modern theatre, and, indeed, the history of post-war Britain. They embodied ideas of cultured citizenship in a self-consciously modern and increasingly affluent nation. They also showed how the arts could be afforded a central place within the modern built environment, physically and conceptually.

New theatres were realized amid debates about the nature of performance. The architect Peter Moro, a key figure in the theatre-building boom, recorded in 1963:

> By all appearances the theatre is undergoing a revolution. Playwrights are exploring new subjects which are presented by producers in unusual ways; old plays are given new interpretations; actors, backed by the new techniques in lighting, use new techniques of acting.[7]

Just as significant—perhaps more so—were the organizational changes which also reshaped British theatre at this time. Before 1939, theatres had been predominantly privately funded and had operated on an essentially commercial basis. The foundation of the Arts Council, coupled with the provisions of the Local Government Act of 1948 (by means of which local authorities were permitted to subsidize the arts), thus represented a sea change. Public funds could now routinely be used to subsidize theatre—or, at least, certain kinds of theatre. In 1963, the *Architectural Review* suggested that 'it is becoming clear that a new pattern of [theatre] organization is emerging in which, outside London and the largest cities,

[2] 'Theatre at Colchester', *Architects' Journal* 156 (5 July 1972), pp. 19–34 (p. 22).

[3] Elain Harwood, 'Theatres in West Germany, 1945–70', in *Setting the Scene: Perspectives on Twentieth-century Theatre Architecture*, edited by Alistair Fair (Farnham, 2015), pp. 103–32.

[4] Frederick Bentham, *New Theatres in Britain* (London, 1970).

[5] N. V. Linklater, 'The Achievement in Drama', in *The State and the Arts*, edited by John Pick (Eastbourne, 1980), pp. 77–94 (p. 87).

[6] Dominic Shellard, *British Theatre Since the War* (New Haven/London, 2000), p. 177.

[7] Peter Moro, 'Is the Proscenium Obsolete?', *ABTT Bulletin* 2nd Year, no. 2 (June 1963), n.p.

commercial interests will have little part'.[8] What was this 'new pattern'? The director Michael Elliott recorded in 1973 that 'nearly all the new theatres [. . .] belong to a race never seen in this land until fifteen years ago—the large publicly subsidised civic theatre serving a new public with new fare'.[9] The result, he argued, was not only that 'regional civic theatre is playing a much larger part than ever before in the national scene' but also that 'the pattern of what used to be an entirely commercial theatre has dissolved into the split European tradition of the serious subsidised theatre and the boulevard commercial'.[10] The 'serious subsidised theatre' typically meant non-profit 'repertory' playhouses with a resident company of actors presenting a wide range of productions. This sort of theatre was favoured by subsidy-givers and so came to dominate the landscape of regional drama after 1950 at the expense of the hitherto-dominant commercial touring circuits and commercial repertory companies. It reflected, as the *Architectural Review* concluded in 1963, 'the idea of the theatre as a social or educational necessity, like a library', an idea that was 'relatively new in this country'.[11]

The historian Anthony Jackson has observed that 'it is a measure of just how extensive and how deep the changes were that so much was reflected so quickly in the buildings alone'.[12] Take, for example, the management of Birmingham Repertory Theatre in 1960:

> The live theatre, if it is to stay live, must in future think along entirely different lines from hitherto. Although careful to preserve the best of its unique and invaluable traditions, it must start right back from the beginning again, from the ground, and build new playhouses fitted for the needs not only of 20th century playwrights and players, but also, even more important, of 20th century playgoers.[13]

Of course, this kind of return to first principles was one of the central premises of modern architecture, and similar ideas were often aired by architects and critics. However, the new theatres really did represent something novel. In their location, in the kinds of spaces they contained, and, indeed, in their modern architecture itself, they suggested progressive intentions. The writer John Elsom noted in 1971 of Bolton's Octagon Theatre that it was 'very much a "new-style" Rep' which transcended traditional typological boundaries: 'a curious blend of youth club, arts centre and theatre, with the coffee bar crowded with teenagers and the manager sweeping the yard at the back'.[14] University theatres, too, were embedded within changing educational practices and evolving views of higher education's purpose.

[8] Peter Jay, 'Theatres: stage and auditorium', *Architectural Review* 133 (March 1963), pp. 174–85 (p. 175).

[9] Michael Elliott, 'On Not Building for Posterity', in *Making Space for Theatre: British Architecture and Theatre Since 1958*, edited by Ronnie Mulryne and Margaret Shewring (Stratford-upon-Avon, 1995), pp. 16–20 (p. 16). (Originally published in *Tabs* 31, no. 2 (June 1973), pp. 41–4.)

[10] Elliott, 'Posterity', p. 19.

[11] Jay, 'Theatres: stage and auditorium', p. 175.

[12] George Rowell and Anthony Jackson, *The Repertory Movement: A History of Regional Theatre in Britain* (Cambridge, 1984), p. 99.

[13] LoB, MS 978/1/6/1/1, 'The Birmingham Repertory Theatre: its present and future', November 1960, p. 3.

[14] John Elsom, *Theatre Outside London* (London, 1971), p. 174.

Modern Playhouses examines these developments and their architectural consequences, in a context in which architecture and planning in Britain were being transformed by the theories and practices of modernism. It explores how theatre buildings were conceived, designed, and received, and so is as much a history of the ideas that informed the design and reception of these buildings as it is an account of the buildings themselves. Nonetheless, while highlighting the modernity of these theatres' conception, planning, and design, it also suggests that continuities were important. In this respect, the argument is informed by recent histories of drama, several of which have emphasized continuities and gradual changes over such supposedly 'landmark' developments as the première of John Osborne's *Look Back in Anger* in 1956 or the abolition of theatre censorship in 1968.[15] Such interpretations reflect a broader revisionism in post-war British history that counters such ideas as the 'swinging sixties' by pointing to the extent to which, for many, cultural preferences and social behaviours were barely altered during the decade.[16] Many of the theatres discussed in this study accommodated productions that were often deliberately 'mainstream' in terms of their content and style, and which played to audiences interested in having a good night out rather than a challenging cultural experience.

The architecture of these theatres, too, can often be conceived in productively 'mainstream' terms, representing modern architecture as it was conceived, constructed, and experienced around Britain. Britain's 'modern playhouses' were embedded in the realities of practice rather than the narrow terms of avant-garde discourse. Even among the better-known of the architects discussed in the following chapters, abstract theorizing was rare. Denys Lasdun, for example, eschewed what the historian Barnabas Calder has described as 'rebarbative theory' for a more moderate approach, as is evident in a letter sent by Lasdun to Alvin Boyarsky at the Architectural Association:

> You want all the time to see architecture in terms of a neat, literary statement, and you can't. There are certain things that you've got to experience and move through; see the light shedding on the place and actually sense the volume, and that's what it's about, but I can't put that into English.[17]

Similarly, Peter Moro remembered a difficult encounter with a group of historians who 'wanted me to theorise, but I just can't because [design] came naturally'.[18] His theatres, like Lasdun's National Theatre and many of the others discussed in this volume, represent an essentially undogmatic modern architecture, a 'practical art'

[15] For example, Dominic Shellard, 'Introduction: the Arts and Humanities Research Council (AHRC) British Library Theatre Archive Project, and the Golden Generation', in *The Golden Generation: New Light on Post-war British Theatre*, edited by Dominic Shellard (London, 2008), pp. 7–18; Claire Cochrane, *Twentieth-century British Theatre: Industry, Art and Empire* (Cambridge, 2011), pp. 2–5.

[16] For example, Dominic Sandbrook, *White Heat: A History of Britain in the Swinging Sixties* (London, 2009), p. xvii.

[17] Quoted in Barnabas Calder, 'Committees and Concrete: the genesis and architecture of Denys Lasdun's National Theatre' (PhD diss., University of Cambridge, 2007), p. 130.

[18] British Library, Architects' Lives, C467/07, Peter Moro interviewed by Louise Brodie, 1996, part 14.

in which the aim (as Moro put it) was 'to breathe life into the banality of functionalism'.[19] By examining these buildings it is possible to arrive at a more rounded understanding of the period's architectural history, one which includes a range of designers rarely considered by historians. It prioritizes what Jessica Holland and Iain Jackson, with reference to the work of Jane Drew and Maxwell Fry, have dubbed a 'steady' modernism, an architecture neither wholly radical nor entirely conservative.[20] The results varied in their forms and materials, but might, for example, demonstrate the persistence of traditional architectural hierarchies, or be shaped by a visual sensibility rather than wordy theories. Such approaches were described disparagingly as 'mainstream' and 'routine' modernism by Reyner Banham in 1966, terms that reveal Banham's avant-garde preferences.[21] Other critics, too, have been less than positive. J. M. Richards in 1940 distinguished what he termed 'the real modern architecture' from stylistic 'jazz-modern', while Misha Black in 1975 bewailed the 'flood of the worst kind of bastardized modern architecture' that followed the Festival of Britain.[22] Yet it is important not to let the posturing of certain groups—not least those dedicated to 'brutalism' and verbosity—overshadow other developments. 'Steady' or 'mainstream' approaches could be entirely productive and appropriate, engaging with practical reality rather than the imagination. Of Warwick Arts Centre, Colin Amery recorded in 1974 that 'the architecture of these new buildings is not formal or dogmatic, it is workmanlike and cheerful (inside)—the fact that it hasn't created a new ethic or -ism may not be such a bad thing'.[23]

The four decades after 1945 represent a moment when public funding allowed regional civic and repertory theatre to assume real prominence in Britain. Whereas many studies of post-war British architecture end in the mid-1970s, amid energy crises, recession, and the critical terms in which modernism was increasingly received, this volume continues into the 1980s. Although by 1976 it was apparent to some contemporaries that the building boom was ending,[24] new theatres continued to be conceived, designed, and built, notwithstanding diminished levels of public expenditure. In this respect, this work echoes a recent positive 'turn' in the historiography of the 1970s, in which several historians have turned away from the idea of a decade of 'crisis' by presenting alternative, more positive narratives.[25] Only in the 1980s—a period whose histories are only now beginning to be studied seriously—did the pace of major theatre construction really slow. The Arts

[19] RIBA, MoP/11, 'Architecture—the practical art', typescript by Moro, 1984; MoP/12, untitled typescript by Moro, 1992.

[20] Iain Jackson and Jessica Holland, *The Architecture of Edwin Maxwell Fry and Jane Drew* (Farnham, 2014), pp. 7–8.

[21] Reyner Banham, *The New Brutalism: Ethic or Aesthetic?* (London, 1966), p. 41.

[22] J. M. Richards, *An Introduction to Modern Architecture* (Harmondsworth, 1940), p. 11; Bevis Hillier, 'Introduction', in *A Tonic to the Nation: The Festival of Britain, 1951*, edited by Mary Banham and Bevis Hillier (London, 1976), pp. 10–19 (p. 12).

[23] 'An Uncertain Ethic', *Architectural Review* 157 (May 1975), pp. 267–8 (p. 268).

[24] 'Exchange Experience', *Architectural Review* 160 (December 1976), pp. 361–2.

[25] For example, Lawrence Black and Hugh Pemberton, 'The Benighted Decade? Reassessing the seventies', in *Reassessing 1970s Britain*, edited by Lawrence Black, Hugh Pemberton, and Pat Thane (Manchester, 2013), pp. 1–24.

Council's 1984 report, 'The Glory of the Garden', proposed a reduction in the number of organizations receiving subsidy,[26] while its 'Housing the Arts' fund, which had been introduced in 1965, was wound up. Nonetheless, most of the theatre-building projects that had been identified at the end of the 1950s as being desirable had been carried out.[27]

Also worth a note is the 'British' focus of the book. With transnational agendas now informing historical analysis in productive ways, it may seem retrograde to look at the architecture of a single state, albeit a state made up of several nations. Architects, consultants, actors, and directors were certainly often aware of developments abroad. However, new theatres were nonetheless created in a specifically 'British' context of funding and legislation, albeit one which played out in different ways. This study looks beyond London and, indeed, beyond England, to Scotland and Wales, and (briefly) to Northern Ireland—not a part of Great Britain *per se* but a constituent part of the United Kingdom. The Arts Council's operations in Scotland and Wales were devolved, while local government and local repertory companies had significant roles in conceiving and promoting new theatres.

Post-war theatre buildings have hitherto been discussed in detail by architectural historians only briefly.[28] In examining them, this study seeks not only to plug the gap but also to build on institutional histories of individual theatre companies, accounts of the workings of the Arts Council, discussions of the cultural politics of central and local government, and analyses of the structures and practices of regional theatre in twentieth-century Britain.[29] It also builds on histories of the

26 ACGB, 'The Glory of the Garden: the development of the arts in England. A strategy for a decade' [1984].

27 'Buildings Update Leisure 1: theatres and performance spaces', *Architects' Journal* 174 (12 August 1981), pp. 309–23 (p. 309).

28 *Making Space for Theatre: British Architecture and Theatre Since 1958*, edited by Ronnie Mulryne and Margaret Shewring (Stratford-upon-Avon, 1995); Elain Harwood, *Space, Hope and Brutalism: English Architecture 1945–1975* (New Haven/London, 2015), pp. 484–508; Marian Pringle, *The Theatres of Stratford-upon-Avon, 1875–1992: An Architectural History* (Stratford-upon-Avon, 1993); Calder, 'Committees and Concrete'; Barnabas Calder, *Raw Concrete: The Beauty of Brutalism* (London, 2016), pp. 273–329. David Wiles, *A Short History of Western Performance Space* (Cambridge, 2003) is helpful, but not focused on particular examples. There is also useful discussion in Rowell and Jackson, *Repertory Movement*. The author's books, essays, and articles are listed in the bibliography.

29 For the Arts Council: Janet Minihan, *The Nationalization of Culture: The Development of State Subsidies to the Arts in Great Britain* (London, 1977); Andrew Sinclair, *Arts and Cultures: The History of the Fifty Years of the Arts Council of Great Britain* (London, 1995); Richard Witts, *Artist Unknown: An Alternative History of the Arts Council* (London, 1998); Euan McArthur, *Scotland, CEMA and the Arts Council: Background, Politics and Visual Arts Policy* (Farnham, 2013). For discussions of cultural politics at a local level, see for example, Nick Hayes, *Consensus and Controversy: City Politics in Nottingham, 1945–1966* (Liverpool, 1996). For the national level, see, for example, Lawrence Black, *The Political Culture of the Left in Affluent Britain, 1951–64: Old Labour, New Britain?* (Basingstoke, 2003); Robert Hewison, *Culture and Consensus: England, Art and Politics since 1940* (London, 1995). Key (auto-)biographies include: Peter Hall, *Peter Hall's Diaries: The Story of a Dramatic Battle*, edited by John Goodwin (London, 1983); Patricia Hollis, *Jennie Lee: A Life* (Oxford, 1997). The structures of theatre are considered in Rowell and Jackson, *The Repertory Movement*; Elsom, *Theatre Outside London*. For studies of this period in theatre, see, for example, Shellard, *British Theatre*; *The Golden Generation*, ed. Shellard; Michael Billington, *State of the Nation: British Theatre Since 1945* (London, 2007); Richard Eyre and Nicholas Wright, *Changing Stages: A View of British Theatre in the Twentieth Century* (London, 2000).

welfare state and its architecture,[30] and, more generally, seeks to refine our understanding of modernism in post-war Britain. As a work of architectural history rooted in the archive, this work considers questions of conception, interpretation and reception,[31] examining built and unbuilt projects as well as texts and images. The analysis is informed by the idea that modernism should not be defined in narrow formal terms but rather should be understood as a diverse field of practices that responded to the condition of modernity itself.[32] In this respect, it recognizes that innovations in terms of style, form, and materials were certainly important in the design and reception of Britain's new theatres, but the discussion nonetheless looks beyond such labels as the currently fashionable 'brutalism' to propose alternative, perhaps more productive (and certainly more historically rooted) ways of considering this period's architecture, such as its social role or the extent to which it might be understood in terms of civic identity and citizenship.

The theatres discussed here represent my selection of what seem to be the key examples, chosen for various reasons including a wish to look at different sorts of building (civic, repertory, and university theatres), the involvement of prominent figures, and the survival of archival records. Although some of the theatres are better served by the archive than others, one of the significant features of a period in which the arts were part-supported by the public purse is that a history of its buildings can draw not only on the records of theatre managements, where they survive, but also the minutes and papers of the bodies that subsidized (and sometimes also planned) theatres. The involvement in theatre-building of local government and the Arts Council not only generated records that in themselves are revealing but also has contributed to the survival of this material, public bodies typically being more likely to have taken steps to preserve their history than sometimes ephemeral commercial organizations. Local record offices and university archives have proved invaluable sources of information, offering up records of council discussions, books of newspaper clippings, and, in some cases, the papers of theatre managements. Many of these collections appeared never before to have been consulted, sometimes because they had only recently been deposited or because access to them had hitherto been restricted. Some papers were carefully indexed; in other cases, it was necessary to trawl several years' (or decades') worth of minutes for relevant nuggets. Also apparently previously unconsulted were many of the papers relating to the Arts Council of Great Britain's 'Housing the Arts' fund. This archive, now at the Victoria and Albert Museum, contains a vast quantity of relevant

[30] For example, Mark Swenarton, Tom Avermaete, and Dirk van den Heuvel, 'Introduction', in *Architecture and the Welfare State*, edited by Mark Swenarton, Tom Avermaete, and Dirk van den Heuvel (Abingdon, 2014), pp. 1–23.

[31] Parallels include William Whyte, *Redbrick: A Social and Architectural History of Britain's Civic Universities* (Oxford, 2015); Miles Glendinning and Stefan Muthesius, *Tower Block: Modern Public Housing in England, Scotland, Wales and Northern Ireland* (New Haven/London, 1994); Robert Proctor, *Building the Modern Church: Roman Catholic Church Architecture in Britain, 1955 to 1975* (Farnham, 2014); Andrew Saint, *Towards a Social Architecture: The Role of School-building in Post-war England* (New Haven/London, 1987).

[32] Sarah Williams Goldhagen, 'Something to Talk About: modernism, discourse, style', *Journal of the Society of Architectural Historians* 64, no. 2 (June 2005), pp. 144–67.

material. Where possible, the papers of architects and designers have also been studied, and key protagonists were interviewed. The records of the Association of British Theatre Technicians similarly formed a useful counterbalance to an overly 'administrative' history.

In what follows, Chapter 1 summarizes the development after 1945 of a 'cultural policy' by way of context for subsequent discussion of local motivations. Chapter 2 looks at the funding of theatre-building projects, including the 'Housing the Arts' fund. Chapter 3 explores theatre architecture in the 1940s and 1950s, before Chapter 4 extends the story into the 1960s, showing how theatres represented new understandings of the contemporary public building. Two specific themes follow. Chapter 5 considers how theatres could be implicated in debates about urban planning and civic identity, while Chapter 6 discusses the extent to which theatre buildings could be intended as a focus for the community, not least on university campuses. Chapter 7 continues the chronological narrative by looking at the 1970s and the 1980s. The focus then turns to auditoria and stages: how could they be understood in 'modern' ways? Chapter 8 examines the rejection of the proscenium arch arrangement that had dominated before 1939, while Chapter 9 nonetheless asserts that the proscenium arch stage could itself be understood to be 'modern'. Finally, Chapter 10 considers 'reactions' to the modern playhouse, including impermanent and mobile theatres, and the restoration of pre-1914 buildings.

Running through these chapters are several themes, including the extent to which theatre buildings suggest continuity as well as change, and flexibility as well as specificity. Also important are the ways in which the arts were implicated in the idea of reforming Britain, both culturally and physically; in this respect, this study charts the expansion of the welfare state project into the realms of culture and leisure. At its core, this is a story of the complexities of modern architecture, the emergence of a modern approach to theatre architecture, and the intended forging of a modern Britain by cultural means. It is also a story of process and collaboration. These theatres were shaped by the ideas of their funders and users, and the realities of their contexts. As with all works of history, my analysis is an interpretation, not a definitive account, and I have had to be selective. Many of the theatres discussed here could well form the subject of a book-length study in themselves. In addition, further work could potentially be done on such subjects as stage technologies, the planning of backstage spaces, or the ways in which the theatres, once constructed, were used and altered. More also remains to be said on such topics as community-led arts projects in the 1970s and 1980s, the conservation of older theatres, and on the experience of 'found space'. But as theatre itself emerges from this study as a diverse enterprise, so too is there room for many interpretations of its architectural history.

1

'An Instrument of Policy and Something Socially Desirable'

Public Funding and Theatre

In 1948, T. S. Eliot reflected on the extent to which culture increasingly appeared to be a politicized matter. 'We observe nowadays', he wrote, 'that "culture" attracts the attention of men of politics: not that politicians are always "men of culture", but that "culture" is recognised both as an instrument of policy and as something socially desirable which it is the business of the State to promote.'[1] Whereas before 1939 theatre in Britain had depended on private patronage, commercial endeavour, and box-office income,[2] by the end of the following decade the principle that theatre might be routinely subsidized by the public purse had been decisively established. The historian Anthony Jackson noted in the early 1980s:

> the three main sources of income for theatres [between the late 1950s and the 1980s] have been the box office, the Arts Council and the local authorities. There have of course been grants, donations and sponsorship from other sources too—from the regional arts associations, from wealthy individuals and from business firms—but with only a few notable exceptions these sources for the [repertory theatre] have been minimal.[3]

Subsidies from the Arts Council and local authorities rarely dominated theatrical balance sheets. In 1970, for example, it was reported that regional theatres typically recovered 75 per cent of their costs from ticket sales, with public funds covering the remaining 25 per cent.[4] Nonetheless, the existence of subsidies prompted significant changes in the organizational structures and viability of professional theatre, and these changes in turn had architectural consequences. In essence, 'revenue' (i.e. operational) subsidy gave the country's regional repertory companies a reasonably stable financial foundation and so allowed them to start to think about either improving their existing buildings or starting afresh in a new theatre, the

[1] Janet Minihan, *The Nationalization of Culture: The Development of State Subsidies to the Arts in Great Britain* (London, 1977), p. 215.

[2] Fred M. Leventhal, '"The Best for the Most": CEMA and state sponsorship of the arts in wartime, 1939–1945', *Twentieth Century British History* 1, no. 3 (1990), pp. 289–317 (p. 289).

[3] George Rowell and Anthony Jackson, *The Repertory Movement: A History of Regional Theatre in Britain* (Cambridge, 1984), p. 110.

[4] ACGB, 'The Theatre Today in England and Wales: the report of the Arts Council Theatre Enquiry' [1970], p. 35.

construction of which would then typically be supported by local authority and Arts Council 'capital' grants. The emergence of the 'civic theatre', provided by the local authority, was another hallmark of this period. So too was a growing number of university theatres, some of which were intended for teaching and student use, others as venues for professional performances.

The advent of subsidy meant that new theatres in post-war Britain could be shaped by the ideas and ambitions not only of actors and directors but also a range of other individuals and organizations, at both the local and national levels. To that end, this chapter focuses on what might be called post-war 'cultural policy' as context for the discussion in subsequent chapters of the more 'local' motivations that also underpinned the construction of new theatres. It outlines the emergence of a system of public support for the arts and then considers how this development was justified, looking particularly at the extent to which the arts were seen to be transformative, before considering the impact of the emergence of subsidy on the structure of British theatre.

THE ARTS COUNCIL OF GREAT BRITAIN AND THE LOCAL GOVERNMENT ACT

The Festival of Britain opened in 1951, offering a post-war 'tonic to the nation'.[5] While the Festival's Lansbury estate offered a glimpse of the future of inner-city housing, the location of the newly completed Royal Festival Hall at the heart of the main Festival site on the South Bank suggested the place of the arts in the new Britain. Indeed, the historian Arthur Marwick has argued that culture had an integral place in the emerging welfare state:

> the ideology of consensus [...] was of a well-disposed, well-educated upper class, cooperating with the various fractions of the middle class and with certain representatives of the working class, in running the country in the best interests of everyone, it being understood that those interests comprised spending money both on welfare services and, to a degree never envisaged before the war, on culture.[6]

By the end of the 1940s, two main routes had been established by means of which public money could be spent on the arts. First, the Arts Council of Great Britain, founded in 1945 and granted its royal charter in 1946, distributed central government funding at 'arm's length' from the political machine.[7] In addition, the Local Government Act of 1948 allowed local authorities routinely to support the performing arts.

[5] Becky Conekin, '"Here Is the Modern World Itself" The Festival of Britain's representations of the future', in *Moments of Modernity: Reconstructing Britain, 1945–1964*, edited by Becky Conekin, Frank Mort, and Chris Waters (London, 1999), pp. 228–46.

[6] Arthur Marwick, *Culture in Britain Since 1945* (Oxford, 1991), p. 16.

[7] For CEMA, see Robert Hewison, *Culture and Consensus: England, Art and Politics since 1940* (London, 1995), pp. 29–48; Charles Landstone, *Off-Stage: A Personal Record of the First Twelve Years of State Sponsored Drama in Great Britain* (London, 1953); Euan McArthur, *Scotland, CEMA and the Arts Council: Background, Politics and Visual Arts Policy* (Farnham, 2013).

The work of the Arts Council of Great Britain built upon the example of the wartime Council (originally Committee) for the Encouragement of Music and the Arts (CEMA), which had initially been an initiative of the Pilgrim Trust but was later wholly supported by government. Although CEMA had intended to support amateur as well as professional practice, it had increasingly focused on the latter under the leadership of John Maynard Keynes. The Arts Council of Great Britain defined its remit in similar terms. In addition, as will be discussed in greater detail shortly, the Arts Council's founding charter referred to 'the fine arts exclusively', which meant that certain judgements were made as to what was worthy of support.[8] In the case of regional theatre, mixed-programme repertory companies were the Arts Council's main beneficiaries. A few theatres and touring companies were directly managed by the Arts Council during the 1950s,[9] but most of its grant-in-aid went to independent organizations, with non-profit groups being favoured over their more commercially minded counterparts. Of the fifty-one major repertory theatre companies whose existence was recorded in 1960, thirty-seven had non-profit status, which made them eligible for support.[10] Of these thirty-seven, twenty-six were then receiving at least some funding from either the Arts Council or their local authority, or, in some cases, both. Nonetheless, just £235,000 was available during the Arts Council's first year,[11] and while overall spending on culture did increase during the Conservative administrations of 1951–64, especially in 1962–3 and 1963–4,[12] the Arts Council's budgets remained modest during these early years.

As far as local-government support for the arts was concerned, post-war developments again had their roots in wartime. In 1942, for example, the British Drama League had proposed a 'Civic Theatre Scheme'.[13] These theatres would be jointly funded by government and local trusts, and would offer 'true repertory', namely a programme in which a number of plays would be shown in rotation, using the same group of actors. Classical plays and new works of 'merit' were to be preferred. The scheme was not taken forward, but Section 132 of the 1948 Local Government Act gave authorities the powers to spend on the arts the product of a rate equivalent (in England) to sixpence in the pound.[14] Those authorities who wished to borrow money for this purpose were required to advertise their intentions before

[8] Hewison, *Culture and Consensus*, p. 43.

[9] N. V. Linklater, 'The Achievement in Drama', in *The State and the Arts*, edited by John Pick (Eastbourne, 1980), pp. 77–94 (p. 79).

[10] ACGB, Annual Report, 1959–1960 ('The Priorities of Patronage'), pp. 26–7.

[11] John Pick, 'Introduction: the best for the most', in *The State and the Arts*, edited by John Pick (Eastbourne, 1980), pp. 9–19 (p. 14).

[12] ACGB, Annual Report, 1961–1962 ('A Brighter Prospect'), p. 3: reference to a £445,000 increase for 1962–3, one-third of which went to repertory theatre; Hansard, HC Deb 27 April 1965, vol. 711, c. 288.

[13] LoB, MS 2339/4/10, 'Unsorted Box 10', British Drama League, 'The Civic Theatre Scheme', 12 November 1942.

[14] William L. Roots et al., *The Local Government Act, 1948* (London, 1948), pp. 87–91. A slightly lower rate of 4–4/5d (approx. 2 new pence) applied in Scotland into the 1960s (see NRS, ED61/72, Nigel Abercrombie to Harold Rossetti, 14 December 1966). The legislation was subsequently updated, for example by the Local Government (Scotland) Act 1973, although the principle remained.

applying for government sanction. The money raised could be spent not only on what were termed 'entertainments', but also buildings. Once again, professional excellence was prioritized, and recipients of grants had to demonstrate 'cultural value'. The status of theatre was thus transformed, potentially becoming akin to other local authority services such as schools or libraries. The result was the emergence of the so-called 'civic' theatre, a term which not only illustrates the role of local authorities as the landlords and funders of these theatres, but also implies a sense of citizenship.

The actors' union, Equity, reported at the start of the 1950s that sixty-four authorities were supporting the arts, with twenty-seven helping the professional theatre.[15] Some were renting venues to local groups (Basingstoke, Bexhill, Bristol), while some had taken theatres into civic control (Canterbury, Hornchurch, Runcorn, Walsall). Some were running arts centres (Doncaster, South Shields, Whitley Bay); another strategy was to offer guarantees against losses. In 1956, the Arts Council's Annual Report noted the support of the authorities for theatre in Bristol, Birmingham, Chesterfield, Coventry, Hornchurch, Salisbury, Dudley, Nuneaton, Guildford, Winchester, and Chippenham.[16] In 1961, it cited several cases where grants had increased recently.[17] By this date, local authorities were increasingly spending money on buildings. In 1964, 43.8 per cent of local authority spending on the arts, some £2.9 million, went on 'halls, theatres, and other entertainment buildings' as opposed to 7.5 per cent on 'cultural entertainments'.[18] When, that same year, Bolton Town Council investigated the provision of a civic theatre, it noted the existence of such venues in Colwyn Bay, Colchester, Halifax, Harrogate, and Rotherham.[19] Many were conversions, but purpose-built theatres had opened in Coventry and Leicester, and more were planned.

Yet how prevalent was local authority support? In 1959, it was suggested that the 1948 Act could yield £9 million annually but that the total amount of municipal patronage amounted to less than £250,000.[20] In 1966, Leatherhead Repertory Company received a local authority subsidy equivalent to just a third of a penny in the pound, while Edinburgh's support for the arts at the level of two pence in the pound in 1967 was described as 'extremely good by British standards'.[21] In these circumstances, the Arts Council reported in 1958 that, much as the overall pattern of patronage had largely switched from private to public sources, the arts nonetheless 'have to take their chance, they have to renew their plea each year [...]'.[22] The Arts Council had a particular interest in emphasizing the patchy nature of local funding, for in this way it could reinforce its own case for larger budgets, but others

[15] LoB, MS 2339/4/10, 'Unsorted Box 10', 'The Theatre and Civic Entertainment', leaflet produced by the Civic Theatres Committee of the British Actors' Equity Association, *c.*1950–1.

[16] ACGB, Annual Report, 1955–1956 ('The First Ten Years'), p. 27.

[17] ACGB, Annual Report, 1960–1961 ('Partners in Patronage'), pp. 19–20.

[18] BoA, ABZ/89/1, Report of a Meeting of the Institute of Municipal Entertainment, 29 April 1964.

[19] BoA, ABZ/45, Box 1/1, Loose papers detailing civic theatres.

[20] Richard Findlater, *The Future of the Theatre* (London, 1959), p. 10.

[21] SHC, 6368/10/6, clippings: *Surrey Advertiser*, 8 October 1966; NRS, ED61/71, Ronald Mavor to Colin McKenzie, 25 August 1967.

[22] ACGB, Annual Report, 1957–1958 ('A New Pattern of Patronage'), p. 8.

made similar arguments. The MP Hugh Jenkins—a noted supporter of theatre—suggested in 1965 that local authorities often remained reluctant to embrace the idea of theatre as an amenity rather than a business (while, he went on, those working in theatre often considered that local authorities were 'peopled by unimaginative morons').[23] His Conservative colleague, Robert Cooke, also asked what could be done to get 'backward' local councils to spend more.[24]

For Labour, the answer was clear: central government should set an example. Following the election in 1964 of a Labour administration under Harold Wilson, Jennie Lee was appointed Minister of State for the Arts, a new post initially located within the Treasury but soon transferred to the Department for Education and Science (DES). In 1965, she presided over the publication of a White Paper, 'A Policy for the Arts: the First Steps', which proposed a 'more coherent, generous and imaginative approach'.[25] It was hoped that local authorities might thus be persuaded to support the arts,[26] especially where buildings were concerned.[27] Under Lord Goodman (chairman, 1965–72), the Arts Council's budget duly rose from £3.2 million in 1964–5 to £9.3 million in 1970–1,[28] allowing N. V. ('Dick') Linklater, its drama director during the 1970s, later to reflect of this time that 'with increasing grant in aid, but never quite enough, it nevertheless seemed possible that the arts might before too long become properly subsidised and cared for'.[29] Increased budgets allowed new initiatives. For example, a 'New Activities Committee' was formed at the end of the 1960s, just as the abolition of theatre censorship allowed innovative and improvised work to be shown beyond the private club settings to which it had been hitherto confined;[30] it was said that 'any artistic experience short of dementia' might be funded.[31] However, perhaps the most radical provisions of the White Paper were concerned with the establishment of a fund for 'Housing the Arts', which (as is discussed in Chapter 2) formalized and increased previous Arts Council spending in this area.

The optimism of this period was short-lived, however, as economic difficulties increasingly disrupted the ambitious state spending programmes that had been inaugurated during the 1960s. In 1975, Tony Crosland, then Secretary of State for the Environment, told Britain's local authorities that 'the party is over' as far as

23 'Civic Theatres, Their Housing and Administration', *Stage and Television Today Supplement*, 4 March 1965, p. 2.

24 Lawrence Black, '"Making Britain a Gayer and More Cultivated Country": Jennie Lee, the creative economy, and the 1960s' "Cultural Revolution"', *Contemporary British History* 20, no. 3 (2006), pp. 323–42 (pp. 328–9).

25 'A Policy for the Arts: the first steps', Cmnd. 2601 [1965], paras 74–6.

26 Hansard, HC Deb 27 April 1965, vol. 711, c. 232.

27 'A Policy for the Arts', para. 52.

28 Andrew Sinclair, *Arts and Cultures: The History of the Fifty Years of the Arts Council of Great Britain* (London, 1995), p. 133; Black, '"Gayer and More Cultivated"', p. 325.

29 N. V. Linklater, 'Obituary: Hugh Willatt', *Independent*, 18 November 1996, <http://www.independent.co.uk/incoming/obituary-sir-hugh-willatt-1353029.html> (accessed 27 January 2017).

30 Sinclair, *Arts and Cultures*, pp. 155–6; Rowell and Jackson, *Repertory Movement*, p. 113.

31 Hewison, *Culture and Consensus*, p. 141, quoting Lord Goodman, then chairman of the Arts Council.

major public expenditure was concerned.[32] The Arts Council's budgets came under pressure, with the 1975–6 Annual Report ('The Arts in Hard Times') announcing that a decade of ever-increasing funding was now drawing to a close.[33] The situation was barely changed in the early 1980s. Although new initiatives were discussed in the Arts Council's special 1984 report, 'The Glory of the Garden', the document also proposed that several long-standing beneficiaries of subsidy should lose their grants and confirmed that 'Housing the Arts' would be wound up.[34] The principle of public subsidy ultimately survived the 1980s, but things were changing, with theatre administrators increasingly having to grapple with notions of the economic value of the arts, the perceived benefits of business sponsorship, and the need to operate in more clearly 'commercial' ways.[35]

CULTURAL LITERACY: JUSTIFYING SUPPORT FOR THE ARTS

The introduction of subsidies for the arts after 1945 reflected the long-standing wish of certain designers, artists, politicians, and educators to encourage an awareness of 'culture' and design among the population at large. Their aim was the reform of taste. For example, although the wartime 'Utility' furniture scheme was the product of necessity and a response to shortages, it had sought to promote an appreciation of good design, quality manufacture, and modernist aesthetics. A similar programme of design education was followed after 1944 by the Council of Industrial Design (COID), which in 1956 created the Design Centre to display products that had secured its seal of approval. Deliberately conceived as a showcase rather than a shop, the centre was presented as a dispassionate environment in which an appreciation of good design—or at least, the COID's view of what constituted it—could be encouraged.

The system of subsidy for the arts took a similar approach in attempting to encourage the forms of cultural practice deemed by policymakers and grant-givers to be especially valuable. The Arts Council's founding charter—as has been noted—referred to 'the fine arts exclusively', and while its revised charter of 1967 stated an ambition 'to improve the knowledge, understanding and practice of the arts', it nonetheless implied a relatively highbrow view that was, if liberal, hardly radical or populist.[36] As Patricia Hollis concluded in her biography of the 1960s Arts Minister, Jennie Lee:

[32] Mark Swenarton, 'Politics Versus Architecture: the Alexandra Road Public Enquiry, 1978–81', *Planning Perspectives* 29, no. 4 (2014), pp. 423–46 (p. 425).

[33] Rowell and Jackson, *Repertory Movement*, p. 113.

[34] ACGB, 'The Glory of the Garden: the development of the arts in England. A strategy for a decade' [1984].

[35] Kate Dorney and Ros Merkin, 'Introduction', in *The Glory of the Garden: English Regional Theatre and the Arts Council 1984–2009*, edited by Kate Dorney and Ros Merkin (Newcastle-upon-Tyne, 2010), pp. 1–14.

[36] Hewison, *Culture and Consensus*, pp. 140–1.

> only the established fine arts (music, drama, painting) could be judged 'excellent'; new activities, such as children's theatre, film and photography, folk song and even literature—all those fields where critical judgement was harder and peer review less clear cut, where performance could be controversial—were deemed not to come within the Arts Council remit.[37]

This frame of reference reflected the suspicion of many on the Left of commercial mass culture.[38] In 1964, Lee described the Federation of Playgoers' Societies as 'a kind of resistance movement against the degradation of the whole level of art and the theatre'.[39] In her view, it was not the role of government to tell people what to like, but 'the good things of art, like the theatre, should be encouraged'. Hence the extent to which repertory theatres would become significant beneficiaries of Arts Council and local subsidies. 'Classic' plays and new works typically dominated in these theatres, rather than light entertainment or variety; a 1944 study described the 'wholesome staple diet' offered in Edinburgh.[40] Repertory thus seemed best to embody the professional excellence and high-culture agenda of the Arts Council's founding charter.

For Lee, like many of her Labour colleagues, access to the arts was a matter of democracy:

> We have only accomplished half a social revolution [...] Too many people are culturally semi-literate, through no fault of their own [...] The opportunity to enjoy art has mostly been restricted to people with money and leisure.[41]

It was, she continued, 'one of the duties of a Socialist government' to open up the bastions of culture to the whole population. Labour's interest in the arts and leisure was not new.[42] However, by the end of the 1950s, a sense that much of the party's initial programme—including the National Health Service, nationalized industry, and state economic planning—had been achieved meant that those on the 'New Left', in particular, advocated greater engagement with leisure. Tony Crosland argued that with 'the passing of the old collective grievances and injustices, [...] we shall turn our attention increasingly to other, and in the long run, more important spheres', including 'the cultivation of leisure'.[43] These ideas informed Labour's 1959 manifesto, 'Leisure for Living', and Lee certainly saw her work in terms that evoked the role of her late husband, Aneurin Bevan, in the creation of the National Health Service. As the 1965 White Paper put it:

> all new social services have to fight long and hard before they establish themselves. Only yesterday it was the fight for a free health service. The day before it was the struggle to win education for all.[44]

[37] Patricia Hollis, *Jennie Lee: A Life* (Oxford, 1997), p. 249.

[38] Lawrence Black, *The Political Culture of the Left in Affluent Britain, 1951–64: Old Labour, New Britain?* (Basingstoke, 2003), pp. 76–82.

[39] ERO, D/Z 455/2/12, clippings: 'Live Theatre "a Kind of Resistance Movement"', *Essex County Standard*, 6 November 1964.

[40] J. H. Burns and D. Sutherland Graeme, *Scottish University* (Edinburgh, 1944), p. 66.

[41] 'A Better Life and Leisure for Our Young People', *The Times*, 24 November 1966.

[42] Minihan, *Nationalization of Culture*, p. 173.

[43] C. A. R. Crosland, *The Future of Socialism* (London, 1956), p. 520.

[44] 'A Policy for the Arts: the first steps', para. 98.

In other words, culture and leisure would be co-opted by the welfare state.

The idea that the arts might have a beneficial effect was broadly a matter of consensus, with the terms used by the Conservatives at times echoing those used by Labour. For example, in 1959, a Conservative Political Centre pamphlet entitled *The Challenge of Leisure* dubbed the arts a 'bulwark against boredom' in an age of affluence and increasing free time.[45] The arts, it suggested, would contribute to the formation of the individual, giving a 'sense of purpose and [...] personal responsibility'.[46] The principal difference between the two parties concerned the extent to which the state should be involved, with Conservatives typically preferring to encourage individual initiatives.[47] Nonetheless, the Arts Council's budgets did increase under the Conservative governments of the 1950s and early 1960s. Support for Labour, furthermore, did not automatically translate into unqualified enthusiasm for theatre subsidies. In Guildford in 1961, a number of Labour councillors opposed a subsidy for the repertory company.[48] And while the financial cuts of 1984 were proposed under a Conservative government, it was actually under the Labour administrations of 1974–9 that the Arts Council's budgets first came under serious pressure, if for economic rather than ideological reasons.

The idea that particular types of cultural activity were of special value circulated beyond central government. In Coventry, for example, the Labour City Council's wish to build a civic theatre reflected several agendas, including a pattern of municipal interventionism that had begun in the late 1930s with the election of a Labour-dominated authority. More immediately, it was suggested that the city's recent physical growth had not been matched by the development of the kinds of social and recreational facilities that would expand residents' cultural horizons and promote a sense of community.[49] Thus in 1949, the town clerk referred to a 'sufficient and properly balanced provision of theatres, cinemas and other places of entertainment,' while in 1958 the mayor, Pearl Hyde, hoped that the then newly opened Belgrade Theatre would end what she described as the city's reputation as a 'burial place of culture'.[50] Similarly in Plymouth in 1969, Alderman Harold Pattinson, one of the chief advocates of the proposed new Theatre Royal, spoke of his vision of a city 'where citizens can be employed, housed, educated and given opportunities for cultural development as well as development of personality'.[51] In Dundee, meanwhile, it was suggested by the theatre management that 'the excellent work

[45] Conservative Political Centre, 'The Challenge of Leisure' [pamphlet, 1959], p. 14.

[46] 'The Challenge of Leisure', p. 5.

[47] 'The Challenge of Leisure', p. 19: 'as Conservatives, we favour voluntary initiative, but we are bound to take account of social and economic changes. [...] more of this type of expenditure will have to come in future from the public purse'.

[48] SHC, 7018/2/4/142, clippings: *Surrey Advertiser*, 4 November 1961.

[49] Nick Tiratsoo, *Reconstruction, Affluence and Labour Politics: Coventry, 1945–60* (London, 1990), p. 7; Alistair Fair, '"A New Image of the Living Theatre": the genesis and design of the Belgrade Theatre, Coventry, 1948–58', *Architectural History* 54 (2011), pp. 347–82 (p. 360).

[50] CHC, CCA/3/1/11161, Town Clerk to Mary Glasgow, 4 May 1949; PA2313/5/2/1, clippings: *Coventry Evening Telegraph*, 5 February 1958.

[51] PCL, uncat., Theatre Royal file, undated clipping (*c.*1969/70), 'The Arts Challenge to Plymouth'.

done by the Rep has helped to temper the philistine image that the rest of the country has of the city'.[52]

These ideas were given particular urgency by a sense that Britons had an increasing amount of money to spend on leisure pursuits. Prime Minister Harold Macmillan famously suggested in 1957 that most people had 'never had it so good', and indeed average weekly earnings increased by 130 per cent between 1955 and 1969.[53] However, affluence represented a potential problem for the Left.[54] It was often suggested that new-found wealth might be directed towards the kinds of apparently low-brow (and perhaps Americanized) leisure activities of which some were wary. Individualism, too, was a problem for the Left, for whom group activities often had particular significance, not least because individualism (and suburbanization) could be associated with Conservative support. Hence the significance for the likes of Lee of encouraging appreciation of 'the good things of art, like the theatre' as a balance to these tendencies. In these circumstances, theatre architecture might have to be rethought for those who had 'never had it so good', with the management of Birmingham Repertory Theatre noting at the start of the 1960s:

> A higher standard of living is making demands for more comfortable football and cricket grounds and countless other centres of sport and entertainment. The old-fashioned theatre, too, has had its day. The public wants something more than a mere playhouse with stalls, circle and gallery. Equal comfort throughout is demanded.[55]

While potential audiences might have more time to devote to theatre-going, the case for attending in the face of an ever-increasing range of leisure activities—many comfortably home-based—evidently had to be articulated more clearly than ever.

Others made similar points. *Punch*, for example, considered that Coventry's Belgrade Theatre represented an act of 'defiance' in the face of materialism.[56] Similarly, the theatre director Stephen Joseph suggested in 1964 that it was not possible to live 'by washing machines alone',[57] while the founders of Centre 42, the arts centre opened in 1966 within the Roundhouse, a former railway building in north London, proposed that 'material improvement is only the first stage in a long effort to make better living conditions [. . .]'.[58] In Derby in the early 1970s, the Town Council thought that the inclusion of a theatre within the Eagle Shopping Centre would temper the development's character, with the Playhouse's administrative director reporting that 'suddenly the Council saw the new theatre as bringing a whiff of culture, of eating and drinking, into what could otherwise

[52] UoDun, MS 316/44/5 (ii), 'The Case for a New Theatre for the Rep', n.d.

[53] Dominic Sandbrook, *White Heat: A History of Britain in the Swinging Sixties* (London, 2006), p. 191.

[54] Otto Saumarez Smith, 'Central Government and Town-Centre Redevelopment in Britain, 1959–1966', *Historical Journal* 58, no. 1 (2015), pp. 217–44 (p. 230); Black, *Political Culture*, p. 118–21.

[55] LoB, MS 978/1/6/1/1, 'The Birmingham Repertory Theatre: its present and future', November 1960, p. 1.

[56] CHC, PA2313/5/2/1, clippings: *Punch*, 9 April 1958.

[57] Stephen Joseph, 'Introduction' to his *Actor and Architect* (Manchester, 1964), pp. 1–29 (p. 28).

[58] RSA, uncat. boxes, Centre 42 Annual Report, 1961–1962, p. 5.

be an over-commercial setting'.[59] That theatre could balance the commercial pressures of modern life was also suggested in Billingham, where facilities for leisure were thought to be as 'essential to the well-being of the community' as shops: 'leisure and happiness' were 'essential ingredients of Billingham's design for living'.[60] In High Wycombe, the anti-suburban viewpoint took on hysterical overtones: 'decentralised housing' had resulted in a 'grey, soaking dullness that leads to neurosis, strikes, low productivity, and a general feeling of helpless aimlessness'.[61] The proposed arts centre of *c.*1970 would apparently be an 'oasis of social sanity' in the face of this problem.

The wish to encourage apparently productive forms of leisure was given additional impetus by a persistent belief that the public now enjoyed ever-increasing amounts of free time. In 1948, Chancellor of the Exchequer Stafford Cripps referred during a conference about theatre to 'shortening hours of labour',[62] while the 'white heat' technological revolution invoked by Harold Wilson in the 1960s similarly prompted confident predictions that mechanization would soon reduce working hours significantly.[63] In Birmingham, the director of the Midlands Arts Centre, John English, proposed at a 1964 conference that the average Briton would soon work only between the ages of twenty-five and fifty, and for just five hours each day.[64] What would people do for the rest of time? A survey for Gallup in 1957 revealed that one in four people was already sometimes at a loss as to how to spend their leisure hours.[65] In Billingham in 1961, the Urban District Council's clerk, architects, and engineer struck a cautionary note when they told councillors that 'unless facilities for leisure and recreation are provided by the Local Authority, they are not likely to be provided by anyone else except industrial firms'.[66] Their choice of words implies a degree of scepticism about what might otherwise be provided by 'industrial firms'.

Cutting across many of these discussions is the idea that theatre-going could be transformative. For example, Theatr Clwyd in Mold was intended to 'ensure that children from the earliest age will be nurtured in the arts', being a 'veritable power house for cultural activities' that would 'have a tremendous effect on the people'.[67] The inquiry into the construction of Bromley's Churchill Theatre similarly referred

[59] 'The New Derby Playhouse', *Artefact* [magazine of the East Midlands Arts Association] 3, no. 6 (n.d.), pp. 4–5.

[60] TA, U/S/1143, 'Billingham—Planned for People' [*c.*1965].

[61] TTT, Roderick Ham archive, Dove box, 'A Professional Arts and Entertainments Centre for South Bucks', n.d.

[62] Minihan, *The Nationalization of Culture*, p. 229.

[63] Sandbrook, *White Heat*, pp. 48–9.

[64] John English, 'Leisure and the Performing Arts', in *Actor and Architect*, edited by Stephen Joseph (Manchester, 1964), pp. 75–86 (p. 79).

[65] Dominic Sandbrook, *Never Had It So Good: A History of Britain from Suez to the Beatles* (London, 2005), p. 132.

[66] TA, U/S/706, letter to Development and Plans Committee members signed by Fred M. Dawson (Clerk), A. J. Elder (architect), Edwin Shaw (engineer and surveyor), H. H. Wright (treasurer and accountant), 23 June 1961.

[67] FA, CC/TC/1/64, 'Proposed Arts Centre, Mold, Flintshire: Preliminary Report' [April 1969], pp. 1, 12.

to its role in 'the stimulation of ideas and the full development of human personality'.[68] Chichester Festival Theatre was essentially privately funded, but its aims were scarcely different: 'the promotion and advancement of aesthetic education and the cultivation and improvement of public taste in drama, opera, music, painting and the other arts'.[69] The same ideas also informed the growing number of university theatres. Higher education generally was often considered to be a formative experience for young adults, and in this respect its role could be understood in terms that went beyond the purely academic to encompass also the social and cultural.[70] Just as the influential 1963 Robbins report on university expansion referred to the creation of 'cultivated' men and women rather than subject specialists, in 1979 an Arts Council report on the support of British universities for the arts discussed the 'conversion of the undergraduate into graduate and, by implication, a useful [...] member of society [...]', with universities producing not only 'well-qualified specialists' but also 'a broader band of the informed public'.[71] Many of the new university theatres of the 1960s and 1970s addressed this agenda. For example, Southampton University proposed that 'the arts can be a unifying power in the intellectual life of a community, in these days when Universities tend to be divided by specialist interests' and that 'the theatre, music and the fine arts have a crucial part to play in bringing together and uniting in common humane interests members of its different Faculties'.[72]

At the same time, with their audiences understood to be at an especially impressionable age, university theatres represented in an especially focused way the intention that access to high-quality drama and music might transform students' cultural outlook. Many of these theatres hosted professional performances, at least on a part-time basis. At the University of Sussex, for example, the Gardner Arts Centre was intended to show that the arts were 'as vital a part of campus life as any lecture hall or seminar room, the library, the sports hall, a refectory or a hall of residence', according to its director, Walter Eysselinck.[73] In 1962, when the university first proposed the construction of a 'Fine Arts Centre' (a revealing choice of words), a report reflected on the need for such a facility:

> The great increase in the numbers of those now receiving a university education is but one aspect of the social revolution in which we are living. More and more students have been brought up in homes from which there is not only an absence of beautiful things, of records, of books, but from which there is also lacking—though the responsibility for this is that of a wider group than the family—any tradition of respect or

[68] BA&LS, 792.094223, W.S. Gage et al., 'Churchill Theatre, Bromley' [ACGB Case Study], p. 14.

[69] WSRO, Box 60, 'The Chichester Festival Theatre Trust', memo of 23 March 1961.

[70] Alistair Fair, '"Brutalism Among the Ladies": modern architecture at Somerville College, Oxford, 1947–67', *Architectural History* 57 (2014), pp. 357–92 (pp. 373–87). Schools could be similarly conceived: Tom Hulme, '"A Nation Dependent on Its Children": school buildings and citizenship in England and Wales, 1900–1939', *Journal of British Studies* 54, no. 2 (2015), pp. 406–32.

[71] W. Forster, *The Universities, the Arts and the Public* (London, 1979), n.p.

[72] HES, MS 2329/ENG/35/1/9–10, 'The Nuffield Theatre'; HES, MS 2329/ENG/35/3/1, Centenary appeal booklet, *c.*1961.

[73] UoSx, SxUOS1/1/5/13/1, Walter Eysselinck, 'Objectives for the Arts Centre', typed paper, n.d.

> appreciation for such things. All these students spend a minimum of three years in a new home, a new family—the university family. This is a magnificent opportunity to repair the omissions of the old.[74]

Consulted in 1964 about the proposals, George Devine, the director of Royal Court in London, suggested that the centre might host events on the theme of 'what is "good taste"' while also 'bring[ing] the students and faculty into touch with the creative arts as a leisure activity'.[75]

This theme is also evident in the case of Manchester University's drama department, whose role was defined by its first professor, Hugh Hunt, as being in part to create 'demand': the 'most vital function of a department of drama is, after all, <u>the creation of an informed audience</u>'.[76] Manchester was one of several new centres for the academic study of drama which were established in post-war Britain. Bristol was first in 1947, its approach drawing on abandoned wartime proposals for a university theatre in Oxford; others including Hull and Manchester followed during the 1960s.[77] At Hull, the university's first lecturer in drama, Donald Roy, stated that his aim was not 'to manufacture Oliviers and Peter Halls' but rather to turn out graduates with an appreciation of literature in context.[78] Reference was made to the potential of drama to offer 'a well-balanced enrichment of the disciplines in the Faculty of Arts'.[79] In addition, university drama departments also offered opportunities for performance to the students themselves.

The encouragement of certain forms of theatre was, therefore, bound up in wider discussions of cultural transformation, which also encompassed other spheres, such as design. These debates were, in turn, shaped in part by concerns about the effects of affluence and increasing leisure. During the 1970s, the terms of the argument would evolve to become less didactic and more participatory. In the meantime, however, the Midlands Arts Centre shows the lengths to which an education in taste might be taken:

> Good talk and good manners will be encouraged. An interest in good food will be stimulated by a restaurant block providing everything from bread and cheese (but with a dozen kinds of bread and a selection of cheeses) to a French restaurant—with waiters in tails who can help form the young taste in choosing a wine for a meal.[80]

74 HES, MS 2329/ENG/52/2/168–71, 'Memorandum on the Proposed Fine Arts Centre in the University of Sussex', July 1962.

75 UoSx, SxUOS1/1/5/13/1, George Devine, 'Memorandum on the Setting Up of a Centre of the Creative Arts at Sussex University', 10 November 1964.

76 JRL, Hugh Hunt uncat. Box 12, text of Hunt's unpublished autobiography, 'Slings and Arrows', p. 269; UoMan, VCA/7/573, folder 2, 'Report on Visits to Departments of Drama in the USA', n.d.

77 Dennis Welland, John Prudhoe, and Donald Roy, 'American Literature: Drama: university courses', *Critical Survey* 3, no. 2 (1967), pp. 114–24 (pp. 120–1).

78 Welland et al., 'American Literature', p. 124.

79 Bodleian, MS. Eng. Misc. c. 1017/2/80, 'Notes on the Job' [note by Coghill, n.d.]; HHC, University Archives, Registrar Uncat. Box 14, folder 33/3, D. Campbell to F. Harris-Jones, 26 October 1965.

80 UoEx, 26/1d/2d, uncredited clipping, 20 June 1962, 'Where Youth and the Arts Can Meet'.

Here was perhaps a particularly clear evocation of the idea that an appreciation of the arts, good design, and good food, together with a rounded education, would contribute, as Lee put it, to a Britain that was 'gayer and more cultivated'.[81]

STRUCTURES OF THEATRE AND THE END OF 'TATTY REP'

Writing during the 1970s, Hugh Willatt recorded that 'of all the changes that came about [as a result of the introduction of subsidy], the reorganisation of the theatre was to be the most dramatic and significant'.[82] Willatt was not alone in noticing this development. In 1963, for example, the director Norman Marshall wrote in *Country Life* about what he dubbed a 'renaissance' in what was then known as 'provincial theatre'.[83] By 1980 subsidized repertory companies were the main providers of drama in the regions. Many of these companies occupied new theatre buildings, and so it is worth summarizing their development.

Repertory theatre had emerged in Britain in the early twentieth century.[84] In these theatres, a company of actors typically worked according to a pattern known as 'weekly rep', in which they would present one play each evening for a week while rehearsing the next week's play during the day. As has been noted, the kinds of play presented in these theatres appealed to the Arts Council's interest in 'the fine arts exclusively', and so they became the main recipients of its grants to regional theatre. Whereas eighteen repertory companies had Arts Council revenue support in 1953, by 1970 the number had increased to fifty-two.[85] The amount of subsidy available to repertory theatres increased seven-fold between 1952 and 1963.[86] These developments came at the expense of regional commercial theatre, which was already being challenged by television (and not least by the regionalized structure of ITV). By 1978, of seventy-two regional theatre companies then in operation, just ten were run commercially,[87] while commercial 'pre-London' touring became increasingly unviable. In such circumstances, the often-large buildings of the commercial theatre, many built before 1914, proved increasingly tricky to operate. They were also increasingly unappealing. In Sheffield, it was noted in 1971:

> the day is long past when one is prepared to go through the physical discomfort of waiting for long hours on stone gallery steps. You couldn't help but think that you were third-class citizens. [...] There were seldom chairs and back-rests in the galleries, and the padding of the benches was of a minimum quality. If you couldn't sit upright

[81] 'A Policy for the Arts', paras 14, 91, and 100.

[82] Hugh Willatt, 'How the Arts Are Promoted', in *The State and the Arts*, edited by John Pick (Eastbourne, 1980), pp. 21–46 (p. 34).

[83] 'Renaissance in the Provincial Theatre', *Country Life*, 1 June 1963, pp. 57–9.

[84] Rowell and Jackson, *Repertory Movement*, pp. 16–53.

[85] ACGB, 'Housing the Arts in Great Britain', 2 vols [1959 and 1961], II, pp. 15–16; 'Theatre Today', pp. 11 and 35.

[86] Rowell and Jackson, *Repertory Movement*, pp. 81–2. See also ACGB, Annual Report, 1962–1963, p. 13.

[87] Linklater, 'The Achievement', p. 80.

> for four hours, then you had to hope that the person behind would permit you to loll against his or her knees. [...] The seats were uncomfortably hard and the view of the stage was atrocious [...].[88]

The previous year, an Arts Council report had concluded that 'theatre of private enterprise' outside London was 'on its last legs, physically run-down and morally disheartened'.[89]

While it might be argued that the targeting of subsidy towards regional repertory suggested an uncritical perpetuation of 'high' cultural forms,[90] this type of theatre was itself significantly transformed after 1950.[91] For example, many repertory theatres during the 1950s had a core company of actors—six to eight in Leatherhead, for example.[92] However, permanent companies working together for a whole season gave way to more fluid groups; actors increasingly sought more flexible terms of employment so as to be able to profit from opportunities in regional television.[93] At the same time, subsidy meant that the need to present a new show each week in order to maximize box-office income was reduced. The Arts Council supported a move away from 'weekly rep' to the presentation of shows for two weeks, not least because the result was that rehearsal periods were correspondingly increased.[94] Derby made the move in 1960, followed in 1961 by Northampton. Bromley, Cheltenham, Colchester, and Leatherhead followed suit in 1962, with Leatherhead then switching to 'three-weekly rep' in 1966.[95] The safety net provided by subsidy also offered greater freedom in play choices, which no longer always needed to be calculated only to attract the maximum box-office return. The higher standards that resulted from longer rehearsals and more stable budgets prompted Colin George, the director of the Sheffield Playhouse, to quip in 1969 that the term 'repertory' no longer suggested a theatre in which the sets fell apart mid-performance.[96] Three years before, the energetic director at Leatherhead, Hazel Vincent Wallace, had made a similar point: 'the old regime of "tatty rep" has gone forever, killed by the competition of television and the higher standards [...] demanded by a far more discriminating public'.[97] Now, repertory was more professional: 'the old policy of mediocre companies playing comedy and thrillers in

[88] John Bertram, 'Theatre Parade', *Sheffield Spectator*, August 1971 [copy in Crucible Theatre archive].

[89] ACGB, 'Theatre Today', p. 11.

[90] Alan Sinfield, 'Culture, Consensus and Difference: Angus Wilson to Alan Hollinghurst', in *British Culture of the Postwar: An Introduction to Literature and Society, 1945–1999*, edited by Alistair Davies and Alan Sinfield (London, 2000), pp. 83–102 (p. 84). See also John Elsom, *Theatre Outside London* (London, 1971), p. 83.

[91] Rowell and Jackson, *Repertory Movement*, pp. 82–3, 91–9.

[92] Hazel Vincent Wallace, interviewed 31 October 2015.

[93] SHC, 6368/10/6, clippings: *Surrey Advertiser*, 13 August 1966; Hazel Vincent Wallace, interviewed 31 October 2015.

[94] Dominic Shellard, 'Stability, Renewal and Change: Gielgud and Olivier in 1957', in *The Golden Generation: New Light on Post-war British Theatre*, ed. Dominic Shellard (London, 2008), pp. 67–91 (p. 91).

[95] 'Project for Leatherhead's New Theatre' [1966] copy supplied by Hazel Vincent Wallace.

[96] SHC, 6368/10/8, clippings: *Daily Mirror*, 17 September 1969.

[97] SHC, 6368/10/6, clippings: *Leatherhead Advertiser*, 14 October 1966.

unattractive theatres is no longer good enough, and the result of the battle for audiences has been a general raising of standards in all surviving theatres'.[98]

CONCLUSIONS: 'NOT IN THE BUSINESS OF MAKING MONEY'

In drawing the themes of this chapter together, it is helpful to begin by reiterating that Arts Council and local government grants and loan guarantees existed within a wider matrix of funding. The Arts Council's 1960 report was published under the title 'Partners in Patronage', and, as has been noted, in 1970 theatres were reported to recover 75 per cent of their costs from ticket sales. Commercial sponsorship grew in importance, too, and in 1976 Jennie Lee was a member of the panel that set up the Association for Business Sponsorship of the Arts (ABSA), declaring that the Arts existed in a 'mixed economy now'.[99] Nonetheless, one writer concluded in 1983 that 'subsidy has, for the majority of regional theatres, become a vital part of their operation'.[100] In 1963, the vice chancellor of the University of Exeter suggested of the new Northcott Theatre, then under construction on campus, that 'it is by no means so vital to produce revenue all the time'.[101] Similarly, in 1956 the management of the Nottingham Playhouse appealed for support from the city authorities on the basis that 'normal business calculations' of the sort that sustained the commercial theatre could not apply to the kind of theatre that they provided.[102] In Reading in 1977, the management of the new Hexagon put it more bluntly: they were 'not in the business of making money'.[103]

Theatre was increasingly presented as a matter for routine public spending. One Leatherhead councillor argued in 1966 that 'the financial provision for minority amenities is a basic function of all local authorities',[104] while Labour councillors in Nottingham reported that 'providing for people's leisure is almost as important as jobs, housing and education'.[105] In response to the growing number of civic theatres, Emile Littler, the owner of a major chain of touring venues, told the *Stage* in 1958 that he thought there might be no more new commercial theatres built.[106] The introduction of the 'Housing the Arts' fund in 1965 seemed only to confirm this

[98] SHC, 6368/10/6, clippings: *Surrey Advertiser*, 13 August 1966; Hazel Vincent Wallace, 'Let's Be Constructive', *Stage*, 2 May 1963, p. 16.
[99] Sinclair, *Arts and Cultures*, p. 172.
[100] Rowell and Jackson, *Repertory Movement*, pp. 114–15.
[101] UoEx, 26/1d/2d, clipping: '100,000 Gift by Devon Millionaire', *Express and Echo*, 12 February 1963.
[102] NA, DD/NP/1/2/1/1, Directors to Nottingham Corporation, 8 October 1956.
[103] RCL, Hexagon file, 'Space Age', *Reading Evening Post*, 13 October 1977.
[104] SHC, 6368/10/6, clippings: Councillor S. J. Taylor, quoted in *Leatherhead Advertiser*, 8 October 1966.
[105] Quoted in Nick Hayes, *Consensus and Controversy: City Politics in Nottingham, 1945–1966* (Liverpool, 1996), p. 167.
[106] Emile Littler, 'The Theatre I Would Build', *Stage*, 27 March 1958; see also Peter Jay, 'Theatres: stage and auditorium', *Architectural Review* 113 (March 1963), pp. 174–85 (p. 175).

direction of travel, with the MP Hugh Jenkins suggesting that 'the new theatre builders [a]re not going to be private organisations but public authorities'.[107] Only a few examples, such as Chichester Festival Theatre, deviated from this pattern (and even then, Chichester did receive a small Arts Council revenue grant).[108] The extent to which the system facilitated local initiatives is important. The Arts Council acted largely responsively, while the 1948 Act allowed local authorities flexibility, with some fully financing a civic theatre, others making grants to repertory companies, and some being notably less generous. Furthermore, civic and repertory theatres remained largely independent in their activities, usually being managed by trusts and boards.[109] Programming remained the responsibility of the artistic director.[110]

The stability and higher standards afforded by even modest levels of subsidy enabled expanded horizons. In mid-1950s Nottingham, for example, a new theatre was thought to be essential as a way to accommodate the growing audience; it was reported that potential patrons were often turned away, either because the class of seat they wanted was unavailable or because the theatre was full.[111] There was also competition between theatres, and in Sheffield, for example, the repertory company in 1965 proposed a makeover in response to the 'exciting new look' of theatres in Nottingham and Coventry.[112] Similarly in Salisbury, the chairman of the town's Playhouse informed the town clerk in 1969 that 'unless we can be rehoused within five years we will have the worst building of any permanent repertory company in the country and it will be increasingly difficult to attract good actors, directors and technical staff here'.[113]

Ultimately, therefore, the advent of a system of public subsidy allowed theatres to be conceived during the 1950s and 1960s as public amenities with a transformative role. There are parallels here with developments elsewhere in Europe after 1945, with culture frequently being seen as something that would foster active citizens.[114] But the recasting of theatres in these terms also meant that questions of use and policy sometimes became almost secondary amid debates about cultural enlightenment, communal identities, civic pride, or the idea of the theatre as a prominent building within the modernized townscape. Thus the critic Colin Amery, reviewing Colchester's Mercury Theatre in 1972, noted:

[107] 'Civic Theatres, Their Housing and Administration', *Stage and Television Today Supplement*, 4 March 1965, p. 2.

[108] WSRO, Box 52, memo re Arts Council grants, 1971/72.

[109] For the formation of the Trust at Coventry in preference to 'direct management', see 'Civic Theatre Plan at Coventry', *Stage*, 11 April 1957, p. 1.

[110] Rowell and Jackson, *Repertory Movement*, p. 116.

[111] NA, DD/NP/1/2/1/1, Directors to Nottingham Corporation, 8 October 1956.

[112] SCA, LD2341, Playhouse Board minutes, 28 January 1965.

[113] W&SA, G23/132/249, W. G. Vizard to G. Richardson, 20 January 1969.

[114] Kenny Cupers, 'The Cultural Center: architecture as cultural policy in post-war Europe', *Journal of the Society of Architectural Historians* 74, no. 4 (2015), pp. 464–84.

> The architect, Norman Downie, [...] has been fortunate in being able to work closely with the director of the repertory company, David Forder, to a specific brief that they could both follow through to completion. Surprisingly, this is quite rare: theatres have often been built without a particular client, the local authority first building a theatre and then appointing a director.[115]

One such theatre 'built without a particular client' was the Belgrade in Coventry, where the city councillors appear to have given little thought to who might use the new civic theatre that they were so keen to build. The city was home to the Arts Council-funded Midland Theatre Company, and although early proposals for the theatre made mention of this group, the Belgrade Theatre was seemingly designed with little reference to them.[116] Its programming policy and management were only decided shortly before the theatre was opened in March 1958,[117] by which time the Midland Theatre Company had been wound up.[118] In Glasgow, too, it was said of the proposed new Cultural Centre in May 1966:

> admittedly [the city authorities] consulted the potential users but it is not clear to what extent they acted on their advice. In the case of the repertory theatre, at least, it seems they merely kept the Citizens' Theatre Company informed of their intentions—'This is what we are providing; we hope you like it'.[119]

In nearby Dumbarton, meanwhile, members of the People's Theatre were only consulted by the local authority after design work on the new civic theatre had begun, and their suggestions were reportedly ignored in favour of those made by Colin Chandler of the Royal Scottish Academy of Music and Drama.[120]

In these circumstances, a degree of vagueness could prevail. A report commissioned for the Arts Council and the Gulbenkian Foundation in the 1970s concluded that 'the majority of Universities seem to have built their theatre buildings with insufficient thought as to what role they are intended to play, both within the University and in the region'.[121] Meanwhile a concerned Alexander

[115] 'Theatre at Colchester', *Architects' Journal* 156 (5 July 1972), pp. 19–34 (pp. 22–4).

[116] 'Criticism: the architects reply', *Architects' Journal* 128 (21 August 1958), pp. 269–70: 'Ideally the director of a theatre should be appointed and policy decided before the architect produces his sketch designs.'

[117] CHC, CCA/TC/1/1/29, clippings: *Coventry Standard*, 23 November 1956; *Coventry Evening Telegraph*, 2 March 1957 and 1 April 1957.

[118] The company was formally wound up in June 1957, closing with a performance of Philip Mackie's *Death in the Family*. *The Times*, 21 June 1957, p. 3 states that the Arts Council had decided to disband the company in anticipation of the new Belgrade opening the following spring, and the *Stage* reported the same on 20 June 1957. Bryan Bailey was appointed to run the Belgrade in July: see *Stage*, 25 July 1957. Presumably there was some continuity in terms of personnel between the Midland Theatre Company and the new repertory company at the Belgrade, which may have made the latter seem like the former in all but name.

[119] 'Capital Catching Up With Its Festival', *Scotsman*, 2 May 1966.

[120] Alistair McNeill, 'Civic Theatre—or White Elephant?', *Scottish Theatre*, September 1969, pp. 19–20.

[121] UoN, 00-0181, Arts Council of Great Britain/Gulbenkian Foundation, 'University Studio Theatres'.

Dunbar of the North-Eastern Association for the Arts wrote of Billingham Forum in 1965:

> I have [...] been concerned to find out exactly what Billingham [Urban District Council] proposes to use the Theatre for. I do not think Billingham had properly considered this; and had hazy notions of having the National Theatre and Sadlers Wells [...].[122]

In this respect, then, the expanded field of organizations and interests that so productively reshaped the practice and landscape of post-war theatre perhaps also muddied the waters when it came to the conception and design of the new buildings that were enabled by the emergence of subsidy.

[122] V&A, ACGB/84/21, Alexander Dunbar to Jo Hodgkinson, 26 November 1965.

2

'Housing the Arts'

Funding Capital Projects

When John Maynard Keynes outlined the ambitions of the Arts Council of Great Britain in July 1945, he highlighted 'the shortage—in most parts of Britain the complete absence—of [. . .] suitable buildings' for the arts.[1] The need to prioritize the reconstruction of housing, schools, and other essential services meant that this 'shortage' remained unaddressed in the short term. Only with the easing of austerity measures in the mid-1950s did attention start to turn to the construction of new theatres. Some of these theatres were conceived in time-honoured tradition as commercial ventures, such as the New London Theatre in the West End (completed in 1972), while others were entirely the product of local fundraising. However, the building boom that changed the landscape of regional British theatre between the 1950s and the 1980s was fundamentally enabled by public funding. Chapter 1 discussed the availability and impact of subsidies for practice, but grants and loans were also increasingly available for building projects. The 1948 Local Government Act enabled local authorities to build civic theatres and also to support the construction of theatres by other organizations, including repertory companies. In 1965, the Arts Council of Great Britain launched a programme of funding for capital projects, which it named 'Housing the Arts'. That said, with the exception of certain civic examples, theatres were rarely built entirely with public money. Most drew on several sources of funding, including donations from individuals, charitable organizations, and businesses.[2] 'Housing the Arts' grants, for example, averaged just 19 per cent of total project costs in the early 1970s.[3]

This chapter examines how major regional theatre-building projects were funded. It discusses local-authority finance, grant-giving trusts, and fundraising by theatre managements and audiences, but its principal focus is the Arts Council's 'Housing the Arts' programme. The fund, which survived into the 1980s, had nationwide impact. Of the 187 projects which it supported between 1965 and April 1973, all but fourteen were outside London.[4] By March 1976, £8,214,500

[1] ACGB, 'Annual Report' [1945], pp. 20–3 (p. 22) (also published as 'The Arts Council: its policy and hopes', *The Listener*, 12 July 1945).

[2] Roderick Ham, *Theatre Planning* (London, 1972), p. 249.

[3] V&A, ACGB/120/43, 'Fifteen Years of Achievements' [report, 1973], p. 3.

[4] V&A, ACGB/120/35, Hugh Willatt to C. W. Wright, 13 November 1973.

had been committed to 291 schemes with a total cost of £42.35 million.[5] Its grants were often seen to be a sign of approval. In Bedford in 1973, for example, the authorities offered funding towards a proposed new theatre on condition that support was also forthcoming from 'Housing the Arts' and from the public.[6] Their stipulation neatly captured the way in which new theatres were conceived and funded as local projects within a national context.

LOCAL-AUTHORITY FUNDING FOR THEATRE BUILDINGS

When Coventry's Belgrade Theatre opened in March 1958, it attracted attention not only as the first major theatre to be constructed in Britain for nearly twenty years, but also as the country's first purpose-built civic theatre. That the city councillors had 'decide[d] to spend £220,000 on a bauble as superfluous as a civic playhouse' was, for the *Observer*'s drama critic, Kenneth Tynan, 'one of the great decisions in the history of local government'.[7] Other authorities followed Coventry's example. By far the most ambitious was the Corporation of London, whose £163 million Barbican Arts Centre (completed in 1982) included theatres, a concert hall, cinemas, a library, and conference facilities. Substantial—if not quite so large—civic schemes were conceived by many other local authorities across Britain. Billingham Urban District Council, for example, used the rates income generated by the town's rapidly expanding chemical industries to build a new town centre, spending more than £20 million on urban development between 1945 and 1965.[8] It was the principal sponsor of the £1 million Forum complex (1968), which included a sports centre and theatre. In north Wales, Flintshire County Council promoted a major arts complex in Mold which included Theatr Clwyd (1976), and set aside £410,000 towards the eventual £2.6 million cost.[9] Meanwhile in Inverness in March 1973, the Borough Council applied to borrow £800,000 towards the costs of Eden Court Theatre, to be paid back from future rates income, with the balance of the cost of the theatre to come from Arts Council and Highlands and Islands Development Board grants (£300,000), and a local campaign fund.[10] Other notable council-led (though not necessarily entirely council-funded) theatres were built in Eastbourne (the Congress, 1963), Swindon (the Wyvern, 1971), Leicester (the Haymarket, 1973), and Plymouth (Theatre Royal, 1982). Key unbuilt examples that were promoted by local authorities include a substantial cultural centre proposed for Glasgow, initial designs for which date from the mid-1960s. Also significant were Edinburgh's

[5] V&A, ACGB/120/3, Council Paper 599: 'Assessment of Architectural and Technical Aspects of Schemes' [March 1976].

[6] V&A, ACGB/120/35, Special Committee report, 12 October 1973.

[7] 'Curtain Up at Coventry', *Observer*, 30 March 1958.

[8] V&A, ACGB/84/21, F. M. Dawson to Nigel Abercrombie, 7 October 1965.

[9] FA, CC/3/9, 'The Official Opening of Theatr Clwyd and Educational Technology Centre, Mold', 21 May 1976.

[10] HA, HCA/D628/1/2, Derek C. Bigg, 'The Pre-history of Eden Court Theatre, Inverness', unpublished MS, p. 3.

plans to build a large theatre, popularly known as the 'opera house', which went through several iterations during the 1960s and early 1970s before being abandoned in 1975.

Whereas a civic theatre would essentially be provided by the local authority, in many other cases a local council would part-fund the construction of a theatre conceived and managed by an independent trust or repertory company. In Birmingham at the end of the 1960s, for example, the City Council contributed £640,000 towards the new £886,000 Repertory Theatre and provided a site for it.[11] In Colchester in 1967, the Mercury Theatre received a site and £60,000; the balance, originally estimated at £200,000, was to come from the Arts Council and a public appeal.[12] In Derby, the Borough Council's decision in 1969 to offer the repertory company a grant of £100,000 plus a site at a peppercorn rent was significant in driving forward the campaign to build a new Playhouse.[13] The council's involvement was crucial. When the Arts Council was initially unable to offer a 'Housing the Arts' grant, the local authority increased its offer to £150,000, made available a loan of at least the same amount again, and offered to guarantee a building society loan.[14] (By 1974, the Arts Council had committed £130,000 to Derby, although severe inflation meant that the final contract cost now edged close to £700,000.) In Bolton, the promoters of the Octagon Theatre were given a site for which no rent would be charged plus a grant of £5000 (towards a total cost estimated in 1966 as £60,000), as well as an annual subsidy.[15] In Farnham, the Urban District Council offered the repertory company a historic building, Brightwell House, plus one-third of an acre on which to expand. On a grander scale, the London County Council (LCC) gave a crucial shot in the arm to the proposed National Theatre in 1961 when it confirmed its offer of a site for the building and a grant of at least £1 million, provided that £1 million was forthcoming from central government.[16] An Act of Parliament promising state funding had been passed in 1949, but little progress had been made, and so the LCC's action essentially forced the hand of the government. By 1967, the deal was such that the Treasury and the Greater London Council would each contribute half of the estimated capital cost, then some £7.5 million.[17]

Nonetheless, local authorities' action was circumscribed by several factors. First, successive governments restricted the availability of credit as a means of economic control, with the need for 'loan sanction' often delaying projects during the 1950s and 1960s.[18] In addition, wider economic circumstances often slowed progress.

[11] LoB, MS 2339/4/9, Robert Aitken to Alexander Dunbar, 5 February 1971.

[12] ERO, C1371/10, clippings: 'Theatre Was Fruit of a Garden Talk', *Evening Gazette*, 10 May 1976.

[13] V&A, ACGB/84/91, A. P. W. Burrows to N. V. Linklater, 22 November 1969.

[14] DRO, D738/4/1, '£600,000 Plan for New Theatre to Go Ahead', *Evening Telegraph*, 1 February 1973.

[15] V&A, ACGB/84/37, G. A. Harrison to Jo Hodgkinson, 15 July 1966.

[16] Barnabas Calder, 'Committees and Concrete: the genesis and architecture of Denys Lasdun's National Theatre' (PhD diss., University of Cambridge, 2007), p. 26.

[17] Calder, 'Committees and Concrete', p. 32.

[18] For example, the Congress Theatre: ESRO, DE/A/5/15, Finance and General Purposes minutes, 29 October 1956, reference to MHLG Circular 55/56; DE/A/5/16, Finance and General Purposes minutes, 28 August 1961, for Circular 37/61. See also V&A, ACGB/120/9, HTA minutes, 20 October 1965.

In February 1968, a civil servant in the Ministry of Housing and Local Government recorded that 'following devaluation [of the pound in late 1967], severe cuts have been made in the amount of capital expenditure available for civic, amenity and cultural projects'.[19] Local government reorganization and national curbs on spending had similar effects during the 1970s.[20] Political arguments, too, could affect progress. After the abandonment in 1975 of much-debated proposals for a new theatre in Lincoln, the architect, Sam Scorer, concluded ruefully that local politics had hammered the final nail into the scheme's coffin.[21] In this respect, local-authority funding for capital projects could be as controversial as supporting the practice of the arts. Potentially, given the greater sums involved and the implication that councillors might also be committing themselves to ongoing revenue subsidy, the debates could be even more fraught. In Plymouth in the 1970s, for example, there were long discussions regarding the proposed Theatre Royal. The city's Labour politicians initially opposed the project on the basis that a repertory theatre might appeal only to elite tastes, an argument that shows how local attitudes might differ from those of the party leadership.[22] Later, however, Labour proved more enthusiastic while the Conservatives opposed the principle of a subsidized theatre, preferring instead a commercially run venue for touring shows; one critic painted a picture of 'sinister, yet blithely accepted running losses'.[23] Peter Moro's design for the Theatre Royal had to navigate these entrenched positions. As built, the auditorium has a variable capacity suited both to large-scale touring shows and smaller, potentially subsidized productions.

The terms of the debate in Plymouth would have seemed familiar to Moro, as the birth of the new Nottingham Playhouse, completed to his designs in 1963, had been characterized by similar arguments.[24] A replacement for the old Playhouse, it was to be funded with the money raised when the municipal gasworks had been nationalized, the proceeds having been earmarked for a scheme that would benefit the city. However, many local Conservatives favoured 'civic minimalism', placing newspaper advertisements during the 1959 election which criticized the use of public money to build a theatre. After a period when Labour's majority teetered on a knife-edge, the party finally lost control of the council in May 1961, and the new Conservative-led administration attempted to give the part-built Playhouse to the Moss Empires chain of commercial theatres. The offer was eventually rejected, however, in part because Moro's design had been conceived for a subsidized repertory company and so lacked the audience capacity needed for an unsubsidized, commercially run touring theatre to be viable. A legal challenge also seemed likely if the

19 V&A, ACGB/84/147, S. J. B. Hurden to J. C. Nelson, 29 February 1968.

20 V&A, ACGB/120/9, HTA minutes, 25 June 1975.

21 V&A, ACGB/84/163, clipping: 'Super-theatre Drama Ending', *Lincolnshire Echo*, 5 November 1975.

22 PCL, Theatre Royal clippings: 'Small Theatre "Would Only Be For Minority"', *Western Morning News*, 5 June 1970.

23 PCL, Theatre Royal clippings: 'Theatre: can it be stopped?', *Western Evening Herald*, 10 February 1978.

24 Nick Hayes, *Consensus and Controversy: City Politics in Nottingham, 1945–66* (Liverpool, 1996), pp. 162–86.

transfer went ahead, while Moss Empires was unwilling to enter local politics and stated that it did not wish to hinder the construction of a civic theatre. As the historian Nick Hayes has concluded, the Conservatives fell victim to their own argument, namely that Nottingham could have either a municipal/subsidized theatre or a private/commercial theatre, but apparently not both.[25]

Even when local-authority support was forthcoming, the miserliness that characterized some councils' subsidies for artistic practice was sometimes also evident when it came to capital projects. In Guildford, the Yvonne Arnaud Theatre building fund in 1962 received just 250 guineas from Surrey County Council, a tiny sum when the theatre was projected to cost £350,000.[26] Furthermore, funding often came with strings attached. The managements of Coventry's Belgrade Theatre and the Nottingham Playhouse were both required to repay the money that had been provided to build their theatres.[27] Jennie Lee was presumably thinking of this sort of example when in 1965, as Minister for the Arts, she called for greater generosity. The increased Arts Council budgets over which she presided were, as was discussed in Chapter 1, intended to encourage local authorities to support the arts, but she was especially keen to promote investment in buildings. The means by which she sought to do so was the 'Housing the Arts' programme.

THE ORIGINS OF 'HOUSING THE ARTS'

The phrase 'Housing the Arts' first appeared formally as the title of the Arts Council of Great Britain's Annual Report for 1954–5. The Arts Council had hitherto occasionally turned its attention to architectural matters, with designs for a prototype Arts Centre being circulated in 1945–6, for example, while a theatre-planning advisory service was launched in February 1950.[28] However, the 1954–5 Annual Report inaugurated a more sustained engagement with buildings. Its focus had been prompted by the recent inquiry into the replacement of London's bombed Queen's Hall, which had called for a coordinated survey of current provision and future requirements, but it was also timely. The recent abolition of the post-war system of building licences allowed a more expansive approach. For now, however, the report painted a bleak picture. No permanent theatres had been built since 1939, 120 theatres had closed, major venues such as Covent Garden were outdated, and the country's spending on the arts was depressingly low. What was needed, it concluded, was to spend £1 million on buildings in each of the next ten years.

The report made brief mention of the role of 'Parliament and local authorities' in deciding what level of spending on buildings was possible, but gave little clue as to where the money would come from, or how it would be apportioned. It called

[25] Hayes, *Consensus and Controversy*, pp. 162–86.

[26] SHC, 7018/2/4/143, clippings: *Surrey Advertiser*, 26 January 1962.

[27] ACGB, 'The Theatre Today in England and Wales: the report of the Arts Council Theatre Enquiry' [1970], pp. 36–7.

[28] ACGB, Annual Report, 1949–1950, pp. 21–2.

for 'prudence and deliberation', arguing that 'a hundred civic theatres manned by second-rate professional actors would not create a renaissance of drama'.[29] Instead, it proposed 'thirty exemplary theatres', in which:

> the living art of drama is more likely to be sustained than it is at present—distributed in penny packets in precarious establishments committed to the suicidal policy of weekly 'rep', or sent forth on vain, if adventurous, mobile missions to play Shakespeare on improvised stages in village halls.[30]

(The Arts Council's then secretary-general, William Emrys Williams, made the same point in a separate report that same year: 'music and drama must have fixed abodes where resident companies can develop their skill and *esprit* and sense of purpose'.[31]) Amateur theatre was to be left to its own devices; similarly, 'show business and the commercial theatre will solve their problems of housing (and everything else) on purely economic calculations'.[32]

For the time being, the Arts Council proposed that it should remain a gatherer of information.[33] It was keen to avoid 'a grandiose plan for building theatres and halls up and down the country—and it would preserve that attitude even if the need to maintain full employment in the building industry should ever make Ministers excessively well-disposed to such ventures'.[34] Nonetheless, it hoped for 'a consolidated national agenda' in which potential schemes could be identified and prioritized. To that end, an enquiry was set up at the request of the then Chancellor of the Exchequer, Harold Macmillan. Led by Llewelyn Wyn Griffith, the novelist and Arts Council vice-chairman, it presented its findings in a two-volume report, again under the title 'Housing the Arts'.[35] The first volume, published in 1959, examined London, Scotland, and Wales, and considered topics including the potential to add certain theatres to the growing lists of buildings of historic interest and the need for a national body to which proposed theatre demolitions could be referred. Volume Two followed two years later and examined 'the needs of the English provinces'. It cited the increasing if still limited interest of local authorities in supporting the theatre, and noted the recent growth of repertory theatre. While it cautioned against the retention of older theatres for sentimental reasons, it suggested that some could successfully become civic venues, with a central loan fund supporting necessary refurbishment. New theatres would remain a matter of local initiative. At the same time, a 'grid' of theatres was proposed, with the implication that this 'grid' might be coordinated (reprising an idea that had appeared in the council's Annual Report for 1953–4), while either the Arts Council or a 'National Trust for Theatres' would fund capital projects.

[29] ACGB, Annual Report, 1954–1955 ('Housing the Arts'), pp. 14–15.
[30] ACGB, Annual Report, 1954–1955, p. 10.
[31] Andrew Sinclair, *Arts and Cultures: The History of the Fifty Years of the Arts Council of Great Britain* (London, 1995), p. 101.
[32] ACGB, Annual Report, 1954–1955 ('Housing the Arts'), p. 9.
[33] ACGB, Annual Report, 1954–1955, p. 16.
[34] ACGB, Annual Report, 1954–1955, p. 9.
[35] ACGB, 'Housing the Arts in Great Britain', 2 vols [1959 and 1961].

In July 1961, the Arts Council was informed that Chancellor of the Exchequer Selwyn Lloyd was prepared to make an allocation for capital works.[36] Meanwhile, the 1961–2 Annual Report recorded that around a fifth of the increase in the following year's budget would be spent on building projects.[37] These developments belie Jennie Lee's later claim that 'not one single penny was set aside for capital expenditure on the arts' under the Conservative governments of the 1950s and 1960s, in spite of talk of '"never having it so good", about the affluent society, and all the rest of it'.[38] Nonetheless, her White Paper of 1965 and the subsequent launch of 'Housing the Arts' were significant, with funding for capital projects being increased and offered on a more systematic basis than hitherto. A sum of £250,000 was to be allocated in 1965 and £500,000 in subsequent years.[39] Lee's particular interest in (theatre) architecture reflected the significant role that she felt it might play in the creation of the 'gayer and more cultivated' Britain that she sought.[40] Architectural grandeur was not necessarily her aim, however. In 1968, it was reported that Lee 'felt that architects were often too concerned with the artistic appearance of a theatre and did not give enough attention to the physical comforts of its occupants'.[41] In this respect, she hoped new theatres would tempt on account of their facilities and the improved quality of work that they would accommodate. Hugh Willatt made much the same point, though referring also to the attractions of architectural modernity:

> all the evidence [. . .] has shown that an entirely new theatre designed to enable a particular working unit to operate efficiently and economically has enormous advantages over an old building, however well converted. Equally important, from the point of view of the audience, and particularly younger people, there is in a new building an appeal which is lacking in an old one, however well modernised.[42]

Ultimately, therefore, 'Housing the Arts' was to be a means by which to build audiences as well as buildings.[43]

'HOUSING THE ARTS' IN OPERATION

What was initially called the 'Capital Grants Committee' began its work in 1965.[44] There were several early expressions of interest. Sheffield, for example, was one of the first off the blocks, writing in April 1965 to see if the fund might support work to the existing Playhouse; ultimately £7500 was offered for improvements to the

36 ACGB, Annual Report, 1961–1962 ('A Brighter Prospect'), p. 30.
37 ACGB, Annual Report, 1961–1962, p. 14.
38 Hansard, HC Deb 27 April 1965, vol. 711, c. 288–99.
39 Patricia Hollis, *Jennie Lee: A Life* (Oxford, 1997), p. 268.
40 Hollis, *Jennie Lee*, p. 268.
41 NRS, ED61/71, 'Lyceum/Castle Terrace Redevelopment, Edinburgh', 27 November 1968.
42 V&A, ACGB/84/28, Hugh Willatt to T. H. Parkinson, 29 October 1968.
43 Hollis, *Jennie Lee*, p. 268.
44 V&A, ACGB/120/9, HTA minutes, 28 July 1965.

sound system and the refurbishment of the bar.[45] Indeed, Lee was able to tell Parliament that same month that £215,000 had already been committed, with recipients in Birmingham (the Midlands Arts Centre), Boston, Bridgnorth, St Austell, Shaftesbury, Weymouth, and Worcester.[46] In March 1965, it was confirmed that commitments would be made to schemes that were also supported by local authorities. Grants would not exceed 50 per cent of the total cost of the project, and would usually be less.[47] Although small awards could be (and were) made, there was a presumption in favour of larger projects. The governors of Pitlochry Festival Theatre, for example, were seemingly encouraged by the Scottish Arts Council in 1965 to 'think big and get ourselves at the head of the queue'.[48] Nonetheless, the limited nature of the annual allocation meant that in practice there was an upper limit on eligible schemes. So-called 'monster projects', such as the proposed Edinburgh 'opera house', were considered separately as special cases.[49] In practice, finding money for such large schemes was rarely straightforward, and few came to fruition.[50]

Applications for capital funding were all considered within the Arts Council's Finance Department in London. From 1969, a dedicated 'Housing the Arts' officer—Peter Longman until 1978, and later Judith Strong—oversaw the assessment process. Funding was offered responsively.[51] Nonetheless, applicants were assessed against an idealized map of provision—quite literally, as Longman maintained a large map of existing and proposed venues.[52] The 1961 report had recommended that towns with a population greater than 250,000 should have a major theatre. A report of February 1976 similarly proposed an 'Abstract Plan' in which towns with a population of more than 200,000 would have a large theatre for touring productions and those with a population of 100,000 or more would have a medium-sized touring venue plus a repertory theatre.[53] Location was not the only factor taken into account, however. Other factors which informed the assessment process included the projected type of facility, the anticipated degree of professional use, an estimate of need, the suitability and technical competence of the design, the feasibility of the project finances, and the implications for revenue subsidy.[54] A report was then presented to the 'Housing the Arts' Committee, which met every two months. It was convened by the council's deputy chairman and

[45] V&A, ACGB/84/246, David Brayshaw to Jo Hodgkinson, 12 April 1965, and Nigel Abercrombie to David Brayshaw, 26 August 1965.

[46] Hansard, HC Deb 27 April 1965, vol. 711, c. 289. The Midlands Arts Centre demonstrated the mixed nature of funding: 80 per cent of its construction costs came from private sources, including the unions and industry. See John Elsom, *Theatre Outside London* (London, 1971), pp. 171–2.

[47] V&A, ACGB/120/47, Secretary-General's note, 24 March 1965.

[48] PFT, uncat. Board minutes, 31 May 1965.

[49] V&A, ACGB/120/3, 'Housing the Arts' [background paper, 1978]; NRS, ED61/82, 'Major Capital Projects for the Arts', 10 April 1970. Also considered thus was a proposed opera house in Manchester in *c.*1965–70. HTA money was sometimes forthcoming in 'monster' cases: see NRS, ED61/87, C. W. Wright to I. M. Robertson, 26 September 1973.

[50] Alistair Fair, '"An Object Lesson in How Not To Get Things Done": Edinburgh's unbuilt "opera house", 1960–75', *Architectural Heritage* 27 (2017), pp. 91–117.

[51] V&A, ACGB/120/9, HTA minutes, 31 January 1973.

[52] Peter Longman, interviewed 30 January 2015.

[53] V&A, ACGB/120/1, 'Paper 442: Survey of Buildings to House the Arts', 18 February 1976.

[54] V&A, ACGB/120/1, 'A Review of Housing the Arts in Wales' [January 1975].

comprised the chairs of the Arts Council's Art, Drama, Music, Regional, and Touring panels, plus representatives of the Scottish and Welsh Arts Councils, and (from the early 1970s) independent members. The report typically included the views of the 'Housing the Arts' officer, as well as a technical assessment by the Association of British Theatre Technicians' Theatre Planning Committee (which is discussed further in Chapter 8).

Although some early applications seem to have been waved through, the Arts Council increasingly engaged critically with schemes. The authorities in Derby were told in 1972 that:

> We would be happier about the whole scheme, and our contributions to the capital and revenue sides, if the capital cost, and therefore the borrowing element, could be reduced. We have in mind the very satisfactory theatre recently opened in Colchester at a total cost of £250,000.[55]

In May that year, it was proposed that the Arts Council might convene a special panel to consider selected proposals in detail,[56] and these panels, which drew on external expertise, turned out to be especially willing to criticize. In June 1973, for example, a group chaired by the director Michael Elliott reported of the proposed theatre at Ipswich that 'the combination of the present site with the present architect and the present budgeted cost would not produce a good result'.[57] The Drama, Finance and Policy Committee took up the theme, concluding that 'it would be preferable to have no theatre there at all than a totally unsatisfactory one'.[58] The issues were multiple. How workable was the proposed adaptable auditorium? Was the budget too small? The theatre's rather anodyne elevations, which were the work of a local firm, Vine and Vine, also came under fire.[59] However, Elliott's panel 'did not feel it proper or possible to insist on a change of architect'.[60] Nonetheless, an experienced technical specialist, Martin Carr, joined the design team, and in December 1975 a revised scheme was presented.[61] Although the auditorium seemed better (if nonetheless 'idiosyncratic'), continuing doubts prompted Peter Longman to propose that the Arts Council should insist on the appointment of a consultant architect.[62] In summer 1976, Vine and Vine were replaced by Roderick Ham, the experienced designer of new theatres at Leatherhead and Derby,[63] ending what Longman dubbed 'one of the longest continuing sagas on the Housing the Arts files'.[64]

The 'saga' in Ipswich played out against an increasing interest in architectural quality on the part of the 'Housing the Arts' Committee. Peter Moro and the theatre

55 V&A, ACGB/84/91, Hugh Willatt to N. S. Fisher, 7 August 1972.
56 V&A, ACGB/120/33, Notes on a meeting at the ABTT, 12 May 1972.
57 V&A, ACGB/84/147, Special Committee report, 28 June 1973.
58 V&A, ACGB/120/9, HTA minutes, 25 July 1973.
59 V&A, ACGB/120/3, HTA minutes, 26 November 1975. SRO, A1/312/4060/486 includes drawings of the Vine and Vine scheme.
60 V&A, ACGB/84/147, Special Committee report, 28 June 1973.
61 V&A, ACGB/84/147, Peter Longman memo, 5 December 1975.
62 V&A, ACGB/84/147, Peter Longman memo, 5 December 1975.
63 V&A, ACGB/84/147, Peter Longman memo, 29 July 1976.
64 V&A, ACGB/84/147, Peter Longman memo, 5 April 1977.

consultant Iain Mackintosh attended its February 1976 meeting to speak on this subject, citing the 'depressing' quality of many theatres.[65] To support such schemes with public money, Moro felt, was unjustifiable. It was not the first time that Moro had demonstrated an interest in design quality. He had been a member of the technical advisory panel convened during the 1960s by Edinburgh Corporation to consider the specification of the city's 'opera house', then being designed by William Kininmonth, but resigned in 1971. It was reported that 'he was unhappy with the architectural expression of it and did not want to be associated with the building which he felt must now result'.[66] Following the 1976 discussion, Moro was asked to join the 'Housing the Arts' Committee, and it was agreed that major schemes would routinely be referred for comment to the Royal Fine Art Commission.[67] In the longer term, the Arts Council in 1984 required that the architect of the new Leeds Playhouse be selected by means of a competition, the jury for which was chaired by Moro.[68]

'Housing the Arts' continued to allocate £500,000 annually until 1973–4, when its annual 'commitment ration' was raised to £750,000, and then to £1.25 million.[69] In practice, the allocation for each year was committed that year but was not claimed until it was actually needed (i.e. when a project had reached a certain stage). A number of rules governed the awards, not all of which were appreciated by recipients, as the Arts Council's Jean Bulwinkle noted in exasperated fashion in 1967:

> I am at a loss to understand why the companies to whom we offer capital grants cannot be told in these first letters that we can pay only 50% of their bills. Finance Department seem to think it sufficient for them to know this condition when 'detailed arrangements governing the offer' are sent. But the letters containing these detailed arrangements are very often not sent until much of the preliminary work has already started, and expenditure incurred.[70]

Potentially also problematic in view of the high rate of inflation in the early 1970s was the way that grants were made as a fixed sum rather than on a percentage basis, although an allowance for inflation was made. Further funding was not guaranteed, although the Arts Council was sometimes able to offer an ad hoc supplementary grant. Leicester, for example, had received £180,000 by 1974 for the new Haymarket Theatre as opposed to the £150,000 originally pencilled in during 1968, reflecting the way in which the total cost of the theatre had increased from an estimated £628,000 in 1968 to £968,000 by 1973.[71]

[65] V&A, ACGB/120/3, 'Architectural Assessment of Applications' [paper by Peter Moro, 16 February 1976], and HTA minutes, 25 February 1976.

[66] NRS, ED61/85, I. M. Robertson memo, 22 February 1972.

[67] V&A, ACGB/120/3, 'Assessment of Architectural and Technical Aspects of Schemes', 17 March 1976; HTA minutes, 27 April 1976.

[68] UoL, BC MS 20c Theatre LP Arc/2, Box 4, File A, part 1, Lord Howard to Charles Barber, 27 March 1984.

[69] V&A, ACGB/120/3, 'Housing the Arts' [background paper, 1978].

[70] V&A, ACGB/84/149, J. A. Bulwinkle to Jo Hodgkinson, 3 January 1967.

[71] V&A, ACGB/120/3, 'Discussion on Supplementary Contributions', paper for meeting of 26 November 1975.

The course of 'Housing the Arts' did not run smoothly during the 1970s. It was reported in April 1970 that the Arts Council had made more commitments than it could really afford.[72] In October that year, it was noted that the commitment rations for 1971–2 and 1972–3 had been taken up by schemes to which some form of indication had been given, while further 'urgent' applications totalling £1.025 million awaited a decision.[73] When the Bolton Octagon applied for funding for a projected Children's Theatre, the reply came back that the council had insufficient funds to enter a commitment, and that its priority had to be those projects already under way or to which a firm indication of support had been given.[74] Furthermore, the nature of the commitment system, in which promises were made against a total 'ration' for the year but might take several years to mature, prompted an appearance before the Public Accounts Committee.[75] Ultimately, a rolling triennial allocation was introduced. As of January 1972, it was proposed to make available £200,000 of the next year's ration, and £200,000 of the following year's allocation.[76]

Worsening public finances then took their toll. In February 1974, the Arts Council was informed that it could not commit any more of the 1974–5 and 1975–6 rations, nor could it reallocate any funds.[77] It had asked for an increased commitment ration, but was told that the cash allocation for 1974–5 would be reduced to £550,000. Although matters had improved by summer 1974,[78] government-imposed restrictions once again affected the programme after July 1976 in the wake of wider cuts in public expenditure.[79] The Department of Education and Science (DES) proposed that 'Housing the Arts' cash grant be cut, but—in what the Arts Council considered a fundamental misunderstanding of the nature of its commitments—it sought to reduce actual annual expenditure rather than the commitment ration.[80] Effectively, the council was to be denied the cash needed to meet commitments it had already made. Furthermore, although the Arts Council had asked to spend £1.35 million during 1977–8, the DES had assumed that the council intended to spend no more than £1 million that year, and so the money that was to be made available was actually some £850,000 below the sum that had been anticipated.[81] The reductions meant that it would take until 1982 to meet all the commitments that had already been made, and would mean that no further commitments could be taken on. Projects to which an indication of probable support had been made (but as yet no formal commitment had been entered into)

72 V&A, ACGB/120/9, HTA minutes, 29 April 1970.
73 V&A, ACGB/120/9, HTA minutes, 25 October 1970.
74 V&A, ACGB/84/37, Hugh Willatt to Robin Pemberton-Billing, 25 June 1970.
75 V&A, ACGB/120/9, HTA minutes, 28 July 1971.
76 V&A, ACGB/120/9, HTA minutes, 26 January 1972.
77 V&A, ACGB/120/9, HTA minutes, 27 February 1974.
78 V&A, ACGB/120/9, HTA minutes, 31 July 1974.
79 E.g. Mark Swenarton, 'Politics Versus Architecture: the Alexandra Road Public Enquiry, 1978–81', *Planning Perspectives* 29, no. 4 (2014), pp. 423–46 (p. 425).
80 V&A, ACGB/120/3, Paper 473, 'Housing the Arts Committee Meeting, 29 September 1976'.
81 V&A, ACGB/120/3, Paper 534, 'The Financial Situation and Future Policy', for meeting on 25 November 1977.

would now not be funded, possibly damaging the Arts Council's reputation.[82] In response to DES's view that only formal promises mattered, the committee noted that 'a strictly legal commitment is not the only commitment which should be honoured',[83] although offers of support had always been made on the basis that payment would be subject to Parliament's granting provision in due course.[84]

Major grants continued to be made, particularly in Scotland, where £200,000 was to be spent in 1979–80.[85] However, the punning title of a discussion paper of March 1978—'W(h)ither Housing the Arts'—highlighted ongoing problems, and it was reported in 1979 that 'cash—or, rather, the lack of it—has continued to be the dominant feature of [...] 1978/79'.[86] 'Many worthwhile schemes have had to be abandoned', it was noted in July 1978.[87] Phased grants, it was reported in 1979, meant that clients had to borrow money to cover the shortfall, incurring interest charges, while in other cases, local authorities took the Arts Council's lack of support as evidence that a scheme was not worth supporting.[88] Furthermore, even those projects which did manage to secure funding could be compromised by severe cost inflation. The lack of cash meant that it was now only rarely possible to make supplementary grants to 'ensure that the quality of the original design is maintained, that the finished building is properly equipped, or that all elements necessary for its proper function are included'.[89]

Several less cash-dependent roles for the 'Housing the Arts' Committee were considered in the early 1980s, including its recasting as an advisory service akin to that provided by the Sports Council.[90] It was noted in October 1983 that the scheme was no longer operating within the terms of its contract,[91] and that it had virtually reached the limits of its ability to take on new commitments.[92] If such a conclusion was intended to encourage greater investment, the money failed to materialize. Although the Belgrade Theatre was told in January 1984 that its application for a contribution to refurbishment costs would be considered,[93] it was concluded in March that 'Housing the Arts' could only survive with larger budgets, and that if such budgets could not be found then the money would be better spent on revenue funding.[94] A decision to phase out the fund soon followed.[95] However, the closure of 'Housing the Arts' was not the disaster that it might have been ten

[82] V&A, ACGB/120/9, HTA minutes, 29 September 1976.
[83] V&A, ACGB/120/9, HTA minutes, 29 September 1976.
[84] Peter Longman, pers. comm., February 2015.
[85] V&A, ACGB/120/41, Harry McCann memo, 13 April 1979.
[86] V&A, ACGB/120/3, 'W(h)ither Housing the Arts', 22 March 1978; ACGB/120/28, 'Housing the Arts, 1978/79'.
[87] V&A, ACGB/120/3, 'Housing the Arts—Council Paper No. 696', 19 July 1978.
[88] V&A, ACGB/120/3, Paper 605, 'Housing the Arts Fund Cash Allocation' [1979].
[89] V&A, ACGB/120/3, Paper 605, 'Housing the Arts Fund Cash Allocation' [1979].
[90] V&A, ACGB/120/3, 'The Role of the Housing the Arts Committee', 17 March 1981; ACGB/120/4, HTA minutes, 27 July 1983.
[91] V&A, ACGB/120/3, 'The Continuing Demand for Capital Funding' [October 1983].
[92] V&A, ACGB/120/4, HTA minutes, 14 October 1983.
[93] V&A, ACGB/84/85, Judith Strong to Robert J. Tarr, 23 January 1984.
[94] V&A, ACGB/120/4, HTA minutes, 26 March 1984.
[95] V&A, ACGB/120/40, HTA minutes, 11 April 1984.

years previously. New sources of funding had emerged, especially if a case could be made for a theatre's possible contribution to economic development, an idea that assumed increasing significance in the 1970s and 1980s. In addition, the majority of the country's major repertory companies had been rehoused, while numerous smaller projects had also been assisted, especially after 'Housing the Arts' widened its terms of reference in the early 1970s to include such things as temporary venues.[96] Grants had also been made towards the restoration of some of the country's older theatres. In this respect, the ambitions of 1955 had arguably been met—and perhaps even exceeded.

OTHER FUNDING SOURCES

In April 1976, Peter Longman counted thirty projects on the year's preliminary 'Housing the Arts' list.[97] Leaving aside three 'monster' projects, their total value was an estimated £12 million, with the Arts Council planning to allocate £2 million and local authorities around £6 million. Allowing for contributions from other grant-giving bodies, around £3 million remained to be found by the appeals planned by twenty-one of the applicants, an average of £150,000 each. In this respect, although the theatre-building boom of the 1960s and 1970s was fundamentally enabled by public subsidies, it was—with the exception of a few civic theatres—rare that a new theatre would be entirely built with public money. What other sources were available?

Some theatres, especially those with a resident repertory company, were able to muster support from their loyal audiences. Guildford's Yvonne Arnaud Theatre was nearing completion in 1965 when one peer told the House of Lords about this 'most elegant and delightful theatre, built almost entirely by local private subscriptions'.[98] Later in the decade, the nearby Thorndike Theatre in Leatherhead secured a larger amount of public funding than had the Yvonne Arnaud (£50,000 from the Arts Council, and £10,000 from the Urban District Council) but nonetheless still had to raise a significant sum.[99] Aided by its large and active Theatre Club, events included antiques fairs, supper parties, a raffle for a colour television set, and a football match, while it was also possible to 'name a seat'.[100] More exotic proposals included the suggestion that a VC10 aeroplane might be chartered for a return flight to New York, with seats to be sold for £80 each.[101] Meanwhile in Sheffield, which received a substantial 'Housing the Arts' grant at the end of the 1960s for the Crucible Theatre, it was reported in September 1970 that 310 bricks had been 'sold' for 10

96 V&A, ACGB/120/9, HTA minutes, 27 November 1974.

97 V&A, ACGB/120/3, 'Report on Professional Fund Raisers in Housing the Arts', 21 April 1976.

98 Hansard, HL Deb 23 June 1965, vol. 267, c. 506.

99 V&A, ACGB/84/149, N. V. Linklater memo, 18 September 1966. The contract price in 1969 was £315,000 (Frederick Bentham, *New Theatres in Britain* [London, 1970], p. 94).

100 SHC, 6368/3/3 documents the activity through the Appeal Committee minutes. See also 6368/4/1, Theatre Club minutes.

101 V&A, ACGB/84/149, flyer advertising the flight.

shillings each, thirty-five seats had been named for £25 each, twenty-two donors had signed up for a priority booking scheme at £50 each, and thirty-six stainless steel tiles had been allocated at £50 each.[102]

Like the Yvonne Arnaud Theatre, Chichester Festival Theatre was almost entirely paid for by a well-organized public appeal between 1959 and 1962,[103] prompting its founder, Leslie Evershed-Martin, to describe it as 'by the people for the people'.[104] Its success owed much to Evershed-Martin's single-minded vision and effort. He worked tirelessly, with his diary recording daily meetings, talks, and fundraising events.[105] These events included a ball at Arundel Castle, but not all were so lavish. The Appeal Committee's efforts were supplemented by those of the Festival Theatre Society, composed of individuals with an interest in the project, which organized events including a sculpture exhibition. Some of their ideas did not go down well, however, prompting the Society to record, with evident feeling, that its jumble sales had been deemed to 'descend to a lower "standard"'.[106]

Grant-giving foundations often supported new theatres, especially those that were built on university campuses.[107] Their involvement in such projects was crucial, because University Grants Committee (UGC) finance was typically limited to fees, furnishings, and equipment, while Arts Council interest was only likely when a significant public programme was intended. When planning its new theatre in 1959, the University of Southampton approached the Nuffield Foundation, which had made grants to universities for other types of buildings. The vice chancellor, Gwilym James, reported that 'it would be a new line for [them], but he [Leslie Farrier-Brown of the Foundation] seemed fairly confident'.[108] Partly by stressing the links that the theatre would make between the university and the town, and perhaps helped by the architect Basil Spence's typically appealing drawings, £130,000 was secured.[109] Other Nuffield-funded theatres followed. Meanwhile in Cardiff, the university's new theatre was part-funded in the mid-sixties by the Sherman Trust, which had been founded by the football pools operator of the same name. Elsewhere, the Calouste Gulbenkian Foundation was a notable benefactor of theatres, and not only of university venues. Having supported the construction of the (amateur) Middlesbrough Little Theatre in 1957,[110] it part-funded the centre for drama teaching at the University of Hull in 1965,[111] and further Gulbenkian-funded buildings and auditoria (often small studio theatres) followed. The Northcott Theatre at the University of Exeter received £50,000 from the

[102] V&A, ACGB/84/246, Appeal Organiser's Review, September 1970.

[103] Subsequently small grants were received from the Arts Council, e.g. £3000 towards the electrical installation in 1964. See WSRO, CFT Box 43, Report by Pieter Rogers, 1964.

[104] WSRO, CFT Box 58, 'Festival' [brochure].

[105] WSRO, CFT Box 62, 'Dates Continued' [handwritten diary].

[106] WSRO, Add Mss 45575, Report by S. Garrard, 1 November 1961.

[107] Susan Todd, 'Strength Lies in Ideas Not Expertise', *Times Higher Education Supplement*, 4 May 1973.

[108] HES, MS 2329/ENG/35/3/162, Gwilym James to Basil Spence, 19 December 1959.

[109] UoB, 28/22/01, letter to Sir William Haley, 13 May 1960.

[110] 'Middlesbrough Little Theatre', *Architectural Review* 123 (April 1958), pp. 272–3 (p. 272).

[111] HHC, University Archives, Registrar Uncat. Box 14, File 33/3, Richard Mills to Brynmor Jones, 19 October 1965.

Gulbenkian Foundation in 1965, around a quarter of the construction cost,[112] but it also demonstrated that there remained a role for the individual patron of the arts, because its name reflected a £100,000 donation by Devon businessman George Northcott. Similarly the University of Sussex's Gardner Arts Centre was named after the local businessman Dr Lyddon Gardner, who made a substantial donation to the building fund.[113]

The effect of the 1970s financial squeezes on 'Housing the Arts' prompted particular emphasis on fundraising from sources beyond local government and the Arts Council. An increasingly popular option was to argue that a theatre would contribute to economic growth in order to unlock state and European funding. This strategy was used with some success in Scotland in the late 1970s, with the likes of Pitlochry Festival Theatre securing funding from the European Regional Development Fund. Another option was corporate sponsorship. Business had previously supported theatre-building projects; the Thorndike Theatre, to take one example, received donations from Ronson and other local firms.[114] However, might business now have a greater role? A report in 1976 by the market research firm Mintel concluded that 'as government is increasingly short of cash, it is to industry that the arts must look'.[115] A paper presented to the 'Housing the Arts' Committee the same year stated that 'successive Ministers' had taken the view that, even with unlimited budgets, it would 'not be appropriate for all financial support for the arts to come from Government sources', and that they had encouraged business and industry to support the arts.[116] It cited the interest in this area of the (Labour) government while noting the recent formation of groups including the Association for Business Sponsorship of the Arts (ABSA). At the start of the 1980s, the new Minister for the Arts, Norman St John-Stevas, confirmed the direction of travel when he stated that 'the arts world must come to terms with the fact that Government policy has decisively tilted away from the expansion of the public to the private sector'.[117]

In September 1976, the Arts Council organized a conference on fundraising. Its secretary-general, Roy Shaw, described the event as a 'nuts and bolts affair designed to teach Arts Administrators [...] what fund raising is, [and] how to go about it [...]'.[118] One hundred and thirty-nine delegates—thirty-nine more than originally anticipated—attended.[119] (The event itself was sponsored, although one of the donations, two crates of sherry, was apparently lost by the host university.[120]) The theme was the need for a 'broadly based campaign'. One speaker, Nigel Slater, contrasted the ideal—a single large cheque—with the reality of multiple small

[112] 'Exeter's New Theatre', *Guardian*, 3 December 1965, p. 6.
[113] UoSx, SxUOS1/1/5/13/1, Vice Chancellor's Address, 8 December 1967.
[114] SHC, 6368/3/3, Appeal Committee, 20 October 1966.
[115] V&A, ACGB/120/20, Report by Mintel entitled 'Sponsorship of the Arts' [1976], p. 42.
[116] V&A, ACGB/120/20, Housing the Arts Paper 593: 'Commercial Sponsorship of the Arts', 18 February 1976.
[117] Quoted in Sinclair, *Arts and Cultures*, p. 248.
[118] V&A, ACGB/120/6, Transcript of opening address.
[119] V&A, ACGB/120/23, Peter Longman memo, 21 June 1977.
[120] V&A, ACGB/120/23, Peter Longman memo, 21 June 1977.

donations. In his view, 'the £50,000 donation has almost become a memory of the super '60s'. While big donations from industry would still be sought, among his suggested strategies were cocktail parties (which he likened to 'a sophisticated series of "Tupperware dos"'), and a grand gala evening 'of such social magnificence that even tone-deaf philistines would be encouraged to attend'.[121] Covenants to the equivalent of 50 pence per week were encouraged, such a sum apparently being acceptable to most members of the public because it was 'less than a packet of good cigarettes and considerably less than the cost of a large pub whisky'.[122]

Who would organize this kind of appeal to business, industry, and the public? In 1976, Peter Longman predicted that two in three of the schemes on the 'Housing the Arts' list would appoint a professional fundraiser.[123] One of the most active was Maurice Hawker.[124] In July 1974, Hawker was involved at Poole Arts Centre, the Unicorn Theatre, the Liverpool Everyman, and in Lincoln, Ipswich, and Bedford.[125] Yet his business collapsed, going into liquidation in England in February 1977 and Scotland in May 1978.[126] Its success had been mixed. In Ipswich, Hawker had aimed to raise £305,000 from business, industry, and private donations, with a further £50,000 coming from charity; the Arts Council would, it was hoped, contribute £150,000 and the local authorities £300,000.[127] However, Longman thought these figures 'a tall order',[128] and indeed during 1974 it became clear that Hawker's total return would be unlikely to exceed £160,000. Dinner parties in people's homes achieved little, the hope of a business donation of £20,000 was not met, and while a Gala Committee was able to raise £50,000, the total achieved from business by March 1976 was £150,000.[129] Furthermore, although the Arts Council had by this date slightly increased their offer to £160,000, the local authority contribution was three-quarters of what had been hoped for. Proposals to sell the naming rights for the theatre to John Player and Sons, the tobacco company, came to nothing, despite the potential for an appropriately punning name in the Players Theatre.[130] How can Hawker's apparent lack of success in Ipswich be explained? The sums were certainly ambitious. Hawker, meanwhile, blamed the economic downturn as well as 'the failure of some people closely involved in the project to recognise their crucial role in setting an early and high standard of giving to establish the levels of financial support necessary'.[131]

[121] V&A, ACGB/120/6, Transcript of conference, 1976.

[122] V&A, ACGB/120/6, Transcript of conference, 1976.

[123] V&A, ACGB/120/3, Peter Longman memo, 21 April 1976.

[124] Longman suggested that Hawker had 'cornered the market': V&A, ACGB/120/3, HTA minutes, 27 April 1976.

[125] V&A, ACGB/120/20, Peter Longman memo, 23 July 1974.

[126] V&A, ACGB/120/20, Peter Longman memo, 22 July 1977; Alexander Dunbar to Anthony Field, 4 May 1978.

[127] V&A, ACGB/120/20, Ipswich and Suffolk New Theatre Trust: Fund Raising Consultants' Final Report, p. 3.

[128] V&A, ACGB/84/147, Peter Longman memo, 31 January 1974.

[129] V&A, ACGB/120/20, Fund Raising Consultants' Final Report, pp. 6–10.

[130] V&A, ACGB/84/147, Peter Longman memo, 28 February 1975.

[131] V&A, ACGB/120/20, Fund Raising Consultants' Final Report, p. 12.

Hawker's outcome in Ipswich was not unique, as his involvement in contemporaneous proposals for a theatre in Bedford demonstrates. Despite the projected cost of the theatre reaching more than £1 million by June 1974, Hawker confidently argued that the building should be constructed in full, as a reduced or phased version would not be such a tempting prospect for donors.[132] He also claimed that the local authorities and the Arts Council would double their planned contributions. Accordingly, as Longman recorded, 'they decided in true Bedford style to carry on with the full scheme'. By December 1974, however, two major local employers, Electrolux and Vauxhall Motors, had decided that the economic situation was such that they could not be seen to be supporting the theatre while making their own cutbacks.[133] It was concluded that the scheme might have to be phased after all. Hawker's contract was terminated in March 1975 when his deputy announced that a smaller appeal would be more time-consuming and would necessitate a larger fee,[134] but by June he had been reappointed. However, confidence in the project had been shattered, and it was soon abandoned.

Appeals had mixed results even before the recession of the mid-1970s. In January 1971, for example, it was noted that Derby Playhouse's public appeal had not prospered, with one Arts Council official asking 'should we contribute to a scheme where we really think that there is an over-optimistic estimate of how much will be raised by appeal (and where, therefore, we are more than likely to find ourselves called upon to provide additional funds to see the project through)?'.[135] In these circumstances, the Arts Council's interest in fundraising in the mid-1970s was perhaps partly to prevent a run on its own funds. The difficulties increasingly being encountered by local authorities meant that the Arts Council's share of costs was in fact rising,[136] and opportunities to 'top up' grants were few.[137] But was the appointment of a professional fundraiser the best strategy? At a 'Housing the Arts' meeting in September 1975, it was suggested that such consultants sometimes 'hindered rather than helped'.[138] Certainly the promoters of the new theatre at High Wycombe might have agreed: there the fundraiser reportedly charged more than was raised.[139] Furthermore, Longman suggested in 1976 that 'in-house' appeals tended to be more consistently successful, perhaps because they were led by committed theatre staff rather than unknown outsiders.[140] Given the terms with which Roy Shaw introduced the 1976 conference, it might be concluded that the event was an attempt to empower theatre managements and, perhaps, to minimize dependence on external consultants.

132 V&A, ACGB/84/18, Peter Longman memo, 14 June 1974.
133 V&A, ACGB/84/18, Peter Longman memo, 19 December 1974.
134 V&A, ACGB/84/18, Peter Longman memo, 21 March 1975.
135 V&A, ACGB/84/91, N. V. Linklater memo, 21 January 1971.
136 V&A, ACGB/120/9, HTA minutes, 25 June 1975 noted a fall from an average 25 per cent to 15 per cent but then a rise to 18 per cent.
137 V&A, ACGB/84/91, Peter Longman to D. V. W. Malin, 6 December 1976.
138 V&A, ACGB/120/3, HTA minutes, 24 September 1975.
139 V&A, ACGB/120/3, Peter Longman memo, 21 April 1976.
140 V&A, ACGB/120/3, Peter Longman memo, 21 April 1976.

Whatever the case, the account of the Salisbury Playhouse that was presented to conference delegates by its manager, Reginald Salberg, summed up the reality of the 'mixed economy'.[141] Planning for a new theatre had begun during 1963, and in 1970 a fundraising consultant was appointed. By October 1973, it was anticipated that the Playhouse would receive £80,000 from each of the District and County Councils, and £80,000 from 'Housing the Arts', leaving the appeal to find at least £500,000. By August 1974, only £70,000 had been raised, and the fundraisers left. A replacement was described by Salberg as 'lovely' but not keen on asking people for money. Nonetheless, £117,000 had been secured by March 1975 and the foundation stone was laid by Peter Hall. By now, the Arts Council had promised £200,000, while the county and city were offering £120,000 each, leaving £250,000 to the appeal. A total of 470 out of 510 seats were 'sold', covenants were secured, an amateur production of *Uncle Vanya* (complete with caviar supper) was staged, and appeals were made to the Women's Institute. The sum was eventually raised, but not from industry ('industry always fails to give', concluded Salberg). Nor was every other idea successful: 'We even tried [...] an advertisement in *The Times* saying—would you like [for] posterity a theatre named after you for £100,000?'[142] While the advertisement remained unanswered, it at least demonstrated the ways in which inventive local initiatives as much as public funding underpinned post-war regional theatre-building.

[141] V&A, ACGB/120/6, Transcript of address by Reginald Salberg.
[142] V&A, ACGB/120/6, Transcript of address by Reginald Salberg.

3

Towards a New Theatre Architecture, 1945–60

In October 1949, representatives of Coventry City Council travelled to London for a meeting at the Arts Council of Great Britain.[1] Inspired (as was discussed in Chapter 1), by Labour councillors' desire to end Coventry's reputation as a 'burial place of culture', the town clerk evidently had in mind the provisions of the previous year's Local Government Act when he wrote in May 1949 of 'the possible establishment of a permanent theatre for the Midland Theatre Company'.[2] Mary Glasgow, then the Arts Council's secretary-general, responded enthusiastically,[3] and it was proposed that a new theatre might be realized as part of the Festival of Britain. There was as yet no detailed design, but the city architect, Donald Gibson, had been working on schemes for the reconstruction of the city centre even before the bombing of November 1940. Drawings produced during 1940 and 1941 show a linked group of wedge-shaped theatres and cinemas on Corporation Street, adjacent to the main shopping area.[4] However, in September 1949 the Arts Council's Charles Landstone told the town clerk that he was 'sorry that you feel despondent about the long term policy for a civic theatre',[5] and by November the project seemed stalled: 'recent national developments [i.e. the devaluation of the pound] will not make it any easier to secure approval'.[6]

Landstone remained 'very hopeful and believe[d] that Coventry may yet be the first city to erect a Civic Theatre'.[7] However, it was to be 1952 before planning for a new theatre in Coventry began in earnest, and a further six years before the Belgrade Theatre opened (see Figure 3.1).[8] The theatre was designed within the city architect's office, which had been set up with Gibson at its head in 1938. The creation of this department demonstrated the extent to which the then newly elected Labour council's interventionism extended to the built environment, something which would remain the case in the post-war period.

1 CHC, CCA/3/1/11161, minutes of 7 October 1949.

2 CHC, CCA/3/1/11161, Town Clerk to Mary Glasgow, 4 May 1949.

3 CHC, CCA/3/1/11161, Mary Glasgow to Town Clerk, 7 May 1949.

4 UoEd, GB 0237/PJM/CCC/A/1/1, 'Plan for the New Coventry: from disorder and destruction—order and design' [booklet, 1941], pp. 9–11; also 'Post-war Coventry: a plan for redevelopment of the centre', *Architects' Journal* 93 (24 April 1941), pp. 278–81.

5 CHC, CCA/3/1/11161, Charles Landstone to Town Clerk, 22 September 1949.

6 CHC, CCA/3/1/11161, Town Clerk to Mary Glasgow, 4 November 1949.

7 CHC, CCA/3/1/11161, Charles Landstone to Town Clerk, 22 September 1949.

8 Alistair Fair, '"A New Image of the Living Theatre": the genesis and design of the Belgrade Theatre, Coventry, 1948–58', *Architectural History* 54 (2011), pp. 347–82. Early ideas included the conversion of existing buildings; meanwhile a scheme shown in 1952 in Yugoslavia was felt 'lacking'.

Figure 3.1. Belgrade Theatre, Coventry: elevations to Corporation Street and an unfinished Belgrade Square in 1958 (Colin Westwood/RIBA Collections)

As a civil servant put it in 1963, 'Coventry think of urban renewal in its widest sense, [...] with a heavy emphasis on the local authority undertaking all the redevelopment itself'.[9] The fundamentals of the theatre design were established before the end of 1954, when Gibson departed Coventry for Nottinghamshire, although in spring 1955 an alternative design was prepared.[10] Whereas the theatre in Gibson's original scheme had little street presence, being hidden behind a four-storey block containing shops with actors' flats above, in these new designs the auditorium was turned through ninety degrees and a small square was created in front of the theatre, flanked symmetrically by wings containing the shops and flats. With construction imminent (if not already underway),[11] such a rethink was clearly impractical. As built, the layout of the theatre and the design of the street-facing block remained essentially that developed under Gibson. Nonetheless, the idea of greater prominence evidently appealed. Gibson's successor, Arthur Ling, arrived from the London County Council in May 1955, and a revised proposal was prepared in which the building previously intended for the neighbouring site was omitted. What would have been a windowless party wall thus became the theatre's principal public front, facing a new public square.[12]

[9] TNA, HLG/71/1287, memo of 8 April 1963.

[10] CHC, AP/PL/38/1458/160–63, drawings of alternate scheme, April 1955.

[11] 'Coventry's New £200,000 Venture', *Stage*, 25 November 1954.

[12] 'The New Coventry's Successful Break with Tradition', *The Times*, 27 April 1956: 'the civic theatre [...] has been redesigned and greatly improved since the plans for it were published last year'.

Topped by a large civic crest and featuring large windows divided by slender stone piers, the Belgrade Square elevation made a prominent statement of the theatre's intended place in the life of the rebuilt city. A symbolic quality was often attached to Coventry's post-Blitz recovery; the city's wartime experience had attracted international attention, leading after 1945 to several 'town twinning' initiatives as well as the gift of Yugoslavian timber that gave the theatre its name. Along with Coventry's pioneering pedestrian precinct and new inner ring road, the theatre—in both conception and form—embodied Lord Reith's wartime dictum that the city should 'plan boldly' in its reconstruction. The artist Martin Froy, commissioned by the Arts Council to work with the theatre architects, reported of the new proposals that 'the theatre at Coventry is part of a much larger project'.[13] His interpretation surely had as much to do with the council's vision of this theatre as a vehicle for cultural enlightenment as the way that, as Froy put it, 'much more has been given to the approach and hence to the prestige of the theatre in its new and more spacious setting'. The contemporary theme continued inside, with airy foyers featuring chandeliers by Bernard Schottlander and abstract mosaic panels by Froy representing the 'Four Seasons' (see Figure 3.2). (Froy's initial suggestion, a mural

Figure 3.2. 'Like an airport': the foyers at the Belgrade Theatre, Coventry, 1958, with Bernard Schottlander's chandeliers and part of Martin Froy's mosaic (on the right) (John McCann/RIBA Collections)

[13] Martin Froy, 'Civic Theatre, Coventry: Report to the Arts Council' [*c.*1956], pp. 2–3. Copy kindly supplied by Martin Froy.

on the themes of war, peace, sowing, and harvest, had been intended for the solid party wall that was originally proposed, but, when that wall was reconceived as the theatre's glazed elevation, he was instead allocated the wall dividing the auditorium from the foyer.[14]) The foyers, too, were novel for their inclusion of a coffee bar and restaurant. They were to be open during the day, not just at performance times, with all patrons sharing a common space, rather than being segregated by ticket price. Similarly innovative were the actors' flats, the provision of which symbolized the theatre's repertory operation. Summing up the Belgrade in the *Observer*, Kenneth Tynan was enthusiastic: 'enter most theatres, and you enter the gilded cupidaceous past. Enter this one, and you are surrounded by the future'.[15]

The Belgrade was the first major expression of the boom in post-war regional theatre-building. Its architectural modernity was echoed by the theatres that followed in its wake. In 1965, the *Stage* discussed the emergence of what it termed a 'new image of the living theatre' made up of 'steel and glass playhouses' whose flowing interior spaces were shared by all.[16] 'Steel and glass' and open planning—standing for the vocabularies and materials of modern architecture generally—might thus express new ideas about performance, the theatre as a building type, and the place of the arts in society. The 'new image', the *Stage* continued, was evident not only in the Belgrade but also the likes of the Yvonne Arnaud Theatre, Guildford (1965). What were its sources? Several writers saw the influence on the theatres of London's Royal Festival Hall (1951).[17] Predominantly intended for concert performances, the Festival Hall was significant as the first major non-austerity building to be realized in post-war Britain. Its design is echoed in the Belgrade's materials (stone and glass), planning (the auditorium revealed as a wedge-shaped volume, visible through and above the glazed elevation), and detailing (the auditorium boxes, angled towards the stage). However, the Belgrade's thin mullions, set like abstracted pilasters below a horizontal cornice, suggest a return to order after the Festival Hall's original loosely patterned elevations, which were altered during the 1960s.

Yet without denying the Belgrade's position as the first major new regional theatre in post-war Britain, it is simplistic to position the Festival Hall as its isolated precursor and then to view these two buildings as the sole sources of the 'new image'. In refining the picture, this chapter begins by briefly setting the new theatres of the 1950s and 1960s in an international context. It then turns the clock back to discuss British examples from the mid-1940s and the 1950s. They suggest that the Belgrade might more productively be seen as the first major outcome of a discourse which, through actual buildings as well as unbuilt schemes, offered initial solutions to the question: how might a modern theatre be designed?

[14] Martin Froy, 'Civic Theatre, Coventry', pp. 2–3; Martin Froy, 'Second Report to the Arts Council', 14 November 1954. Copy supplied by Martin Froy.

[15] 'Curtain Up at Coventry', *Observer*, 30 March 1958.

[16] 'Theatre for All', *Stage*, 19 August 1965.

[17] For example, CHC, PA2313/5/2/1, clippings: *News Chronicle*, 6 February 1958.

MODERN THEATRE ARCHITECTURE

In discussing the modern theatre, our starting point has to be modern architecture in Britain itself. During the 1950s, the immediate post-war focus on reconstruction gave way to a broader concern with modernization, as expansiveness was facilitated by the easing of austerity, by the end of the system of building licences in 1954, and by economic recovery. Consciously 'modern' approaches to the planning, structure, materials, and forms of new buildings dominated. Theatre design reflected these broader developments in architectural culture and practice. Whereas the theatre-building boom of the late nineteenth and early twentieth centuries had been led by a coterie of specialist architects who built little else, now the appointment of architects inexperienced in theatre—famously Denys Lasdun at the National Theatre—brought new ideas. Even such architects as Peter Moro who were known as theatre specialists were involved in a range of work, and their wider practice therefore shaped their approach to theatre design.[18] An interest in modernity was not unique to architects. Theatre directors and city councillors could also seek to innovate architecturally. The 1957 design brief for the new Nottingham Playhouse, for example, stated that 'a theatre built to play a part in the life of Nottingham from the 1960s onwards should be different from a theatre built in another sort of town, at another time'.[19]

Post-war British architecture was forged in an international context, and so too were its new theatres. Sweden was an important early source. Its social-democratic ethos chimed with the philosophy of the nascent welfare state in Britain, and its wartime neutrality meant that there was a stock of recent buildings from which to draw inspiration. During 1948, the promoters of the National Theatre toured venues in Malmö and Gothenburg as well as Helsinki in Finland, with a record of their impressions being passed much later to Lasdun, while a detailed description of the Malmö theatre, seemingly dating from the late 1940s, survives in the archive of the historian and theatre consultant Richard Southern.[20] Similarly, Bryan Westwood, who with his brother Norman designed Eastbourne's Congress Theatre, reported in 1957 that he planned to visit theatres and concert halls in Scandinavia.[21] However, northern Europe was not the only potential source of ideas. Accounts were published in Britain of theatres in locations from Ireland to Iceland.[22] The major new theatre at Strasbourg in France was visited by a group from the amateur Questors Theatre in Ealing, west London, in 1954.[23]

[18] For a parallel in church architecture, see Robert Proctor, *Building the Modern Church: Roman Catholic Church Architecture in Britain, 1955 to 1975* (Farnham, 2014), p. 48.

[19] NA, DD/NP/1/2/1/1, Architect's Brief, n.d., p. 1.

[20] RIBA, LaD/170/4, record of Scandinavian tour; RSA, folder 'RS—Reports and Articles on Theatres', 'Description of the Malmö Municipal Theatre'.

[21] ESRO, DE/A/18/6, Entertainments and Pleasure Grounds [hereafter 'E&PG'] Committee, 14 June 1957.

[22] See e.g. 'A National Theatre for Iceland', *Architects' Journal* 111 (4 May 1950), p. 542; 'Rebuilding the Abbey Theatre in Dublin', *Architects' Journal* 129 (19 February 1959), pp. 305–7.

[23] Questors Theatre archive, uncat., 'Notes on a Visit to Strasbourg, July 7th to 9th 1954'.

It also formed an important reference point for the Nottingham Playhouse.[24] (The Strasbourg theatre's influence may be partly explained by the role in its construction played by the prominent director Michel Saint-Denis, who had been based in London at the Old Vic in the late 1940s.) Norman Westwood, meanwhile, planned to travel to Italy.[25] There were also discussions of North American theatres and sometimes visits, too, despite the high cost of transatlantic travel. In spring 1945, members of the Oxford University Drama Commission travelled to Cleveland, Iowa, and New Haven in order to glean ideas for the theatre that they hoped the university might construct,[26] while the well-travelled Norman Westwood also hoped to cross the Atlantic in 1957.[27] That said, it was not until the 1960s that North America formed a more frequent reference point for British theatre designers and then typically for those designing university venues. The absence of much in the way of public subsidy meant that there were few examples of the civic/repertory type on which to draw, while the flexibility of many commercially run American theatres was often deemed unnecessary in Britain.[28]

By the late 1950s, the principal source of continental inspiration was West Germany, something that remained the case into the 1970s.[29] In 1963, John Harrison, director of the Birmingham Repertory Theatre, suggested that 'the pilgrim must go to Western Germany to see modern theatres, and we have lately followed one another along the circuit like earnest seekers after grace'.[30] Peter Moro, too, referred to the 'inevitable' tour of West German theatres.[31] There was a long-established tradition of civic patronage of the arts in Germany, and the construction of major state-supported buildings for performance occurred on both sides of the Iron Curtain. Between 1946 and 1967, seventy-three theatres were constructed in West Germany, while nearly 200 more were repaired after war damage.[32] Theatre equipment could be of as much interest as the buildings themselves. Richard Pilbrow and Richard Brett travelled during 1967 to see technical installations at first hand, their findings informing their proposals for the National Theatre's stage specifications.[33] Meanwhile, there was written coverage of projects for those who could not visit.

[24] Elain Harwood, *Space, Hope and Brutalism: English Architecture 1945–1975* (New Haven/London, 2015), p. 496.

[25] ESRO, DE/A/18/6, E&PG Committee, 14 June 1957.

[26] Bodleian, MS. Eng. Misc. c. 1017/2/119–36, Report of the Oxford University Drama Commission.

[27] ESRO, DE/A/18/6, E&PG Committee, 14 June 1957.

[28] For the dominance of campus studios in British accounts, see e.g. Percy Corry, 'Stages in America', *Tabs* 19, no. 2 (September 1961), pp. 18–31. See also Stephen Joseph, 'Introduction', in his *Actor and Architect* (Manchester, 1964), pp. 1–29 (p. 11 for the distance of America from Britain and the potential influence of campus drama studios); Peter Moro, 'Theatre Today', *Architectural Design* 30, no. 9 (September 1960), pp. 358–68 (p. 358).

[29] For Robert Matthew's trip after securing the commission to design a major theatre in Edinburgh: NRS, ED61/88, Progress Report 10, 8 February 1974.

[30] 'Theatre Theatre', *Guardian*, 25 July 1963.

[31] RIBA, MoP/6, 'Nottingham Playhouse', typescript, n.d.

[32] Elain Harwood, 'Theatres in West Germany, 1945–70', in *Setting the Scene: Perspectives on Twentieth-century Theatre Architecture*, edited by Alistair Fair (Farnham, 2015), pp. 103–32 (p. 103).

[33] Richard Pilbrow, *A Theatre Project* (New York, 2011), p. 160.

Articles appeared in English-language architectural periodicals,[34] theatres featured in surveys of German architecture,[35] and there were detailed accounts in specialist publications.[36] Information could be obtained in other ways, too. For example, in 1963 there was a proposal to stage an exhibition of German theatre design at Leatherhead Repertory Theatre.[37]

Much as they were visited and studied, West German theatres were often thought to be of limited value as models.[38] Supported by the *Wirtschaftswunder* with subsidies of up to 80 per cent and designed for an epic style,[39] these buildings were certainly larger than their British equivalents. Gelsenkirchen's Nationaltheater, opened in 1959, provided 4.15m^2 of site for every seat, whereas Coventry's Belgrade Theatre, praised in Britain for its spaciousness, offered 1.45m^2.[40] Even allowing for variables in costs and what might be included in the published figures, Gelsenkirchen cost some £1.6 million, whereas the Belgrade was completed the previous year for £270,000.[41] Nonetheless, there were lessons to be learned, if only in terms of general disposition and architectural vocabulary, and there are certainly examples in which German influence is apparent. They include the stacked boxes in the auditorium at Billingham Forum (1968), which have been likened to contemporary West German opera houses,[42] and the sledge-like auditorium side slips in the 1974 proposals for the new theatre at Castle Terrace, Edinburgh, which, as sketched by the architect Robert Matthew, are labelled using the German term, *Schlitten*.[43] Meanwhile the mechanized stage of the Churchill Theatre, Bromley, was inspired by venues which director David Poulson and architect Kenneth Wilson had seen on an Arts Council-supported tour of Germany.[44]

All this notwithstanding, domestic examples and debates could often be more important than international precedents. Conferences and societies offered opportunities for discussion. In 1951, for example, an exhibition of theatre architecture was staged in Coventry, while like-minded individuals came together in such groups as the Council of Repertory (later 'Regional') Theatres (CORT), founded in 1944, and the Society for Theatre Research (1948). The magazine

34 E.g. 'Reverberators: Post-war German concert halls and opera houses', *Architectural Review* 126 (August 1959), pp. 87–99; Ernst Priefert, 'Shape and Acoustics in Recent German Concert Halls', *Architectural Design* 30, no. 7 (July 1960), pp. 282–8; Victor Glasstone, 'Auditoria Galore', *Architectural Design* 33, no. 11 (November 1963), pp. 547–56.

35 E.g. Ulrich Conrads and Werner Marschall, *Modern Architecture in Germany* (London, 1962).

36 E.g. Peter Moro, 'New Theatre at Bonn', *Tabs* 23, no. 4 (December 1965), pp. 11–15.

37 SHC, 6368/4/1, Leatherhead Theatre Club minutes, 1 August 1963.

38 RIBA, MoP/10, Moro, 'A Sense of Proportion', p. 125–6; Harwood, 'Theatres in West Germany', pp. 126–7.

39 P. Fischer, 'Doing Princely Sums: structure and subsidy', in *The German Theatre: A Symposium*, edited by Ronald Hayman (London, 1975), pp. 215–34.

40 Roderick Ham, *Theatre Planning* (London, 1972), p. 252.

41 Werner Ruhnau, 'Das neue Stadttheater in Gelsenkirchen', *Bauwelt* 51 (1960), pp. 407–11 (p. 408).

42 Paul Iles, 'Towards the Prevention of a Theatre Demolition', text of 2002, <http://www.laughingaudience.co.uk/billingham_forum_theatre.html> (accessed 10 March 2017).

43 UoEd, RHM 29, uncat. drawings of Castle Terrace Theatre.

44 BA&LS, 792.0942178, 'Churchill Theatre, Bromley: opened by HRH The Prince of Wales', brochure, 1977.

Tabs, published several times a year under the auspices of the technical firm Strand Electric, included accounts of recent buildings at home and abroad. Archives and published accounts alike record the sometimes extensive trips around Britain that were undertaken by artistic directors, theatre boards, and/or their architects.[45] At the start of our period, the sources were interwar. Elisabeth Scott's Shakespeare Memorial Theatre at Stratford-upon-Avon (1932) had not proved an unqualified success in its planning,[46] while its Dudok-inspired brick modernism was hardly the flavour of the 1950s, but it nonetheless suggested how a theatre might be treated as a prominent public building. Meanwhile Erich Mendelssohn and Serge Chermayeff's De La Warr Pavilion at Bexhill-on-Sea of 1935, a key work of the International Style, had not only an auditorium but also extensive refreshment and exhibition areas, and so anticipated the enhanced facilities of post-war theatres. Not only that, but the explicitly public terms in which the ninth Earl de la Warr had conceived the building addressed themes that would become commonplace after 1945. So too did the Pioneer Health Centre, Peckham, of 1935. Intended as a building in which citizens might improve their physical well-being through recreational activities and exercise, it showed how architecture could supply a venue for self-transformation and productive leisure. Along with the likes of the Building Centre (1932) and the Housing Centre (1934), it was one of a growing number of 'centres' that promoted new ways of living.[47]

FIRST STEPS TOWARDS A NEW IMAGE, *c.*1945–60

It would be a mistake to see the architectural history of British theatre as one of inactivity until the mid-1950s. The original Pitlochry Festival Theatre, for example, opened in 1951 (see Figure 3.3). It was one of several tented venues in use at this time, including John English's Arena Theatre in Birmingham. Subsequently encased in a steel and asbestos structure, the Festival Theatre's tent was the product of necessity when government approval for a more permanent, conventional building was withheld;[48] it was intended to be temporary, but in fact remained in use until 1981. Elsewhere, the Theatre Royal, Hanley, was reopened in spring 1952 after a major fire,[49] while the architect Pierre Sonrel reconstructed the Old Vic at the

[45] E.g. CHC, PA2313/5/2/1, clippings: *Local Government Chronicle*, 10 May 1958, for visitors to the Belgrade; HA, BI/1/1/101, Town Council minutes, 5 May 1967, for a tour of theatres including Coventry and Nottingham; FRO, CC/TC/1/164, 'Proposed Arts Centre, Mold' [1969], p. 12, for visits to Basildon, Croydon, Bolton, Manchester, Birmingham, Chester, Nottingham, and the University of York.

[46] Marian Pringle, *The Theatres of Stratford-upon-Avon, 1875–1992: An Architectural History* (Stratford-upon-Avon, 1993), pp. 43–4.

[47] Elizabeth Darling, 'Spaces of Citizenship in Inter-war England', paper presented to the 'Architecture, Citizenship, Space' conference, Oxford, 15 June 2017. The Design Centre (1956) can be understood in similar terms.

[48] PFT, uncat., memo submitted to the Scottish Arts Council, 28 September 1971.

[49] 'Opening a Theatre', *Tabs* 10, no. 1 (April 1952), p. 24.

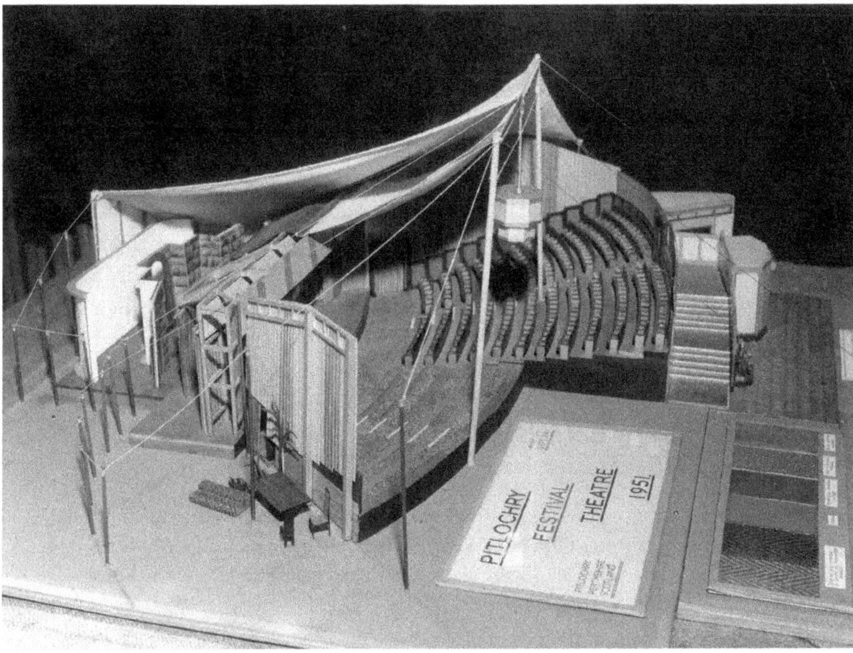

Figure 3.3. Pitlochry Festival Theatre: the tented theatre of 1951 (Architectural Press Archive/RIBA Collections)

start of the decade as the home of the newly founded National Theatre Company.[50] The Shakespeare Memorial Theatre at Stratford-upon-Avon, too, was significantly altered between October 1950 and March 1951, with new side slips being added to the previously blank auditorium walls by Brian O'Rorke, who was then also working on designs for the National Theatre.[51] The University of Bristol, aided by a $20,000 Rockefeller grant, appointed Richard Southern in December 1949 to convert a squash court into a flexible studio for its pioneering Drama Department.[52] The creation of the Drama Department in 1946 had been the initiative of Vice Chancellor Philip Morris, who was also chair of the Bristol Old Vic Trust.[53] Amateur dramatics were served by new venues such as Hall Green Little Theatre in south

[50] 'Theatre: reconstruction of the Old Vic, London', *Architects' Journal* 112 (30 November 1950), pp. 455–9. Judi Loach, who has investigated the Sonrel papers at the British Library, has suggested in correspondence with the author that no one in Britain was thought sufficiently knowledgeable about theatres, and that Sonrel may well have been recommended by the director Michel Saint-Denis, then based at the Old Vic and who subsequently commissioned him to design the new theatre at Strasbourg.

[51] 'Shakespeare Memorial Theatre, Stratford-upon-Avon', *Tabs* 9, no. 3 (December 1951), pp. 5–9.

[52] RSA, Box 'University of Bristol Studio Theatre', Winifred Shapland to Richard Southern, 8 December 1949; 'Theatre for Drama Department, Bristol University', *Architects' Journal* 114 (5 July 1951), p. 14.

[53] Martin White, 'Professor Glynne Wickham', *Independent*, 11 February 2004, <http://www.independent.co.uk/news/obituaries/professor-glynne-wickham-37973.html> (accessed 14 December 2015); Archives Hub catalogue of the papers of Sir Philip Robert Morris, <http://archiveshub.ac.uk/data/gb3-dm588> (accessed 14 December 2015).

Birmingham (1951) and Greenock Arts Guild (a converted swimming pool of 1955).[54] Middlesbrough Little Theatre (1957) was intended for amateur and professional use, while student drama was staged in such venues as the basement theatre in the University of Edinburgh's newly built Adam House (1954).[55]

Among the notable unbuilt projects of the period was Frederick Gibberd's proposed Oxford University Playhouse. In 1944, the president and vice president of the university's Film Society received a letter sent on behalf of the film mogul Sir Alexander Korda.[56] Korda seems to have been thinking of supplying the society with lecturers, films, and equipment, but the project soon assumed greater significance when Korda was put in contact with Nevill Coghill, a scholar of English literature and an active theatre director. There had been discussion of a university theatre in the late 1930s, but the construction of the New Bodleian Library had taken priority.[57] Now a more ambitious scheme was formulated. Korda believed that the film industry in Britain would prosper only if it was supplied with sufficient graduates:

> so that the immense work of disseminating cultural and institutional ideas through out [sic] the world by the medium of Cinema could be supported by an outflow from the Universities of educated and intelligent people who had acquired [...] some knowledge of and interest in dramatic and film work.[58]

Korda's views were perhaps informed by the way in which such wartime films as Laurence Olivier's *Henry V* had functioned as propaganda. It was later reported that he considered film to be a key medium 'through which the English view and way of life can find expression'.[59] He potentially also wanted to safeguard the British film industry in the face of a likely onslaught from Hollywood. At the same time, his form of words also may have been calculated to make the idea of a drama school seem palatable to a university not known for its interest in vocational subjects. Indeed, the small group that formed to discuss the idea concluded in May 1944 that 'the approach must be such as the University can accept as academic'.[60] A professor would work with the existing schools of Languages and Literature, focusing on the teaching of 'dramatic literature' by means of a university theatre 'envisaged chiefly as a laboratory for research and demonstration'.[61] In addition, some six plays would be produced each term, split between classical drama, works in English, and plays in other modern languages.

[54] Brian Gavin, 'New Life for an Old GAG!', *Theatres* 11 (Spring 2007), pp. 6–9.

[55] Clive Fenton, 'Appleton's Architects: building the University of Edinburgh (1949–65)' (PhD diss., University of Edinburgh, 2002), I, pp. 127–35. See also B. T. Pentreath, 'Classical Modernism in Fifties Edinburgh: Adam House, by William Kininmonth', *Architectural Heritage* 5 (1995), pp. 97–111.

[56] Bodleian, MS. Eng. Misc. c. 1017/1/48, 'Pre History of the Offer in Sir David Cunynghame's Letter Before Council', 4 July 1944. See also Don Chapman, *Oxford Playhouse: High and Low Drama in a University City* (Hatfield, 2008), pp. 127–8.

[57] Bodleian, MS. Eng. Misc. c. 1017/1/4–5, Minute of 16 June 1944.

[58] Bodleian, MS. Eng. Misc. c. 1017/1/4–5, Minute of 16 June 1944.

[59] Bodleian, MS. Eng. Misc. c. 1017/1/42, Notice of Sir Alexander Korda's benefaction.

[60] Bodleian, MS. Eng. Misc. c. 1017/1/1–2, Notes of meeting on 10 May 1944.

[61] Bodleian, MS. Eng. Misc. c. 1017/1/1–2, Notes of meeting on 10 May 1944.

When it came to the appointment of an architect, the committee sought a designer 'with Theatre and Laboratory experience who is good enough to put up a building in Oxford'.[62] Their first thought was the former Bauhaus director, Walter Gropius, who had codesigned the arts centre at Dartington Hall (1938) and was now based at Harvard, but they resolved in the interests of speedy progress to ask the Royal Institute of British Architects to suggest a young architect who might produce an initial study and costing.[63] Two names came back: A. F. B. Anderson of Robert Atkinson's practice, who had experience of theatre reconstruction and the design of film studios; and Julian Leathart, whose principal qualifications included several cinemas and a stage for experimental drama at Doncaster Grammar School.[64] Two further suggestions—William Holford and Frederick Gibberd—were made by the 'Editor of the *Architectural Review*', presumably Nikolaus Pevsner in J. M. Richards's absence on war service.[65] Gibberd was then president of the Architectural Association and was well regarded for his pre-war flats in south London, but his eventual appointment was the product of a sense that he would approach the task in an open-minded way.[66] His design was published in 1948.[67] Although a university theatre of this kind was essentially a new building type in Britain, Gibberd proposed something that was civic in scale and reasonably conventional in design, save, perhaps, for its inclusion of an outdoor amphitheatre. In plan and appearance, it recalled the Shakespeare Memorial Theatre; it also anticipated a theatre designed by Gibberd for a site in Harlow New Town in 1948.[68] The main auditorium, seating 687 in a single rake with boxes to the rear, was to be fan-shaped, though with unusual stepped sides. A large foyer would include space for exhibitions. The exterior was to be faced in a mixture of rough Bladon stone and smooth dressed ashlar 'to obtain contrast in form, colour, and texture',[69] a picturesque approach typical of Gibberd. The result would have been a little like Giles Gilbert Scott's recently completed New Bodleian Library in synthesizing contextual influences with the precepts of international modernism. The theatre remained unexecuted, the victim of its apparently vocational overtones as well as post-war austerity and shortages. Nonetheless, the ideas that had shaped its design turned out to be influential. In the late 1940s, Glynne Wickham, an Oxford graduate who had been president of the Oxford University Dramatic Society when the theatre

[62] Bodleian, MS. Eng. Misc. c. 1017/1/7, Notes of meeting on 11 July 1944.

[63] Bodleian, MS. Eng. Misc. c. 1017/1/7, Notes of meeting on 11 July 1944.

[64] Bodleian, MS. Eng. Misc. c. 1017/1/17, Notes of meeting on 27 July 1944; MS Eng. Misc. c. 1017/1/20–21, Notes on the architects. The Doncaster project was not fully implemented owing to the outbreak of the war.

[65] Bodleian, MS. Eng. Misc. c. 1017/1/19, Agenda of 21 August 1944: reference to letter sent to Coghill.

[66] Bodleian, MS Eng. Misc. c. 1017/1/28, 'Draft Report of the Committee on the Drama', 11 September 1944'.

[67] [Oxford University Drama Commission], *Report of the Oxford University Drama Commission* (Oxford, 1948), esp. pp. 15–23 for report by Gibberd. See also 'Theatre for Oxford University', *Architects' Journal* 108 (4 November 1948), pp. 421–5.

[68] 'Physical Planning Supplement: Harlow New Town: the masterplan', *Architects' Journal* 107 (5 February 1948), pp. 127–31.

[69] 'Theatre for Oxford University', p. 424.

was being discussed, became the first lecturer in Drama at Bristol.[70] Echoing Coghill, he proposed that the subject would enrich a general humanities education.[71] The terms in which the university Drama Department at Hull was created in the early 1960s in turn drew on Bristol. Hull's professor of English, Ray Brett, had come to Hull from Bristol, and Wickham advised Hull about its proposals.[72]

Gibberd's contextual elevations were not unique in 1940s British architecture. A 'regional' trend had been evident since the late 1930s, the idea being to develop enriched forms of modern architecture which were sympathetic to local and national traditions of form and material use. A prototype Arts Centre, published by the Arts Council in 1945 and based on designs by Geoffrey Jellicoe, was very much in this vein.[73] The planning of this building suggested a more radical rethinking of architecture for performance than Gibberd's Oxford theatre, embodying the new ideal of the subsidized arts as a beacon of cultural aspiration at the heart of Britain's regional communities. It was to include a 600-seat hall, space for exhibitions, and a 200-seat restaurant. Several possible layouts were suggested, with potential exterior treatments including rough stone and timber cladding. However, the ultimate example of the tendency towards an 'enriched' modern architecture was the Royal Festival Hall in London, the designs for which were published two years before its 1951 opening.[74] The Festival Hall was significant, both as an architectural model and also for what it suggested of the place of culture in the post-war world. Constructed as part of the Festival of Britain and funded by the London County Council (LCC), it enjoyed a prominent location within the Festival site.[75] Its design was steered decisively within the LCC Architects' Department by Robert Matthew. He originated the concept of the 'egg in the box', in which the auditorium was elevated above the foyers and backstage areas in order to insulate it from the vibration of passing mainline and underground trains. Developed under Matthew's deputy, Leslie Martin, and with Peter Moro joining the team to lead the detailed work on the public areas, the Festival Hall's planning drew on Scandinavian examples visited by Matthew, while its deliberate juxtapositions of colour and pattern recall the work of Berthold Lubetkin's practice, Tecton, for which Moro had worked in the late 1930s. The building contrasted in its informality and lightness with pre-war British concert halls, such as Sheffield's City Hall, a piece of monumental stripped classicism by E. Vincent Harris (1920–32), or the Philharmonic Hall at Liverpool by Herbert J. Rowse (1939), which adopted a brick *moderne* style. For John Summerson, it was 'the first monumental place of public assembly in central

[70] George Brandt, 'Glynne Wickham', *Guardian*, 25 February 2004, <http://www.theguardian.com/news/2004/feb/25/guardianobituaries.highereducation> (accessed 14 December 2015).

[71] Glynne Wickham, 'Conclusion: retrospect and prospect', in *The Universities and the Theatre*, edited by D. G. James (London, 1952), pp. 102–15 (p. 106).

[72] Donald Roy, email to author, 18 January 2016; HHC, University Archives, 17/4, parcel 118, Building Committee, 2 July 1964.

[73] [ACGB], 'Plans for an Arts Centre' [London, 1945].

[74] E.g. 'London's New Concert Hall', *Architects' Journal* 109 (5 May 1949), p. 400.

[75] The definitive account is found in Miles Glendinning, *Modern Architect: The Life and Times of Robert Matthew* (London, 2008), pp. 88–109.

Figure 3.4. National Theatre design by Brian O'Rorke, with the theatre located between Waterloo Bridge and the Festival Hall (RIBA Collections)

London to be designed with deeply held loyalty to the principles of the modern movement'.[76]

The Festival Hall's planning and style were influential. For example, the 512-seat Middlesbrough Little Theatre, opened in 1957 and designed by Albert J. Elder and Enrico de Pierro, is essentially a miniature Festival Hall.[77] Although entirely contained within a simple cube and faced in red brick rather than stone and tile, the arrangement of solid and void on the main elevation is very similar, as is particularly clear in photographs of the model.[78] These images suggest that the exterior was to be rendered or painted white, evoking the colour of the Festival Hall's stone cladding. On a bigger scale, the influence of the Festival Hall is also felt in Brian O'Rorke's 1950s proposals for the National Theatre, so much so that designs of 1951 were deemed to be too similar to the Festival Hall by the Royal Fine Art Commission (see Figure 3.4).[79] A location for the theatre on the South Bank had been identified in 1943 and was codified in Patrick Abercrombie and J. H. Forshaw's *County of London Plan*, replacing an earlier site in South Kensington and being intended as part of a riverside cultural quarter.[80] Edwin Lutyens had produced designs for the Kensington site in collaboration with Cecil Masey, a specialist in cinema design, and the pair now turned their attention to the South Bank. After Lutyens's death in 1944, a classical scheme was produced by Hubert Worthington, before Abercrombie, Forshaw, Charles Holden, and Pevsner selected

[76] John Summerson, 'Introduction', in Trevor Dannatt, *Modern Architecture in Britain* (London, 1959), pp. 11–29 (pp. 19–20).

[77] Elder, a local architect, was subsequently involved at Billingham. De Pierro taught at the Architectural Association and later designed Corby Civic Centre (1965), which included a theatre.

[78] 'Theatre: Middlesbrough', *Architectural Review* 119 (January 1956), pp. 18–21.

[79] Daniel Rosenthal, *The National Theatre Story* (London, 2013), pp. 37–8.

[80] Elain Harwood, '"Reviving a Great Sector of London to the Benefit of the Community": the London County Council's rebuilding of the South Bank as a cultural quarter, 1945–76' (PhD diss., University of Bristol, 2009), p. 44. For pre-1939 attempts to create a National Theatre, see Rosenthal, *National Theatre*.

Brian O'Rorke to take over the project. As Barnabas Calder suggests, 'O'Rorke was safely, uncontroversially modern in the manner that one might expect from an architect chosen by this committee of establishment architectural figures.'[81] Nonetheless, he was a modernist, with a strong reputation as an interior designer. Although it was intended that he would work with Masey, it soon became clear that O'Rorke's approach was incompatible with that of the somewhat older Masey, who was paid to withdraw. As of July 1949, the year in which government support was promised (if in vague terms) for the project, two auditoria were required, one with a proscenium arch and 1200 seats on three levels, the other seating 500 in a single tier and potentially having an open stage.[82]

O'Rorke arranged the auditoria back-to-back on a site between County Hall and the Festival Hall.[83] He reportedly saw the National as a cross between a yacht club and a 'Victorian conservatory',[84] i.e. a lightweight, festive structure. (His mention of a 'yacht club' brings to mind Joseph Emberton's Royal Corinthian Yacht Club at Burnham-on-Crouch of 1930.) Yet the designs also have a classical character. Drawings of spring 1952 show a portico-like projecting section with thirteen bays. There is an arcade at entrance level and, above, triple-height glazing with balconies looking over the Thames.[85] There are various versions of the sides of the building, some delicately detailed, others tending towards a more austere stripped classicism.[86] By the early 1960s, the larger auditorium had assumed a circular plan and now featured an open stage.[87] One scheme places the theatre adjacent to County Hall, the open-stage auditorium being housed in a rotunda with a series of rather jolly, radiating gabled roofs.[88] The foyers and backstage areas are arranged around an internal court, while the riverfront elevation has double-height foyers opening onto a terrace. Other versions took account of the then-emerging proposals to organize pedestrian circulation across the South Bank on an elevated podium, with parking below.[89] In one, the theatre, still with a circular auditorium and internal courtyard, moved to a site closer to Hungerford Bridge and the Festival Hall.[90] To the west would have been the opera house then proposed for Sadler's Wells. It was to be separated from the National by a 'theatre square', the theatre and opera house together framing views of the Shell Tower from the river in an arrangement that anticipates Denys Lasdun's first proposals for the site in the 1960s.

[81] Barnabas Calder, 'Committees and Concrete: the genesis and architecture of Denys Lasdun's National Theatre' (PhD diss., University of Cambridge, 2007), p. 24.

[82] SBTA, DR1103/2/5/3, 'The National Theatre, July 1949'.

[83] Some of O'Rorke's schemes are illustrated in 'The Long Dream', *Architectural Review* 161 (January 1977), pp. 65–8 (p. 67).

[84] Rosenthal, *National Theatre*, p. 38.

[85] RIBA, PA823/13/1–6, drawings by Brian O'Rorke, March–April 1952.

[86] RIBA, PA823/14/1-29, drawings by O'Rorke *c.*1950–5.

[87] E.g. RIBA, PA824/2/10, section, *c.*1962. See also Harwood, *Space, Hope and Brutalism*, pp. 490–1.

[88] RIBA, PA824/2/3, National Theatre, perspective sketch by O'Rorke, *c.*1960/61.

[89] SBTA, DR1103/2/5/3, Fordham Flower to Brian O'Rorke, 22 September 1961, mentions a 'podium' and 'something about building over garages. No site plans were produced, and I was absolutely without a clue about what they were talking'.

[90] RIBA, PA824/2/1, National Theatre and Opera House plan by O'Rorke, and PA 824/2/4, perspective, *c.*1961/62.

None of O'Rorke's proposals was built, although a foundation stone was laid in 1951. His early schemes were not well received by planners, while there were ongoing discussions about the theatre site. There also remained the question of who would actually pay for the building: the credit squeeze of 1957 was one among many setbacks.[91] It was claimed by some that the money would be better spent on the Old Vic and in the regions. However, another project with echoes of the Festival Hall had better luck, at least in being constructed if not necessarily well-received. Croydon's Fairfield Halls complex, which included the 740-seat Ashcroft Theatre, was designed in the mid-1950s by Robert Atkinson and Partners.[92] This firm had become prominent during the 1930s with a series of stripped-classical buildings, not least in central Croydon, and it continued working in this style into the 1950s. The style was, however, increasingly unfashionable, and their proposals for the University of Cambridge's Sidgwick Site were passed over in 1953 in favour of more consciously modern designs by Hugh Casson and Neville Conder.[93] Perhaps in the light of this experience (as well as the typological parallel), Fairfield Halls represented a more overt engagement with the 'Festival style' on the part of the firm—now without Atkinson, who died in 1952. The Festival Hall's influence is evident in several ways that move beyond style alone, including the concert hall's angled side boxes, the continuation of the foyer beneath the auditorium, and the articulation of the auditorium as a solid mass. The use of a variety of facing materials is also similar, as is the complex projection and recession of the windows on the main elevation.

Upon its opening in 1962, however, Fairfield Halls seemed problematic to some.[94] By the early 1960s, the 'Festival style' was considered in negative terms by some younger architects and writers including the prominent critic Reyner Banham, who concluded in 1976 that it 'had bottomed out in 1961'.[95] The juxtaposed forms and materials that typified the style were increasingly thought to be not only old-fashioned but also lacking in theoretical rigour, as is evident from the reception given to Eastbourne's Congress Theatre (1963) (see Figure 3.5). This theatre had been conceived in the late 1940s as a complete reconstruction of the town's Winter Garden, but, quite apart from the restrictions on capital expenditure

[91] Rosenthal, *National Theatre*, pp. 38–9; Harwood, *Space, Hope and Brutalism*, pp. 490–1. The foundation stone was later moved to the eventual National Theatre site, now east of Waterloo Bridge. The various changes in the site prompted some critics to quip that the stone might productively be put on wheels, while the delays provided cartoonists with ample fodder. Kenneth Tynan and Richard Findlater staged a mock 'funeral' for the National in 1958, being pictured in 'mourning' next to the stone.

[92] MoC, FS70 (711) RED, clipping: 'Fairfield Halls', *Surrey Life*, February 1964, pp. 14–16; Pf570 (792) FAI, Robert Atkinson and Partners, 'Report on Plans for the Fairfield Halls', 4 April 1961. The job architect was David Beaty-Pownall.

[93] Alistair Fair, '"The Ideal Campus": the Sidgwick Site, Cambridge', *Twentieth Century Architecture* 11 (2013), pp. 103–21 (pp. 106–8).

[94] MoC, FS70 (711) RED, 'Public Halls Design Criticised', 15 May 1959 (cites the *AJ*: 'cliché-ridden essays in the new-fangled modern style'); also 'Fairfield Halls Architect Has Died Aged 89', *Croydon Advertiser*, 26 March 1993.

[95] Reyner Banham, 'The Style: "flimsy...effeminate"?', in *A Tonic to the Nation: The Festival of Britain, 1951*, edited by Mary Banham and Bevis Hillier (London, 1976), pp. 190–8 (p. 196).

Figure 3.5. 'Too many materials'? Congress Theatre, Eastbourne, 1963 (Architectural Press Archive/RIBA Collections)

then in force, early designs by Murray Easton and Howard Robertson had demonstrated the significant cost of such a venture, and the decision was taken instead to construct a concert hall that would also be suitable for conferences.[96] A seafront location was considered in 1955,[97] but ultimately a site adjacent to the Winter Garden won out.[98] During 1956, Bryan and Norman Westwood replaced Easton and Robertson, who were now reported to be too busy.[99] The brief was finalized in November 1956, with a two-tier auditorium for 1650 people 'who would be able to see in comfort all activities on the stage'; by now, these 'activities' also included 'theatrical productions'.[100] Sketch plans were shown in March 1958 while the detailed design was largely complete by summer 1959.[101]

96 ESRO, DE/A/43/52, E&PG Committee, 14 April 1949; DE/A/18/6, E&PG Committee, 14 February 1951, 22 December 1952, and 18 November 1955: 'the primary purpose [...] would be to provide accommodation for concerts and other seated entertainments and the business season of conferences'.

97 ESRO, DE/A/18/6, E&PG Committee, 5 January 1955; DE/A/20/4, Joint Committee, 6 January 1955 and 14 September 1955.

98 ESRO, DE/A/18/6, E&PG Committee, 18 November 1955 and 18 May 1956.

99 ESRO, DE/A/18/6, E&PG Committee, 28 June 1956. Howard Robertson reportedly recommended the Westwoods. He had himself been recommended by the RIBA, along with Charles Cowles-Voysey, Brian O'Rorke, Stanley C. Ramsey, and Denman and Son. See E&PG Committee, 15 June 1951.

100 ESRO, DE/A/18/6, E&PG Committee, 29 November 1956.

101 ESRO, DE/A/18/6, E&PG Committee, 14 March 1958 and 17 July 1959; DE/A/18/7, E&PG Committee, 11 December 1959.

The Congress was in the mould of the Festival Hall. Its front elevation of stone and glass is especially similar, while the auditorium is partly entered at first-floor level, like the Festival Hall (although the reason for this arrangement was reportedly to make the most of a sloping site).[102] Yet while the *Architects' Journal* was positive about the spatial interest of the galleried foyers, it criticized the use of 'too many materials and different finishes' on the theatre's exteriors, which it thought 'distracting' and 'inextricably complex'.[103] The south elevation, for example, featured several different stone finishes as well as brick, slate, and dark aggregate panels, while the rear of the theatre featured textured brick patterns. In the *AJ*'s view, it would have been better to have used one material consistently for structural elements and another for infill areas. In this respect, the Congress Theatre might be compared to the Nottingham Playhouse, opened in 1963 to Peter Moro's designs. The latter's austere materials and rigorously geometric planning suggested a somewhat different approach, as will be discussed in Chapter 4.

'A "NEW LOOK" IN THEATRE BUILDINGS'

Although stylistic labels are rarely straightforward in architectural history, many of the examples discussed in this chapter suggest the so-called 'New Empiricism', a style that emerged in the late 1940s as a fusion of Modern Movement principles with ideas drawn from recent Scandinavian design and a picturesque sensibility. It was characterized by a lively approach to materials, colour, texture, and decoration, with, as the historian Robert Proctor has neatly put it, 'brick and stone, concrete window frames, slate hangings and chequered slot or lozenge patterns, enlivened by modern sculpture or murals'.[104] The result was a pragmatic, 'empirical' architecture founded to some extent on visual effect rather than dogmatic theory. This idea at an urban scale informed the 'Townscape' approach favoured by the *Architectural Review* between the mid-1940s and the early 1970s. By the late 1950s, the 'New Empiricism' had been co-opted by the welfare state. Proctor has suggested that it formed the basis of a 'municipal modernism', in which its use for a range of building types by autonomous but essentially 'public' bodies including local government located these buildings within a broader programme of modernization. Not only that, but the designers of buildings for non-state institutions, such as the various churches, sometimes deliberately deployed this style in order to suggest the place of these buildings within the broader civic endeavour.[105] Because the 'New Empiricism' had dominated the Festival of Britain, both on the South Bank and at the Lansbury 'live architecture' housing estate, it could be understood as a new national style.

New theatres, while not always civic ventures, were fundamentally brought into the purview of the state through the introduction of subsidy and the emerging interest of politicians in leisure and culture. The Belgrade, in particular, might be

[102] 'Congress Theatre, Eastbourne', *Architects' Journal* 138 (31 July 1963), pp. 235–50, 252.
[103] 'Congress Theatre, Eastbourne', pp. 239, 243.
[104] Proctor, *Modern Church*, p. 70. [105] Proctor, *Modern Church*, pp. 69–78.

thought to embody 'municipal modernism' in several ways. The first of these was its promotion by the local authority, rather than a pre-existing repertory company. As was noted in Chapter 1, the Midland Theatre Company was barely consulted about the building, and there were a number of problems in the backstage planning as a result. Also significant was its design by the city architect, its evocation of the Festival Hall (a building also designed by local-authority architects), and the way that its architecture was considered in terms of its surroundings. In its modernism, its use of brick and mosaic, and in the setting back of the shops behind a colonnade, the Belgrade's forms and materials were consistent with other developments in the rebuilt Coventry. In this respect, the Belgrade took on the vocabulary of its neighbours as a statement of its intended position within the new city. It was to be a focal point, but one that was visually consistent with the broader setting. The effect would have been yet more obvious had the Westmorland slate cladding of early designs been adopted for the *pilotis*, because this material was used on contemporaneous buildings throughout the city centre. The Belgrade also demonstrates that, much as this 'municipal modernity' might seem at first glance to be a kind of homogenizing influence that flattens the distinctions between building types, perceptions of the theatre as a special type of building did not vanish. Such things as its chandeliers and its physical prominence within the modern townscape, facing the new public square, placed it, like Fairfield Halls, the Congress Theatre, or indeed the Festival Hall, within a tradition of grand public architecture.

Similar conclusions might be reached of the early designs for Billingham Forum. As was discussed in Chapter 1, leisure was thought by the town's councillors to have an integral place in Billingham's 'design for living'. It was thus reported in 1959 that 'the full development of [the town centre] would give to the public a centre for shopping, education and culture; entertainment; sport and recreation; and local government administration, on all of which the future of a progressive town depended.'[106] A letter signed by the town clerk and others in 1961 claimed that 'unless the Town Centre Development is seen as a complete exercise in sociological planning, the full benefits will not be realised'.[107] Modernity was to the fore: 'Billingham Urban District Council realised that people wanting to work in the town's new and fast expanding industries would not expect only a house—they would demand an environment to match the exciting and up-to-date conditions in their place of work.'[108] So too, as in Coventry, was the wish to promote community in a fast-growing town: 'bricks and mortar were not by themselves sufficient, a sense of identification with the community had to be encouraged, a feeling that Billingham is a place in which one "lives"'.[109]

[106] TA, Billingham Urban District Council [hereafter 'UDC'] minutes, Development and Plans Committee, 5 October 1959.

[107] TA, U/S/706, letter to Development and Plans Committee members signed by Fred M. Dawson (Clerk), A. J. Elder (Architect), Edwin Shaw (Engineer and Surveyor), H. H. Wright (Treasurer and Accountant), 23 June 1961.

[108] TA, U/S/1143, pamphlet: 'Billingham—Planned for People'.

[109] TA, U/S/2409, pamphlet: 'Billingham Urban District Council, 1923–1968'.

The leisure facilities that might engender this 'feeling' were to be designed, like the rest of the new town centre, by Albert J. Elder, the co-designer of Middlesbrough Little Theatre, and Thomas Lester. Their 1959 proposals located the civic theatre in a fan-shaped building on axis at the end of the Queensway precinct, where it was to be flanked by two blocks, one containing a ballroom and shops, and the other containing shops and offices.[110] Colonnades would connect these three buildings with each other and with the swimming baths and shops that were to be located behind the theatre. Nearby would be bus stops and a petrol station. The architects' drawings show a consistent architectural language in which the civic structures and other buildings—such as shops—would look very similar. Elevations would be brick and tile, there would be a mixture of flat and shallow-pitched roofs, while 'Townscape'-inspired planting and street kiosks would figure in a Coventry-like pedestrianized area. In this way, the theatre would be embedded in the wider municipal modernity of the town centre, while nonetheless being distinguished by its axial position.

The proposals for Billingham, like the Belgrade and the other theatres considered in this chapter, were thus fundamentally modern in appearance and in their relationship with wider urban developments, but without being radical. Given the extent to which avant-garde tendencies are often privileged in architectural criticism, such an interpretation might seem negative, perhaps implying a diluted approach conceived to appeal to popular sensibilities and good taste. (Eastbourne Borough Council certainly conceived the Congress Theatre in somewhat genteel terms, hoping that it would contribute to 'that atmosphere of dignity and refinement which is justifiably considered one of the main attractions and amenities of the town'.[111]) In this respect, Reyner Banham's hardly fulsome discussion of what he termed 'mainstream' or 'routine' modernism was noted in the Introduction.[112] This kind of implied hierarchy is also evident in some historians' writing. Joseph Mordaunt Crook, for example, has suggested of the 1930s that 'when modern went modernistic, it became respectable', appealing to 'fashion rather than function, stylistics rather than ergonomics',[113] while David Dunster, analysing the post-war work of Alison and Peter Smithson, has proposed 'good taste' as the antithesis of avant-garde radicalism.[114] The reception afforded to Basil Spence's contemporaneous Coventry Cathedral might be understood similarly. For some critics, Spence's design compared poorly with some of the apparently more radical proposals over which it triumphed in the 1951 competition, such as the design by the Smithsons; it represented a blend of 'Gothic revival structure with Baroque tricks and modernistic detail'.[115] Yet, beyond the circles of architectural criticism,

[110] TA, U/S/706, 'Billingham Urban District Council: Town Centre Development', 1959.

[111] ESRO, DE/C/1/2, Development Plan Written Analysis, 1951, p. 97.

[112] Reyner Banham, *The New Brutalism: Ethic or Aesthetic?* (London, 1966), p. 41.

[113] Joseph Mordaunt Crook, *The Dilemma of Style: Architectural Ideas from the Picturesque to the Postmodern* (London, 1987), p. 252.

[114] David Dunster, 'Introduction', in Alison Smithson and Peter Smithson, *The Shift* (London, 1982), p. 7.

[115] Peter Kidson, Peter Murray, and Paul Thompson, *A History of English Architecture* (Harmondsworth, 1965), p. 318; Nicholas Bullock, *Building the Post-war World: Modern Architecture and Reconstruction in Britain* (London, 2002), pp. 76–82.

Spence's fusion of tradition and innovation was seen as successfully modern.[116] Its popularity was such that Spence's account of the building, *Phoenix at Coventry*, was serialized in the *Sunday Times*, with sales of the book reportedly paying for the construction of his weekend cottage at Beaulieu.[117] Coventry Cathedral demonstrates the persistence and popularity during the 1950s and 1960s of an undogmatic, visually oriented modernism in Britain, and Spence was not alone in pursuing such an approach.[118] It offers an important balance to the ostensibly tougher and often more theoretically inflected strains of modernism that emerged during the 1950s and which have attracted greatest critical attention.

The architectural press was sometimes guarded in its response to the new theatres of the late 1950s and early 1960s. The example of the Congress has already been noted, and while J. M. Richards was positive about the Belgrade's appearance, he nonetheless took issue with aspects of the theatre's planning.[119] However, as at Coventry Cathedral, the non-architectural press was often more supportive. The *Stage* thought the Congress 'superior-looking',[120] and while the *Daily Mail* thought that the Belgrade was 'unlike a theatre' (being instead 'an unglamorous glass-doored building'), it seems to have intended this description in positive terms, comparing the new theatre with 'those ornate old monuments of faded plush, tarnished gilt and mirrors, crumbling marble pillars and creaking boards which still serve for so much British drama'.[121] Meanwhile Kenneth Tynan invoked modern and scientific parallels in his assessment of the Belgrade:

> Rather than a museum, it suggests an observatory. The lobbies are long and capacious, like those of a good airport. The auditorium, cherry plush underseat and polished wood overhead, is both resplendent and practical. The sightlines are impeccable, and the acoustics have a high-fidelity bite which makes most West End theatres seem like schools for deafness. The stage is deep. The wings are wide. The opportunity is enormous.[122]

Country Life, finally, began a 1963 article on the 'Provincial Theatre' in classic Puginian fashion with two contrasting images: a grainy line drawing of Sunderland Empire ('gilt and plush') and a photograph of the foyer at the Belgrade.[123] Unlike Pugin's *Contrasts*, however, in which an idealized medieval history was preferable to the (nineteenth-century) present, now the latter suggested a welcome improvement on what had gone before.

It is clear, therefore, that the architecture of the likes of the Belgrade and the Congress was understood as something fundamentally new, which, despite (or perhaps

[116] Robert Furneaux Jordan, 'Coventry Cathedral', *Guardian*, 20 May 1962.

[117] Louise Campbell, *Coventry Cathedral: Art and Architecture in Post-war Britain* (Oxford, 1996), pp. 257–8; '50,000 visit Coventry Cathedral', *Guardian*, 28 May 1962; Louise Campbell, Miles Glendinning, and Jane Thomas, *Basil Spence: Buildings and Projects*, p. 149.

[118] Iain Jackson and Jessica Holland, *The Architecture of Edwin Maxwell Fry and Jane Drew* (Farnham, 2014), pp. 7–8; Christine Hui Lan Manley, *Frederick Gibberd* (London, 2017).

[119] 'Theatre in Corporation Street, Coventry', *Architects' Journal* 128 (7 August 1958), pp. 199–214 (p. 204).

[120] 'The Congress, Eastbourne', *Stage*, 13 June 1963, p. 15.

[121] CHC, PA2313/5/2/1, clippings: *Daily Mail*, 13 March 1958.

[122] 'Curtain Up at Coventry', *Observer*, 30 March 1958.

[123] 'Renaissance in the Provincial Theatre', *Country Life*, 1 June 1963, pp. 57–9 (p. 57).

because of) its relationships with broader currents in modernism, was distinctive to modern theatres. In part, the difference between these theatres and those of twenty years before was one of architectural fashion, and indeed in 1958 the Arts Council borrowed the language of contemporary couture in referring to the Belgrade as an example of an emerging 'new look' in theatre design.[124] It is not surprising that the new theatres of the late 1950s and early 1960s contrasted with their pre-war predecessors, because few buildings of this date reprised the forms of nearly three decades before. However, because no permanent professional theatres had been built in the interim, the change would perhaps have seemed more dramatic. At the same time, the 'new look' was not necessarily superficial, but could potentially help the theatre survive in an age of competing leisure activities. A 1960 memorandum on the future of Birmingham's Repertory Theatre suggested that 'centres of public performance must be imaginative and inviting if a new audience is to be secured and held'.[125] Indeed, architectural reform was almost official policy, with the 1965 White Paper criticizing the 'cheerless unwelcoming air' of older cultural buildings.[126] Although clearly thinking in terms of art galleries ('no greater disservice can be done to the serious artist than to present his work in an atmosphere of old-fashioned gloom and undue solemnity'), it suggested that architectural 'gaiety and colour, informality and experiment' would appeal to the young.[127]

Furthermore, these first post-war theatres also connoted through their modern architecture the new context of theatre-making and funding. The *Stage*, for example, thought that 'the modern trend in theatre-going for all' was reflected by the 'new image of the living theatre' that it discerned in 1965.[128] *The Times* made a similar point in 1961, arguing that 'the obsolescence of playhouses confronting the passer-by with a playfully aristocratic façade of rococo volutes and plaster cupids may be all for the best'.[129] Local authorities, it went on, could not be expected to support the 'minority art' for which such buildings had been constructed. It would be far better, it concluded, for new theatres to 'proclaim their dual function as workshop and palace of the arts' by means of their architecture, which would seem far more relevant to contemporary audiences increasingly accustomed to modern design. They would also 'fit snugly into the urban scene', in the manner of Proctor's 'municipal modernism'. The positive use of the forms and materials of modern architecture to signify the new context of theatre funding and practice is also evident in the critic John Elsom's 1971 assessment of the new Birmingham Repertory Theatre, in which the theatre's modernity reflected both its subsidized status and the resurgence of regional theatre:

> To move the Company from that dignified inadequacy [the 'old Rep'] to its gleaming new home is symbolic of a wider change—the end of one phase in the repertory movement and the start of another, where state patronage (and municipal) has started

124 ACGB, Annual Report, 1957–1958 ('A New Pattern of Patronage'), p. 27.
125 LoB, MS 978/1/6/1/1, 'The Birmingham Repertory Theatre: its present and future', p. 1.
126 'A Policy for the Arts: the first steps', Cmnd. 2601 [1965], para. 4.
127 'A Policy for the Arts', paras 5–8.
128 'Theatre for All', *Stage*, 19 August 1965.
129 'Should We Build New Theatres?', *The Times*, 3 February 1961.

> to replace private, where the provincial theatre need not feel always resentful of the greater glories of London and where even a certain optimism ought not to be considered unreasonable.[130]

One might conclude, therefore, that the 'new image' of post-war theatre that emerged during the 1950s was far more than the product of architectural fashion alone, and that the results were far more than derivative examples of the 'Festival style'. As in John Osborne's 1957 play *The Entertainer*, in which the dying music hall forms a metaphor for the state of the nation, the *Daily Mail*'s 'ornate old monuments' might thus symbolize the struggling regional theatre of the past, with its social assumptions and sometimes poor-quality productions, whereas the likes of the Belgrade—'unlike a theatre'—seemed to promise a new beginning.

[130] John Elsom, *Theatre Outside London* (London, 1971), p. 24.

4

'The Second Positive Stage'

Modern Public Buildings, *c.*1958–71

In December 1963, *The Times* reported of the newly opened Nottingham Playhouse that 'local residents have nicknamed it the bunker'.[1] History does not record whether this term—which was presumably inspired by the Playhouse's exposed concrete surfaces—was positively meant; one suspects not. Peter Moro's design presented a different 'new image' of theatre from that discussed in Chapter 3, relying on pure geometry and the honest expression of materials rather than the kind of decoration that was evident in examples such as the Congress Theatre, Eastbourne. One possible interpretation of this difference might look to wider developments in architectural culture. In this respect, the second half of the 1950s witnessed growing unease with the so-called 'New Empiricism' among some critics and architects. Having in January 1955 criticized the style for 'its misuse of traditional materials and its "veneer" of modern details',[2] *Architectural Design* was more strident two years later, bewailing the 'lack of rigour and clear thinking' that it saw in 'the romantic pasticheries of the Festival of Britain and its offspring, the free empirical manner derived from Sweden'.[3] What was the alternative? In 1955, the critic Reyner Banham defined 'the New Brutalism' in terms of 'formal legibility of plan' and 'clear exhibition of structure'.[4] At the same time, some younger architects, such as Alison and Peter Smithson, cultivated an interest in working-class culture, seeking architectural and urban forms rooted in human behaviour in response to what they saw as the abstract functionalism and urbanism promoted since the 1930s by the Congrès Internationaux d'Architecture Moderne (CIAM). Subsequently, 'brutalism', distinct from the 'New Brutalism', has acquired a wider and sometimes vague currency. In place of Banham's 'ethic', it has come to mean a bold, massy aesthetic drawing on sources including the post-war work of Le Corbusier.[5]

One of the most striking examples of an aesthetic brutalism is the small but dramatic Theatr Ardudwy (1973), designed by Colwyn Foulkes and constructed on a college campus in Harlech.[6] Located on a steeply sloping site, it is boldly

[1] 'A Theatre That Promises to Work', *The Times,* 10 December 1963.
[2] 'The New Brutalism', *Architectural Design* 25, no. 1 (January 1955), p. 1.
[3] 'Thoughts in Progress: the New Brutalism', *Architectural Design* 27, no. 4 (April 1957), p. 111.
[4] Reyner Banham, 'The New Brutalism', *Architectural Review* 118 (December 1955), pp. 354–61.
[5] E.g. Barnabas Calder, *Raw Concrete: The Beauty of Brutalism* (London, 2016). See also Reyner Banham, *The New Brutalism: Ethic or Aesthetic?* (London, 1966), p. 89.
[6] 'Fourth Theatre Opens', *Guardian*, 28 September 1973.

massed with a cantilevered auditorium and external staircases, while its elevations have different concrete finishes. Concrete did not always dominate, however. For example, Theatr Gwynedd, Bangor (Percy Thomas Partnership, 1975), had unadorned walls of brown brick. Entrances and windows of various widths were punched through the front elevation at ground level, while to one side a projecting section containing stairs, lit by a deliberately off-centre slit window, was daringly supported on a thin sliver of concrete. It was demolished in 2015. Similarly dominated by brick is the Denny Civic Theatre, Dumbarton (Alan Reiach, 1965), a straightforward brown brick box with pleasingly chunky flights of steps in board-marked concrete.[7] Bricks are similarly prominent at Newcastle University's Theatre of 1971 (see Figure 4.1), where the choice of material echoes other campus buildings by the same architect, William Whitfield. Before recent alterations, the theatre was composed from curved and rectilinear brick-faced volumes topped by large copper-clad roofs.[8] It was also intended to connect to a network of pathways elevated above the surrounding roads, a planning strategy typical of the 1960s which was advocated by Colin Buchanan's influential 1963 report *Traffic in Towns*.

Figure 4.1. Newcastle University Theatre: view from the Civic Centre in 1971 (Colin Westwood/RIBA Collections)

[7] HES, AR17/1–3, drawings of 1962–5 illustrating the project.
[8] 'University Theatre', *Architects' Journal* 153 (5 May 1971), pp. 1005–16 (p. 1006).

This kind of vertical separation of pedestrians and motor vehicles is often associated with brutalism, and not only because its popularity coincided with the high-water mark of brutalist fashion. The Smithsons and others were keen to reclaim the ideal of the street as a place for human interaction, safe from traffic, and elevated decks and podiums offered one way to do that. In addition, the interrelationship of buildings with raised circulation routes appealed to those architects who were interested in 'megastructures', i.e. multifunctional, multilevel buildings of complex appearance and section that spread into the surrounding cityscape.

Chichester Festival Theatre (1962) might at first glance suggest the formal clarity and material honesty of Banham's brutalism. Its architects, Powell and Moya, had been responsible for prominent projects including the Churchill Gardens estate in Westminster and the Princess Royal Hospital, Swindon, but the job came their way because Powell's father was a canon of Chichester Cathedral.[9] Powell was initially reluctant, quipping that the practice knew more about operating theatres than drama theatres.[10] A tent having been deemed impractical, the requirement was an economical structure that would 'express as clearly as possible the internal planning and design of the building'.[11] As built, the theatre comprised little more than a hexagonal volume containing the auditorium and stage, which was elevated to avoid expensive excavation. The foyers are tucked underneath, their stepped concrete ceilings revealing the seating tiers above. Its appearance is the direct product of its plan, extruded into three dimensions. The hexagonal plan, in turn, resulted from the arrangement of the audience around the three sides of the theatre's 'thrust' stage (which is discussed in Chapter 8).

Yet how helpful is the brutalist tag? In 2015, Christopher Stevens, the job architect at Chichester, pointed to the theatre's small budget as the reason for its directness, recalling that 'it was simply a case of finding the least expensive way to solve a need and if possible two'.[12] Nor is Stevens alone in rejecting the label. Peter Moro, for example, seems not to have ever considered his work in these terms.[13] As a result, this chapter, like the two that follow it, proposes that there are more productive ways to consider theatres of the 1960s and early 1970s than through a stylistic lens alone. For Moro, Nottingham Playhouse was significant for what it said about the nature of modern public buildings. In 1963, he wrote:

> To those who find it difficult to get away from preconceived ideas of what a civic building should look like, this building may come as a shock at first. But when one realises that such ideas are based on associations with a period entirely different

[9] Elain Harwood, *Space, Hope and Brutalism: English Architecture 1945–1975* (New Haven/London, 2015), pp. 65, 497.

[10] Christopher Stevens, interviewed for the 'Chichester Festival Theatre RENEW Project', 7 December 2014. Transcript supplied by the theatre.

[11] 'Elizabethan Theatre for Chichester', *Architects' Journal* 131 (11 February 1960), pp. 259–60 (p. 260).

[12] Christopher Stevens, email to author, 18 May 2015.

[13] Alistair Fair, '"A London Architect Who Has Specialised": Peter Moro and festivity in theatre design, *c.*1955–82', in *Setting the Scene: Perspectives on Twentieth-century Theatre Architecture*, edited by Alistair Fair (Farnham, 2015), pp. 133–62.

from our own it will not be surprising that this difference will express itself architecturally.[14]

To that end, this chapter asks what a selection of the new theatres of this period might reveal about attitudes to the design of public buildings and the place of those buildings within an evolving modern architecture. In 1948, the critic J. M. Richards suggested that:

> Modern architecture has now won its battle against period revivalism and against the denial of the technical revolution that the use of reminiscent styles implies. But in so doing it has only achieved the first negative stage of the struggle for a contemporary architectural language. The second positive stage has still to be undertaken, the development of an idiom rich and flexible enough to express all the ideas that architecture—especially representational architecture—ought to be capable of expressing. The modern idiom, as we find it at present, can express little except utilitarian ideas.[15]

Public buildings—'representational architecture', as Richards put it—were potentially the vehicles for the development of this vocabulary, as Sigfried Giedion, the secretary of CIAM, also argued:

> The people want buildings representing their social, ceremonial and community life. They want their buildings to be more than a functional fulfilment. They seek the expression of their aspirations for joy, for luxury and for excitement.[16]

Giedion's reference to 'joy [...] luxury and [...] excitement' suggests that theatres, in particular, might have a special role to play in this 'second positive stage' of modern architecture. In this respect, Moro reflected in 1989 that:

> in the less utilitarian buildings it is essential to evoke deliberately an emotional response from those who use them and see them. [...] theatres [...] are failures when they have no magic.[17]

In 1964, he had similarly referred to the 'emotional content' of theatre design, and the need to create 'appropriate atmosphere' in order to heighten the theatrical experience.[18]

Moro was not alone in emphasizing the theatricality of theatre. In 1959, for example, Richard Findlater wrote that while functionality was important in modern theatres, it should be achieved 'without sacrificing a shred of atmosphere',[19] while in Ealing, the management of the Questors Theatre noted that they were 'not willing to surrender that quality which can best be described as "theatre atmosphere".

[14] V&A TC, Nottingham file, uncat., *Guardian Journal Souvenir Supplement*, 11 December 1963.

[15] [J. M. Richards, ed.], 'In Search of a New Monumentality: the Symposium', *Architectural Review* 104 (September 1948), pp. 117–28 (p. 117).

[16] 'New Monumentality', p. 120.

[17] RIBA, MoP/10, Peter Moro, 'A Sense of Proportion: memoirs of an architect', unpublished MS, *c.*1989, p. 76.

[18] RIBA, MoP/11, 'Speech for Nottingham Rotary Club, 20.1.64', and 'Lecture', n.d., typescripts by Moro.

[19] Richard Findlater, *The Future of the Theatre* (London, 1959), p. 19.

The interior and its arrangement must suggest a place of entertainment, not a workshop'.[20]

One strategy was to reinterpret the established trappings of theatre in modern dress. Moro noted that 'one registers how the old Victorian theatres sparkled and you try to translate it into modern equivalents'.[21] However, excessive ornamentation or obvious expense, especially within a partly publicly funded building, might suggest wastefulness as well as poor taste and undesirable historicism. Thus at Nottingham Playhouse, Moro reported that 'by the manipulation of the spaces, and by careful lighting, we have created an atmosphere which is both dignified and festive without being ostentatious'.[22] In this way, the Playhouse moved beyond the purely utilitarian in order to express its function as a theatre as well as its status as a public building.

This chapter examines the ways in which clients and architects responded to the public and civic nature of modern theatre. It begins by discussing three theatres designed by Basil Spence before considering in detail how public architecture—and specifically 'monumentality'—could be rethought in progressive terms, with specific reference to the Belgrade Theatre, the Nottingham Playhouse, and the National Theatre. These examples demonstrate that 'mainstream' modernism did not necessarily mean that the buildings themselves faded into the mainstream. Rather, an undogmatic approach did not preclude the idea that theatres were special. In fact, it could encourage a traditional view of architectural hierarchy, in which certain types of buildings were privileged and so were accorded a rich treatment. For other designers, however, public buildings—and new theatres—could be understood in more everyday terms. The chapter therefore concludes with two examples that show how an enriched modernism might be developed into a new vernacular.

'NO QUESTION OF A "UTILITY" APPROACH'

In August 1962, the chairman of the Royal Shakespeare Company (RSC), Fordham Flower, reflected on the designer of a new theatre in Notting Hill, west London, which had been commissioned by the Ballet Rambert for its own productions and to accommodate visits by the likes of the Comédie Française. He wrote: 'the architect is a man called Seifert, who I would say is extremely bright and undoubtedly successful, tho' whether he would be my choice for the designer of a new and exciting theatre is another thing'.[23] Richard Seifert, best known for his office buildings, had become involved at the beginning of the 1960s when the Ballet Rambert, having apparently learned that it was unlikely to receive much in the way of public

[20] Questors Theatre archive, uncat., 'Memorandum to Advisory Panel—No. 3'.

[21] PCL, Theatre Royal clippings: *Western Evening Herald/Western Morning News*, Theatre Royal Supplement, 5 May 1982.

[22] V&A TC, Nottingham file, uncat., clipping from *Guardian Journal Souvenir Supplement*, 11 December 1963.

[23] SBTA, DR1108/2/4/1, Fordham Flower to Edward Thompson, 27 August 1962.

funding for the theatre that it sought to construct, approached a commercial developer, Atlas Securities, to help them realize the project.[24] Seifert's drawings show a polygonal tower, not unlike his later NLA Tower in Croydon (1970) but faced in glass and without that building's alternating geometries.[25] It was described as a 'beacon', tempting audiences with a dazzling show of brightly lit foyers.[26] However, faced with rising costs, the Ballet Rambert turned to the RSC, which was keen to establish a purpose-built London base.[27] It was thought that the RSC might contribute to the cost of the building, named the New Mercury Theatre.[28]

Flower was not alone in his scepticism of Seifert. In August 1962, the RSC's director, Peter Hall, reported 'reservations', which were apparently shared by the Ballet Rambert.[29] Seifert's specialism in office design often counted against him, isolating him from many of his architectural peers. In essence, his commercial focus was at odds with the social agendas of the welfare state, especially in view of his infamous skill in maximizing developers' returns through canny planning and a thorough grasp of planning policy. Who might replace him? Hall suggested Basil Spence,[30] which appealed to Flower, who, as the Deputy Lieutenant of Warwickshire and sometime chairman of Coventry Cathedral's Reconstruction Committee,[31] was well aware of Spence's work.[32] Flower reported in March 1963 that:

> Spence is the right chap for the job. His prestige is so high after Coventry, and his reputation now so world-wide, that the association of his name with the scheme is bound to give it enormous impetus. Now that we know that he is not only willing, but mad keen to do it, it would in my view be a psychological error to make an announcement without mentioning him.[33]

Spence was no stranger to theatre design. In 1950, he had worked on proposals for a new Theatre Royal on Edinburgh's Leith Street, although they remained unexecuted.[34] After 1957, his office designed the Nuffield Theatre at the University of Southampton, which formed part of the bigger campus development for which

[24] RDC, RDC/AD/01/01, minute of 23 June 1960. Atlas Securities' chairman, Alfred Esdaile, was an impresario who had redeveloped London's Prince of Wales Theatre in 1937, and was lessee of the Royal Court. The firm was behind the Prince Charles Theatre in the West End. Jack Cotton was also approached: RDC, uncat. 'New Mercury 1' folder, W. O. Hart to Sir David Waley, 22 July 1960. The Ballet Rambert had previously discussed the project with Elidir Davies.

[25] RDC, uncat., photographs of Seifert's drawings, *c.*1962.

[26] RDC, uncat. clippings: 'New "Dream" Theatre for West London?', *West London Observer*, 23 February 1962.

[27] SBTA, DR1108/2/4/1, Peter Hall to Fordham Flower et al., 10 August 1962.

[28] RDC, RDC/AD/01/01, minute of 22 March 1962.

[29] SBTA, DR1108/2/4/1, Peter Hall to Fordham Flower et al., 10 August 1962.

[30] SBTA, DR1108/2/4/1, Peter Hall to Fordham Flower et al., 10 August 1962.

[31] 'Obituary: Lt-Col. F. Flower', *The Times*, 11 July 1966; Basil Spence, *Phoenix at Coventry: The Building of a Cathedral* (London, 1962), p. 90.

[32] SBTA, DR1108/2/4/1, Fordham Flower to Lord Cottesloe, 15 March 1963: 'I worked closely with Basil Spence at Coventry for twelve very exciting years.'

[33] SBTA, DR1108/2/4/1, Fordham Flower to Hugh Willatt, 7 March 1963.

[34] Louise Campbell, Miles Glendinning, and Jane Thomas, *Basil Spence: Buildings and Projects* (London, 2012), p. 301.

they were also responsible and opened in 1964.[35] In Notting Hill, Seifert ('v. cross and hurt') withdrew,[36] although Spence was hardly more fortunate. Fundraising proceeded slowly before the project collapsed in late 1964 when the RSC was offered the use of the theatre proposed for the new Barbican Estate in central London.[37] In the meantime, Spence had refused to be considered as a potential designer of the National Theatre on account of pressure of work.[38] His practice was certainly busy, but did he also think that he already had a theatre on his books, one that might be more likely to come to fruition than the much-delayed National?

The terms in which Spence was praised by Flower demonstrate the extent to which the Ballet Rambert and the RSC conceived their theatre in relatively traditional terms. In 1960, for example, the Ballet Rambert proposed that:

> the price of seats should be on the high side and the whole premises strikingly attractive. There would be no question of a 'utility' approach [...].[39]

A large number of drawings dating from 1963 in Spence's hand illustrate his typical method in which, once questions of layout and massing had been determined, a design was interrogated for its aesthetic possibilities.[40] Numerous potential treatments of the theatre's elevations are shown. In this respect, Spence's approach hardly accorded with the theoretical preoccupations of the younger generation, as is illustrated by the visit of a group of Architectural Association students to the University of Sussex in 1962. The students queried the extent to which the structure of Spence's buildings was honestly expressed, prompting Spence (who confessed to the Architectural Association's Edward Carter of being 'afraid of your boys') to reply that as a 'down-to-earth Scot' his view of structure was that it should be 'durable' and 'bond with the architecture to create a unit, look beautiful and not be too expensive'.[41] In the case of the New Mercury Theatre, Spence noted that the building was intended as a theatrical 'nursery' for 'the boys in leather' and would not necessarily have a 'plush' auditorium.[42] His response, however, was hardly

[35] HES, SPE ENG/35/1/1, photograph of site layout, 1957; 'The First University Theatre', *Architects' Journal* 139 (22 January 1964), p. 174.

[36] SBTA, DR1108/2/4/1, Fordham Flower to Basil Spence, 22 March 1963.

[37] SBTA, DR1108/2/4/2, Fordham Flower to Hugh Willatt, 6 May 1964: 'Peter and I had an odd approach the other day from the City. It was very unofficial and tentative and concerned the building of a theatre and a concert hall as part of the rebuilt Barbican scheme.' See also HES, MS 2329/ENG/56/4/19–20, Peter Chamberlin to Basil Spence, 18 February 1965, and RDC, RDC/AD/01/01, minute of 10 December 1964. At the end of the 1960s, the project was revived as a collaboration with Arup Associates; the theatre was to be designed by Peter Moro and was to be located within an office building. See RDC, RDC/AD/01/02, minutes 1967–71.

[38] Barnabas Calder, 'Committees and Concrete: the genesis and architecture of Denys Lasdun's National Theatre' (PhD diss., University of Cambridge, 2007), pp. 43–4.

[39] RDC, uncat., folder: 'New Mercury Theatre 1', 'Memorandum on a New Theatre at Notting Hill Gate' [February 1960]. The choice of words suggests the wartime 'utility' design programme, which had not been universally popular.

[40] E.g. HES, SPE ENG/56/2/6/1–10, exploratory studies, *c.*1963; SPE ENG/56/2/8/1–11 and SPE ENG/56/2/9/1–6, drawings of September 1963–January 1964; SPE ENG/56/2/5/1–11, façade treatments. Documentation relating to the project is at HES, MS 2329/ENG/56/1–5.

[41] HES, MS 2329/ENG/52/2/179, Basil Spence to Edward Carter, 14 November 1962.

[42] HES, MS 2329/X/19/7/64–66, Basil Spence to J. M. Richards, 7 February 1964.

Figure 4.2. 'Dramatic effect': perspective by Basil Spence of the proposed New Mercury Theatre, Notting Hill, 1963 (©HES. Sir Basil Spence Archive)

utilitarian (see Figure 4.2). Writing in early 1964, he emphasized the importance of the theatre's materials, planning, and appearance in creating an appropriately theatrical environment:

> Generally speaking I feel the Theatre should have a strong plastic cast concrete exterior, probably with a granite aggregate and a ribbed surface. The foyer and restaurant will be lit by windows of brilliant coloured glass cast in the concrete and taking the shape of tall narrow slits of light. [...] Inside, the dramatic effect should be heightened by the sharp dynamic forms which I wish to use. I clearly admit I am influenced by Scharoun's concert hall in Berlin, but emotionally I am attuned to this sort of treatment as I used it in the Sea and Ships Pavilion at the South Bank [in 1951].[43]

There are parallels here with Spence's contemporaneous designs for the Nuffield Theatre. Described as an 'amphitheatre' on an early site layout, the Nuffield has similarly ribbed walls, though of brick, while its over-scaled, copper-clad auditorium and fly tower create the same kind of 'dramatic effect' and dynamic roofscape that was intended in Notting Hill.[44] There are also similarities with other projects

[43] HES, MS 2329/X/19/7/64–66, Basil Spence to J. M. Richards, 7 February 1964.

[44] HES, SPE ENG/35/1/21, photograph of perspective by Spence, 1959, shows the theatre without the ribbed walls of the executed design. Interior perspectives by Spence include SPE ENG/35/1/60 of 1961.

by Spence, which were similarly conceived as *Gesamtkunstwerke*, such as Coventry Cathedral, where carefully chosen materials, lighting, stained glass, and art are all combined to stunning effect.

Spence's design for the Notting Hill theatre reflected not only his visual sensibility but also his long-established belief in the traditional value of architectural 'decorum' or hierarchy, in which certain high-status types of buildings would be distinguished by their rich treatment. When Hugh Casson praised Spence's work at Sussex, Spence replied that he appreciated such compliments 'in these days of Universities like hospitals or technical colleges'.[45] It is therefore not surprising that the campus centrepiece, Falmer House, evokes the grandeur of antiquity in its large arched openings. Similarly, it takes the materials—brick and concrete—used by Le Corbusier in a deliberately rough way at the Maisons Jaoul (1954) and reprises them in a more refined fashion appropriate to Falmer House's symbolic and ceremonial function. Spence was not alone in privileging buildings for ceremony and culture. Robert Matthew, for example, conceived the Festival Hall as a prestigious cultural 'Acropolis' in which the essence of London would be concentrated and distilled.[46] Similarly in Coventry, the introduction of the square adjacent to the Belgrade Theatre might be taken to indicate the theatre's status as an important public building, something that would have been less immediately obvious had the theatre's only public face comprised a doorway in a row of shops, as was originally proposed.

After the abandonment of the New Mercury project, Spence went on to design the Gardner Arts Centre at the University of Sussex. The Gardner, which was completed in 1969, is located west of Falmer House, on a site that had been earmarked for arts and sports buildings.[47] It comprises a series of brick-clad drums and wedge-shaped blocks with few windows, and so has a strong presence, notwithstanding Spence's view that it should 'merge and sit naturally on the site' (see Figure 4.3).[48] Its solidity was evidently important to Spence, who resisted calls by the centre's director, Walter Eysselinck, for greater transparency. In late 1965, Eysselinck feared that:

> it would look like a big brother of the stunning Chemistry theatre which serves an entirely different, sterner function. I wonder whether we do not need more glass so that people outside become more aware of what is happening in the Centre. This impression of informality and openness was something we all agreed upon. It is not a matter of mere aesthetics but of an identity and a function clearly expressed also in the external form.[49]

[45] HES, MS 2329/ENG/52/2/146, Basil Spence to Hugh Casson, 16 May 1963.

[46] Miles Glendinning, *Modern Architect: The Life and Times of Robert Matthew* (London, 2008), pp. 89–90.

[47] HES, SPE ENG/52/2/12/1, a site plan, shows the arts facilities arranged around a 'Theatre Court' (not unlike the courtyard of Falmer House), as well as a gymnasium.

[48] HES, MS 2329/ENG/52/5/35, Basil Spence to Walter Eysselinck, 7 December 1965.

[49] HES, MS 2329/ENG/52/5/37, Walter Eysselinck to Basil Spence, 25 November 1965.

Figure 4.3. Polygonal monumentality: the Gardner Arts Centre, University of Sussex, in 1970 (Henk Snoek/RIBA Collections)

In another report, he made the same point:

> I have stressed the need for a light and simple building, not only as an economic necessity but as a matter of artistic principle. I prefer Chichester to Nottingham, I am more interested in the suggestiveness of a small touch, the care of a detail, the quality of equipment than in gadgets and marble floors.[50]

Spence, however, disagreed. In 1969, he rebuffed a suggestion that the surfaces might be softened with wood: 'I am more than surprised to have your suggestion that such a temporary material as wood (which smacks of a roadhouse) should be used for this building which is very solid in conception.'[51] Its solidity reflected the building's function and status, and perhaps also the extent to which it had been funded by a substantial donation from a local businessman, Dr Lyddon Gardner, whose death was to give the building the status of a memorial. In these respects, it was far removed from the commercialized low culture of the 'roadhouse' of which Spence was so disparaging.

[50] UoSx, SxUOS1/1/5/13/1, Walter Eysselinck, 'Toward an Arts Centre', 3 June 1965.
[51] HES, MS 2329/ENG/52/5/6–7, Basil Spence to Walter Eysselinck, 16 July 1969.

The Northcott Theatre, Exeter, is, like the Gardner, housed in a building of somewhat monolithic form. This theatre, which opened in 1967, came into being when the University of Exeter realized that the £100,000 donated by the businessman George Northcott to maintain live theatre in the city could be used to help build a theatre on its own site, a long-held ambition.[52] Like many other buildings of the same date on campus, the theatre was the work of William Holford's office. The university authorities were evidently keen that it be designed by Holford, perhaps for consistency's sake, as in June 1963 they concluded that 'a general architect of high standing, rather than a specialist, should be appointed'.[53] Holford's name headed the list of possible architects, but apart from John Crowther and Associates of Truro, all of the others who were considered, in fact, had theatre experience: Louis de Soissons (Welwyn Garden City); Peter Moro (listed as 'Peter More'); Elidir Davies (the Mermaid); R. W. Hurst (LAMDA); John Brownrigg (the Yvonne Arnaud, Guildford); and Robert Atkinson (Fairfield Halls).[54] Initially, the building was to be faced with white concrete blocks. It was reported that the architects 'thought that this was appropriate [...] this theatre was to be the focal point of the centre of the University'.[55] However, concerns about streaking (of the concrete, by rainwater) meant that the same brown bricks found elsewhere on campus were eventually used for the theatre, lest the building become, as the architects put it, 'sordid'.[56] Nonetheless, its windowless walls and wedge-shaped, blocky massing still contrast with the stripped classicism and delicate detailing of Holford's earlier work for the university, suggesting its special status. Holford referred to the theatre as the 'apex of a succession of buildings for meeting and assembly'.[57]

The Northcott's wedge-like form and the Gardner's composition as a cluster of drums and wedges both bring to mind the historian Philip Goad's suggestion that some modern architects deployed geometric clarity and 'significant form' in order to suggest status and meaning in public architecture 'in the absence of a sanctioned ornamental language'.[58] In this reading of modern architecture, as in certain kinds of modern art, forms and geometries carry meaning and assume the communicative role hitherto played by ornamental detail. In the case of modern architecture, these forms and geometries might suggest monumentality and civic status. In this respect, Goad's analysis reflects the extent to which the search for a so-called 'modern monumentality' was significant in post-war architectural discourse. It is to this idea that we now turn.

[52] UoEx, 26/1d/3c, Roderick Ross to P. Stower, 27 January 1958.

[53] UoEx, 26/1d/3c, 'Minutes of an Informal Meeting Regarding Northcott Theatre and Arts Centre', 25 June 1963.

[54] UoEx, 26/1d/3c, Addendum attached to the 'Minutes of an Informal Meeting Regarding Northcott Theatre and Arts Centre', 25 June 1963.

[55] UoEx, 26/1d/2d, Transcript of interview with Stower and Riches, 16 March 1967.

[56] UoEx, 26/1d/2d, Transcript of interview with Stower and Riches, 16 March 1967.

[57] UoLiv, D147/C74/3, Interview transcript [presumably Holford], n.d.

[58] Philip Goad, 'Post-war and Polygonal: special plans for Australian architecture, 1950–70', *Architectural Theory Review* 15, no. 2 (2010), pp. 166–86 (p. 177).

MODERN MONUMENTALITY IN THEORY AND PRACTICE

In 1973, Colin Amery noted that 'some of the many new [theatres] encourage patrons by allowing much of the glitter inside to show through glass walls and canopies'.[59] Thus, for example, in the case of Guildford's Yvonne Arnaud Theatre—designed by Scott Brownrigg and Turner after 1958 and opened in 1965—it was intended that views into the building would, in effect, advertise the theatre, with reference being made to 'a tempting invitation to the colour and excitement within'.[60] In this respect, the closely spaced vertical fins at either side of the full-height foyer windows suggest pleated curtains which have been pulled back, while a projecting balcony blurs the inside/outside distinction by allowing audience members and day-time visitors to spill out onto the adjacent riverbank (see Figure 4.4). Sketches by the architects render the glass almost invisible and place the audience on full view.[61] The theatre is, in effect, demystified by its transparent elevations, something that resonates with Jennie Lee's intention that it should be accessible to all.

Figure 4.4. Yvonne Arnaud Theatre, Guildford, viewed from the millpond in 2006 (Alistair Fair)

[59] 'Old Vic + New: Theatre Royal, Bristol', *Architectural Review* 153 (February 1973), pp. 123–30 (p. 130).

[60] SHC, 7018/2/3/142, clippings: 'This is the Yvonne Arnaud Theatre', *Surrey Advertiser*, 29 April 1961.

[61] SHC, 4580/8-14, sketches by Scott Brownrigg architects, n.d., especially 4580/10.

The Yvonne Arnaud Theatre's transparency not only serves as an invitation to potential patrons but can also be understood within the context of wider debates about monumentality. In 1951, John Summerson wrote of the Festival Hall that 'the river-front hesitates on the brink of monumentality'.[62] Summerson's choice of words was surely deliberate. Monumentality was a significant topic in post-war architectural discourse, partly because it could be associated with totalitarianism,[63] and also because it could seem backward in both scale and values. The *Architectural Review* explored the subject in a 'symposium' in 1948.[64] CIAM's 1951 conference, held at Hoddesdon and entitled 'The Heart of the City: the Humanisation of Urban Life', also considered monumentality as part of a broader discussion of urban design. Several definitions of a so-called 'modern monumentality' emerged. The most straightforward was that advanced by Henry-Russell Hitchcock, in which the monument was 'a testimonial consciously or unconsciously provided for the future'.[65] A building's scale and decoration were thus less significant than its potential for meaning, and there is evidence of community centres, playing fields, and even bus shelters being understood as 'living monuments'.[66] The Arts Council thought that cultural buildings could be conceived in this way, proposing that there might be 'no better memorial of a war to save the freedom of spirit of the individual than a central group of buildings for drama and music and art'.[67]

Sigfried Giedion, meanwhile, proposed a slightly different approach. He suggested, in his contributions to the 'Heart of the City' conference and elsewhere, that civic projects offered particular opportunities for the development of a new monumentality.[68] Within these buildings, places, and structures, people would 'play as important a role as the spectacle itself' in 'a unity of the architectural background, the people, and the symbols created by artists'.[69] In other words, Giedion's 'modern monumentality' was a fundamentally humanized architecture, in which a building's occupants effectively added to (and perhaps completed) its architectural meaning through their presence and actions. Giedion discussed Le Corbusier's *Unité d'habitation* in these terms, citing a party during which the building came 'to its full strength when animated by this vibrant throng'.[70] Others made similar arguments. For example, everyday life was conceived in animating terms in the Arts Council's 1945 Arts Centre prototype, whose 'large continuous windows [...] frame the picture of the street'.[71]

[62] Harwood, *Space, Hope and Brutalism*, p. 489.

[63] John Summerson, 'The Mischievous Analogy', in his *Heavenly Mansions and Other Essays on Architecture* (London, 1949), pp. 195–218 (pp. 203–5).

[64] [Richards], 'New Monumentality', pp. 117–28.

[65] 'New Monumentality', p. 119.

[66] Selina Todd, 'Phoenix Rising: working-class life and urban reconstruction, *c.*1945–1967', *Journal of British Studies* 54, no. 3 (2015), pp. 679–702 (p. 688); Elain Harwood and James O. Davies, *England's Post-war Listed Buildings* (London, 3rd ed., 2015), p. 118.

[67] ACGB, Annual Report, 1945–1946, p. 22.

[68] E.g. Sigfried Giedion, 'The Need for a New Monumentality' [1944] in his *Architecture, You and Me: The Diary of a Development* (Cambridge, MA, 1957), pp. 25–39 (p. 31).

[69] Giedion, 'The Need for a New Monumentality', p. 39.

[70] Sigfried Giedion, 'Social Imagination', in his *Architecture, You and Me: The Diary of a Development* (Cambridge, MA, 1957), pp. 157–77 (p. 165).

[71] [ACGB], 'Plans for an Arts Centre' [London, 1945], p. 9.

One of the speakers at Hoddesdon was Arthur Ling, who four years later would replace Donald Gibson as Coventry's city architect.[72] While, as was shown in Chapter 3, Ling did not inaugurate the revisions to the Belgrade Theatre design that led to the construction of the adjacent public square, the way in which the gathering audience was placed on view through the large windows of the revised design brings to mind Giedion's call for a humanized monumentality. The same is true of Martin Froy's foyer mosaics, which reflected 'a scheme of artist-architect co-operation' in which it was intended that 'the decoration of a public place would develop naturally with the plans for the building itself'.[73] Not only do the mosaics thus suggest the integral place of art in Giedion's new monumentality, but as 'an indeterminate but evocative background to the people assembled in front' (to quote Froy), they were also intended to create an effect 'of expectancy like that given on the empty stage when the cyclorama is used, lights being played upon it'.[74] The mosaics were to be seen from the theatre square as a single, non-figurative composition spanning both foyer levels, with the audience in the foreground. In this way, they contributed to the humanization of a building which in any case had been conceived in explicitly civic, communal terms. Furthermore, Ling's apparent interest in Patrick Geddes's Outlook Tower—a place which through the provision of views allowed individuals to relate themselves to the city beyond—suggests that views in the other direction were also significant, especially in the light of the city authorities' concern that new residents felt little connection to Coventry.[75] Looking out at the surrounding streets would allow theatregoers and those drinking coffee during the day to perceive their place in the rebuilt city.

Although Peter Moro seems not to have referred explicitly to modern monumentality and was certainly no fan of elaborate theory, his description of Nottingham Playhouse as 'a building to be used and enjoyed, not a building to subdue and impress' suggests a progressive approach.[76] The same is true of his description of the Playhouse upon its opening in 1963: 'whereas civic buildings tended to be heavy and pompous, modern methods of construction and a change of spirit produce exciting solutions, elegant and adventurous'.[77] The project's origins lie in the mid-1950s, when the Repertory Company—newly in receipt of Arts Council subsidy—started to outgrow the old Playhouse. Initial discussions with Moro took place during 1956 with a view to refurbishment and reconstruction, but by June 1957 it had been decided to construct a new theatre, and a site on Wellington Circus was selected.[78] In 1958, Moro's appointment was formally confirmed.[79] There had

[72] Arthur Ling, 'Satisfying Human Needs at the Core', in *Heart of the City*, edited by Jacqueline Tyrwhitt, J. L. Sert, and Ernesto Rogers (London, 1952), pp. 94–6 (p. 95).

[73] Martin Froy, 'Belgrade Theatre' [typescript, 1958]. Copy kindly supplied by Martin Froy.

[74] Martin Froy, 'Belgrade Theatre: interior decoration' [typescript, 1958]. Copy kindly supplied by Martin Froy.

[75] Alistair Fair, '"A New Image of the Living Theatre": the genesis and design of the Belgrade Theatre, Coventry, 1948–58', *Architectural History* 54 (2011), pp. 347–82 (p. 366).

[76] V&A TC, Nottingham file, uncat., clipping from *Guardian Journal Souvenir Supplement*, 11 December 1963.

[77] V&A TC, Nottingham file, uncat., *Guardian Journal Souvenir Supplement*, 11 December 1963.

[78] NA, DD/NP/1/2/1/1, memo of 8 October 1956; Nottingham Theatre Trust to J. L. Hodgkinson, 3 January 1957; letter to Bertrand Hallward, 29 June 1957.

[79] NA, DD/NP/1/2/1/1, letter to Bertrand Hallward, 11 May 1959.

been pressure to select a local architect, but a figure with a national reputation was preferred. Mention was made of William Holford and Leslie Martin, as well as Donald Gibson, who was now Nottinghamshire's county architect but had overseen the initial designs for the Belgrade Theatre in his previous role at Coventry.[80] Moro was nonetheless uniquely qualified. With the detailed design of the Festival Hall to his name along with television studios for Associated Rediffusion, he was described as 'a London architect who has specialised in matters of this sort'.[81] Furthermore, it was hoped that the new Playhouse would 'make some contribution to theatre architecture nationally and internationally',[82] and so the Festival Hall's prestige and prominence surely also counted in Moro's favour.

The Nottingham Playhouse is one of the best theatre buildings of its date. Its design repeats the Festival Hall's essential *parti* in that its auditorium is articulated as a solid object at the building's core. The auditorium is housed in a concrete drum which rises through and above a block housing the foyers and backstage areas (see Figure 4.5). To one side of the building, a long wing stretches forwards, housing the restaurant. An intended upper level here was to provide actors' flats. The flats were more economically conceived than those which had been built at the Belgrade, apparently lacking *en suite* facilities, but were eventually omitted to save money. The composition of the Playhouse as a collection of cuboids and a cylinder echoes Gunnar Asplund's Stockholm Public Library (1922–8) as well as Claude Nicolas Ledoux's Rotonde de la Villette (1784–8). More immediately, Moro's mentor, Berthold Lubetkin, stressed the potential significance and value of form

Figure 4.5. Nottingham Playhouse, newly completed in 1963 (RIBA Collections)

[80] NA, DD/NP/1/2/1/1, letter to Bertrand Hallward, 11 May 1959.
[81] NA, DD/NP/1/2/1/1, memo of 8 October 1956.
[82] NA, DD/NP/1/2/1/1, letter to Bertrand Hallward, 11 May 1959.

and geometry in architecture. Drawing on constructivist theory, he argued that 'the sharp-edged regularities of crisp geometric formulations have universal meaning independent of whims or moods' and so serve to locate buildings within a historical continuum.[83] If it is accepted that Moro was thinking along the same lines as Lubetkin, from whom he professed to have learned a significant amount, and bearing in mind Philip Goad's argument that monumentality for modern architects could be the product of a 'reversion to significant form via geometry',[84] then it might be concluded that the simply articulated volumes of Nottingham Playhouse (and Moro's subsequent theatres) serve to suggest the dignity appropriate to civic architecture without the use of traditional ornament or historically specific forms.

Moro's Playhouse also appeals to Giedion's view of modern monumentality as 'a unity of the architectural background, the people, and the symbols created by artists'. The foyers and restaurant are predominantly glazed at street level, with Moro reportedly being interested in the ways that these spaces would be seen from the street.[85] A drawing of the theatre, published in 1961, renders this glazing almost imperceptible, meaning that the interior is on full view,[86] and this quality is also evident in the completed theatre. Writing in the *Guardian*, Diana Rowntree concluded that:

> Glass walls allow the eye to link the colonnaded spaces within with the faintly ecclesiastical Victorian circus outside. The passer-by can see the audience festooned on the leisurely staircase or in dramatic silhouette against the rough concrete of the drum.[87]

As Rowntree pointed out, the stair has a particularly important role in animating the elevation. Located adjacent to the windows, it is clearly visible. The Playhouse's entrance is at an intermediate level between the upper and lower foyers, meaning that all patrons must either ascend or descend after entering the building. The stair's shallowness—alluded to by Rowntree's use of the word 'leisurely'—lengthens the experience of its use, both physically and temporally, and maximizes its effect. The upper part of the elevation is treated as a projecting *piano nobile*. Drawings and a model of 1959 show a single horizontal band of windows, vaguely Corbusian in character, which would have offered only a partial glimpse of the upper foyer.[88] Whereas the expansive glazing of the Belgrade Theatre offers fairly open views, at Nottingham Playhouse the view was to be more deliberately framed by the width of the slot. The executed design is slightly different in form, but the view remains deliberately framed. Small square windows alternate with narrow vertical slits, reprising the pattern of the wood panelling in the Festival Hall's auditorium in metal transoms, white panels, and glass. This pattern—more complex than that

83 John Allen, *Berthold Lubetkin: Architecture and the Tradition of Progress* (London, 2012), p. 141.
84 Goad, 'Post-war and Polygonal', p. 177.
85 Michael Mellish, interviewed 15 February 2013.
86 Peter Moro, 'The Nottingham Playhouse', *Builder* 203 (12 May 1961), pp. 893–5.
87 'The Building', *Guardian*, 29 November 1963.
88 'Project for the Playhouse Theatre, Nottingham', *Architects' Journal* 130 (17 September 1959), pp. 209–10.

proposed in 1959—means that views of the Playhouse's upper foyer take on a more abstract quality, in that patrons are viewed (and see out) through a mixture of vertical and horizontal windows in what might be considered as a game of revelation and concealment.

The foyers themselves, meanwhile, are not without spatial and formal interest in their own right, but they also serve as a carefully designed backdrop for visitors and audiences. The briefing document provided to Moro emphasized the experience of being in and moving through these spaces, and of being seen in them, referring to the 'importance as a feature' of 'staircases and places designed for the mingling and circulation of the audience'.[89] The upper foyers are pulled back from the auditorium drum in the manner of galleries, with corresponding views within and between the different levels, and of the staircase. Within this environment, Moro's choice of materials is significant. Board-marked concrete dominates, not least on the curved wall of the auditorium drum. It is relieved only by an abstract aluminium 'sculpture' by Geoffrey Clarke, whose jagged forms and rough textures embody the same direct materiality as Moro's architecture. Whereas in Coventry Martin Froy's mosaic covered—even 'decorated'—the equivalent wall at the Belgrade Theatre, with Froy romantically conceiving the auditorium as a jewel-encrusted, wood-lined box of treasures, no attempt was made in Nottingham to hide the Playhouse's construction materials. However, the exposed concrete is not simply an expression of brutalist honesty. Moro conceived his later Plymouth Theatre Royal as 'a building teeming with people and the walls are a foil to that',[90] and Nottingham Playhouse invites a similar interpretation. The *Architectural Review* concluded that its 'neutral concrete surfaces and spotty lighting' served to 'show to advantage persons dressed in the sub-formal styles and in the quasi-formal postures of current British social life'.[91] There are echoes here of the way in which some of Moro's contemporaries sought, as Alison and Peter Smithson put it, to 'invite the occupiers [of buildings] into the game of architecture', with the permanent building forming a backdrop for transient expressions of occupation.[92] In a similar vein, although the unbuilt designs of 1965 for a major cultural complex in Glasgow by the city architect, Archibald Jury, suggest a somewhat conventional view of monumental design in their vast scale and grand arcades, mention was nonetheless made of the way that the audiences gathering in the foyers would be seen through their glazed elevations. 'Kaleidoscopic' effects would apparently result from patrons moving behind the coloured glazing of the staircase towers.[93]

The experience of these spaces in use could be understood in overtly theatrical terms. In 1959, Elidir Davies told the British Drama League that it was essential to conceive the public as actors and actresses who would enjoy the excitement of

[89] NA, DD/NP/1/2/1/1, Nottingham Playhouse architects' brief, p. 6.

[90] PCL, Theatre Royal clippings folder: 'Peter Moro: man of the night people', *Western Evening Herald* Special Supplement, 5 May 1982.

[91] 'ID: Nottingham Playhouse', *Architectural Review* 807 (May 1964), pp. 337–42 (p. 342).

[92] Alistair Fair, '"Brutalism Among the Ladies": modern architecture at Somerville College, Oxford, 1947–67', *Architectural History* 57 (2014), pp. 357–92 (pp. 378–80).

[93] V&A, ACGB/120/41, 'Description of the Design and Layout of Glasgow's New Cultural Centre', 29 September 1965.

approaching a theatre building and being on view within it.[94] In this way, he went on, staircases should be considered as stages, and cloakrooms as dressing rooms. The *Architectural Review* was clearly thinking along these lines when, in a discussion of the 'theatrical experience' at the Nottingham Playhouse, it described the theatre's main stair as a 'display shelf' for the audience.[95] Similarly, the upper part of the Playhouse's auditorium is entered through a rectangular opening in the concrete drum which reads as a kind of mini proscenium arch. Standing here, patrons might momentarily cast themselves as 'actors' in a way that brings to mind Martin Froy's provision of a mirror in the Belgrade Theatre foyer in order that 'the audience might see themselves as actors taking part in the theatre, and that the excitement of the floating staircase might be enhanced by their percieving [sic], in reflection, their situation in relation to it'.[96]

Something of this quality is also evident in the architect Denys Lasdun's description of the National Theatre's foyers and terraces as its 'fourth theatre', the essential counterpart to its three auditoria.[97] The *Architectural Review*'s January 1977 special issue not only photographed the building in use but also illustrated the abstract stepped forms of Edward Gordon Craig's interwar stage sets, making the theatrical parallel yet more obvious,[98] while the critic Mark Girouard commented that:

> [the audience] comes into its own in the intervals. It then becomes the play, and each member of it is at once actor and spectator. One parades up and down through a series of inter-connecting stage sets, striking conscious or unconscious attitudes and watching others do the same.[99]

It is, therefore, to the National Theatre that we now turn.

'INCOMPLETE WITHOUT PEOPLE': THE NATIONAL THEATRE

Designed largely between 1964 and 1967 and opened in 1976, the National Theatre might be interpreted as a canonical example of brutalism on account of its omnipresent board-marked concrete, although Lasdun refused to consider it thus.[100] Its history has been described by Barnabas Calder as being 'long and messy'.[101] As was discussed in Chapter 3, the architect Brian O'Rorke produced several designs during the 1950s and early 1960s following the government's promise of

[94] LoB, MS 978/1/3/2/10, Elidir Davies, 'Architecture and Space', presented to the British Drama League on 31 December 1959.

[95] 'ID: Nottingham Playhouse', p. 342.

[96] Froy, 'Belgrade Theatre: interior decoration' [typescript, n. 74 above].

[97] Denys Lasdun, 'Humanising the Institution', *Architectural Review* 161 (January 1977), pp. 25–6 (p. 25).; 'Detailing the Drama', *Architectural Review* 161 (January 1977), pp. 31–4 (p. 31).

[98] 'Detailing the Drama', p. 31.

[99] Mark Girouard, 'Cosmic Connections', *Architectural Review* 161 (January 1977), pp. 5–7 (p. 5).

[100] Calder, *Raw Concrete*, p. 323.

[101] Calder, *Raw Concrete*, p. 278. My discussion of the National draws on Calder's 'Committees and Concrete' as well as *Raw Concrete*, pp. 278–329, plus William J. R. Curtis, *Denys Lasdun: Architecture, City, Landscape* (London, 1994), pp. 108–57. Daniel Rosenthal, *The National Theatre Story* (London, 2013) is also helpful.

support in 1949. However, little more was achieved until the London County Council (LCC) forced central government to commit to the project in 1961 by offering a substantial grant on condition that Parliament at least matched the sum. In this respect, the National finally came into being as the product of an unlikely alliance between the left-wing LCC under Isaac Hayward, whose agenda was the democratization of 'culture' and the desire to have 'the biggest and best civic theatre in the country',[102] and right-wing parliamentarians keen to suggest Britain's cultural superiority and to cement their own legacy. In 1963, a National Theatre Company was formed at the Old Vic under Laurence Olivier. It was intended that Sadler's Wells Opera and the Royal Shakespeare Company would both join the project, although the RSC soon withdrew.

A formal project board was set up to oversee progress. It rejected the idea that there should be two auditoria shared by the theatre and opera companies, instead asking the opera and theatre directors to set out their views on what was required. Olivier, however, was reluctant to undertake this task alone, and so formed a building committee whose members, as Calder puts it, apparently comprised 'those whose criticisms he feared rather than those who would be the most cooperative and useful members'.[103] It included experienced directors (not least Peter Hall and Peter Brook of the rival RSC), designers, and, later, technicians.[104] The committee proved a disruptive influence, attempting to usurp the board's position as the official client body.[105] As is discussed in Chapter 8, it sought to shape decisively the design of the National's auditoria, yet its members rarely agreed with each other. In addition, Olivier and Norman Marshall were weak chairmen.[106] The architect Denys Lasdun was to record of its meetings in 1964 that they comprised a series of 'interesting personal vignettes, some of them cancelling out, some not'.[107]

Whereas O'Rorke had seemed safely modern in the late 1940s, by the early sixties he had been overshadowed by a new generation of architects.[108] A design competition was proposed, but the Building Committee, true to belligerent form, intervened with a demand that the competition should select a designer, not a design.[109] Many of the committee's members, not least Peter Brook, had a fundamental distrust of architects and feared that a design would be foisted upon them. Their view carried the day. The intended panel of assessors was downgraded to become an advisory panel, and a three-stage process was set up. First, architects would express their interest; several were also invited to compete. The second stage would comprise interviews, with outline designs then following in a third round. Up-and-coming young designers (many suggested by the director George Devine) were pitted against more established firms (see Table 4.1).[110] Several competitors, such as Peter Moro, had experience of theatre design, but many did not. Bill

[102] Calder, 'Committees and Concrete', p. 29.
[103] Calder, *Raw Concrete*, p. 284.
[104] Calder, 'Committees and Concrete', pp. 67–71.
[105] Calder, 'Committees and Concrete', pp. 73–7.
[106] Calder, 'Committees and Concrete', pp. 78–85.
[107] Calder, 'Committees and Concrete', p. 73.
[108] Calder, 'Committees and Concrete', p. 38.
[109] Calder, 'Committees and Concrete', p. 41.
[110] Calder, 'Committees and Concrete', pp. 41–62.

Table 4.1. October 1963 shortlist

Ahrends Burton and Koralek	Nominated by the Building Committee and John Piper of the assessors' panel. Made it to the final eight, and considered possible designer of the opera house or experimental theatre.
Architects' Co-Partnership	Thought to be 'first-rate, but not for this work' by the interview panel. Made it to the final eight.
Arup (Philip Dowson)	Designer of buildings for Oxbridge colleges; thought 'reasonably good, but not outstanding' by the interview panel.
Bridgewater, Shepheard, Epstein	
Burnet Tait and Lorne with Werner Ruhnau	Ruhnau had designed new theatres in Germany; potentially, as with Davies and Moro, this counted against him.
Peter Carter	
Casson and Conder	Nominated by the assessors' panel.
James Cubitt and Philip Johnson	
Elidir Davies	Had experience of theatre (Mermaid Theatre, 1959), which may have counted against him.
Eldred Evans and Denis Gailey	Nominated by the Building Committee (i.e. George Devine).
Frederick Gibberd	Proposed by the assessors' panel, and had experience of theatre design in Oxford. No comment recorded on his interview.
Ernö Goldfinger	No comment recorded on his interview, but perhaps his famously tough personality did not appeal.
Howell Killick Partridge and Amis	Nominated by the Building Committee, and made it to the final eight.
Denys Lasdun	Nominated by the assessors' panel.
Richard Llewelyn-Davies	Nominated by the assessors' panel. Thought to be 'first class analytically but not creative enough' after the interview. Made it to the final eight.
Peter Moro	Nominated by the assessors' panel. His experience of theatre counted against him, as did his apparently 'pessimistic' interview.
Brian O'Rorke	Presumably included on account of his previous work, and unlikely to have been considered a serious contender.
Richard Sheppard, Robson and Partners	Then known for their educational buildings. Deemed 'analytical, but not very creative' by the interview panel, but still made it to the final eight.
James Stirling and James Gowan	Nominated by the Building Committee, and by John Piper of the assessors' panel. Made it to the final eight.
Yorke Rosenberg and Mardall	Nominated by the assessors' panel. Made it to the final eight.

Notes: The Building Committee's other nominations (largely made by George Devine) were: Powell and Moya; Alison and Peter Smithson; Lyons Israel and Ellis; Chalk, Crosby, and Herron (of Archigram); and Cedric Price.

The assessors' panel comprised Robert Matthew, Hubert Bennett, William Holford, John Piper, and Norman Marshall. It also proposed Basil Spence, Leslie Martin, and Ralph Erskine.

Of the architects who were invited to compete, refusals were received from Spence, Powell and Moya, and Martin.

The files record comments on other architects, including the Smithsons (thought to be too theoretical) and Richard Seifert ('too commercial. No convictions').

Source: Calder, 'Committees and Concrete', pp. 41–62.

Howell, for example, wrote that 'we have never built a theatre, but considering the record of those who have, we do not think this is necessarily a fatal drawback'.[111] Lasdun emerged victorious in November 1963. His interview was to become legendary. Whereas most of the competitors arrived *en masse*, Lasdun appeared alone, spoke quietly, and expressed his willingness to collaborate with the Building Committee. He emphasized the National's 'spiritual' aspect, Olivier later recalling that 'we all fell for that'.[112] Nonetheless, he would also have seemed like a safe pair of hands. Having worked with Berthold Lubetkin in the 1930s and 1940s, he had set up his own office in the early 1950s, and his work was consistently acclaimed. His contemporaneous designs for the University of East Anglia would have demonstrated his ability to handle a large public project. In addition, the recently completed Royal College of Physicians was a building of considerable richness and subtlety, which suggested that Lasdun could tackle a prestigious project with success. The committee was unanimous in favouring him, and decided to abandon the proposed third round of the competition.

Lasdun's design for the National was rooted in the material and planning trends of the 1960s but also represented an exploration of various established preoccupations of his office, including the refined use of concrete, deeply modelled elevations, stepped sections, and carefully controlled geometries.[113] Glimpses into his evolving ideas survive in a small number of early sketches and a published scheme of 1965 in which the theatre and opera house are located between Hungerford Bridge and County Hall, framing views of the Shell office tower. Revised proposals of 1967 feature the theatre alone, moving it to the east of Waterloo Bridge. These designs largely accord with the building that opened in 1976.[114] As built, the National is organized around its two main auditoria (the design of which, along with the smaller studio theatre, is discussed in Chapter 8), which are arranged at 45 degrees to each other (see Figure 4.6). These auditoria are set within a structure described by Lasdun as being 'without facades but with layers of building, like geological strata'.[115] The public areas essentially have six levels, but the arrangement of the strata on the riverside elevations is varied. In some areas they are omitted altogether, in other places they are obscured by external walkways, while the use of a 3:2 section further complicates the relationship between the foyer levels and those of the walkways and riverside terraces. The elevations contrast in their horizontality with the vertical accents of the fly towers, which rise above the two main auditoria. That serving the Olivier Theatre—the National's largest auditorium—is the more complex in form. Two corners are chamfered and

[111] Calder, 'Committees and Concrete', p. 55.

[112] Laurence Olivier, 'The Great Experiment', *Architectural Review* 161 (January 1977), pp. 15–16 (p. 15).

[113] William Curtis, 'Perspective', *Architectural Review* 161 (January 1977), pp. 52–8.

[114] The decision to use the eastern site was taken on 9 March 1966: see Rosenthal, *National Theatre*, p. 106. A model was shown on television on 22 November 1967 (Rosenthal, *National Theatre*, p. 137). For an image of the paired scheme, see 'The Long Dream', *Architectural Review* 161 (January 1977), pp. 65–8 (p. 68).

[115] Quoted in William Curtis, 'Past and Prejudice', *Architectural Review* 161 (January 1977), pp. 8–14 (p. 11).

Figure 4.6. National Theatre, aerial view in 1976 with the Olivier Theatre on the diagonal axis and the Lyttelton Theatre to the right (Lasdun Archive/RIBA Collections)

the other two are extended by 'ears' containing stage equipment. This shape hints at the form of the 'open' (i.e. non-proscenium arch) stage and amphitheatre-like auditorium below. Inside the building, the foyers are alternately constrained and open, dark and light, with views between the various levels and out to the riverside. The foyers repeat the board-marked concrete surfaces of the exterior, adding 'diagrid' coffered ceilings and floors of brick and carpet.

Lasdun described his approach in progressive terms: 'we have tried to offset the current scepticism about the permanent housing of institutionalised culture and the doubts about architectural form-making by a response away from the isolated monument [...]'.[116] His agenda was partly urbanistic, with the strata being 'connected in such a way that they flow into the surrounding riverscape and city'.[117] In his view, 'a fundamental aspect of the design will be concerned with movement',[118] and so, whereas the neighbouring buildings were 'closed boxes with walkways', the National's strata 'are open [...] you enter the strata'.[119] Mark Girouard borrowed from E. M. Forster in using the phrase 'only connect' to describe the visual and

[116] Curtis, 'Past and Prejudice', p. 11. [117] Curtis, 'Past and Prejudice', p. 11.
[118] Memo of 1963, quoted in Calder, 'Committees and Concrete', p. 165.
[119] Calder, 'Committees and Concrete', p. 165.

physical links that the strata create.[120] In addition, as an 'architecture of landscape [...] without facades', the National was also for Lasdun an attempt to 'humanis[e] the institution'.[121] Of the foyers and strata, he suggested:

> people and events will be the decoration. Time will make its marks of weathering. The building is placed in time but modifies time and moves in it.[122]

Indeed, J. M. Richards concluded in 1976 of the National that 'it's been deliberately made incomplete without people'.[123] Lasdun referred to a 'townscape sculpture' whose visitors were 'movable ornament'; their relationships 'continually shift' as they move 'forcing an entirely different reading' of the building.[124] The result would be 'ASSYMETRICAL, DYNAMIC, SCULPTURAL' as well as 'SCENOGRAPHIC'. (Similarly 'dynamic' was a proposal made in 1974 by Peter Hall, who had succeeded Olivier as the National's director, that it might be interesting to turn off the floodlighting at regular intervals in order to project newsflashes onto the building.[125])

Yet for all that the National suggests a progressive public architecture, its status remained important. Despite earlier claiming that it was 'NOT a monument', in 1996 Lasdun concluded that 'it has to be monumental because [...] it is a civic matter'.[126] He had made a similar point in 1964. When Peter Brook argued that a 'bombed site in Bethnal Green' might make a more immediate and authentic venue for performance than a new building, Lasdun concluded that 'we could do it on the South Bank, but is this a National Theatre?'[127] Thus, for example, Lasdun was keen to achieve a high standard of board-marked concrete in order to distinguish the National from more workaday concrete buildings, and accordingly an extremely detailed specification was intended to deliver exact results in terms of texture, colour, and weathering capability.[128] The richness of these surfaces was amplified by the original lighting strategy, which brought out the precision with which the concrete had been finished and celebrated it in unashamedly aesthetic terms. The planning of the foyers, too, is important. Those serving the Olivier Theatre have a more axial character than those which are adjacent to the proscenium arch Lyttelton Theatre.[129] Axiality was not new in Lasdun's work, but typically it was subverted. At the earlier Royal College of Physicians, for example, the processional route is blocked in what Calder terms 'a gesture of modernist hostility to the tradition of axiality'.[130] In the case of the Olivier foyer, however, the axial route

[120] Girouard, 'Cosmic Connections', pp. 6–7. Girouard was less fond of the Belvedere Road elevations, which as built were strataless for economy.

[121] Lasdun, 'Humanising the Institution', pp. 25–6.

[122] Quoted in Curtis, 'Past and Prejudice', p. 13.

[123] Quoted in Curtis, *Lasdun*, p. 154.

[124] RIBA, LaD/167/1, handwritten note by Denys Lasdun, n.d.

[125] RIBA, LaD/164/2, telephone conversation between Peter Hall and Denys Lasdun, 22 May 1974.

[126] Quoted in Calder, 'Committees and Concrete', p. 201.

[127] RIBA, LaD/167/4, Building Committee, 4 March 1964.

[128] Calder, 'Committees and Concrete', pp. 186–9.

[129] Barnabas Calder, 'The Limits of 1960s Radicalism: the Fun Palace versus the National Theatre', in *Setting the Scene: Perspectives on Twentieth-century Theatre Architecture*, edited by Alistair Fair (Farnham, 2015), pp. 164–78 (p. 171).

[130] Calder, 'The Limits of 1960s Radicalism', p. 171.

Figure 4.7. 'Deliberately incomplete without people': the National Theatre's Lyttelton foyer in 1976 (Lasdun Archive/RIBA Collections)

survives intact, beginning on the riverside walk, ascending via the external stair on the building's western 'prow', and entering the foyers, which are disposed on essentially symmetrical lines around the route, with the circle foyer being especially grand in its double height. By contrast, the Lyttelton foyers and circulation are more informal and often low-ceilinged (see Figure 4.7). When they open onto a triple-height galleried area, they lack the symmetries of the Olivier foyers. Furthermore, the Lyttelton foyer's stairs do not have the same processional quality. Instead, they rise in largely enclosed towers from which there are only glimpses of the foyers beyond. The point at which the two areas intersect is, to quote Calder again, 'a gloriously complex piece of planning which reads—and is experienced—as a free composition in slanted slab-columns and cut-away decks'.[131] Here, perhaps most clearly, it is possible to discern Lasdun's concern with, on the one hand, the kind of material and spatial register and tone appropriate to a major public building and, on the other, the refashioning of this kind of building in contemporary terms.

Critics certainly interpreted the National in terms of both continuity and innovation. William Curtis invoked the idea of monumentality. With modern architecture having dispensed with the 'domes, porticoes, grand orders, [...] stressed

[131] Calder, 'The Limits of 1960s Radicalism', p. 172.

entrances, [and] axial symmetry' that traditionally implied civic status, the National instead achieved monumentality through its scale, processional routes, materials, and 'partial symmetry'.[132] The result was 'grandeur of effect with simplicity of means', offering 'a possible language for public buildings of all sorts'.[133] Monumentality was also discussed by Mark Girouard, for whom the National was (despite its urban connections) also 'a piece of abstract sculpture', a 'landmark' which was accomplished and serious-minded.[134] As he saw it, 'regardless of what goes on inside it, the National Theatre also exists as an object, a new and prominent addition to the townscape'.

In 1976, Curtis concluded that 'at present, monuments are treated with suspicion in England—as if they were dinosaurs from a previous age or the products of *prima donnas* intent on self-aggrandisement'.[135] Were what might be intended as examples of a progressive monumentality always interpreted as such? The theatre historian Victor Glasstone thought not, concluding in 1969 that the new breed of civic theatres typically took the form of 'aloof monument[s]'.[136] Consciously anti-monumental approaches were further developed during the 1970s, as is discussed in Chapters 7 and 10. However, this chapter concludes with two examples, conceived at the end of the 1960s, which show how the National's 'human' and 'urban' qualities could be refined in the pursuit of a different kind of enriched modern public architecture.

'TAKING ON A NEW WARMTH': POPULAR MODERNISM

Writing in 1947, J. M. Richards linked the development of modern architecture—of which modern monumentality formed one part—with the need not only for richness but also a new vernacular:

> The frigidity of the modern aesthetic must take on a new warmth. Whilst not abating one jot of our hard-won standards of refined taste and scientific exactitude, we must reach out for the things that ordinary people like and admire, and elevate them to an honoured place in our aesthetic. A new vernacular art must come to birth, an art embracing everybody, the artist and the engineer as well as the common man.[137]

As the historian Jessica Kelly has discussed, Richards believed that architects needed to tap the 'popular vernacular' in order to 'find a way of grafting its vitality on to the sound stock of contemporary functionalism' though 'without having to accept its aesthetic and ethical vulgarities'.[138] These ideas are clearly evident in the

132 Curtis, 'Perspective', p. 56.

133 Curtis, 'Perspective', p. 58; William Curtis, 'Criticism', *Architectural Review* 161 (January 1977), pp. 22–4 (p. 24).

134 Girouard, 'Cosmic Connections', p. 7.

135 Quoted in Curtis, 'Past and Prejudice', p. 8.

136 'Theatre Architecture in Britain', *RIBA Journal* 50 (1968), pp. 501–7.

137 'Wanted: a new vernacular', *Architects' Journal* 105 (9 January 1947), pp. 27–8.

138 Jessica Kelly, 'Vulgar Modernism: J. M. Richards, modernism and the vernacular', *Architectural History* 58 (2015), pp. 229–60 (p. 231). See e.g. 'The Next Step?', *Architectural Review* 107 (March 1950), pp. 165–81 (p. 168).

decorative forms of the New Empiricism. They also bring to mind the interest of the likes of the Smithsons and Banham in popular culture and the historical vernacular. Bill Howell, writing in October 1957, stated his wish for 'more vulgarity (I should prefer this to [...] anaemic good taste [...]) but we should also get some splendid eccentricities—a department in which we used, as a nation, to excel'.[139] Although Howell's argument was in part that the 1947 Town and Country Planning Act was stifling creativity, it also reads as a call for a more popular, even witty modernism. Otto Saumarez Smith has seen this quality in contemporaneous projects by Howell Killick Partridge and Amis (HKPA), including the Senior Common Room at Downing College, Cambridge (1966–70, led by Howell), which provided the famously neoclassical college with an abstracted version of a temple in response to initial disquiet at a previous, more overtly modern scheme.[140]

Howell Killick Partridge and Amis's Young Vic in London (1970) can be understood in terms of this search for a 'modern vernacular'.[141] The project originated with the director Frank Dunlop. In 1966, the Arts Council's 'Young People's Theatre Enquiry' under Constance Cummings had recommended greater engagement with young people's theatre, a conclusion that appealed to Dunlop. After working at Nottingham Playhouse and with the Pop Theatre, he became an associate of the National Theatre in 1967 on condition that Olivier help him realize a young people's theatre for those 'whose incomes or inclinations make existing theatres seem expensive or forbidding'.[142] Whereas the National 'proper' emerged from lengthy committee discussions, Dunlop had considerable authority as the client for the Young Vic. A vacant site was found near to the Old Vic, a five-year lease was arranged, and 'Housing the Arts' funding was secured.[143] HKPA was appointed in 1968 after the stage designer, Patrick Robertson, who was involved in developing the concept, suggested to Dunlop that Howell might be suitable for the project.[144] Howell had studied with Robertson at Cambridge and had designed an 'Old Vic Theatre Centre' as a student at the Architectural Association. HKPA's work more generally, meanwhile, was highly regarded.

Access to the theatre was to be through the one structure on the site that had survived the Blitz, a former butchers' shop. For the auditorium, Howell designed an octagonal building of bare blockwork walls within an exposed steel framework:

[139] 'Freedom to Build', *The Times*, 1 October 1957.

[140] Otto Saumarez Smith, 'A Strange Brutalist "Primitive Hut": Howell Killick Partridge and Amis's Senior Common Room at Downing College, Cambridge', *Twentieth Century Architecture* 11 (2013), pp. 149–65 (p. 157).

[141] For the following account I draw on Rosenthal, *National Theatre*, pp. 159–66, and Geraint Franklin, *HKPA* (London, 2017), pp. 132–7.

[142] Copy of Application for Capital Grant, May 1968, among the papers of the late John Partridge.

[143] V&A, ACGB/120/9, HTA minutes, 28 February 1968.

[144] Rosenthal, *National Theatre*, pp. 160–1, and 'Obituary: Patrick Robertson', *Guardian*, 22 April 2009, <http://www.theguardian.com/stage/2009/apr/22/obituary-patrick-robertson> (accessed 18 March 2015). See also letters between Bill Howell and Frank Dunlop of 17, 21, and 23 May 1968, and record of a meeting at the National Theatre offices, 27 May 1968, among the papers of the late John Partridge.

> After beating about the bush for a bit, I finally summoned up the courage to slide out my little drawing. Frank took one look at it and said, 'Good God, it looks just like a gasworks with flags on'. After a moment's pause, he said, 'Come to think of it, that's pretty much what the Globe must have looked like'.[145]

On the one hand, the Young Vic's structural and material honesty recalled the unadorned surfaces of Old Vic's nearby annexe building (Lyons Israel and Ellis, 1958) and anticipated Lasdun's National Theatre. It was also a statement of radical economy, being originally intended to cost £60,000 (although the final account came to £93,000), while the architects' file begins with the note that 'THIS IS A TEMPORARY BUILDING'.[146] Indeed, the construction of an agricultural-type shed had initially been considered. In this respect, the Young Vic was an important example of a 'frugal' tendency which gathered speed in the 1970s (and which is further discussed in Chapter 7). Howell's interest in 'vulgarity'—i.e. a 'popular' approach—is also evident. At one stage, he proposed the theatre's blockwork walls could be adorned with a collage of posters showing 'large jolly objects' and such images as 'baked-bean advertisements', rather than theatre publicity.[147] He recalled that the borough architect was 'absolutely horrified and took a lot of persuading that I hadn't gone off my rocker'.[148] A similar interest in the ordinary had shaped the work of Alison and Peter Smithson and other members of the revisionist Team X group of architects in the mid-1950s, of which Howell was briefly part. In this context, Howell's proposed advertisements reinterpreted the numerous posters and billboards of inner-city London, placing everyday items on prominent view as a way to deinstitutionalize the new theatre in a somewhat iconoclastic fashion. In its answer to Richards's much earlier call for a vulgar modernism, the Young Vic thus suggested a way forward for modern architecture.

Something similar is also evident in a final example, the Crucible Theatre, Sheffield, which opened in 1971 (see Figure 4.8). This theatre replaced the city's Playhouse, which had been outgrown by the Arts Council-supported Repertory Company and was also threatened with demolition for a road-widening scheme.[149] A site on the city's new ring road, near to the civic centre and adjacent to the older Lyceum Theatre, was selected in 1966.[150] Early the following year, the architects Renton Howard Wood (RHW) were commissioned to design the theatre.[151] The architectural longlist had included designers with local and national reputations as well as several with experience of theatre.[152] The initial shortlist featured a Sheffield firm, Hadfield Cawkwell Davidson, as well as Arup Associates, RHW (then

[145] Franklin, *HKPA*, p. 136.

[146] Memo entitled 'Architects' Notes', among the papers of the late John Partridge.

[147] Copy letter from Bill Howell to Frank Dunlop, 18 October 1968, among the papers of the late John Partridge.

[148] Copy letter from Bill Howell to Frank Dunlop, 18 October 1968, among the papers of the late John Partridge.

[149] SCA, LD2341, Board minutes, 24 August 1966.

[150] V&A, ACGB/84/246, N.V. Linklater meeting note, 26 September 1966.

[151] V&A, ACGB/84/246, Building Committee Report to Trustees, February 1967.

[152] V&A, ACGB/84/246, Building Committee Report to Trustees, February 1967. It comprised Lasdun, Moro, Ling, Arup, RHW, Whitfield, Hadfield Cawkwell Davidson, Spence, Casson, Gollins Melvin Ward, Stillman and Eastwick-Field, Devereaux and Davies.

Figure 4.8. Crucible Theatre, Sheffield, view towards Park Hill in 1971 (Architectural Press Archive/RIBA Collections)

working on a scheme for Sheffield University), William Whitfield, and Denys Lasdun. The director, Colin George, later recalled that RHW's lack of experience of theatre was important: '[it] encouraged us [. . .] [otherwise] they might say, "I've done all this" and you think you're just going to get the same old thing'.[153] In June 1967, several design options were presented.[154] At this stage, the new theatre was to have an adaptable proscenium arch stage like the Nottingham Playhouse. (The subsequent change to a thrust stage is discussed in Chapter 8.)

[153] Colin George, interviewed 26 June 2006. Lasdun reportedly declined to be considered, presumably because the National Theatre was at a critical stage.

[154] V&A, ACGB/84/246, Building Committee Report to Trustees, June 1967.

As built, the core of the Crucible is its octagonal auditorium, the geometry of which repeats in the foyers, studio theatre, and backstage areas that are wrapped around it to create a strong silhouette. Initially, brown facing brick was proposed but ultimately 'Forticrete' blocks were used, influenced by Colin St-John Wilson's recently completed house in Cambridge and thought by the architects to reflect the industrial character of Sheffield.[155] The elevations are topped by a 'cornice' of glass-reinforced plastic panels, which have recently been restored to their original brown colour. The sobriety of the exterior contrasts with the theatre's foyers, which were conceived in a spirit of theatrical exuberance, with gloss-painted ceilings, strip lights, and a unique patterned carpet in the upper foyer by Clare Ferraby (since replaced), which echoed in bright colours the diagonals of the theatre's plan (see Figure 4.9).

Figure 4.9. Pop informality: the upper foyer at the Crucible Theatre, Sheffield, in 1971, with the Clare Ferraby-designed carpet (John Donat/RIBA Collections)

[155] Nick Thompson, interviewed 20 June 2006.

The auditorium is accessed through large doors with dramatically over-scaled, coloured arrows above them. Colin George had earlier noted that the white, grey, and black tones of the foyers in Tyrone Guthrie's theatre at Minneapolis served to heighten the 'harlequin' colours of the auditorium there.[156] He sought to reverse the pattern in Sheffield: the auditorium was subdued in its finishes, but the foyers were enlivened with colour in an almost brash fashion. Of the result, one theatre consultant reported that 'comments about "flashiness" do not seem to be misplaced'.[157] An early proposal was yet more vibrant, with zebra-skin patterned wallpaper intended to suggest 'brassiness' rather than restraint.[158]

At the same time, the Crucible raises an important point about the relationship between theatres and their setting. Girouard's emphasis on connections at the National has already been noted, in terms of views as well as the extent to which some of the theatre's external terraces acted to connect physically the building with its setting. The Crucible went further. Although as much an 'object' as the National in that the building faced a new public square and was visible across the Sheaf Valley from the Park Hill flats, the Crucible was also intended to be embedded in its setting. Views into and from the building were significant, but even more important was the way in which the lower foyer was intended to form part of a longer notional pedestrian route linking the railway station with the shopping area.[159] Its hard surfaces not only contrasted with the brightly coloured carpets of the upper foyer, but also blurred the boundary between interior and exterior space. Potential patrons were thus not simply given views into the building, but were quite literally routed through it in a way that suggested not only a humanization but also an urbanization of the modern monument. It is that 'urban' aspect of theatre design which forms the focus of Chapter 5.

[156] V&A, ACGB/84/246, Reports by Colin George and David Brayshaw on American theatre, n.d.
[157] NRS, ED61/87, Martin Carr to Brian Annable, 10 July 1973.
[158] Nick Thompson, interviewed 20 June 2006.
[159] Nick Thompson, interviewed 20 June 2006.

5

'A New Image of the Town Centre'

Theatres, Civic Pride, and Urbanity

In 1964, Bolton Town Council commissioned the prominent architect-planner Graeme Shankland to make proposals for the development of the town centre.[1] Shankland's appointment reflected the extent to which British towns and cities were conceived in increasingly 'planned' terms after 1945. This trend was the product of several factors, including the requirement for planning imposed by such legislation as the 1947 Town and Country Planning Act, the professionalization since the 1930s of the role of the planner, the drive to clear slums, the significant place often ascribed to urban matters within modernist architectural discourse, and the argument that cities needed to be reconstructed to accommodate an ever-increasing number of motor vehicles. In Bolton, Shankland proposed new development and selective conservation, his aim being 'a new image of the town centre [...] built up from a framework of the best of the existing fabric and clearly distinguishing Bolton from elsewhere'.[2] There had already been calls for 'cultural' activities to complement 'commercial and business uses' in the town,[3] and to that end, Shankland suggested that:

> an Arts Centre be formed around the already proposed Civic Theatre [...]. Such a centre would be a great asset to the town, providing a focal point for educational, cultural and purely social events. It could be a gathering place in the town centre in the evening, and establish the prestige of Bolton town centre.[4]

The arts centre would be a substantial public building, prominently stating the place of leisure in Bolton's 'new image' and suggesting the 'prestige' of the town centre through its presence. As a focal point, it would not only reflect well on the town for providing it, but would also serve as a vehicle for active, engaged citizenship by inculcating civic pride among residents. In addition, by being what the report described as a 'gathering place', it might also contribute to a sense of urbanity. This term reflects the urban quality which was increasingly prized by architects and planners during the 1950s and 1960s, in part as a reaction to the low density

[1] Otto Saumarez Smith, 'Graeme Shankland: a sixties architect-planner and the political culture of the British left', *Architectural History* 54 (2014), pp. 393–422 (p. 411).

[2] BA, 711 BOL, Shankland Cox and Associates, 'Bolton: Town Centre Map. Planning Consultant's Final Report', July 1965, p. 27.

[3] BA, ABZ/45, Box 1/10, 'Notes on "Theatre for Bolton"', *c.*1965.

[4] BA, 711 BOL, Shankland Cox 'Final Report', pp. 14–15.

of development in the first post-war new towns. Urbanity was the product of a fundamentally non-suburban density of development and liveliness of usage. At the same time, the term also evokes a sense of urbane sophistication; one thinks of Jennie Lee's 'gayer and more cultivated' Britain.

This chapter places theatre architecture in a series of 'urban' contexts. Like the previous two chapters, it focuses on the period between the late 1940s and the early 1970s. It begins with the idea of civic pride and the symbolic role of theatres in establishing new images of the modern city, before continuing with the physical place of theatre buildings within the planned urban landscape. These two themes could be related. In 1955, seven years after the Local Government Act had enabled the routine creation of civic theatres, the Arts Council commented on the way in which this type of theatre was sometimes planned:

> There is a disposition among many of our city planners to include in their blue-prints a civic theatre cheek-by-jowl with the new town hall, the fire station, the technical school, the youth club and the shopping centre. The living theatre should not be indiscriminately included in this municipal box of bricks. Nothing but disillusion would be the outcome of erecting theatres in the well-meaning manner that our grandfathers ran up art galleries and museums all over the place.[5]

The issue was the conception of new theatres in terms of civic pride alone, but mention of a 'municipal box of bricks' also raises the question of location. Did financial support for these buildings by municipal authorities imply not only new understandings of their role and their place in narratives of civic pride, but also a new approach to their setting? 'Civic centres' emerged in Britain from the 1920s onwards, grouping together local-authority functions and facilities in complexes that were often substantial in size and whose multifunctional nature implied order and efficiency. But was it right to build a theatre within such a civic cluster in order to connote its status as a public amenity, or should theatres be located in more 'everyday' environments?

CIVIC PRIDE

Reflecting on the Belgrade Theatre's first year in operation, the theatre's Annual Report concluded that 'the tributes paid to Coventry as the first city to build a civic theatre and to create a new theatre centre at a time when many theatres are facing difficulties and are closing has undoubtedly given the citizens of the city a rightful sense of pride'.[6] The report's optimistic tone was unsurprising but nonetheless reflected the way in which civic pride, new construction, and innovation were closely linked in Coventry. For example, the *Financial Times* in 1958 noted a 'resurgence of civic pride after wartime destruction created an unwavering determination to build adventurously for the future'.[7] At the same time, the report's mention of 'citizens'

[5] ACGB, Annual Report, 1954–1955 ('Housing the Arts'), pp. 14–15.
[6] CHC, CCA/TC/5/4/2/1, Belgrade Theatre Annual Report, 1957–1958.
[7] CHC, PA2313/5/2/1, clippings: *Financial Times*, 28 March 1958.

suggests an inclusive view of civic pride. Reconstruction was not necessarily an imposed, top-down experience.[8]

In an article about the redevelopment of British towns and cities during the 1950s and 1960s, the historian Peter Shapely has argued that the concept of civic pride—more usually associated with the nineteenth century—was frequently invoked.[9] Reconstruction formed a potent vehicle for the expression of interurban rivalries; boosterist narratives were developed by councillors, technocrats, and developers alike. As Shapely puts it, 'civic pride was no longer mirrored in the choice of Gothic or classical styles of design, but through the dirt-free and the modern, promised by concrete and glass'.[10] Shapely focuses on shopping centres, but theatres were also frequently discussed in these terms. In the *Architects' Journal* in 1972, Colin Amery noted that:

> There are elements of local prestige involved too; now that grandiose municipal buildings are out of favour, patronage of the arts has become a suitable aspiration for local councillors. If Birmingham can have a glittering playhouse, why not Manchester too?[11]

Similarly, the director Stephen Joseph suggested in 1968 that 'a civic theatre, in particular, is looked on as a trump card in the game between rival communities'.[12] Yet for Joseph this 'game' did not always have a positive outcome: 'there is a belief that provided the front of the theatre is trumpery no other expenditure need be considered'. Certainly the Belgrade Theatre's backstage facilities were thought lacking almost immediately,[13] as if to confirm that the designers had been preoccupied with the public face of the building and the City Council's aspirational ideals rather than the mechanics of theatre. *Tabs*, reviewing new theatres in Birmingham, Sheffield, and Swindon in 1971, highlighted the importance attached to impressiveness: 'they are objects of Civic Pride and considerable trouble has been taken to make them architecturally important'.[14]

Civic pride was invoked by a range of organizations and individuals, not only by councillors and council officials. In Derby, the construction of the new Playhouse was described, if only for strategic reasons, by the repertory company's chairman as something that would contribute 'to the proper modernisation of the town and [the] improvement of its image'.[15] Similarly, the directors of the Nottingham Playhouse suggested to the City Council in 1956 that a new theatre would aid the city's 'greater reputation',[16] while the chairman of Sheffield's New Theatre Trust

[8] See e.g. Selina Todd, 'Phoenix Rising: working-class life and urban reconstruction, *c.*1945–1967', *Journal of British Studies* 54, no. 3 (2015), pp. 679–702.

[9] Peter Shapely, 'Civic Pride and Redevelopment in the Post-war British City', *Urban History* 39, no. 2 (2012), pp. 310–28.

[10] Shapely, 'Civic Pride', p. 315.

[11] 'Theatre at Colchester', *Architects' Journal* 156 (5 July 1972), pp. 19–34 (p. 22).

[12] Stephen Joseph, *New Theatre Forms* (London, 1968), p. 22.

[13] Norman Marshall, 'Planning Adaptable Theatres', *Drama* 62 (1961), pp. 38–41 (p. 39).

[14] 'Triptych', *Tabs* 29, no. 3 (September 1971), pp. 114–24 (p. 114).

[15] DRO, D738/4/1, D. V. W. Malin to Norman Fisher, 30 June 1969.

[16] NA, DD/NP/1/2/1/1, Playhouse Directors to Nottingham City Council, 8 October 1956.

reported in 1971 that the soon-to-be-opened Crucible Theatre would enhance 'Sheffield's image as an emerging city with an international reputation' by 'demonstrat[ing] that this is a city which supplies not only quality in its products, but quality in the life it offers to its citizens'.[17] The Crucible's thrust stage was cited as evidence of a progressive, international outlook; it was noted that it was inspired by the example of Stratford, Ontario. The press, too, often raised the idea of civic pride. In Edinburgh, for example, the *Scotsman* argued in 1974 that:

> Edinburgh's opera house is more important to the future condition of the city than many of the citizens imagine. If the project is abandoned or downgraded so that a second-best substitute is considered adequate, it will be a sign—yet another sign—of civic acceptance of mediocrity. Conservation of parts of Edinburgh's heritage is not enough for a capital, Festival city.[18]

In Plymouth, a letter sent in 1965 to a local newspaper argued that the city needed a new professional theatre if it was 'to progress and become a city worthy of the name'.[19] Echoing the theme of the 1951 Congrès Internationaux d'Architecture Moderne (CIAM) conference, 'The Heart of the City', the author continued: 'the essential work of rebuilding the City Centre and providing administrative and shopping facilities having been completed, now is the time for the council to get down to the job of putting a real heart into the city'.

It was often suggested that a new arts building would somehow elevate a town or city above its rivals, through its presence and on account of the ideas and ambitions it represented. For example, in Croydon in 1961, it was felt that the recently completed Fairfield Halls complex was, along with a new road scheme, indicative of a 'worthy county borough' that ought to retain its independence.[20] (Local government reforms were then under consideration, though Croydon's bid to remain outside the proposed Greater London Council area failed.) Similarly, it was suggested in May 1973 that Bromley's proposed new theatre would be 'of enormous use, benefit and prestige to the borough'.[21] In Farnham at the end of the 1960s, it was noted that 'a new and well publicised theatre enhances a town's name and reputation for being an enterprising and forward-looking community [...]'.[22] In Birmingham, meanwhile, it was proposed that a substantial new theatre 'would enhance the reputation of the city'.[23] Civic pride and cultural ambition were especially closely linked in Poole, in a building that forms the centrepiece of an account of the town's post-war history, *Poole's Pride Regained*.[24] Following the

[17] Antony Hampton, 'Most Forward-looking Theatre in Europe Emerges in City', *Quality of Sheffield* 18, no. 2 (1971), pp. 22–3.

[18] 'Second-best City', *Scotsman*, 10 August 1974.

[19] PCL, Theatre Royal clippings: 'Time For Action', *Western Evening Herald*, 21 June 1965.

[20] '"Fight for Status", Developers Asked', *Croydon Advertiser*, 15 December 1961.

[21] 'Backstage Drama', *Bromley Times*, 3 May 1973.

[22] SHC, 6894/7/1/2, 'Appeal to Farnham Businessmen', n.d. [late 1960s]. Such expansive comments did not result from municipal munificence: the Urban District Council grant in 1970 was only £500. See SHC, 6894/2/3, Farnham Repertory Company minutes, 6 July 1970.

[23] LoB, MS 978/5/20–1, minute of 12 August 1959.

[24] John Hillier and Martin Blythe, *Poole's Pride Regained, 1964–1974* (Poole, 1996).

announcement of the 'Housing the Arts' fund in 1965, the Libraries Committee proposed the construction of a new Arts Centre, and in July 1970 a petition calling for the centre to be built was launched. In April 1972, a public debate was attended by 700 people. Poole's rivalry with the nearby town of Bournemouth was ever-present. The ever-increasing scale of the proposed Arts Centre demonstrated Poole's ambition. As built to the borough architect's designs, it included a 1700-seat concert hall and a 640-seat theatre, as well as facilities for exhibitions, meetings, and banqueting. The real coup came when the Bournemouth Symphony Orchestra announced its intention to take up residence in the centre, which finally opened in 1978. However, such ambition was not always welcomed. Claims that Inverness Town Council was proceeding with the construction of a new theatre as 'a prestige project, [...] a status symbol for Inverness' represented criticism of the scheme.[25]

'Civic pride' in one sense had a somewhat abstract quality, relying on an implicit (and positive) association between new public architecture, local authority spending, the prestige of a town or city, and an active citizenship. More tangible, however, were suggestions that development would attract visitors. In Guildford, for example, support for the construction of the Yvonne Arnaud Theatre not only reflected the town's rivalry with Kingston-upon-Thames and desire to be the 'cultural centre of south-west Surrey',[26] but also the hope that it would 'attract theatregoers from all over the country, as well as overseas visitors'.[27] In York in the mid-1960s, the refurbishment of the Theatre Royal was motivated in part by the need to improve conditions for performers and in part because 'the York of the future is seen as the cultural and tourist centre of the North. If it is to be so, an up-to-date theatre is reckoned to be a must'.[28]

A variation on this line of thought promoted the construction of theatres as part of a drive to attract new businesses and residents to an area. In Mold, for example, it was believed at the end of the 1960s that the new transport links and infrastructure that were then proposed for north Wales, including the construction of a barrage across the River Dee, would cause the local population to increase by 250,000 in the thirty years to 1999.[29] In a brochure of the early 1970s entitled 'Flintshire: a County with a Future' (a title that proved optimistic, at least in administrative terms, because Flintshire was subsumed into the new Clwyd County Council in 1974), the local authority's chief executive outlined his hope that industry would invest in the area and emphasized the contribution made by the County Council to the 'aesthetic side of life'.[30] At the same time, the traditional language of civic pride remained. The new arts centre, Theatr Clwyd, was described by its hardly unbiased promoters as 'the initiative of a progressive and enlightened

[25] National Library of Scotland, GEB.57 [1], 'Eden Court Theatre: Report and Decision Letter on the Public Local Inquiry' [1975], p. 19.

[26] V&A TC, Guildford file, uncat., Guildford Repertory Theatre, 'The First Two Years, 1946–1948'; E. R. Chamberlin, *Guildford* (Chichester, 1982), pp. 131–2, 191.

[27] SHC, 7018/2/2/114, Yvonne Arnaud Theatre fundraising brochure, 1961.

[28] 'Theatre Royal at York', *Architects' Journal* 148 (4 December 1968), pp. 1335–42 (p. 1336).

[29] FRO, CC/TC/1/164, 'Proposed Arts Centre, Mold, Flintshire: Preliminary Report' [April 1969], p. 3.

[30] FRO, FC/13/20, 'Flintshire: a county with a future', n.p.

Council',[31] an interesting turn of phrase on the part of the new Clwyd County Council given that the project had been conceived by its Flintshire predecessor. Bold claims were made that the centre 'may well be unique and probably [would be] a prototype for the whole of the Country'.[32]

Bolton's Octagon Theatre, which opened in 1967, can similarly be understood as an attempt to transform perceptions of the town in the interests of its future development. The theatre had been conceived by several students at Loughborough University who were originally from Bolton and wanted to found a new theatre there.[33] They enlisted the support of one of their lecturers, Robin Pemberton-Billing, and presented their proposals for a 350-seat theatre to the Town Council. The site that had been earmarked for a civic theatre in Shankland's plan for the town was turned over to Pemberton-Billing, whose ideas were developed by the borough architect, Geoffrey Brooks. The result—since altered—was a modest building of unrelieved brick with aluminium-framed curtain glazing; the sole ornamental feature was a copper-clad flèche.

Shankland had included a theatre in his plan for Bolton for several reasons. First, a survey had identified that many local residents would like there to be a theatre in the town.[34] Second, it was believed that a theatre might attract new businesses, something which may have been particularly significant in the face of the contraction of Bolton's traditional textile industries.[35] Third, Bolton was thought to be in competition not only with neighbouring towns but also the proposed 'Central Lancashire New Town',[36] particularly because, as Shankland noted, increased car ownership meant that residents now had easier access to a wider choice of shopping and leisure facilities.[37] Intertown competition was thus a real issue that related not only to perceptions of Bolton but also its future success. The *Stage* touched on this idea in its report of the opening of the Octagon, which emphasized the potential of the theatre to attract 'people and trade': 'Lancashire towns were already improving: Blackburn or even Wigan or Bury might any year be stealing a march on Bolton'.[38] The importance of a modern, attractive town centre had been further highlighted by proposals in 1963 to build Britain's first out-of-town 'regional' shopping centre at nearby Haydock.[39] Though the idea was rejected by the County Council and then the Minister for Housing and Local

[31] FRO, CC/3/9 'The Official Opening of Theatr Clwyd and Educational Technology Centre, Mold', 1976.

[32] FRO, FC/13/20, 'Flintshire: a county with a future', n.p.

[33] Robin Pemberton-Billing, *The Octagon Theatre: Concept to Reality* (Bolton, 2011), pp. 19–33.

[34] BA, ABZ/45, Box 1/3, Leisure Survey Results.

[35] BA, ABZ/45, Box 1/2, 'Draft Report on Civic Theatre'.

[36] BA, 711 BOL, J. B. McLoughlin, 'Report to the Chamber of Commerce of a General Survey of the Final Report of the Shankland Plan' [1965], p. 3.

[37] BA, 711 BOL, Graeme Shankland Associates, 'Bolton: Draft Town Centre Map' [November 1964], pp. 19–20.

[38] 'The Octagon, Bolton', *Stage*, 23 November 1967, p. 17.

[39] University of Manchester Department of Town and Country Planning, *Regional Shopping Centres in North West England* (Manchester, 1964).

Government,[40] it demonstrated that traditional urban structures could no longer be taken for granted and that the threat to Britain's town centres came not only from American-style suburbia, but also American-style out-of-town malls.

Shankland outlined how Bolton town centre should appeal to different groups. Of secondary-age pupils, he wrote:

> It is important that boys and girls at this age should come to see the town centre as the centre of entertainment, leisure and recreation. If it has no role in their lives at this stage, it is unlikely to have one when they are young workers or are married, and it may well remain a middle-aged mecca.[41]

This vision of vibrant urbanity accords with the anti-suburban rhetoric of the Left more generally,[42] but Shankland's arguments became explicitly inflected with the idea of civic pride when he discussed the appeal of the town to young adults. Shankland believed that Bolton needed to retain 'the higher educated'.[43] As he put it:

> This is the category that may well consider leaving Bolton unless they can maintain their pride in it. They may not themselves want to visit art galleries and chamber concerts, but they are among the groups who want to be able to say that Bolton has them, when visiting the coffee bars, concert halls and theatres of Manchester. They will certainly spend time in Manchester, but the facilities of Bolton from which they are absenting themselves will give them the pride to return or remain.[44]

Was there a belief, perhaps, that the town of the future might be less dependent on manufacturing, and that the 'higher educated' would be important in the shift to a post-manufacturing economy? Was there also a sense that the 'higher educated' might be wealthy, and that their presence would be beneficial for this reason, too? The council certainly suggested that 'the presence of cultural facilities weighs with the executives of large firms and their families'.[45] In this respect, it seems that culture was intended to attract new residents, who would in turn provide a ready audience for it. A new theatre would not only set Bolton aside from its competitors, but would contribute to the reshaping of the town's social and industrial profiles, and to its ongoing vitality and economic growth.

These same ideas played out at Bedford in the early 1970s as part of a broader narrative that placed ever-increasing emphasis on the economic value of the arts. The recently designated new town at Milton Keynes was less than 20 miles away. Would its development be to the detriment of the historic county town?

[40] '140-acre Shopping Centre Opposed', *The Times*, 18 September 1963; 'Out-of-town Shopping Centre Rejected', *The Times*, 28 July 1965.

[41] BA, 711 BOL, Shankland Cox, 'Final Report', p. 76.

[42] Saumarez Smith, 'Graeme Shankland', p. 394.

[43] BA, 711 BOL, Shankland Associates, 'Draft Town Centre Map', p. 42.

[44] BA, 711 BOL, Shankland Cox, 'Final Report', p. 76.

[45] BA, ABZ/45, Box 1/2, 'Draft Report on Civic Theatre', n.d. Not all welcomed this: would town centre improvements only appeal to 'a small minority of highly educated and sophisticated professionals'? See BA, 711 BOL, J. B. McLoughlin, 'Report to the Chamber of Commerce of a General Survey of the Final Report of the Shankland Plan' [1965], p. 11.

Some in Bedford certainly thought so. It was reported to the Arts Council by the advocates of the new theatre that:

> The future growth of Milton Keynes is said to be threatening to destroy Bedford's individuality. A vibrant theatre in the town will help maintain Bedford's identity and help to prevent it being reduced to mere dormitory status.[46]

The Arts Council took a fairly dim view of this reasoning, with a pencil note on its copy of the theatre's report recording that 'this is aimed at Bedford's pride—not really on rational basis [sic]' and that Bedford 'has managed OK up to now'.[47] Nonetheless, the annotation suggests that the intended message was understood. There was also a suggestion of the people to whom a theatre might appeal, though interestingly it was the Arts Council which recorded that many of the 'executive and managerial workers from Milton Keynes do in fact live in Bedford'.[48] One wonders if their conclusion repeated information given to them by the theatre's proponents, and whether this was a pragmatic view—the 'executive and managerial workers' being more likely to have money for theatre—or an opinion that challenged the purported inclusiveness of post-war theatre.

THEATRE AND CITY

Civic pride was very much in evidence in the case of Billingham Forum, which formally opened in 1968. Its sports facilities reflected the recommendations of the Wolfenden report on local authority support for sport, published in 1960, which had called for 'experimental multi-sports centres'.[49] Billingham Urban District Council framed its ideas grandly: the swimming pool was to be big enough to host international competitions, for example.[50] Similarly expansive (and also no doubt expensive) was the council's intention to host concerts at the Forum by leading orchestras such as the Royal Philharmonic and the Leipzig Gewandhaus.[51] Indeed, the Urban District Council's entire approach to the new town centre offers a striking example of modern civic ambition: 'by providing buildings of architectural merit the Council will be taking over the role of public benefactors who were patrons of architecture in earlier times'.[52] What was termed a 'revolutionary shopping precinct' was inspired by the recent example of Coventry's pedestrian area.[53] Together with the new civic centre it would establish Billingham's claim to be 'among the most forward-looking authorities in the country'.[54] 'Here is a town brimming over

[46] V&A, ACGB/84/18, 'Bedford Theatre Project', n.d.
[47] V&A, ACGB/84/18, 'Bedford Theatre Project', n.d.
[48] V&A, ACGB/120/35, Discussion of the Bedford project, 11 September 1973.
[49] [Wolfenden Committee], *Sport and the Community: The Report of the Wolfenden Committee on Sport* (London, 1960), pp. 38–9, 108.
[50] TA, U/S/706, Billingham UDC, Report for Subcommittee, 27 October 1964.
[51] TA, Billingham UDC minutes, Main Council, 23 December 1964.
[52] TA, U/S/2409, 'The Miracle of Billingham' [n.d.].
[53] TA, U/S/2409, 'Billingham Urban District Council, 1923–1968', n.p.
[54] TA, U/S/2409, 'The Miracle of Billingham' [n.d.].

with confidence in a great future, not satisfied with its immense achievements', it was reported.

While Billingham Forum thus demonstrates the potential contribution of leisure buildings to narratives of modern civic pride, its physical location is also important (see Figure 5.1). The rates income from Billingham's booming chemical industries underwrote the construction of the new town centre, within which the Forum made a prominent statement about the place of leisure: 'the Council felt that bricks and mortar were not by themselves sufficient, a sense of identification with the community had to be encouraged, a feeling that Billingham is a place in which one "lives"'.[55] In January 1959, as was noted in Chapter 3, the town centre architects, Elder and Lester, reported that the principal axis ought to be closed 'by a building of some architectural merit', potentially a civic theatre.[56] By March 1961, it had been decided that these facilities might be organized within 'a single group which would be structurally joined together at the low floor levels and enjoy the same ancillary services', on account of the practical advantages of such an arrangement as well as the potential for 'an impressive and fitting termination to the view down

Figure 5.1. Billingham Forum, model including the theatre (bottom right) and the Queensway precinct (at the foot of the photograph) (Architectural Press Archive/RIBA Collections)

[55] TA, U/S/2409, 'Billingham Urban District Council, 1923–1968' [*c.*1968], n.p.
[56] TA, U/S/706, 'Billingham Urban District Council: Town Centre Development'.

the shopping precinct'.[57] During 1962, the scheme was developed, though progress was hampered by restrictions on local government expenditure.[58] Sketch plans were not ready until late 1963, when it was estimated that the completed building would cost £782,949, including an ice rink, swimming pools, and theatre. Of this figure, the theatre accounted for £125,784.[59] On the one hand, then, the Forum was a substantial structure. At the same time, it was conceived as an integral part of the town centre, and was designed by the same architects. Its foyers and courtyard served, perhaps, as an extension of the town's pedestrian precinct.

The example of Billingham is not unique. Stevenage's Arts and Leisure Centre was originally conceived in 1965 as a modest civic theatre but during 1968 was re-envisioned in Billingham-like terms.[60] It opened in 1975 to the designs of Leonard Vincent, Raymond Gorbing and Partners as a sizeable combined arts and sports centre, through which passed the elevated walkway linking the town centre and railway station (see Figure 5.2). More generally, theatres often assumed a significant place within the planned urban environments of post-war Britain. The immediate foundations for this development had been laid in wartime amid broader campaigns for post-war planning. In a popular paperback, *Living in Cities* (1942), which

Figure 5.2. Stevenage Arts and Leisure Centre in 1975, with a cyclist whizzing along the elevated pedestrian walkway (Architectural Press Archive/RIBA Collections)

[57] TA, Billingham UDC minutes, Development and Plans Committee, 6 March 1961.
[58] TA, Billingham UDC minutes, Development and Plans Committee, 7 January 1963.
[59] TA, Billingham UDC minutes, Development and Plans Committee, 2 December 1963.
[60] The project history can be traced in V&A, ACGB/84/260. See also 'Three Sports Centres', *Architects' Journal* 154 (8 December 1976), pp. 1075–88.

documented a CEMA-supported exhibition of the same name and included drawings of an ideal planned city, the architect Ralph Tubbs illustrated a substantial theatre forming one side of a public square.[61] The conception of the South Bank in London as a cultural quarter, discussed in Chapter 3, was codified in the 1943 *County of London Plan*, whose co-author, Patrick Abercrombie, was to make similar proposals elsewhere. For example, in his 1949 plan for Edinburgh, written with Derek Plumstead, a cultural complex would offer 'a proper setting for three important public buildings—a civic theatre and concert halls, new Theatre Royal, and the principal Catholic Church'.[62]

The emergence at the end of the 1940s of the municipally supported civic theatre as a distinct architectural and institutional type prompted the location of theatres within larger civic centre developments alongside municipal offices. Harlow's civic square of 1963 was flanked by the technical college, town hall, a church, and the theatre,[63] while Frederick Gibberd's original masterplan of 1948 for the town had located the theatre and civic hall in a single linear structure with the municipal offices.[64] In Motherwell, a hall and theatre were integrated into the civic centre, completed in 1970 to the designs of Peter Williams from the Glaswegian firm of Wylie and Shanks.[65] In Reading, the Hexagon was built alongside the council offices by the same architects, Robert Matthew, Johnson-Marshall (RMJM); nearby were other civic buildings. Approached via an elevated pedestrian podium (see Figure 5.3), the Hexagon gives the impression of one of Archigram's 'walking city' pods that has become marooned in the civic landscape. In Solihull, the Library Theatre (Stanley Sellers, 1978) is located alongside the civic hall, council offices, register office, magistrates' courts, and police station. Its elevations, which have blind brick arcades and concrete bands, suggest the influence of Basil Spence's University of Sussex and were reprised on other municipal structures in the town during the 1980s.[66] Finally, Hornchurch's Queen's Theatre (1975, by the borough architect's office) replaced a converted theatre of 1953 and is located facing a small park,[67] around which are also located such 'public' facilities as the telephone exchange and fire station, while the offices of the former Hornchurch Urban District Council, abolished in 1965 but subsequently used as a register office, are close by. The influence of Mies van der Rohe is suggested by the location of the main foyer on an

61 Ralph Tubbs, *Living in Cities* (Harmondsworth, 1942), p. 35 and endpaper.

62 Patrick Abercrombie and Derek Plumstead, *A Civic Survey and Plan for the City and Royal Burgh of Edinburgh* (Edinburgh, 1949), p. 60.

63 Elain Harwood, *Space, Hope and Brutalism: English Architecture 1945–1975* (New Haven/London, 2015), p. 25.

64 'Harlow New Town: the masterplan', *Architects' Journal* 107 (5 February 1948), pp. 127–31 (p. 130).

65 North Lanarkshire Council, history of Motherwell Theatre, <http://www.northlanarkshire.gov.uk/entertainment/index.aspx?articleid=22412> (accessed 5 June 2015).

66 Solihull Library, R.027.4, 'Solihull Library and Arts Centre' [recollections by Stanley Sellers], 2008.

67 Cinema Treasures, 'Queen's Theatre', <http://cinematreasures.org/theaters/30243> (accessed 20 June 2017). See also 'Queen's (ii)', Theatres Trust database, <https://database.theatrestrust.org.uk/resources/theatres/show/2050-queen-s-ii> (accessed 17 October 2017), which describes the theatre as 'rather good, and well detailed for its date', and suggests that it has a 'worthy civic presence'.

Figure 5.3. Reading Hexagon in 1979, connected by the elevated pedestrian podium to the rest of the civic centre (to the left) (Martin Charles/RIBA Collections)

elevated *piano nobile*, slightly cantilevered beyond the lower part of the building, and by the slender mullions that divide the foyers' large windows; there are particular echoes of Mies' 1953 scheme for a theatre at Mannheim, West Germany.

Mold's civic centre was constructed not in the town centre but on its rural fringe. The site had been acquired for civic purposes in 1948,[68] with the county offices being completed there in the late 1960s.[69] The construction of an arts centre on the site was proposed during 1969. As has been discussed, the aim was partly to attract new businesses and residents, but it was also thought that local children were not receiving a rounded cultural education, especially where a specifically Welsh culture was concerned, and in this respect the centre was to assist in teachers' cultural training.[70] The general shortage of major professional arts venues in rural Wales was also noted.[71] Proposals of April 1969 included a theatre

[68] FRO, FC/A/9/2, 'New Shirehall—Flintshire County Council, Llwynegrin', n.d.
[69] FRO, FC/1/68, Flintshire County Council minutes, Annual Meeting, 26 April 1966.
[70] FRO, FC/1/69–70, Flintshire County Council minutes, Education (Primary and Secondary Schools) Subcommittee, 25 July 1967 and 7 January 1969; FC/1/71, County Civic Centre Committee, 6 May 1969 and 30 September 1969.
[71] FRO, CC/TC/1/164, 'Proposed Arts Centre, Mold, Flintshire: Preliminary Report' [April 1969], p. 1.

for 400 to 450 (smaller than that which was eventually built).[72] There was also eventually to be a 1000-seat concert hall with a flat-floored stage and retractable choir seating (described as being on the lines of New York's Lincoln Center, an incredible ambition for a town with a population of 7000), as well as an exhibition suite and crafts centre. Theatr Clwyd, which opened in 1976, was, even without the concert hall, the largest theatre built since 1945 in Wales.[73] Designed by the county architects, it is no less monumental than its earlier civic neighbours, although it lacks their formal symmetries; in addition, its brick-clad elevations contrast with their concrete panels (see Figure 5.4). The primary reason for constructing the arts centre here seems to have been practical, with Theatr Clwyd able to share the services already provided on-site, and to make evening and weekend use of the vast car parks required during the working week by civic centre employees.[74] No doubt the location also made clear the role of the local authority in conceiving and funding the centre. The choice of site was not, however, universally

Figure 5.4. Theatr Clwyd, Mold, in 1976: a major theatre within an out-of-town civic centre (Architectural Press Archive/RIBA Collections)

[72] FRO, CC/TC/1/164, 'Proposed Arts Centre, Mold, Flintshire: Preliminary Report' [April 1969], p. 2.
[73] 'Clwyd', *Stage*, 26 February 1976, pp. 28–31.
[74] FRO, CC/TC/1/164, 'Proposed Arts Centre, Mold, Flintshire: Preliminary Report', April 1969, p. 4.

welcomed. The *Guardian* thought it remote and pointed to the apparent lack of any regular bus service.[75]

If the civic centre at Mold took civic isolationism to the extreme, that at Swindon was conceived in a more integrationist vein. A press release of 1968 reported that:

> the setting which has been devised for the Arts Centre reflects the thinking for the whole of the Civic Centre—a plan to redevelop a central part of Swindon to form a core through which people naturally flow when about their normal business and in which commerce and culture and entertainment can flourish side by side.[76]

Eventually, there was to be a large civic hall, a new post office, as well as shops and offices, all connected to existing municipal buildings by pedestrian bridges across a widened inner relief road.[77] Hugh Casson and Neville Conder were appointed in October 1964 to design the civic complex, and during 1966 it was decided following discussion with the local Theatre Guild and with the encouragement of the borough librarian to add a theatre; around the same time, the Minister for Housing and Local Government decided that Swindon should be expanded by 75,000 people.[78] Priority was given to the arts centre when it appeared that loan sanction for the rest of the civic centre would be delayed. The sloping site allowed the creation of a podium with servicing beneath, segregating pedestrian and vehicular movement in the manner then being popularized by Colin Buchanan (see Figure 5.5). Yet while it was thus informed by 1960s planning fashions, the Wyvern Theatre's brown-brick elevations and lead-sheet cladding have much in common with Casson and Conder's late-1950s university buildings in Cambridge and Birmingham. Similarly, upon the completion of the complex in late 1971, the *Architects' Journal* praised its 'civilised and humane approach', citing its 'pedestrian alleys, little irregularly-paved squares, ramps and bridges with semi-mature trees planted wherever possible'.[79] These terms bring to mind the picturesque 'Townscape' planning for which Casson and Conder had been known since the early 1950s. The new public buildings were, the *Architects' Journal* concluded, 'successfully integrated into the daily life, business and leisure of the town'.

A combination of road improvements, civic offices, and cultural provision also featured in Ipswich, though there the civic site was not so well-related to the rest of the city centre as was the case in Swindon. As the *Architects' Journal* wrote of the recently completed Wolsey Theatre in 1979:

> the new theatre is on the grandly named Civic Drive [...]. As you approach this edge of Ipswich between the railway and the old shopping streets the view is pure 1950s-planners' dreams.[80]

[75] 'No Holds Bard', *Guardian*, 1 March 1976.

[76] W&SA, G24/894/5, undated press release [probably 1968].

[77] W&SA, G24/100/72, Finance, Law and General Purposes Committee minutes, 17 February 1966; 'Stage in its Setting', *Architects' Journal* 154 (22 December 1971), pp. 1392–3.

[78] W&SA, G24/100/71, Borough of Swindon, Finance, Law and General Purposes Committee minutes, 26 October 1964; G24/100/73, Libraries, Museums and Arts Committee minutes, 25 August 1966; Finance, Law and General Purposes Committee minutes, 30 November 1966.

[79] 'Wyvern Theatre and Arts Centre', *Architects' Journal* 154 (22 December 1971), pp. 1420–3 (p. 1421).

[80] 'Wolsey Theatre', *Architects' Journal* 171 (6 February 1980), pp. 277–92 (p. 282).

Figure 5.5. Wyvern Theatre and Arts Centre, Swindon: model of Casson and Conder's proposals including the shopping precinct (to the left) and civic hall (right) (Architectural Press Archive/RIBA Collections)

One reason for the location of the theatre here seems to have been practical: a possible site was bluntly described by one local official as 'a conveniently shaped gap in the Civic Centre building plans'.[81] Another seems to have been the foundation of the project in what was termed 'civic pomp and dignity' as much as 'the need for a new theatre'.[82] Some also thought that the site had practical advantages and would perhaps make the civic area seem less isolated. In 1964, when an 'amenity block' incorporating a 570-seat theatre was planned, it was noted that this facility:

> will provide an attraction during the evenings and at weekends when the Civic Centre and its environs might otherwise tend to become rather dead. The existence of the theatre will enable the Civic Centre to express more clearly its role in the life of the town [...].[83]

The Arts Council was less sure, its 'Housing the Arts' special panel writing in 1973 that the civic centre site was remote from the commercial heart of Ipswich and lacked 'sympathetic' character: 'the theatre would be at a considerable disadvantage'.[84]

[81] V&A, ACGB/84/147, J. T. Hill to Jo Hodgkinson, 19 July 1965.
[82] SRO, A1/312/4060/486, Chief Education Officer to Clerk and Chief Executive, 22 December 1971.
[83] V&A, ACGB/84/147, 'Report (No. 3/1964–65) of the Estate Committee', 7 October 1964.
[84] TTT, Roderick Ham archive, Wolsey box, HTA paper R3/321 'Housing the Arts: Ipswich and Suffolk New Theatre Trust', 28 June 1973.

The location of Birmingham's new Repertory Theatre of 1971 near to council offices and the Central Library was largely for symbolic reasons. The Repertory Company had been founded early in the twentieth century and had constructed a theatre—now known as the 'Old Rep'—in 1913. It began to receive Arts Council subsidy in 1951 and increasingly looked to modernize and expand, led by its administrator, Nancy Burman, while changes to the city's road network made the Old Rep seem increasingly off the beaten track.[85] The possibility of a new building was discussed during 1957, with the subsequent opening of the Belgrade Theatre in nearby Coventry and the Mermaid in London giving added impetus to the idea.[86] Where should the new theatre be built? Proposals for Birmingham's civic area, which was the subject of several plans between the 1920s and the 1980s, included a civic theatre, Philharmonic Hall, and a city hall in a linked structure on the north side of Broad Street.[87] By 1962, the plan had been rejigged but the principle of a theatre remained (as did the adjacent concert hall), and by summer 1963 it had been decided that the theatre should definitely be built here.[88] This decision had been preceded by a degree of debate. In April 1961, it was reported that the chairman of the city's Public Works Committee favoured a site closer to the Old Rep and Birmingham Hippodrome, which together might form an entertainment quarter.[89] It was also feared that ongoing construction in the civic area meant that a theatre there could be isolated for some time.[90] Indeed, the now-demolished Central Library was not completed until 1974, while the International Convention Centre and Symphony Hall opened only in 1991. However, the theatre management favoured the civic site, believing that it reflected their idea of theatre as an art.[91] They were also keen to distinguish themselves from commercial forms of entertainment and suggested that the building they required would be of a different form to that likely to be provided by a developer. The example of Bolton suggests a further theme that may have also shaped the decision in Birmingham, one which underscores the continuities that could inform the conception of new theatres. In Bolton, one of Shankland's colleagues suggested that mixing culture and commerce might not strike quite the right note: 'to site [the theatre] obviously amongst shops may be to lose for it that sense of occasion that most people like for a night out'.[92]

It was thought essential that the theatre should relate closely to the overall plan for Birmingham's civic quarter, and so its architect, Graham Winteringham of

[85] Claire Cochrane, *The Birmingham Rep: A City's Theatre, 1962–2002* (Birmingham, 2003), p. 12.

[86] LoB, MS 978/5/20–1, minute of 12 August 1959.

[87] 'Plan for New Civic Centre', *Architects' Journal* 127 (5 June 1958), p. 860.

[88] LoB, MS 2339/3/4/4, Folder entitled 'Correspondence on Grants, New Theatre', paper entitled 'Proposed New Repertory Theatre' [1962] and same title [1963]. See also Gordon E. Cherry, *Birmingham: A Study in Geography, History and Planning* (Chichester, 1994), pp. 215–17.

[89] LoB, MS 2339/3/4/4, Chair of Public Works Committee to Alderman Watton, 24 April 1961; 'Report of Subcommittee Appointed by Minute No. 6 [...]' 25 April 1961.

[90] LoB, MS 2339/3/4/4, City/Repertory/Arts Council Subcommittee minutes, 28 March 1961.

[91] LoB, MS 2339/3/4/4, City/Repertory/Arts Council Subcommittee minutes, 24 November 1960; 'Report of Subcommittee Appointed by Minute No. 6 [...]' 25 April 1961. Writing in the *AJ*, Winteringham referred to a 'prestige site'.

[92] BA, ABZ/45, Box 1/1, J. M. Welbank to Wilfred Harrison, 30 July 1964.

S. T. Walker and Partners, was instructed to consult the city architect, Alwyn Sheppard Fidler.[93] His first designs were ready by October 1965.[94] Winteringham's initial proposals responded to the Beaux-Arts Classicism of the adjacent buildings by giving the theatre a straightforward colonnade, but as built the arrangement is slightly more complex. The theatre has single-storey arched and glazed openings at ground-floor level, separated by very slender columns. These arcades are inverted and stretched to two storeys above. Recalling the Lincoln Center or the Presidential Palace at Brasilia, they look a little like a series of giant tuning forks reflected in a mirror (see Figure 5.6). The use of concrete was controversial: there were debates during 1966 about the appropriateness of concrete for a civic structure, with the city planners favouring the use of Portland stone.[95]

Although the theatre's large windows suggest the kind of humanized 'modern monumentality' that was discussed in Chapter 4, the Rep is also an example of the kind of unashamedly untheoretical modernism noted in the Introduction. It was certainly interpreted as an example of a 'stylistic', even flashy architecture. Colin Amery in the *Architects' Journal* thought it 'a mess, a melée of misunderstood

Figure 5.6. Birmingham Repertory Theatre in 1971, as the civic quarter slowly takes shape around it (RIBA Collections)

93 Graham Winteringham, interviewed 12 December 2013.
94 LoB, MS 2339/4/3, Directors' Meeting, 26 October 1965.
95 LoB, MS 2339/4/3, Directors' Meeting, 31 March 1966.

stylistic gimmicks'.[96] One is reminded of John Summerson's suggestion in 1957 that any attempt to create a 'Palladio of modern architecture' could only lead to a 'rag-bag of aphorisms, platitudes and fancy jargon'.[97] Yet, as Amery pointed out with some evident surprise, the Rep was popular. After all, the brief had required an architecture of entertainment, not theoretical purity, and perhaps the extent to which it echoed the confident commercial modernism springing up across Birmingham's city centre at this time served to tie the theatre into the wider reconstruction project.

In Leicester, proposals for a theatre to be built within the civic centre were abandoned in favour of a location in the Haymarket shopping centre. Initial plans for this site had been drawn up during 1960, but in 1961 a larger Comprehensive Development Area was declared.[98] Tenders were invited; of the two received in early 1966, that by Taylor Woodrow was preferred.[99] It included a 500-seat cinema, a motel, and an office tower, as well as a 650-seat theatre. In October 1966, the City Council approved in principle the inclusion of a civic theatre to replace the small, temporary Phoenix Theatre.[100] The Phoenix, which had opened in 1963 at a cost of less than £30,000, had been intended to demonstrate that there was an audience for live drama in Leicester until such a time as a more substantial building could be realized. It was the work of Stephen George, the city architect, who was also to be responsible for the Haymarket Theatre. The Haymarket's project architect was Kenneth King, who had earlier worked on the Belgrade in Coventry, while the shopping centre was the work of the Building Design Partnership. By September 1967 the theatre's capacity had grown to 710 seats, and by April 1969 its estimated cost was £627,000, some three times the figure quoted in 1966.[101]

The inclusion of a theatre within the Haymarket scheme had been requested by the city's Town Planning (Development) Subcommittee in March 1965.[102] It had practical advantages in that services such as parking could be shared, thus reprising an argument that could also be made of a civic location (as had been the case at Mold). In addition, its upper floor location also allowed the construction of revenue-generating shops below the theatre, facing the street. The idea was championed by Stephen George and by the planning officer, Konrad Smigielski, who in March 1964 invoked the idea of a megastructure ('one continuous highly complex building') in which the presence of an 'entertainment centre' would 'help keep the city centre alive in the evenings'.[103] In opposition was Peter Chamberlin, the architect of Leicester's civic centre, which as of 1961 was to include a theatre, art gallery, and restaurant. In May 1965, Chamberlin concluded that 'the exclusion of the Theatre

[96] 'Repertory Theatre, Birmingham', *Architects' Journal* 154 (22 December 1971), pp. 1431–7 (pp. 1433–5).

[97] John Summerson, 'The Case for a Theory of Modern Architecture', *RIBA Journal* 64 (1957), pp. 307–13 (p. 307).

[98] LA, 49/35, 'Notes for City Planning Officer' [n.d.].

[99] LA, 49/35, 'Haymarket CDA' [n.d.], which includes a timeline.

[100] LA, 49/35, 'Haymarket CDA'.

[101] LA, 49/35, 'Haymarket CDA'.

[102] LA, DE 3277/214, Town Planning (Development) Subcommittee minutes, 31 March 1965.

[103] LA, DE 3277/214, Report of the City Planning Officer, 4 March 1964.

from the Civic Centre would seriously affect the intention of creating a precinct which would be alive by night as well as by day [...]'.[104] The Town Planning Subcommittee was unmoved, concluding that the quietness of the civic centre in the evenings might in fact harm the theatre. They heard from the city architect that:

> Successful theatre is a careful blend of commercial and artistic enterprise appealing to the widest cross section of public taste. It must be always striving to increase the scope of its appeal. In this connection, its position in the town and relationship to other buildings, is of paramount importance.[105]

Furthermore, a city centre site might attract the young: 'a theatre sited among the popular entertainments which they enjoy would help immeasurably to banish the image of theatre as a middle class culture for the older generation'.[106] Smigielski, in turn, argued that the new proposals were more innovative: 'more than four years have since elapsed [since the 1961 civic theatre plan] and trends in the cultural and commercial life of the City have changed'.[107] He concluded that 'to treat a civic theatre as a cultural activity for the highbrows is an obsolete idea'. In Smigielski's mind, the Haymarket was evidently no less a representation of modern Leicester than his contemporaneous, perhaps more speculative proposals for high-speed monorails and helipads: 'the shopping of the future will be under cover, heated and probably air conditioned'.[108] Yet was the theatre too integrated into its surroundings for its own good? Colin Amery suggested that the theatre, finished in the same bright red brick as the shopping centre and entered at first-floor level, lacked an identity of its own (see Figure 5.7).[109]

Like the Haymarket, Derby Playhouse (1975) was constructed within a shopping centre (see Figure 5.8). Accessed from the marketplace and screened by a row of shops, it was built to house the town's repertory company, which by the end of the 1960s was in need of more space. The architect, Roderick Ham, was commissioned in 1967.[110] Ham's Thorndike Theatre, Leatherhead, was then under construction (it will be discussed in Chapter 6). In 1970, Ham explained that the Playhouse had been designed as an integral part of the replanned city centre, reporting that:

> the first scheme was related to a somewhat tentative town planning layout whereas the latest proposals are related to a redevelopment scheme of the central area which has reached an advanced stage of preparation [...] the fundamental change is that the theatre is no longer a separate building but now includes a row of shops.[111]

[104] LA, DE 3277/214, Town Planning (Development) Subcommittee minutes, 20 May 1965.
[105] LA, DE 3277/215, 'Observations of the Officers of the Corporation on the Siting of a Civic Theatre in the Haymarket Development Area' [June 1965].
[106] LA, DE 3277/215, 'Observations'. [107] LA, DE 3277/215, 'Observations'.
[108] LA, DE 3277/214, Report of the City Planning Officer, 4 March 1964.
[109] 'Haymarket Theatre', *Architects' Journal* 159 (20 March 1974) pp. 607–22 (p. 612).
[110] V&A, ACGB/84/91, Gordon Moult to Jo Hodgkinson, 22 June 1967: 'we are to ask Mr Roderick Hamm [sic] the Architect to produce some sketches'.
[111] DRO, D738/4/1, 'Derby Playhouse Design Report', April 1970, p. 2.

Figure 5.7. 'Trends have changed': Haymarket Theatre, Leicester, 1973 (Architectural Press Archive/RIBA Collections)

Figure 5.8. Model of Derby's Eagle Centre, showing the Playhouse and covered market (middle-left) (Architectural Press Archive/RIBA Collections)

The inclusion of the theatre within the shopping centre had been discussed by the Borough Council's Estates and Development Committee in December 1968,[112] and may well have owed something to the example of nearby Leicester. Various by now familiar reasons were cited in its favour, including the need to achieve a 'balance' of uses, to temper the commercial, and to bring life into the shopping centre in the evenings, while for the theatre's management, the location promised a steady stream of potential patrons during the day.[113] Similarly in Chester, the Gateway Theatre (1968) formed part of comprehensive development plans and in its executed form was proposed by the developer of the Forum shopping centre.[114] Within this 3.5-acre complex, which also included a market hall and offices, the theatre, designed by Michael Lyell Associates, fronted a small public square located on an elevated deck at the end of the new shopping mall.[115] This example makes clear the potential financial advantages of this model for local authorities and theatre managements, as it received funding not only from the Arts Council (£15,000) and the local authority (£105,000) but also the private developer of the shopping centre (£80,000).[116]

The way in which Smigielski and George were opposed in Leicester by Peter Chamberlin is interesting, and perhaps surprising. Chamberlin, along with his professional partners, Geoffry Powell and Christof Bon, was active in the Society for the Promotion of Urban Renewal (SPUR).[117] With David Gregory Jones and Graeme Shankland, then both working for the London County Council, Chamberlin Powell and Bon in 1958 produced a hypothetical proposal for the reconstruction of the London suburb of Boston Manor as a high-density centre in the manner of Vällingby, Stockholm. Adjacent to the underground station was to be a market square and entertainment complex, including a small theatre. Although Chamberlin's wish to accommodate culture within Leicester's civic centre was perhaps inspired by SPUR's rejection of rigid functional zoning in urban planning, the same could be said of the Haymarket proposals, which similarly combined different uses. Why, then, did Chamberlin oppose them? Apart from a natural inclination to defend his own scheme, he may have privileged high culture over commercial forms. It was recorded in Leicester that 'his concern that the theatre may be swamped by the other popular entertainments is an emotional reaction to the concept of the Haymarket centre'.[118]

[112] DRO, D4538/4/21, Estates and Development Committee minutes, 11 December 1968.

[113] 'correct balance': DRO, D4538/4/22, Estates and Development Committee minutes, 19 May 1970.

[114] John Elsom, *Theatre Outside London* (London, 1971), p. 180; 'Gateway Theatre, Chester', Theatres Trust database, <https://database.theatrestrust.org.uk/resources/theatres/show/2171-gateway-chester> (accessed 17 October 2017); V&A, ACGB/84/78, HTA Chester file.

[115] 'Chester Gateway: a creation for theatre and social life', *Stage*, 28 November 1968, pp. 18–19.

[116] 'Chester Gateway', pp. 18–19.

[117] John R. Gold, *The Practice of Modernism: Modern Architects and Urban Transformation* (Abingdon, 2007), pp. 93–104.

[118] LA, DE 3277/215, 'Observations of the Officers of the Corporation on the Siting of a Civic Theatre in the Haymarket Development Area' [June 1965].

Certainly Chamberlin Powell and Bon's contemporaneous Barbican Estate in the City of London offered a distinctive view of what a city neighbourhood might be, with few commercial elements. Its focal point, as elaborated in proposals of 1956, 1959, and 1968, was an arts centre.[119] For the architects, provision for 'recreation' was essential if the Barbican was to be 'a genuine residential neighbourhood'.[120] Initial Arts Centre designs include pavilion-like structures, which were to be shared by professional performers and the students of the Guildhall School of Music and Drama (GSMD), but as built in the 1970s the Arts Centre grew to include a substantial professional theatre (for the Royal Shakespeare Company), a concert hall, a gallery, and conference halls. These facilities were squeezed into the centre of the estate, whose walkways passed around and through the centre, and whose pick-hammered concrete surfaces continued into the foyers and auditoria.

Similarly conceived in terms of urban reconfiguration were the contemporaneous proposals for a major cultural centre in Glasgow, including a concert hall, repertory theatre, and civic (touring) theatre. The initial aim was the replacement of St Andrew's Halls, a well-regarded concert venue which had been destroyed by fire in 1962.[121] At the start of 1963, the *Architects' Journal* published a design by the architect of Cumbernauld's town centre, Geoffrey Copcutt, which located a new civic centre and St Andrew's Halls in a megastructure above the city's Central railway station.[122] His scheme was surely hypothetical, but the proposals put forward after 1964 by the city architect, Archibald Jury, and then by Leslie Martin, were scarcely less ambitious in their scale. On a site north of Renfrew Street, later to accommodate a bus station, Jury proposed two levels of parking, above which the halls and theatres would face an elevated pedestrian plaza, which in one version of the design would have rivalled the city's George Square for size (see Figure 5.9).[123] Underscoring the ambition of the scheme, reference was made to precedents at home (Coventry, Liverpool, Manchester, and the South Bank) and abroad (Lincoln Center, Berlin, Toronto, Tel Aviv, Jerusalem).[124] Along with the new housing and motorways that were being constructed at this time, the project formed part of a broader attempt to reform Glasgow in a modern, technocratic image.[125]

Jury's proposals provoked a storm of criticism, partly because of their rather dull elevations,[126] but also because of the relationship (or lack thereof) between the multilevel structure and its surroundings. Although some images show pedestrian bridges extending beyond the elevated square into the surrounding city blocks, the basic concept of monofunctional 'zoning' in urban planning was increasingly

[119] Elain Harwood, *Chamberlin Powell and Bon* (London, 2011), pp. 122–30.

[120] GLL, CoCoRep 1968/48, Report of the Rates, Finance, Barbican and Music Committees, 1968.

[121] Florian Urban, 'Glasgow's Royal Concert Hall and the Invention of the Post-modern City', *Journal of Architecture* 18, no. 2 (2013), pp. 254–96 (pp. 255–6).

[122] 'Glasgow: twenty year development plan', *Architects' Journal* 137 (30 January 1963), pp. 222, 228–9.

[123] V&A, ACGB/120/41, 'Description of the Design and Layout of Glasgow's New Cultural Centre', 29 September 1965.

[124] Urban, 'Glasgow's Royal Concert Hall', p. 266.

[125] Urban, 'Glasgow's Royal Concert Hall', p. 257.

[126] 'Glasgow Cultural Centre: the great debate', *Architects' Journal* 143 (4 May 1966), p. 1171.

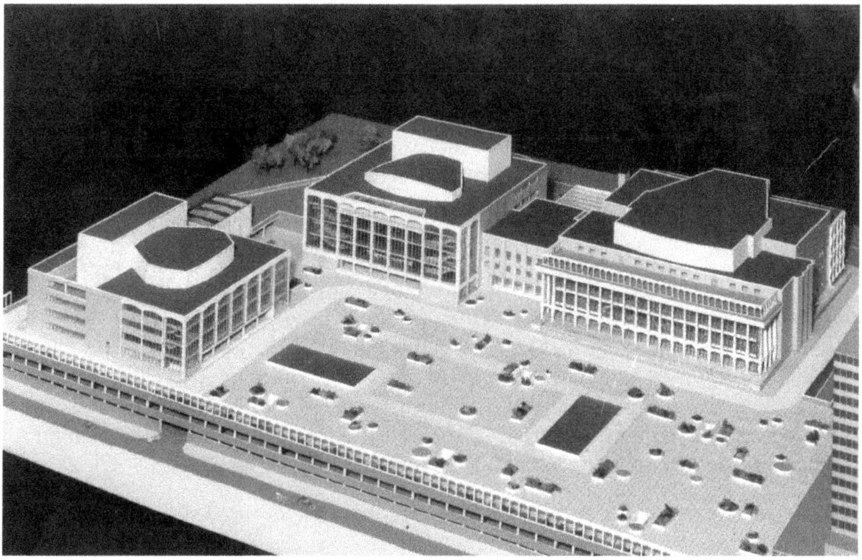

Figure 5.9. Divorced from the 'urban pudding'? Archibald Jury's proposals for the Glasgow Cultural Centre, *c.*1964 (RIBA Collections)

being questioned by the mid-1960s. In an article entitled 'Cultural Centre or Cultural Ghetto', the *Architects' Journal* asked 'why should a concert hall, a civic theatre, a repertory theatre and an exhibition gallery be placed together?'[127] It went on: 'should Glasgow have a religious centre, a restaurant centre or a political centre? Nothing could be more ridiculous'. Rather, it concluded, the new civic and cultural buildings should be integrated into the 'urban pudding'. By October 1966, it seemed that the scheme was 'dead', at least in the form imagined by Jury.[128] Advice was sought from a group of prominent Scottish architects, namely Jack Coia, Ninian Johnstone, Alan Reiach, and Walter Underwood, who recommended that Leslie Martin be approached.[129] Having been Robert Matthew's deputy at the London County Council during the period in which the Festival Hall was built, and having subsequently replaced Matthew, Martin had become professor of Architecture at the University of Cambridge in 1956. He built relatively little in his own right, but was often sought out, especially by institutional clients, to advise on possible architects. Working with a close circle of Cambridge academics, he had also developed a strong interest in urban form, manifested in a series of theoretical propositions in which high densities of accommodation were achieved through the use of low-rise courtyard forms without tower blocks, and also in a proposal for the reconstruction of the government centre at Whitehall in central London. This scheme, conceived by the Conservative government

[127] 'Cultural Centre or Cultural Ghetto?', *Architects' Journal* 143 (5 January 1966), pp. 3–4.
[128] RCS, IA/3/6/1, W. M. Cumming to G. T. L. Scott, 13 October 1966.
[129] GA, Corporation minutes, Finance Committee, 11 December 1967.

in 1963, subsequently stalled under Labour and had been abandoned by the end of the decade.

In early 1968, Martin was appointed as consultant to the project, initially with special responsibility for 'developments in the vicinity of the site'.[130] The urban aspect of the project apparently appealed.[131] Perhaps the grid-iron arrangement of central Glasgow was especially attractive, given the title of Martin's classic 1972 essay, 'The Grid as Generator'. A meeting note, made soon after his appointment, recorded that:

> here, more than any other city in the British Isles, existed an opportunity to realise the construction of a Cultural or Arts Centre closely associated with the life of the City, and to its street and traffic patterns. A group of buildings, or rather the need for them, had come together, naturally, at a point in time and in one City space, and given the same drive and enthusiasm as that given to Urban Renewal generally in the City, the ways seemed open for a significant group of buildings for Music and the Arts with adjacent, [sic] Shopping, Exhibition and Hotel facilities.[132]

Martin sought to avoid 'the idea of a cultural centre occupying some isolated or separated area as if it were something apart from the working life of the city'.[133] Initial planning proposals were presented in November 1968 and were approved in May 1969, with Martin then being appointed to oversee the whole scheme.[134] Martin took as his site an area to the south of that proposed by Jury, closer to the city's shopping areas. His designs, developed in association with Colen Lumley and then Ivor Richards, went through various iterations during the 1970s, but they all proposed the construction of a single building containing all the various parts of the cultural centre. They also all included the creation of a new public space at the junction of Buchanan Street and Sauchiehall Street. As of 1973, the concert hall was to form the centrepiece of the complex, with the new 650-seat Citizens' Theatre and 200-seat studio theatre being built to the west, and the Royal Scottish Academy of Music and Drama (RSAMD) to the south.[135] They were to be connected by a glazed atrium, with drawings showing a sheer wall of glass facing Buchanan Street and Sauchiehall Street (see Figure 5.10).[136] Although the proposals were more modest than the Whitehall schemes, they nonetheless developed many of the same themes: separation of traffic from pedestrians; megastructural thinking ('an overall physical form');[137] and the remaking of the urban landscape in the image of modernity. One drawing shows a space-frame roof covering part of Buchanan Street, creating a sheltered shopping area.[138] Other drawings illustrate

[130] GA, Corporation minutes, Finance Committee, 29 January 1968.
[131] RCS, IA/3/6/1, Ian Ballantyne to G. T. L. Scott, 10 December 1969.
[132] RCS, IA/3/6/1, Ian Ballantyne to G. T. L. Scott, 10 December 1969.
[133] 'Plans Soon for Recreational and Arts Centre in Glasgow', *Herald*, 1 July 1970.
[134] GA, Corporation minutes, St Andrew's Halls replacement subcommittee, 27 May 1969.
[135] RIBA, Leslie Martin box 36/2, 'New Halls and Centre for Music and Drama, Glasgow: Third Report, July 1973'.
[136] RIBA, Leslie Martin box 50/4, Cultural Centre drawings.
[137] RIBA, Leslie Martin box 36/2, 'New Halls and Centre for Music and Drama, Glasgow: Third Report, July 1973'.
[138] RIBA, Leslie Martin box 50/1, March 1975 perspective drawing.

Figure 5.10. Leslie Martin's proposals for the Glasgow Cultural Centre, *c.*1972, on a site south of that earlier proposed by Archibald Jury. Viewed here looking up Buchanan Street, the Citizens' Theatre is rear-left, the concert hall rear-right, and the Royal Scottish Academy of Music and Drama is to the right (RIBA Collections)

roads, service areas, and pedestrian walkways cutting through the complex on various levels. Jury's isolated pavilions-on-a-podium were thus abandoned for a more complex engagement with the city, one that related to the existing street layout and sought to make a positive contribution to the urban experience.

However, concerns about the cost of the scheme were soon aired. The authorities in Glasgow had received money from their insurers in order to replace St Andrew's Halls, but the city's finances were already stretched.[139] At the same time, as a 'monster project' with an estimated cost of nearly £20 million by 1974,[140] the cultural centre was well beyond the scope of the 'Housing the Arts' programme and so would be dependent on a special government award. Extracting promises of such funding seems never to have been simple and rested on claims to 'national' significance which could easily be rebuffed, but making this kind of case was especially tricky in the recession of the mid-1970s.[141] The proposals had already been scaled back: for example, the idea of two theatres—one a 'civic' venue, the other for the Citizens' Theatre—had been dropped as early as July 1970.[142] By 1975 it was clear that the money was unlikely to be forthcoming,[143] and in June 1976, the Secretary

[139] RCS, IA/3/6/2, Edward Taylor to Iain Barber Fleming, 30 November 1970; Urban, 'Glasgow's Royal Concert Hall', p. 271.

[140] NRS, ED61/88, 'Edinburgh Castle Terrace Theatre/Opera House' [March 1974].

[141] Alistair Fair, '"An Object Lesson in How Not To Get Things Done": Edinburgh's unbuilt "opera house", 1960–75', *Architectural Heritage* 27 (2017), pp. 91–117.

[142] 'Plans Soon for Recreational and Arts Centre in Glasgow', *Herald*, 1 July 1970.

[143] NRS, ED61/89, J. Fearn memo, 18 February 1975.

of State announced that the full scheme would be indefinitely postponed.[144] In 1978, with the theatre costed at £6.4 million and the whole scheme at £29 million, the theatre was abandoned.[145] Its site was given over to a commercial development, as was that intended for the RSAMD. The inclusion of a shopping mall in the development, explored by Martin after 1977, was evidently an attempt to offset some of its capital and running costs.[146] The Citizens' Theatre went on to reconstruct its existing premises in the Gorbals, while the King's Theatre—acquired by the city at the end of the 1960s as a stopgap—became a permanent civic theatre. The RSAMD took a separate site on Renfrew Street, opening in 1987; Martin's proposals were developed by William Nimmo and Partners. Meanwhile the concert hall was eventually completed to Martin's designs in 1990.[147] As built, both the concert hall and the RSAMD share an architectural vocabulary, their abstracted and perhaps unduly sober classicism and external staircases evoking Harvey Court, Cambridge, the university residences that Martin had co-designed in the early 1960s. The parallel is not only stylistic, however. Harvey Court was based on an earlier unexecuted scheme for central Cambridge and functioned as a kind of prototype for Martin's urban theories, with its plan and section being tightly organized to create a spatially complex but rational urban landscape in which high densities were achieved. Certainly urban considerations remained key for Martin in Glasgow, even as the scheme was truncated. In 1979, he commented that the hall's 'proximity to a major shopping centre' would be advantageous, the complex serving to 'reinvigorate this important area of the city'.[148] In this respect, and subsequently in making the case for Glasgow as a post-industrial 'city of culture', the Royal Concert Hall, like many of the new theatres of the 1950s, 1960s, and 1970s, demonstrated the potential connections between cultural buildings, the urban environment, and the very idea of urbanity.

[144] GA, Glasgow District Council minutes, Finance Committee, 14 September 1976.

[145] RIBA, Leslie Martin box 36/2, 'New Halls and the Development of the Cultural Centre Site, Glasgow', typescript, n.d.

[146] E.g. drawings marked 'C Hall Solo' in RIBA, Leslie Martin drawings box 50/1.

[147] The shopping centre was eventually not built to Martin's designs; the concert hall was executed by RMJM.

[148] 'Concert Hall Overtures', *Herald*, 15 November 1979; RIBA, Leslie Martin box 36/1, 'Design Report 1979', p. 2.

6

'The Modern Concept of a Community Theatre'

The Social Centre

In 1971, the architects of the then-proposed Warwick Arts Centre, Renton Howard Wood, wrote of their design that:

> In order to generate the maximum activity and social benefit, the Arts Centre and other cultural and social buildings should straddle the main pedestrian route between the existing residential and teaching buildings. Such an arrangement would allow the Arts Centre to develop into the social focus of the University.[1]

The planning of the centre such that the 'main pedestrian route' passed through its foyers recalls the way in which the same architects' Crucible Theatre formed part of a notional route through Sheffield city centre. However, the intention that the Arts Centre would be a 'social focus' is also important, as is its intended 'social benefit'. Through 'a mixed programme of professional and amateur drama, dance, music, and other performance art', it would 'attract an audience drawn not only from the University but also the community at large'.[2] Warwick Arts Centre, which opened in 1974, was not alone among post-war British theatres in being described in these terms. In 1966, for example, it was reported of the new theatre then proposed for Leatherhead that it would be a 'social centre'.[3] Such a social centre could be understood as the embodiment of contemporary thinking, as the chairman of Derby Playhouse made clear when he referred in 1969 to 'the modern concept of a community theatre which through the provision of restaurants, bars, exhibition galleries, lunch time concerts, etc., becomes the focal point of the town throughout the day'.[4]

This chapter begins by discussing the social centre in broad terms before continuing with a close examination of university theatres, in which social ideals were often especially significant. It concludes with three examples by the theatre architect Roderick Ham, focusing in particular on the Thorndike Theatre, Leatherhead, which presented itself as 'Surrey's New Social and Cultural Centre' in the late 1960s. These examples together suggest that the idea of the social centre could be

[1] MRC, UWA/NAD/AC/ARC/2, 'University of Warwick: Arts Centre', 17 March 1971.
[2] MRC, UWA/NAD/AC/2/1, University of Warwick Arts Centre: Annual Report 1974/75.
[3] SHC, 6368/10/6, clippings: *Surrey Advertiser*, 30 July 1966.
[4] DRO, D738/4/1, D. V. W. Malin to Norman Fisher, 30 June 1969.

interpreted in two distinct but potentially interrelated ways. First, the term referred to a place in which individuals would socialize, with generously sized foyers often containing bars, a restaurant, a gallery for exhibitions, a club room, and ample seating. Under the banner 'Your Theatr Clwyd', for example, the new theatre at Mold proclaimed in 1976 that it was open from 10 a.m., six days a week, with a licensed bar available to all.[5] At the same time, the concept of a social centre could also be related in a more abstract way to ideas about society itself. In effect, theatres could be understood as a kind of secular meeting place, at least for those who actively chose to meet there. They would thus form the focus of an urban or university community, and might have a transformative role in shaping civic and social identities. They could also be a magnet within the urban environment, serving to counter the attractions of suburbia.

The significance of these examples goes beyond the immediate history of theatre design. Modern architecture itself could be conceived in fundamentally social terms. Pioneering schemes of the 1930s, such as Elizabeth Denby and Maxwell Fry's Kensal House, west London, had been designed with an eye on the one hand to the development of family life within the individual flat, and, at the same time, the promotion of community through the provision of social spaces for children and adults.[6] The planning and design of housing during the 1950s and 1960s, too, was frequently informed by the desire to encourage social equality and to promote community. An idea dubbed the 'new sociability' was sometimes invoked, namely that the time liberated by modern labour-saving devices might productively be spent with family and friends, in education, or in playing sport.[7] Such ideas were not unique to the design of housing but formed a significant (and evolving) strand in the period's architectural and planning discourses, for example in 'neighbourhood' planning or the concern to recover the traditional role of the street as a place for play and neighbourly chat. As a result, just as Chapter 4's examination of Britain's new theatres as 'public' structures suggested how this period's architecture might be interpreted in ways that move beyond style and appearance alone, so too might a discussion of the influence on theatre design of ideas relating to society and community also lead to a better understanding of post-war modern architecture more generally.

'MORE THAN A PLAYHOUSE'

The idea that theatres might be more than places of performance was established early in Britain's post-war theatre-building boom. The Arts Council's 1945 Arts Centre prototype, for example, included a 200-seat restaurant.[8] Similarly, Bryan

[5] FRO, CC/TC/1/163, 'Eich Theatr Chi—Theatr Clwyd' [brochure].

[6] Elizabeth Darling, *Re-forming Britain: Narratives of Modernity Before Reconstruction* (Abingdon, 2007), pp. 137–74.

[7] John R. Gold, *The Practice of Modernism: Modern Architects and Urban Transformation* (Abingdon, 2007), pp. 204–27.

[8] [ACGB], 'Plans for an Arts Centre' [London, 1945].

Bailey, the first artistic director of Coventry's Belgrade Theatre, reported in 1958 that the Belgrade was intended to be 'more than a playhouse',[9] while the theatre's first Annual Report concluded that 'it is rapidly becoming a social centre'.[10] Coffee and snacks were served from 10 a.m. till noon, while the restaurant opened at lunchtimes on days when a matinée was scheduled and again in the evenings from 6 p.m.[11] By October 1959, Bailey was able to tell the Nottingham Playhouse's board that more catering was being offered than had originally been envisaged, although he advised that the first-floor location of the restaurant was proving problematic.[12] Without its own entrance, it could not be opened independently of the theatre. Peter Moro's design for Nottingham Playhouse was well advanced by this date, but Bailey's comment can only have confirmed the wisdom of Moro's decision to locate that theatre's bar and restaurant in a projecting wing which could easily be isolated from the rest of the building.

Although large foyers were common in contemporary West German theatres, the Belgrade contrasted with many older, commercial theatres in Britain, whose foyers were often not only segregated by ticket price but were also typically cramped and open only at performance times. Commercial exigencies had hitherto demanded that the majority of a theatre's site be given over to the auditorium. By contrast, the Belgrade's public funding provided the means of realizing a more generously conceived social centre whose spacious public areas provided for eating, drinking, and socializing, during the day as well as in the evening. The Belgrade's civic status also supplied the rationale for these facilities. There had already been a number of initiatives in Coventry intended to promote a sense of community and a civic identity among the city's expanding population, including 'Know Your City' bus tours and the launch of a free newspaper, *Civic Affairs*.[13] In this respect, the Belgrade was perhaps conceived as a Soviet-style 'social condenser', a place where individuals might mix and from which they might emerge as a community. This idea may well have been known in Coventry, because several councillors had travelled behind the Iron Curtain, the city had 'twins' in eastern Europe,[14] and the theatre's name reflected Coventry's links with Yugoslavia. Seen in these terms, the theatre was almost a non-religious counterpart to Basil Spence's new Coventry Cathedral, which was then under construction.

Many of the subsidized theatres which followed the Belgrade had foyers that were just as spacious, if not more so, and in this way they, too, contrasted with older, commercial theatres. Ideas of sociability pervaded the terms in which they were described. For example, the Yvonne Arnaud Theatre, Guildford, was to be 'a cultural and social centre, open all day, and a lively meeting place for all whose

[9] CHC, PA2313/5/2/1, clippings: *Tribune*, 23 May 1958.

[10] CHC, CCA/TC/5/4/2/1, Belgrade Theatre Annual Report, 1957–1958.

[11] NA, DD/NP/1/2/1/1, Bryan Bailey to Hugh Willatt, 26 October 1959.

[12] NA, DD/NP/1/2/1/1, Bryan Bailey to Hugh Willatt, 26 October 1959.

[13] Nick Tiratsoo, *Reconstruction, Affluence and Labour Politics: Coventry, 1945–60* (London, 1990), pp. 46, 51–9.

[14] E.g. George Hodgkinson, *Sent to Coventry* (London, 1970), pp. 206–10 for a visit to Dresden. These links reflected first, a shared sense of wartime suffering at the hands of Nazi aggression, and second, Coventry's left-wing local government.

interests lie in the humanities'.[15] The Nottingham Playhouse's design brief similarly proposed that 'the building can be a friendly as well as an exciting place to go to, welcoming theatregoers, and others interested in the Arts generally or responsive to the appeal of the building in itself'.[16] Nonetheless, a degree of caution is needed in interpreting these ambitions. Anthony Field, the Arts Council of Great Britain's finance director, was evidently sceptical of the idealistic tone of at least some of the proposals that landed on his desk. The feasibility study for Stevenage's Arts and Leisure Centre he thought '"worthy" in the dreariest sense' in late 1968.[17] He went on, presumably quoting the study:

> Whilst I applaud the philosophy of a centre making 'an appeal to all members of the community [...] bringing all members of the family unit together in the same area', I should still very much like to see such a Centre in actuality. Please arrange a visit to an Arts Centre for me where Mum and Dad, Johnny, Sis and Baby Bunting together with Granny and Uncle Fred all come delightedly three times a week to an Arts Centre catering for their individual needs.[18]

In this respect, pragmatic considerations also explain the rise of social centres. With—as was discussed in Chapter 1—the limited nature of subsidy meaning that theatres typically generated the majority of their income through the box office, it clearly made financial sense to open during the day. Certainly Nottingham Playhouse's directors suggested in 1956 that the sale of refreshments would bring in useful revenue.[19] Their hopes proved well founded. It was reported in 1966 that the Playhouse had budgeted the previous year for a £9000 loss but had actually made a £1500 profit.[20] Not least among the reported reasons for this success, along with the 'theatrical and exciting' building and the quality of the Playhouse's productions, was the fact that it was 'a busy social centre'.[21]

In Bromley, too, reference was made to 'increasing the earning capacity of the theatre',[22] and it was reported that 80 per cent of the Churchill Theatre's bar and restaurant takings came from people who were not seeing a play.[23] The anticipated increase in leisure time made such considerations especially important:

> it was felt that with the continuing increase in leisure time, no theatre of the future would only work for the now normal 2½ hours each day, and means would have to allow the building fuller usage. To this end technical facilities are provide to give instant set shift electromechanically so that changing from one completely furnished and fully dressed set to another can take place in 30 seconds.[24]

[15] V&A, Theatre Collections Guildford file, untitled/undated sheet with information about the new theatre.
[16] NA, DD/NP/1/2/1/1, Nottingham Playhouse architects' brief, p. 8.
[17] V&A, ACGB/84/260, Anthony Field memo, 19 December 1968.
[18] V&A, ACGB/84/260, Anthony Field memo, 19 December 1968.
[19] NA, DD/NP/1/2/1/1, Playhouse Directors to Nottingham City Council, 8 October 1956.
[20] 'The Under-Rated Theatre', *Guardian*, 24 March 1966.
[21] 'The Under-Rated Theatre', *Guardian*, 24 March 1966.
[22] BA&LS, 792.094223, W. S. Gage et al., 'Churchill Theatre, Bromley' [ACGB Case Study], p. 27.
[23] BA&LS, 792.094223, Gage et al., 'Churchill Theatre', p. 94.
[24] BA&LS, 792.0942178, 'Bromley's New Theatre' [brochure].

The implication here is that the theatre would routinely be used for daytime performances, with technology allowing stage sets to be changed rapidly so that several shows could be presented in close succession, perhaps for quite different audiences. However, by implication, the theatre's foyers would see correspondingly increased use, and indeed it was suggested that the aim was 'a theatre open to the public all day long in which several quite unrelated events could take place in one day [...].'[25] The theatre is integrated with the borough's central library in a tower, a form originally suggested by Bromley's consultant architect, Donald McMorran.[26] The design, developed by Kenneth Wilson in the office of the borough architect, housed the library stacks, offices, and meeting rooms in the concrete-clad tower, which is boldly massed with striking angled sides, while a lower block, faced in tiles, contains shops, reading rooms, and spacious theatre foyers overlooking the adjacent park. It opened in 1977 after a somewhat protracted period of construction.

The provision of drinks and meals, in particular, was thought to allow theatre to offer a distinctive kind of experience. In Bromley, for example, it was felt that 'the concept of a total evening out for playgoers means the provision of full restaurant and bar facilities if a theatre is to compete successfully with television'.[27] In 1959, four years after the launch of commercial television and with the number of television sets in Britain rapidly increasing, Birmingham Repertory Theatre's management made a similar argument. Their ambitions balanced a relatively traditional view of theatre-going as a glamorous and glitzy way to spend an evening with an evident desire to respond to the challenge of television by rethinking what theatres might offer:

> when improvements in [the] artistic and technical quality of television and the possibility of a third [television] channel had made television increasingly popular, [...] a good play well done might no longer in itself be enough to attract an economic audience. However, there would always be a demand for 'a night out' which was a real occasion with first class entertainment, and facilities for good food and drink in comfortable surroundings under the same roof. The present building could not provide all these requirements.[28]

It was hoped that the theatre's foyer would:

> act as the main concourse creating the first link between the life of the City and the theatre. It is here that it is hoped to ensure that the building is regarded as more than a mere theatre but rather as a centre with facilities for a meal and a drink, a place for conversation and other things which provide a complete evening's entertainment all under one roof.[29]

Actually implementing this idea, however, was not straightforward. A 1975 report revealed that the catering contractor had been removed after problems with staff

25 Artistic director, David Poulson, quoted in BA&LS, 792.094223, Gage et al., 'Churchill Theatre, Bromley', p. 27.
26 Sheila Dunn, *The Theatres of Bromley* (Greenwich, 1984), p. 49.
27 BA&LS, 792.094223, Gage et al., 'Churchill Theatre, Bromley', p. 30.
28 LoB, MS 978/5/16–17, minute of 6 April 1959.
29 V&A, ACGB/84/28, brochure about the new Repertory Theatre, n.d.

and the quality of food on offer.[30] In this respect, the report suggested that Birmingham Rep was not unique in attracting critical comment. In Leatherhead, the Thorndike Theatre sold 'boil-in-the-bag' meals for £1 and was open daily from 10 a.m. until 9.30 p.m., but apparently struggled to cope with demand.[31] There were apparently more serious problems elsewhere, with 'heavy losses' at Billingham, Coventry, and Guildford, culinary mediocrity at Liverpool Playhouse, and not only a 'pretentious restaurant' but also a 'terrible buffet' at the Crucible, Sheffield.

Pragmatism and idealism coincided in discussions of the extent to which space for sociability might attract young people. In London in 1966, Peter Hall hoped that 'even greater numbers of the better-educated and critical younger generation' would come to the then-proposed Barbican to see the Royal Shakespeare Company,[32] but often a new building was seen as being as attractive as the performances staged within. The director of the Colchester Repertory Company, David Forder, suggested in 1966 that 'an exciting contemporary building with the amenities of a social centre is the incentive many youngsters of today need to give theatre-going a try—not just for the play but as an enjoyable night out'.[33] As he put it: 'future audiences depend on how we can encourage into the theatre the youngsters of today'. Similarly, it was hoped that the expanded foyers of York's Theatre Royal would draw in the young. At a meeting between theatre staff and city officials in 1965 it was suggested that 'the idea would be to have the place alive during the day, [...] a young persons' centre, etc.', while *Glass Age*, reviewing the project in 1969, dubbed the foyers 'a focal meeting point for the bright youth of York'.[34] A coffee bar, in particular, was thought to attract youthful patrons, with the *Stage* reporting the view of Lord Willis in 1972 that:

> Civilised arts centres such as have sprung up at Coventry, Greenwich, Leatherhead, Nottingham, Guildford and other places attract the brightest minds and the keenest intellects in the community and every effort is made to attract the younger generation. They drop in for coffee and soon become part of the Local Theatre. It is their place, and they guard it with a jealous possessiveness [...].[35]

An apparently more genteel but not dissimilar approach was evident at Chichester Festival Theatre, where in 1962 'additional restaurant facilities for coffee and snack bars for the younger generation' were being considered, 'especially facilities for afternoon tea at the end of matinees'.[36]

One is tempted to speculate in some of these cases that an attempt was being made to draw young patrons away from the temptations of the public house or local cafés. In this respect, some context is important. The 1944 Education Act

[30] V&A, ACGB/120/22, Russell Brown and Bruce Copp, 'Theatre Catering Survey' [*c.*1975].

[31] V&A, ACGB/120/22, Russell Brown and Bruce Copp, 'Theatre Catering Survey' [*c.*1975].

[32] V&A, Theatre Collections Peter Hall file, clipping from *Sunday Telegraph*, 17 July 1966.

[33] ERO, D/Z 455/2/13, clippings: 'Why Colchester Must Plan Now for a New Repertory Theatre', *Essex County Standard*, 9 December 1966.

[34] YSJU, Theatre Royal Archive, Meeting of Corporation officials and Theatre Royal staff, 15 April 1965; also clipping: 'Annex: York Theatre Royal', *Glass Age* 12, no. 2 (1969), pp. 36–8.

[35] 'A Local Theatre Can Be Good for Culture and Commerce', *Stage*, 27 April 1972.

[36] WSRO, CFT Archive, Box 54, Draft 1962 Review, p. 5.

expanded the provision of free secondary education in England and Wales, leading *Tabs* in 1950 to suggest that the result would be a larger audience for cultural activities of a high standard.[37] At the same time, above-inflation increases in earnings meant that the population had on average a greater amount of money to spend on leisure by the late 1950s.[38] The architect-planner Graeme Shankland coupled these two developments in 1964: 'rising incomes will give most people more spending power and the growth of education could well lead to increases in artistic and intellectual pursuits'.[39] In particular, the amount of disposable income enjoyed by young people rose disproportionately and, as the decade wore on, a growing proportion of this age group sought to define their own cultural identity, not least through their leisure activities.[40] With the 'baby boom' generation of the late 1940s reaching maturity during the 1960s, the idea of the social centre thus took on particular significance, not least in the new university theatres of the period.

'THE DEVELOPMENT OF SOCIAL AWARENESS': UNIVERSITY THEATRES

In March 1964, the opening of Southampton's Nuffield Theatre—designed by Basil Spence's office—marked the beginning of a wave of university theatre construction.[41] These buildings were often ambitiously conceived and substantial in scale. In Chapter 1, it was noted that university education was often conceived during the 1960s in broad terms. Graduates would not only have knowledge but would also, it was hoped, be rounded, cultured citizens. In this respect, the expansion of higher education represented the same kind of paternalism that also underpinned the practice of subsidy for the arts, in which theatre-going was thought to have a transformative effect. For example, at the New University of Ulster in Coleraine, it was reported in 1976 that while 'much of the important business of the University is conducted in lectures and seminars', just as important was students' 'general cultural education and the development of social awareness'.[42]

Discussions of 'community' and 'association' permeated 1960s architectural culture, but were particularly prominent where university planning was concerned. Both architects and academics often understood universities in utopian terms as 'total institutions' in which students would be immersed in an 'ideal' community that was set apart from the 'real' world.[43] The greenfield sites favoured for the new universities

[37] 'The National Theatre', *Tabs* 8, no. 3 (December 1950), pp. 4–7.

[38] Arthur Marwick, *The Sixties: Cultural Revolution in Britain, France, Italy, and the United States, c.1958–c.1974* (Oxford, 1998), p. 258.

[39] Quoted in Lionel Esher, *A Broken Wave: The Rebuilding of England, 1940–1980* (Harmondsworth, 1983), p. 229.

[40] Marwick, *Sixties*, pp. 41–80.

[41] 'The First University Theatre', *Architects' Journal* 139 (22 January 1964), p. 174.

[42] PRONI, NUU/3/2/1/7, Report to the University Court, 1975–76.

[43] Stefan Muthesius, *The Postwar University: Utopianist Campus and College* (New Haven/London, 2000).

of the 1960s by the University Grants Committee gave this idea particular clear physical form. In university planning generally, designers and their academic clients were thus concerned with the organization of 'human communities'.[44] In Cardiff, for example, it was suggested that 'to rub shoulders in daily living with fellow students [is] perhaps one of the most vital educational processes offered by universities and other institutions for higher studies'.[45] Within this context, a theatre or arts centre might be understood not only as a place for socializing along the lines of the examples already discussed, but also in symbolic terms that recall the idealistic conception of the Belgrade Theatre. For example, Lancaster's Nuffield Theatre was to be 'a focal point in the University, [...] a unifying power'.[46] Again, the idea of the social condenser may be a helpful analogy. Within university campuses that were often understood and planned as miniature cities, a theatre could play a quasi-civic role, physically and also as a communal building that brought together students from different subjects and backgrounds.

A theatre might also build bridges between academia and the wider world, especially when professionally run theatres were located on university campuses. For example, the Northcott Theatre at Exeter University was described by the vice chancellor as 'an opportunity to bring the university into closer contact with the life of the region'.[47] His choice of words may have been strategic. As was noted in Chapter 4, the Northcott replaced the city's Theatre Royal, with the university taking advantage of a sizeable benefaction given to support theatre in Exeter generally in order to build itself a substantial, well-equipped auditorium. Nonetheless, Exeter was not unique in framing its ambitions in this way. Sussex's Gardner Arts Centre, for example, was to 'provide a link between the University and the community in which it lives'.[48] Furthermore, the centre would offer 'the ideal opportunity [...] to re-examine the relationship between [...] the creative artists working here and the public using the building as a social environment'.[49]

Another example is found by taking a brief detour beyond Britain, at the New University of Ulster, where the Riverside Theatre was to serve the Coleraine-Portrush-Portstewart area, then slated for development as a new town. Intended as 'a cultural amenity for members of the University and the community', the theatre was to stage 'normal scale, epic and large scale drama productions, and also chamber opera and ballet, musicals, pantomime, music hall, variety, cabaret and [...] chamber concerts'.[50] The vice chancellor hoped in 1975 that it would inaugurate

[44] Robert Proctor, 'Social Structures: Gillespie Kidd and Coia's halls of residence for the University of Hull', *Journal of the Society of Architectural Historians* 67, no. 1 (2008), pp. 106–29 (p. 106).

[45] CUA, Address by Dr C. W. L. Bevan to the Court of Governors, 10 November 1967, filed with Reports of the Council.

[46] RSA, uncat. box entitled 'Theatres, Printed Information, M–Z', brochure entitled 'The Nuffield Theatre'.

[47] UoEx, 26/1d/2d, clippings: '100,000 Gift by Devon Millionaire', *Express and Echo*, 12 February 1963.

[48] UoSx, SxUOS1/1/5/13/1, George Devine, 'Memorandum on the Setting Up of a Centre of the Creative Arts at Sussex University', 10 November 1964.

[49] 'The Gardner Arts Centre', *Focus: The News Magazine of the University of Surrey*, November 1969, p. 9, <http://www.sussex.ac.uk/internal/bulletin/downloads/1960-1969/1969/November/196911.pdf> (accessed 24 June 2017).

[50] PRONI, D4327/2/1/32, NUU Council minutes, 12 January 1972, with attached Theatre/Arts Centre Committee report.

'an era of greatly increased community involvement in the University'.[51] Early versions of the university's development plan located the 500-seat theatre conveniently close to the main entrance to the campus.[52] As built, however, the theatre retreated to a more central position on the university site, adjacent to 'The Diamond' (the university's main social building). Here the Riverside Theatre opened in 1975; it was designed by Peter Moro's office and benefited from a large Gulbenkian Foundation grant. A low-slung structure built into a hillside and distinguished by a tall, illuminated column, it is a typical example of the accretive massing and polygonal forms favoured by Moro's office during the 1970s (see Figure 6.1). Its eight-sided plan develops that of the architects' Gulbenkian Centre at Hull University (1969) and is very much in the mould of Moro's contemporaneous proposals for theatres in Brentford and Plymouth, which are discussed in Chapter 7. It also anticipated the form of Moro's later Taliesin Arts Centre, Swansea (1984),

Figure 6.1. Riverside Theatre, New University of Ulster, Coleraine, in 1976: the illuminated pole was intended to signify the theatre's presence on campus (Architectural Press Archive/RIBA Collections)

[51] PRONI, NUU/3/2/1/6, Report to the University Court, 1974–75.

[52] PRONI, NUU/3/2/2/1A, The New University of Ulster: Interim Report on Development Plan, August 1967; Miles Glendinning, *Modern Architect: The Life and Times of Robert Matthew* (London, 2008), pp. 340–3.

whose foyers—which included a bookshop and bank as well as a café and gallery—were similarly intended to form part of the day-to-day life of the university.

Manchester's University Theatre, completed in 1965, represents an early essay in these themes, with its foyers being intended as a meeting place for 'town and gown'.[53] The creation of the university's Drama department had been catalysed by an approach during 1959 from Granada Television, whose educational programming was then led by the former Festival of Britain director-general, Sir Gerald Barry.[54] Granada reportedly offered seven years' funding. It was keen to promote the 'academic' study of drama rather than a more vocational approach, although it nonetheless 'would not wish to disguise that, indirectly, they would welcome an increase in the number of people available as writers, producers, etc.'[55] Hugh Hunt, an Oxford graduate who had directed at the Old Vic in the late 1940s before spending five years in Australia, was appointed as professor in early 1961.[56] Hunt was keen to expand students' cultural horizons, and here his ideas on the potential for drama to enrich humanities teaching echoed the 1948 report on the University of Oxford's unbuilt theatre.[57] He also sought to forge links beyond the university. Soon after his appointment, Granada Television paid for him to visit universities and colleges in the United States, whose auditoria often also served local communities with a diet of amateur and professional drama.[58] Back in Manchester, Hunt proposed that a university theatre could serve 'a valuable function by bringing together the city and the university and by extending the range and quality of available entertainment'.[59] His intentions were clearly shaped by North American practice. He later recorded that 'the opening of the theatre gave me the chance to put my American dream into practice by establishing a professional company on the University campus'.[60]

A teaching studio was initially planned at Manchester, perhaps along the lines of the studio at Bristol University (or Hull's later Gulbenkian Centre),[61] but the university also sought to replace the Arthur Worthington Hall with a small theatre, for which funding was secured from the University Grants Committee. This building, Hunt suggested, 'could, in fact, provide a satisfactory theatre for the Department of Drama as well as for the University Dramatic Societies'.[62] He further proposed that it might also house a professional company that would present 'plays of general

[53] RSA, uncat. box entitled 'Nuffield Theatre and Manchester University Theatre—Plans and Correspondence', Notes of meeting on 31 March 1962.

[54] UoM, VCA/7/573, Drama folder 1, William Mansfield Cooper to Profs Brook and Kermode, 21 December 1959.

[55] UoM, VCA/7/573, Drama folder 1, William Mansfield Cooper to Profs Brook and Kermode, 21 December 1959.

[56] UoM, VCA/7/573, Drama folder 1, Sidney Bernstein to William Mansfield Cooper, 20 October 1960; Cooper to Gerald Barry, 15 February 1961.

[57] JRL, Hugh Hunt box 12, Hugh Hunt, 'Slings and Arrows' [unpublished autobiography], p. 269.

[58] JRL, Hugh Hunt box 12, Hunt, 'Slings and Arrows', p. 272.

[59] UoM, VCA/7/573, Drama folder 2, 'Manchester University Theatre Project' [1961].

[60] JRL, Hugh Hunt box 12, Hunt, 'Slings and Arrows', p. 275.

[61] UoM, VCA/7/573, Drama folder 1, 'Notes on Bristol University Drama Department' [February 1960].

[62] UoM, VCA/7/573, Drama folder 3, Hugh Hunt to William Mansfield Cooper, 18 July 1962.

value to the University and to the city'.[63] Design work began in 1962. The architects were the Building Design Partnership, who were also designing new humanities buildings on the adjacent site. The theatre—which was dramatically remodelled in the late 1990s—was originally straightforward in its planning and appearance. It comprised a modest, brick-faced box with two levels of foyers at one end of the auditorium, whose flexibility, discussed in Chapter 8, was informed by the ideas of Hunt's colleague, Stephen Joseph. The foyers, it was reported, were designed with regard to 'the dual function of the theatre, a work place by day for students and lecturers, and a setting for the occasion of the evening performance with a public audience playing its part'.[64] With two levels, they included a small bar as well as provision for the sale of hot sausage rolls and other snacks.[65] The Century Theatre was an early professional 'resident'; later came the 69 Theatre Company (subsequently to move to the Royal Exchange), and then the Contact Theatre Company, whose work addressed young people and after whom the theatre was renamed.[66]

Warwick Arts Centre, as was noted at the start of this chapter, was intended to be a focus for the campus and beyond. The University of Warwick was founded as one of the 1960s 'new universities', with the initial buildings on its greenfield site being designed by Yorke Rosenberg and Mardall (YRM). Financial pressures meant that communal facilities were at first few and far between, and only at the end of the 1960s was there a concerted attempt to make greater provision for leisure on campus.[67] A 'theatre studio' and conference hall were planned, and Gulbenkian and Nuffield funding was secured, but a £400,000 benefaction in 1968 allowed the university to contemplate a larger development.[68] It was proposed that YRM might work with the prominent American architects Skidmore Owings and Merrill.[69] Their potential involvement suggests that the Arts Centre was seen in more elevated terms than YRM's otherwise fairly uniform academic buildings, an interpretation supported by the appointment as consultants of the Royal Shakespeare Company's Peter Hall and John Bury.[70] However, the centre was conceived at a difficult moment for Warwick. There was growing criticism by students of the university's apparently 'corporate' ethos, which YRM's rectilinear, white-tiled, 'International Style' architecture seemed to embody.[71] There were also technical problems with the white tiles themselves.[72] By 1970, the university was looking for new designers.[73] Gabriel Epstein took over as planner, while the firm of Renton

63 UoM, VCA/7/573, Drama folder 4, memo by Hunt on the university theatre, n.d.

64 JRL, Hugh Hunt box 12, 'University Theatre: University of Manchester October 5th 1965'.

65 JRL, SJ/1/43, Stephen Joseph to J. Gleave, 19 August 1964.

66 E.g. UoM, VCA/7/573, Drama folder 6, 'Application by the 69 Theatre Company [...] to Run the Professional Company', December 1967.

67 Muthesius, *Postwar University*, p. 122.

68 MRC, UWA/M/B/3/1, 'Arts Centre Stages 1 and 2' [paper of July 1970].

69 MRC, UWA/M/B/3/1, 'Arts Centre Stages 1 and 2'; also MRC, UWA/M/B/1/1, Building Committee, 5 November 1968, 13 January 1969, 4 February 1969.

70 For the uniformity of the YRM buildings, see Muthesius, *Postwar University*, p. 117.

71 Muthesius, *Postwar University*, p. 182; also 'An Uncertain Ethic', *Architectural Review* 157 (May 1975), pp. 267–8 (p. 267): 'factories for the production of corporate, managerial men'.

72 MRC, UWA/M/B/1/1, Building Committee, 20 October 1969.

73 MRC, UWA/M/B/1/1, Building Committee, 10 February 1970.

Howard Wood (RHW, later Renton Howard Wood Levin) was recommended for the Arts Centre by Hall and Bury.[74] RHW's Crucible Theatre in Sheffield counted in their favour, as did their experience of university design.

In its asymmetric massing, rough 'Forticrete' blocks, and 'craggy battlemented quality' (as the *Architectural Review* put it),[75] the Arts Centre productively contrasts with the slickness of YRM's buildings. Whereas YRM had favoured monofunctional zoning and individual 'object' buildings set within a grid-iron layout, RHW adopted a more complex planning strategy. The Arts Centre was arranged as part of a group with the Chaplaincy and administrative offices, with (as previously noted) a cross-campus pedestrian route not only connecting these buildings but also passing directly through the Arts Centre's foyers. As it approaches the centre from the north, the path is squeezed between buildings, evoking the narrow alleyways of the Italian hill towns that had apparently inspired the architects.[76] Once inside, however, spacious foyers open up on several levels in what the *Architectural Review* dubbed a 'concourse' that connects the centre's two auditoria, conference hall, and bookshop (see Figure 6.2).[77] The foyers originally included a coffee counter

Figure 6.2. 'Stepping into Las Vegas': Warwick Arts Centre, 1974 (Architectural Press Archive/RIBA Collections)

[74] Muthesius, *Postwar University*, p. 122; MRC, UWA/M/B/1/1, Building Committee, 27 April 1970.
[75] 'An Uncertain Ethic', p. 267.
[76] Nick Thompson, interviewed 20 June 2006.
[77] 'Warwick Arts Centre', *Architectural Review* 157 (May 1975), pp. 259–66 (p. 262).

and also a large bar. The original décor, which featured gloss-painted ceilings, exposed strip lighting, and unplastered blockwork, reprised the 'pop' ambiance of the Crucible, if in slightly less vibrant form, and its hard surfaces similarly blurred the boundary between inside and outside. The *Architectural Review* likened the effect to 'stepping from the dull, grey English countryside into Las Vegas'.[78] Although there are thus clear echoes of the Crucible in the Arts Centre's appearance and planning, RHW's design also suggested a kind of accessibility which responded to the intention that the centre might attract a wide audience. Indeed, in this respect, its name was significant:

> The very name 'Arts Centre' suggests to many a place where there is community participation in creative arts, rather than a place where excellent performances may be seen. Some are attracted by the word 'University', while many are to be wooed in spite of it [...]. Many think of it as a remote place, which might be hard of access and unwelcoming to the humble.[79]

And although growing student vociferousness warned against paternalism,[80] a desire to shape students' tastes had not entirely vanished. The vice chancellor in 1968 noted a 'gradual decline in the quality and general standard of life' on campus, with 'blaring music' audible in the afternoons.[81] In this context, the Arts Centre would perhaps be a civilized space in which students might congregate. (Congregate they did when the building opened, albeit for a 'sit-in'.)

Newcastle University Theatre would, it was hoped in 1968, similarly bring the public onto campus.[82] The university had become fully independent earlier in the decade and began a major development of its city-centre site. A benefaction originally intended for residences was diverted in 1964 to the construction of an 'experimental' theatre,[83] initially intended to serve the needs of university societies and occasionally to accommodate small visiting productions.[84] The university's architect, William Whitfield, began work during 1965.[85] By 1968, it was also proposed that the building provide 'adaptable facilities for the teaching of drama and opera of different countries and periods'.[86] However, achieving everything that was required within the £125,000 budget proved increasingly challenging.[87] It was suggested that the Tyneside Theatre Company might occupy the building for at least part of the year.[88] This decision necessitated an increase in the size of

78 'An Uncertain Ethic', p. 268.
79 MRC, UWA/NAD/AC/2/1, University of Warwick Arts Centre: Annual Report 1974/75.
80 MRC, UWA/R/5/1, 'Whose Arts? Whose Ents?' [1974 paper]: 'EVERY ASPECT OF THE CULTURAL LIFE OF THE STUDENT COMMUNITY IS UNDER FIRE AT THE MOMENT. NOW IS THE TIME TO ORGANISE' [capitals original].
81 MRC, UWA/M/B/1/3, 'The Halls and Social Buildings', paper of 1968.
82 UoN, 00-1196, letter to Councillor Arthur Grey, 4 October 1968.
83 UoN, 00-1196, letter to Councillor Arthur Grey, 4 October 1968; UoN, King's College Council minutes, 22 October 1962 (for the benefaction); Report of the Site Development Committee, 23 March 1964 (use for any building).
84 UoN, 00-1110, 'A Future for the Newcastle Playhouse'.
85 UoN, Site Development Committee minutes, 29 March 1965.
86 UoN, Council minutes, 4 March 1968.
87 UoN, Council minutes, 4 March 1968.
88 UoN, 00-1196, letter to Councillor Arthur Grey, 4 October 1968.

the auditorium but brought the potential for rental income. It also opened the door to a 'Housing the Arts' grant, because the theatre would be used by a professional company. Construction began in 1970: the combination of Arts Council funding, the original benefaction, and other grants allowed the theatre to go ahead at a time when many university building projects had stalled owing to restrictions in public expenditure on higher education.[89] As built, a single foyer was tucked below the auditorium rake (see Figure 6.3). It included a bar and snack counter, and informal groups of seating, although the theatre was distinctive for its inclusion of two further 'promenade' bars within the auditorium itself. The foyer bar was open during the day, with brochures describing it as an 'ideal lunchtime meeting place'.[90]

Many of these same themes were also given an airing in Wales, where major new theatres were located on institutional campuses in Aberystwyth (1972), Bangor (1975), Cardiff (1973), Harlech (1973), and Swansea (1984). For example, at University College, Cardiff, it was reported in December 1969 that the theatre then proposed for a site adjacent to the Students' Union would be an 'ideal meeting

Figure 6.3. Socializing in the foyer at Newcastle University Theatre, 1971 (Architectural Press Archive/RIBA Collections)

[89] UoN, 00-0053, Press Release, 22 April 1970.
[90] Reproduced in [ACGB], 'The Arts Council of Great Britain: the first twenty-five years' [report, 1972], p. 36.

place for all those interested in the performing arts'.[91] In a city where the main theatre had apparently recently been turned over to the showing of adult films, the university's plans were deemed 'essential to the well-being of our ever-renewed but permanent community'.[92] As elsewhere, this 'well-being' related both to the formation of students' cultural tastes and to what was described as 'the corporate life'.[93] The theatre was funded by the Sherman Trust, whose name it took. Initially planned with one auditorium, a further donation in July 1970 allowed the inclusion of a second. Designed by Alex Gordon and Partners, the Sherman was originally clad in dark brick, with rectangular forms and flat roofs, and was deemed 'sombre' and 'chastely detailed' by the *Architects' Journal*.[94] Its foyers were set between its two auditoria and were, in fact, relatively modest in size. They included only a bar and 'lounge', perhaps because the more extensive facilities of the Students' Union were adjacent to the theatre and were connected to it by an exhibition gallery.

The same architects were also responsible for Theatr-y-Werin at Aberystwyth. Here the theatre's community ambitions were made clear in its name, which (in the tradition of the German *Volksbühne*) translates as 'theatre of the people'. Indeed, *werin* has a specific Welsh cultural connotation of mythic 'simple folk', or peasants, being promoted by Iorwerth Peate at the Welsh Folk Museum, amongst others. The name of the building is also significant within the specific context of the university at Aberystwyth, which promoted the study of Welsh language and literature as academic subjects. The theatre was intended to respond to 'the present and future needs of the town [...], the county areas, and the University College' by providing facilities for staff and student drama, local amateur groups, and visiting professional companies.[95] It would also form a focal point, being located adjacent to (and sharing foyers with) the Great Hall (by the Percy Thomas Partnership, 1970). Its concrete exterior echoed the Great Hall's materials but swapped the hall's sculptural forms for a rather more banal blocky massing, prompting the *AJ* to conclude that the theatre felt like a 'poor relation'.[96] It was presumably deliberately subordinate to the Great Hall, which was the university's main ceremonial centre. Nonetheless, the *AJ*'s conclusion that both Theatr-y-Werin and the Sherman were architecturally 'straightforward [...] in a consistent, unaffected idiom' suggests that they might be understood as examples of the same kind of undogmatic modernism as many other new theatres of this period.

How successful were these venues in bringing together 'town and gown'? In Bangor, Theatr Gwynedd's wine bar was reported in 1978 to be popular with students, college lecturers, and the staff of nearby offices, 'who simply call in for a bite to eat'.[97] However, other examples suggest the need to tread cautiously. At Newcastle, it was noted that the theatre's chunky brick architecture was 'often criticised for the

[91] CUA, UCC/R/F/71, Draft Press Release, December 1969.
[92] CUA, UCC Misc/Pub/1, 'The Sherman Theatre is Five'.
[93] CUA, Address by Dr C. W. L. Bevan to the Court of Governors, 10 November 1967, with Reports of the Council.
[94] 'Sherman Theatre; Theatr-y-Werin', *Architects' Journal* 160 (24 July 1974), pp. 207–23 (p. 216).
[95] 'Sherman Theatre; Theatr-y-Werin', p. 210.
[96] 'Sherman Theatre; Theatr-y-Werin', p. 217.
[97] 'Theatr Gwynedd', *Stage*, 9 March 1978.

enigmatic face it presents to the passer-by', although it 'generally delights those who enter it' (see Figure 4.1, Chapter 4).[98] There was apparently a sense that local people viewed it as a 'university' venue, rather than somewhere for the public at large. Students, too, could be hard to please, as the example of the University of Stirling demonstrates. There, the Macrobert Arts Centre (RMJM, 1971) occupies a central place on campus, being located, like Warwick Arts Centre, astride the pedestrian route that connects the teaching and residential buildings. Originally conceived as a hall for graduation ceremonies, it was quickly concluded that a more intensively used arts centre would be a better use of money.[99] Such a centre appealed to the interest in the arts of the university's principal, Tom Cottrell, and better addressed the idea, expressed in the 1966 development plan, that the newly founded university should engage with the local community.[100] However, *Architectural Design* wrote in 1973 that 'many students feel that the Centre does little to assist town and gown relationships'.[101] In the light of Anthony Field's observations on the dreary worthiness that sometimes pervaded discussions of the social centre, as noted earlier in the chapter, we might therefore ask: did this sort of venue ever work well? The extent to which ideas of community participation started to change during the 1970s and 1980s is also significant, as Chapter 10 will consider.

CONCLUSIONS: A 'SOCIAL AND CULTURAL CENTRE'

This chapter has explored a recurring theme in the conception of new regional and university theatres, namely the idea that these buildings could be understood as community and social centres, with potentially expansive public facilities. This idea found particularly clear expression in the example of the Thorndike Theatre, Leatherhead, and so the chapter concludes with a discussion of this theatre, and with two other theatres by the same architect, Roderick Ham.

The Thorndike Theatre—named after the renowned actress, Sybil Thorndike—replaced the old Leatherhead Repertory Theatre in 1969. When the new theatre was under construction, the site hoardings described it as 'Surrey's New Social and Cultural Centre', as was noted at the start of the chapter.[102] The placement of 'social' before 'cultural' was significant. Leatherhead's energetic director, Hazel Vincent Wallace, was an early advocate of the theatre as a social centre, arguing in 1958 that women theatre managers had a greater aptitude for creating a welcoming

[98] UoN, 00-1196, 'The University Theatre, 1970–71' [report to University Council].

[99] UoSt, UA/File/1, Development Committee Paper D/5 [November 1966], p. 7: 'the likely usage of a hall designed mainly for graduations (which occur relatively seldom) suggests that the building should be designed for other important communal purposes, and be used if possible for graduation ceremonies. The main suggested purpose of the building was that it should be an arts centre for the University.'

[100] UoSt, uncat., University of Stirling Interim Development Plan, 1966, paras 3.1–3.7.

[101] Peter Murray, 'University of Stirling', *Architectural Design* 43, no. 3 (March 1973), pp. 154–75 (p. 170).

[102] See also 'The Theatre That Had to Happen', *The Times*, 8 September 1969.

and convivial atmosphere than their male counterparts.[103] Having worked successfully in London, she had moved to Leatherhead in 1951, taking over the Victoria Hall.[104] Built in 1890 as a theatre, the hall had become a cinema in the 1920s before reverting to live drama in the 1940s after the opening of the nearby Crescent Cinema. Wallace ran the theatre as a private club, partly in order to satisfy the fire regulations; by the 1960s there were 14,000 members. A bar had opened in the basement before Wallace's arrival, and a coffee bar followed in the early 1950s with such success that one local café owner complained that she was depriving him of custom. Her approach was partly rooted in common sense. Food and drink attracted new patrons, and in this respect Wallace reported that pre- and post-theatre suppers had contributed to the growth of the audience as well as its diversification: 'after about three years, the audience was 50 per cent male, instead of being made up of old ladies,' she later remembered.[105] The men, she went on, 'came along originally because they liked the food and the bar—and then started to enjoy the plays!' However, the old theatre was too small in the face of growing audience demand, while its somewhat makeshift backstage facilities were increasingly inadequate. In 1964, Wallace was therefore pleased to receive a proposal from a local property firm, the Reeves Trust, to convert the Crescent Cinema, which it owned, into a theatre.[106]

Wallace's idea of a 'social and cultural centre' informed her vision for the new theatre. 'I believe so much in creating a happy atmosphere, with plenty of personal contact, food, and a well-stocked bar', she noted at the time.[107] In the *Illustrated London News*, she described the theatre as 'a community project', explaining that 'we're concentrating on our restaurant facilities, exhibitions, film shows and concerts, as well as the best in drama'.[108] However, the initial plans for the new theatre, prepared by the Reeves Trust's architect, Norman Minter of C. Lovatt Gill,[109] failed to impress. Wallace wrote in April 1965 that they had 'no architectural value' as well as 'snags' including a shallow stage, poor workshop facilities, and inadequate rehearsal and public spaces.[110] Minter was swiftly replaced by Roderick Ham. He had acted and directed whilst a student,[111] and his interests had led to a meeting with Sir Greville Poke, the founding secretary and later chairman of the English Stage Company at the Royal Court. As it happened, Poke also chaired the board at Leatherhead, perhaps making Ham's appointment inevitable when the Minter

[103] 'The Women Score Over the Men', *Stage*, 4 September 1958, p. 12.
[104] Hazel Vincent Wallace, interviewed 26 October 2006.
[105] 'The Theatre That Had to Happen', *The Times*, 8 September 1969.
[106] SHC, 6368/3/9, Hazel Vincent Wallace to L. Lamden, 22 May 1964.
[107] 'The Theatre That Had to Happen', *The Times*, 8 September 1969.
[108] V&A, Theatre Collections Thorndike file, clipping from the *Illustrated London News*, 15 March 1969.
[109] C. Lovett Gill had been one of the architects of the Crescent Cinema in 1939. See 'Leatherhead Theatre', <http://cinematreasures.org/theaters/24800> (accessed 5 November 2015). He practised with Albert Richardson until the latter's death in 1960.
[110] SHC, 6368/3/9, Hazel Vincent Wallace note, 6 April 1965.
[111] Roderick Ham, interviewed 5 October 2005.

scheme proved problematic.[112] In addition, Ham's membership of the Association of British Theatre Technicians' Theatre Architecture and Planning Committee meant that he had reviewed Minter's designs in January 1966.[113] Within a month, Ham had taken over the job, and in April that year an application was made for 'Housing the Arts' funding.[114] However, the bulk of the money was raised locally, with Wallace quipping that the new theatre was built on 'goodwill and coffee mornings'.[115] In this respect, the size of the theatre club and the loyalty of its members were key. Wallace—described as 'the first woman to build a theatre in Britain'—ascribed much of the success of the fundraising drive to the efforts of women members of the club.[116]

In August 1966, a preview of Ham's scheme appeared in the *Architects' Journal*, and relatively little changed between then and the opening of the theatre three years later (see Figure 6.4).[117] The Thorndike is set behind a four-storey block of shops and offices, which replaced the cinema's frontage (and was not designed by Ham). A corridor running through this block gives access to the theatre. The auditorium was constructed within the walls of the former cinema auditorium. To its rear and sides, Ham added the facilities needed by the repertory company, including spacious workshops (since demolished).[118] The essentially hidden nature of the theatre, located behind shops and partly within the shell of an older building, meant that Ham's opportunities for external expression were limited. The principal new elevation is to the side, and here Ham produced a bold, even playful composition. A pair of doors is framed by slender piers which seem almost too slim to support the concrete-fronted balcony above, while a projecting 'box' of solid concrete, some two storeys tall, hovers improbably above a large area of glass.

The foyers were inserted into the gap between the shops and the auditorium (see Figure 6.5), where they rise through three storeys. Ham referred to 'one large open space with open galleries and staircases in it giving all kinds of interesting views and relationships'.[119] The dominant materials are brick and board-marked concrete, the latter used not only for walls but also as an upstand to the galleries, where its visual weight is complemented by chunky timber balustrades. During the day, light filters into the foyers through glass-topped square ceiling boxes, whilst at

112 Roderick Ham, video of 1999 interview by the Association of British Theatre Technicians (copy at the V&A Theatre Collections, viewed in 2007); Hazel Vincent Wallace, interviewed 26 October 2006.

113 ABTT Archives, Notes on a review of the proposed Leatherhead Repertory Theatre, 10 January 1966. The auditorium was described as being fan-shaped at the front and rectangular at back, with a central gangway and wide proscenium arch.

114 V&A, ACGB/84/149, Greville Poke to J. L. Hodgkinson, 28 February 1966; Hazel Vincent Wallace to J. L. Hodgkinson, 20 April 1966.

115 'The Theatre That Had to Happen', *The Times*, 8 September 1969.

116 'The Theatre That Had to Happen', *The Times*, 8 September 1969.

117 'Leatherhead—Cinema into Theatre Conversion', *Architects' Journal* 144 (24 August 1966), pp. 448–9.

118 Hazel Vincent Wallace, interviewed 31 October 2015.

119 SHC, 6368/3/9 [Roderick Ham], 'New Leatherhead Theatre'.

Figure 6.4. Axonometric drawing by Roderick Ham of the Thorndike Theatre, *c.*1967, showing its compact planning, with the auditorium constructed within the shell of the former Crescent Cinema (The Theatres Trust)

night the pattern is ingeniously reversed, with fluorescent lighting illuminating the gaps between the now-darkened boxes. The foyers can be understood as an example of 'modern monumentality', providing a three-dimensional setting which demands to be populated and animated by the theatre's patrons. However, it is surely the

Figure 6.5. A spatial tour-de-force: the Thorndike Theatre foyer in 1969 (Richard Einzig/Arcaid)

extensive space given to social activity which is the most significant feature of the Thorndike. A coffee bar—which was originally open all day and served snacks—is tucked below the auditorium, while the upper part of the building included a restaurant and club room. Exhibitions were staged in the upper foyer. The restaurant was evidently soon in demand: in a comment that would surely have pleased those who saw new theatres as a rebuttal of Americanization, *Concrete Quarterly* recorded that, on the day of its reporter's visit, the Thorndike's bar was busy while the local Wimpy hamburger restaurant was empty.[120] That said, not all welcomed the focus on the social. One patron's complaint about the noise of small children in the foyers was rebuffed by Wallace: this was, she said, a 'community centre'.[121]

The Thorndike was an accomplished design which definitively established Ham's status as a specialist in theatre architecture, just as Nottingham Playhouse had done for Peter Moro earlier in the decade. Like Moro, Ham sat on key committees and shared his knowledge in print, notably in his 1972 book, *Theatre Planning*.

[120] 'Thorndike Theatre, Leatherhead', *Concrete Quarterly* 84 (Spring 1970), pp. 34–40 (p. 38).
[121] SHC, 6368/4/1, Leatherhead Theatre Club minutes, 9 October 1969.

After 1967, he worked on designs for the new Derby Playhouse,[122] followed by proposals for theatres at High Wycombe (unbuilt), Bedford (also unbuilt), and Ipswich. Derby Playhouse, whose location within the city's Eagle Centre was discussed in Chapter 5, was conceived like the Thorndike as 'a community theatre',[123] and had similarly extensive foyers. Like the Thorndike, it presented little in the way of a public 'front': a set of doors, topped by an illuminated canopy, was all that distinguished the entrance to the theatre from the adjacent shops. (Only from the rear can much more of the theatre be seen externally, with its virtually windowless purple brick walls having a monolithic quality.) Ham reported that he had 'decided that the best way of treating the entrance to the foyer was to restrict it so that there is a sense of surprise as one emerges from the relatively narrow neck into the large double height open space of the foyer'.[124] Here, the Thorndike's mixture of brick and concrete gave way to a preponderance of brick (since plastered), while curving stairs and walls introduced a more sinuous note than is evident at Leatherhead. A coffee bar served snacks, while a restaurant was planned with seating arranged in booths. In the *Architectural Review*, Colin Amery welcomed the Playhouse's architectural directness and simplicity, concluding that it featured an 'unpretentious architectural sensibility' and was 'refreshingly free of architectural and theatrical dogmas'.[125] He noted the three-dimensional quality of the foyers and the views between its different levels, although one of these views was apparently less than successful in that it seemed to focus on a large free-standing ashtray.

By June 1969, Ham was also busy with designs for the Dove Arts Centre at High Wycombe (see Figure 6.6). This centre was promoted by a group of residents and business representatives, who evoked a familiar trope in claiming that South Buckinghamshire had 'nothing much to offer a society whose leisure expands all the time and will expand even more with ever increasing automation'.[126] Roderick Ham was commissioned to remedy the situation.[127] Whereas his theatres in Derby and Leatherhead had been relatively hidden, the Dove was to be built on a prominent site in the town centre, adjacent to a railway viaduct and facing a new dual carriageway. Elevations of yellow brick were to be topped by a deep band of strongly textured concrete. The colour of the brick was a deliberate choice, Ham believing that it would highlight the shadows created by the building's curved forms.[128] The auditorium and stage were located on the widest part of the site, with the foyers tapering symmetrically towards a circular exhibition gallery at the building's apex, the form of which was echoed in a sunken coffee bar. The symmetries in these

[122] DRO, D738/4/1, 'Derby Playhouse Design Report', April 1970, p. 2.
[123] DRO, D738/4/1, D. V. W. Malin to Norman Fisher, 30 June 1969.
[124] DRO, D738/4/1, 'Derby Playhouse Design Report', April 1970, p. 10.
[125] 'Theatre, Inverness; Theatre, Derby', *Architectural Review* 160 (October 1976), pp. 212–15 (p. 215).
[126] TTT, Roderick Ham archive, 'THE DOVE: a professional arts and entertainments centre for South Bucks' [1970].
[127] TTT, Roderick Ham archive, 'HIGH WYCOMBE THEATRE AND ARTS CENTRE' [October 1969].
[128] TTT, Roderick Ham archive, Roderick Ham to Fred Pooley, 18 October 1971.

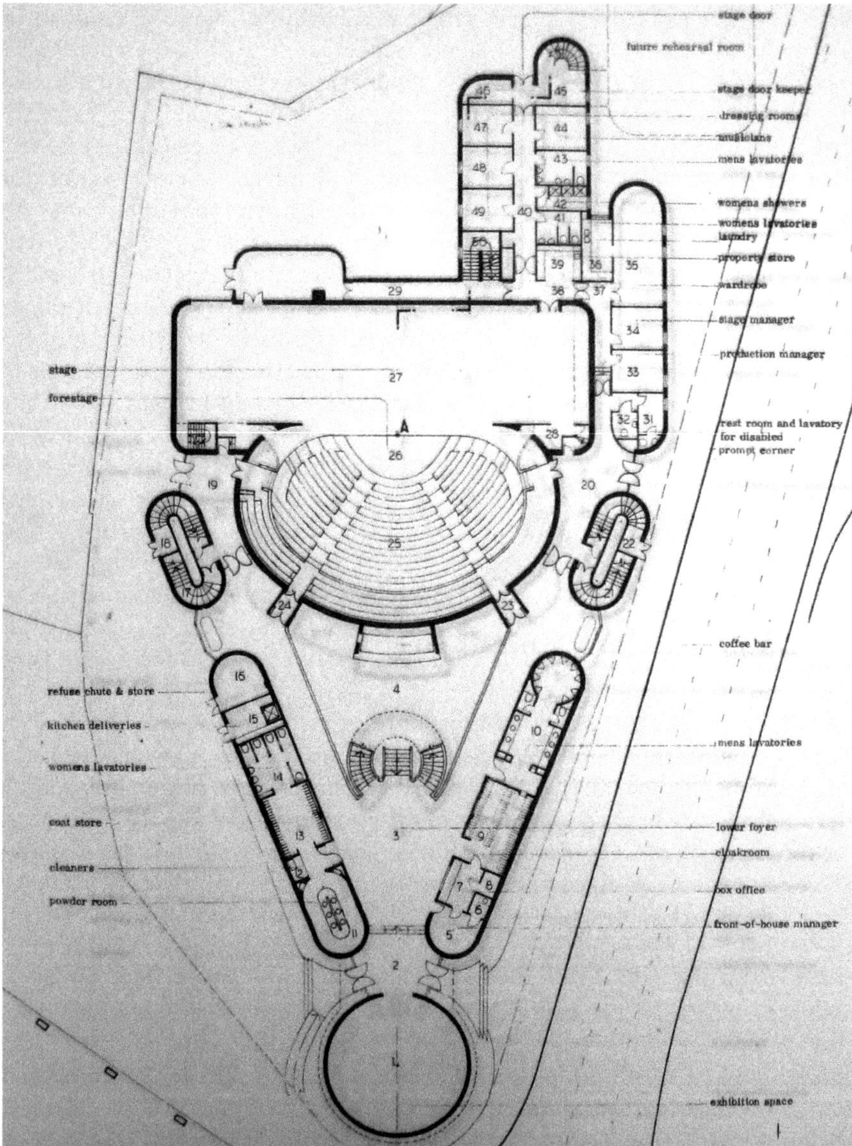

Figure 6.6. Beaux-Arts symmetry: ground floor plan of Roderick Ham's Dove Arts Centre, High Wycombe, *c.*1971 (The Theatres Trust)

spaces have an almost Beaux-Arts formality, not least in their grand central stair, but were conceived in evidently informal terms:

> The building is the place where all sorts of things happen, where it is fun to go, where there is always something unexpected possible. There will be plays, films, pop concerts, ballet, musicals, recitals, cabaret, exhibitions of paintings, photographs and sculpture, good food and drink and a place to drop in and meet friends at any time.[129]

Again, therefore, sociability was important in the centre's conception, as it had been in the other examples considered in this chapter. However, Buckinghamshire County Council proved reluctant to part-fund the project, and despite the adoption of innovative fundraising methods, including a local football pools 'pontoon', it was eventually abandoned.[130] It would not be the only time that one of Ham's projects was to remain unrealized during the 1970s, as Chapter 7 discusses further.

[129] TTT, Roderick Ham archive, Roderick Ham to Fred Pooley, 18 October 1971.
[130] 'A Flutter on the Dove?', *Bucks Free Press*, 19 January 1973 [copy in the Roderick Ham archive at the Theatres Trust].

7

'At the End of a Boom?'

Frugality and Contextualism, *c.*1968–85

In 1974, a team which included the architect Peter Moro was selected to design and build an entertainment and commercial centre in central Plymouth.[1] To be realized by a developer with private investment on a site next to Plymouth's recently completed civic centre, the complex was to include a new Theatre Royal. The developer soon withdrew, but the city authorities decided to build a theatre on the site anyway, and Moro retained the job. Fierce arguments about the merits of the project raged among councillors and in the local press. As was discussed in Chapter 2, the size and use of the theatre were much debated.[2] Its basic design principles had been established by the start of 1978, when, to cut costs, a metre-wide strip was shaved from the perimeter of the building.[3] The Theatre Royal, which opened in 1982, exemplified many of the ideas that have been explored in previous chapters (see Figure 7.1). Conceptually, the project was motivated by ideas of civic pride, the wish to create a 'heart' within a city centre that had been substantially reconstructed after wartime damage, and a desire to attract tourists and conferences to Plymouth. The theatre's facilities and planning, too, reprise familiar themes: for example, its spacious foyers include a large restaurant. Furthermore, the design of the theatre developed principles evident in earlier projects by Moro's office. Its volumetric massing and strongly geometric form evoke the Nottingham Playhouse of nearly two decades before, while the octagons that dominate its plan bring to mind other Moro theatres such as the Gulbenkian Centre at Hull and the Riverside Theatre, Coleraine. The composition of its external elevations also recalls Nottingham Playhouse. The lower foyer elevation is glazed, with the main stair being located next to it as a way to animate the building. The upper elevations' slot-like windows reprise Moro's initial proposals for Nottingham. They were originally faced in bronze, perhaps as a 'luxury' foil to the concrete blockwork used elsewhere, not least on the exterior of the theatre's two auditoria.

[1] PCL, Theatre Royal file, 'Civic Theatre Goal Within Sight', *Western Morning News*, 13 December 1974. For a full account, see Alistair Fair, '"A London Architect Who Has Specialised": Peter Moro and festivity in theatre design, *c.*1955–82', in *Setting the Scene: Perspectives on Twentieth-century Theatre Architecture*, edited by Alistair Fair (Farnham, 2015), pp. 133–62.

[2] E.g. PCL, Theatre Royal file, 'Theatre: can it be stopped?', *Western Evening Herald*, 10 February 1978.

[3] PCL, Theatre Royal file, 'Theatre "Shrink" Operation Close to £750,000 Cut', *Western Morning News*, 4 February 1978.

Figure 7.1. Business as usual? Theatre Royal, Plymouth, 1982 (RIBA Collections)

Yet is a conclusion of 'business as usual' justified? The context in which new theatres were conceived and built during the 1970s and early 1980s was often challenging. In December 1969, Roderick Ham met with the Arts Council of Great Britain's finance director, Anthony Field, to discuss the rising costs that were increasingly affecting theatre-building projects.[4] Ham predicted an increase of some 29 per cent during the following eighteen months, partly because of wage claims being lodged by the unions. This development would, he said, 'have a profound effect on Housing the Arts schemes'. Hugh Willatt in November 1973 suggested that building costs had in fact increased by over 70 per cent since 1970, and a pencil note on the archived copy of his letter states that this number was an underestimate.[5] As was noted in Chapter 2, inflation was accompanied by pressure on the Arts Council's 'Housing the Arts' commitment ration as well as cuts in government expenditure. In several cases, too, fundraising appeals failed. In such circumstances, Willatt noted in his 1973 letter, economy was advisable.

Willatt's recommendation reflected a growing sense of pessimism. The 1970s has sometimes been characterized as a dismal decade in British history, a period of

[4] V&A, ACGB/84/149, Meeting of Roderick Ham, Greville Poke, Michael Marriott, and Anthony Field, 19 December 1969.

[5] V&A, ACGB/120/35, Hugh Willatt to C. W. Wright, 13 November 1973.

economic and political turbulence beset by strikes, inflation, and unemployment.[6] The perception of crisis that pervaded some contemporary commentaries extended to discussions of the built environment.[7] From the late 1960s, modern architecture and planning were increasingly criticized. Several prominent failures called into question recent material and structural innovations. Critics also attacked the foundations on which modern architecture had been built.[8] Had attempts to rethink urban planning genuinely resulted in a humane environment? Were post-war institutional buildings really an improvement on their predecessors? What did the residents of high-rise housing think of their homes? Had modern architects' apparent rejection of overt historical references led to buildings which failed to 'fit in' with their surroundings? Plymouth Theatre Royal, to take one example, was in 1982 deemed by Dan Cruickshank to turn a 'chilling concrete shoulder' to its surroundings,[9] although the most infamous example of this line of thinking came in the form of the Prince of Wales's attack in 1984 on the proposals for the extension of the National Gallery. At the same time, inflation caused many of the grander visions of the 1960s to be curtailed, leaving unfilled gaps in town centres and half-completed institutional development plans. As the 1980s dawned, the neo-liberal ideology of Margaret Thatcher's government set itself in opposition to the welfare state consensus of the previous three decades. It implied a reduction in the size of the public sector and, by extension, the number of major state-led building projects.

In recent years, however, social and political historians have productively challenged both the declinist view of the 1970s and the association of the 1980s with Thatcherism alone. Alternative frameworks have been established, such as 'de-industrialization not decline', along with chronologies that look beyond political milestones to emphasize positive developments in such areas as women's rights.[10] Architectural and urban historians are also increasingly engaging with the 1970s and 1980s, exploring in detail how the assumptions of the previous two decades were challenged.[11] Yet there were also important continuities in this period's architecture and planning. Overtly referential 'postmodern' styles coexisted with subtle contextual modernisms that drew on a longer tradition of regionalism in modern architecture. The 'high tech' aesthetic married the structural rationalism of nineteenth-century engineering with the 1960s technological fantasies of Archigram to create what was, in effect, a rebooted modernism. And within the sphere of planning,

[6] Lawrence Black, 'An Enlightening Decade? New histories of 1970s Britain', *International Labor and Working-Class History* 82 (2012), pp. 174–86 (pp. 174–5).

[7] E.g. Malcolm Macewen, *Crisis in Architecture* (London, 1974).

[8] E.g. the *Architectural Review*'s MANPLAN series of the late 1960s and the early 1970s.

[9] 'Raising the Roof', *Architects' Journal* 175 (12 May 1982), pp. 32–4 (p. 32).

[10] Black, 'An Enlightening Decade?'; Matthew Hilton, Chris Moores, and Florence Sutcliffe-Braithwaite, 'New Times Revisited: Britain in the 1980s', *Contemporary British History* 31, no. 2 (2017), pp. 145–65; Jim Tomlinson, 'De-industrialization Not Decline: a new meta-narrative for post-war British history', *Twentieth Century British History* 27, no. 1 (2016), pp. 76–99.

[11] E.g. Elain Harwood and Alan Powers, 'From Downtown to Diversity: revisiting the 1970s', *Twentieth Century Architecture* 10 (2012), pp. 9–36; Simon Gunn, 'Ring Road: Birmingham and the collapse of the motor city ideal in 1970s Britain', *Historical Journal*, early online publication 2017.

the 'conservative urban surgery' which increasingly supplanted the comprehensive redevelopments of the 1960s also had a modernist pedigree.

As far as theatre-building is concerned, both pessimistic and optimistic interpretations are possible. George Rowell and Anthony Jackson's history of the repertory movement concluded in 1984 that the late 1970s marked the end of thirty years of 'optimism and expansiveness', while the director Michael Elliott commented in 1976 that 'we are at the end [...] of a theatre building boom'.[12] Nonetheless, the construction of major subsidized civic and repertory theatre buildings continued through this period; indeed, the 1970s was the key decade in Scotland. Those theatres figure large in this chapter, which argues that the concept of the modern playhouse survived through the 1970s, and that it continued to evolve. The discussion begins with several notable unbuilt examples before continuing with a selection of theatres that demonstrate the continuing creativity of theatre managements and architects in sometimes challenging circumstances.

'THE VOLUME OF PUBLIC RESOURCES': UNBUILT THEATRES AND MONSTER PROJECTS

In 1963, the Lincoln architects Denis Clarke Hall and Sam Scorer were asked to survey the city's Theatre Royal.[13] They concluded that a new building would be a better investment than patching up the old theatre. In 1965, a site for the 'New Lincolnshire Theatre' was identified on the waterfront,[14] and £100,000 was promised by the Arts Council.[15] Grants were secured from the city and county authorities, and from other local districts, hence the emphasis in the theatre's name on 'Lincolnshire' as opposed to Lincoln alone. Scorer's design featured a roof suspended by means of cables from two massive poles,[16] demonstrating the structural virtuosity for which he had become known as a result of such projects as a petrol station at Markham Moor, whose bold concrete roof form was realized with the engineer Dr K. Hajnal-Kónyi. However, the New Lincolnshire Theatre was not to be. One local newspaper referred in early 1976 to a 'very expensive and pointless trip into fantasy'.[17] By October 1975, the Arts Council had withdrawn its offer of funding, and soon the Lincoln Theatre Association was in liquidation.[18] Although the project had become entangled in politics following local government reorganization in 1974, with the new Lincoln City Council seeking to dispose of the site which

[12] George Rowell and Anthony Jackson, *The Repertory Movement: A History of Regional Theatre in Britain* (Cambridge, 1984), pp. 91, 96–8; 'Exchange Experience', *Architectural Review* 160 (December 1976), pp. 361–2.

[13] V&A, ACGB/84/163, 'The Facts—The Lincolnshire New Theatre' [1971].

[14] V&A, ACGB/84/163, 'The Facts'.

[15] V&A, ACGB/84/163, Peter Longman memo, 13 May 1975.

[16] 'Lincoln Theatre Near Denouement', *Architects' Journal* 156 (15 November 1972), pp. 1108–9.

[17] V&A, ACGB/84/163, clipping: '£100,000 Bill for No-hope Trust Project', *Lincoln Chronicle*, 4 November 1976.

[18] V&A, ACGB/84/163, Roy Shaw to P. H. Newlove, 29 October 1975; also clipping: 'New Theatre Hope in Lincs', *Lincolnshire Echo*, 10 January 1976.

its predecessor had earmarked for the theatre,[19] the principal cause of the project's demise was financial. In 1971, it was estimated that the theatre would cost £446,000, but by September 1974 the figure had risen to £1.25 million.[20] The local authority referred to the state of the economy: 'the volume of public resources [...] was too great, taking into account the current economic situation, other claims upon money, and, in particular, public dissatisfaction with the rates'.[21] Attention turned instead to the refurbishment of the Theatre Royal.

The New Lincolnshire Theatre was not the only project to suffer these kinds of difficulties at this time. For example, Peter Moro's office prepared several schemes for an arts centre in Brentford, west London, between 1975 and 1977.[22] As proposed in September 1975, the centre was to include an octagonal multipurpose hall (with a studio theatre below), separated from a large theatre by a spacious foyer that stepped down to the River Thames. The public and backstage areas were wrapped around the two auditoria and were to be faced with large concrete panels whose round windows had appropriately nautical overtones. By October 1976, the brief had been scaled back to save money. Moro now proposed a building which was square in plan, with a single octagonal auditorium. Its elevations were also simplified, with strip windows and large areas of glazing to the foyers. Though the designs were published in January 1978, fundraising difficulties persisted, and the project collapsed.[23]

Scotland's two biggest schemes of the 1970s were similarly abandoned. However, these projects caution against simply assuming that all unbuilt theatres were the victims of economic circumstance alone. The first example is the unbuilt Glasgow Cultural Centre, first proposed in the mid-1960s. As was discussed in Chapter 5, the centre was to rehouse the Citizens' (repertory) Theatre alongside a concert hall and a new Royal Scottish Academy of Music and Drama (RSAMD). After the city architect's proposals were rejected, the prominent architect and educator Leslie Martin took over. However, the price tag was more than the city could bear, and was also well beyond the scope of 'Housing the Arts'. Only the concert hall was eventually built on the intended site. Edinburgh's contemporaneous ambitions to build a major theatre met a similar fate after several false dawns and protracted debate in the local press about the wisdom of the project and the apparent inability of those in authority to enable it.[24] One civil servant reflected on the saga upon its end in 1975 that 'few of those who have been personally involved [...] will be anxious

[19] V&A, ACGB/84/163, clipping: 'Legal Battle Is Forecast Over Brayford Site', *Lincolnshire Echo*, 8 April 1975.

[20] V&A, ACGB/84/163, Councillors' meeting, 26 September 1974.

[21] V&A, ACGB/84/163, Philip Watts to A. Wickstead, 15 April 1975.

[22] Peter Moro Partnership, 'Report Presented to the Hounslow Arts Trust Limited', September 1975, and 'Report Presented to the Hounslow Arts Trust Limited', October 1976. Copies kindly supplied by Andrzej Blonski. See also 'Hounslow Arts Centre, Brentford', *Architectural Review* 163 (January 1978), p. 48.

[23] Watermans Arts Centre was subsequently opened in 1984 to the designs of Oscar Garry and Partners, being part-financed by the developer of an adjacent office building.

[24] The following summarizes Alistair Fair, '"An Object Lesson in How Not To Get Things Done": Edinburgh's unbuilt "opera house", 1960–75', *Architectural Heritage* 27 (2017), pp. 91–117.

to repeat the experience'.[25] In 1949, two years after the city's inaugural Festival, the planner Patrick Abercrombie proposed the construction of a substantial theatre adjacent to the Usher Hall, and several proposals followed. A commercial developer, Meyer Oppenheim, offered in 1960 to build the theatre as part of a bigger development; it would then be sold to the city. By 1964, Oppenheim's proposals had been abandoned amid doubts about their viability, but the city authorities remained keen to build a theatre for large-scale drama and operatic performances. The so-called 'opera house' was taken over by the City Council, which retained Oppenheim's architect, William Kininmonth of Rowand Anderson, Kininmonth and Paul (RAKP).[26] RAKP's 1966 proposals look not unlike Le Corbusier's monastery at La Tourette, while a revised design of 1968 has a vaguely Art Deco character, with horizontal strip windows and a series of column-like vertical bands at the entrance. It seemed as if construction would soon begin, and the site was cleared. However, the so-called 'hole in the ground' was not to be quickly filled.

As in Glasgow, the project was more expensive than Edinburgh could afford, and so an appeal was made to central government.[27] Jennie Lee expressed interest but failed to make a firm commitment, while the 1970 general election introduced a further delay.[28] A promise of funding eventually materialized in August 1971. The Corporation was offered either 50 per cent of an agreed final capital cost, or the equivalent of £2.25 million at current prices.[29] However, the tide now turned against Kininmonth. A campaign, partly orchestrated from within the Scottish Office, was waged against his design and perceived managerial competence.[30] Attempts to force the architects to form a 'limited project partnership' proved unsuccessful, and RAKP withdrew in late 1972. Several alternative architects' names entered the frame: the two front runners were Renton Howard Wood, and Robert Matthew, Johnson-Marshall (RMJM). The former had recently completed the well-received Crucible in Sheffield, while the latter was a major firm that had a large office in the city. It duly secured the project.

RMJM's designs for what was now a 1400-seat theatre with a 250-seat studio auditorium were published in summer 1974.[31] The main face of the building was to comprise a wall of glass, tilted back from the pavement and curved around the corner of two streets, prompting inevitable comments about 'a space age scheme' (see Figure 7.2).[32] However, the Royal Fine Art Commission for Scotland was

[25] NRS, ED61/59, J. Kidd memo, 11 July 1975.

[26] By the late 1960s, Kininmonth's office was also designing the Brunton Theatre, Musselburgh, which opened in 1971. For their 'opera house' designs, see Fair, '"An Object Lesson"'.

[27] NRS, ED61/72, I. M. Robertson memo, 2 December 1966.

[28] 'Lyceum £2m. Aid Hopes Soar', *Edinburgh Evening News*, 2 December 1966; 'Give Us Our Opera House', *Scotsman*, 18 July 1970.

[29] NRS, ED61/85, I. M. Robertson to Town Clerk, 20 August 1971.

[30] NRS, ED61/85, I. M. Robertson memo, 27 September 1971; 'Opera Architect Accuses Civil Servants', *Scotsman*, 21 October 1972. Fair, '"An Object Lesson"', gives a detailed account.

[31] HES, RMJM uncat. boxes 197 and 198.

[32] 'Opera House on Show', *Edinburgh Evening News*, 5 July 1974.

Figure 7.2. Spaceship modern: RMJM's 1974 design for the Castle Terrace Theatre, Edinburgh (RIBA Collections)

concerned about the extent to which the building would dominate its site.[33] The volume of accommodation required was such that the foyers were cantilevered above the surrounding streets. By 1975, RMJM had reduced the height of the fly tower, which had come in for particular criticism, while the elevations were now to be composed of horizontal stone and glass bands (see Figure 7.3).[34] These bands, which stepped back in apparent emulation of the National Theatre's terraces, reduced the building's bulk; they also evoke the horizontality of contemporaneous 'civic' projects by RMJM, including Edinburgh's Commonwealth Pool (1970). However, by now the cost of the project had risen substantially, to the dismay of the Scottish Office.[35] It was estimated that some £20 million was needed not only to build the theatre but also to connect it to the Usher Hall and the Lyceum Theatre, which was to be refurbished.[36] Local government reorganization in 1975 also proved unhelpful. The new Edinburgh district authority had a limited appetite

[33] 'Commission Object to Scale of Opera House', *Scotsman*, 8 August 1974.

[34] HES, RMJM uncat. box 446, and reproduced in Fair, '"An Object Lesson"'.

[35] NRS, ED61/88, Robert Hughes memo, 29 July 1974: 'It may be that [...] the successor authority [...] will have second thoughts and relieve us of having to make a decision.'

[36] NRS, ED61/88, Robert Hughes memo, 29 July 1974.

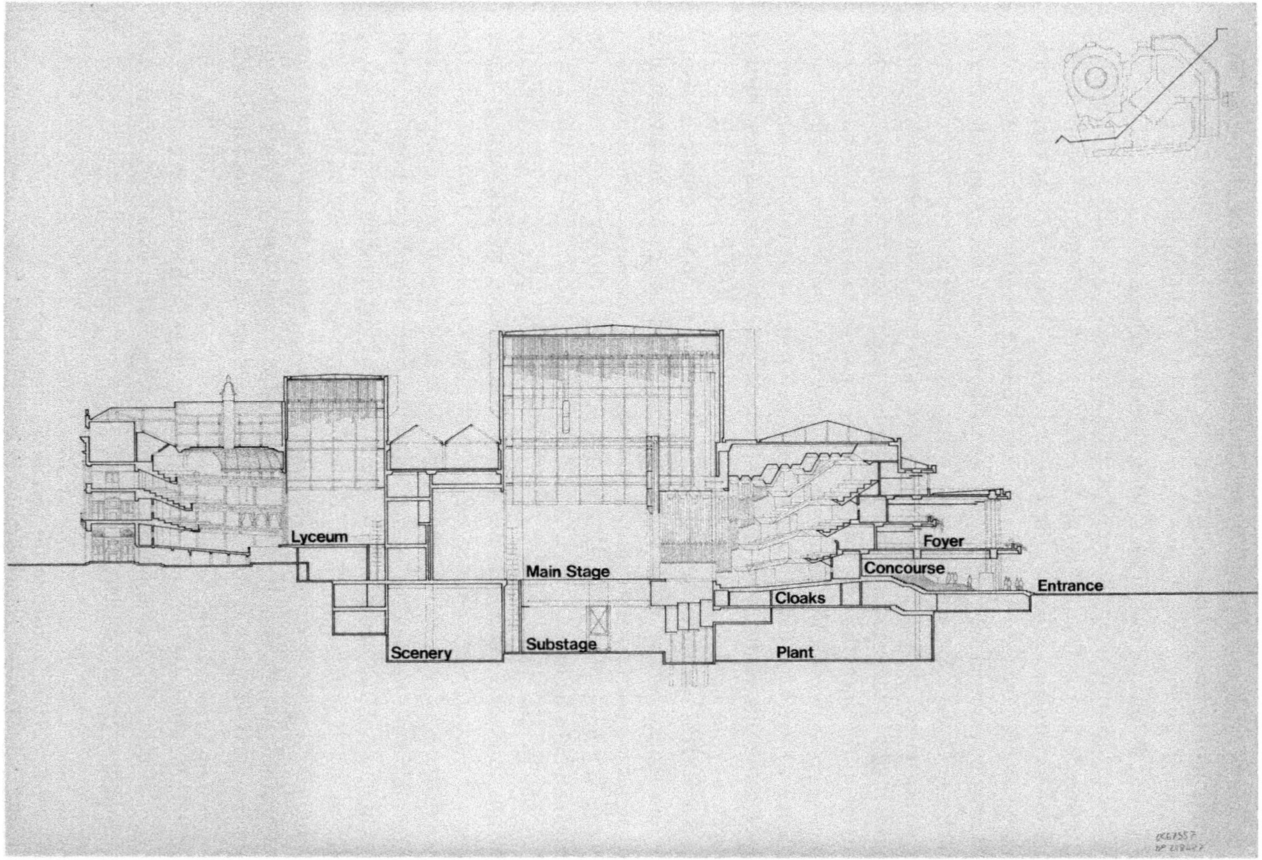

Figure 7.3. Civic horizontality: section through RMJM's 1975 design for the Castle Terrace Theatre, Edinburgh (©Historic Environment Scotland [Robert Matthew, Johnson-Marshall & Partners Collection])

for a scheme devised by its predecessor, while the newly created Lothian Regional Council proposed instead to improve the city's Playhouse, which dated from the 1920s.[37] Alexander Dunbar of the Scottish Arts Council concluded in November 1975, shortly after central government had withdrawn its promise of funding, that the creation of an overarching body like the South Bank Theatre Board, as oversaw the National Theatre, would have been helpful.[38] In his opinion, this kind of scheme was simply too big for local authorities to manage.

While projects of this scale were perhaps too easily the victims of economic circumstance and politics, they also reveal a more fundamental problem. By virtue of its size and expense, the Castle Terrace Theatre was far bigger than could be accommodated within the annual 'Housing the Arts' allocations. So was the Glasgow Cultural Centre, as well as stillborn opera houses in Cardiff and Manchester.[39] The intention was always that such 'monster projects' would be considered separately. However, little thought seems to have been given to how these projects might be managed, or where the money might come from. Amid growing economic turbulence, the time taken to agree a government contribution allowed doubts to grow about RAKP's scheme, while the sums involved gave civil servants an excuse to press for Kininmonth's departure on the basis that the amount of money being offered required an exemplary design. Progress was then further hampered by the need to appoint a new architect after RAKP's departure. By the time that RMJM's designs were ready, not only was the economic climate unfavourable to a scheme whose 'opera house' tag increasingly suggested an undesirable elitism, but the tide had also firmly turned away from large-scale modernist developments in Edinburgh. Had funding been forthcoming in 1968, the theatre would surely have been built.

Ultimately, the evident failure of government to engage more systematically with this kind of scheme suggests a mismatch between rhetoric and practice. Culture and leisure were afforded a significant place in political discourse, but the 'Housing the Arts' programme—although clearly successful in promoting regional theatre-building—was modestly conceived. It had, after all, only ever been intended as a stimulus to local fundraising. It certainly seems that funding was promised to Edinburgh only grudgingly. In 1971, the Paymaster General advised that a decision to make a grant to Covent Garden meant that 'it would be difficult to refuse this offer [to Edinburgh]'.[40] In addition, cheaper proposals to improve Edinburgh's Playhouse and Glasgow's Theatre Royal were seized upon within government, with Scottish Opera being praised for having raised so much money for the latter itself.[41] These examples hint not only at the difficulties of the 'monster project' but also at the value of a more financially modest approach, something which was increasingly to the fore during the 1970s.

[37] NRS, ED61/89, I. M. Robertson to Alexander Dunbar, 18 April 1975.

[38] 'Arts Council Still Have Opera Hopes', *Scotsman*, 13 November 1975.

[39] NRS, ED61/71, 'Lyceum Theatre/Castle Terrace Theatre Redevelopment, Edinburgh', 27 November 1968.

[40] NRS, ED61/84, Paymaster General to Home Affairs Select Committee, 23 April 1971.

[41] NRS, ED61/88, Scottish Minister draft letter to send to Chief Secretary to the Treasury, n.d.

'A MODEST BUDGET BUILDING': ECONOMY AND THEATRE

In August 1969, *Plays and Players* reported that Colchester's proposed 500-seat Mercury Theatre was to be 'a modest budget building'.[42] There had long been talk of a new theatre for the town's repertory company, which was housed within a converted art gallery. The loss of the old theatre's backstage accommodation to redevelopment in 1966 gave the project added impetus, and a New Theatre Trust was formed the following year.[43] The local authority offered £60,000 on condition that the same sum was raised by the theatre, and a site in St Mary's Rectory garden was selected in 1967.[44] The director, David Forder, envisaged the new theatre as a social centre of the kind discussed in Chapter 6: 'the most successful theatres of all are those with new buildings and which can make a real night out, providing a real social occasion with restaurant, bar and exhibitions'.[45] It was to be a contextual building; reference was made to 'the best contemporary regional rather than metropolitan work'.[46] The architect, Norman Downie, was Colchester-based. His design coupled dark brickwork with slate cladding, and was judged by the *Financial Times* to offer 'a blessed relief [from] the usual concrete' and 'vast areas of antiseptic glass' (see Figure 7.4).[47] Economy was to the fore: 'at an early stage it was decided to favour the provision of space [...], economise on the cost of finishes, and leave the installation of more sophisticated equipment to the future'.[48] Though hardly cramped, the theatre is compact, with the foyers and backstage areas being tightly gathered around the hexagonal auditorium. Brick and concrete are left exposed, prompting Colin Amery to observe that 'austerity was the theme for the public areas'.[49] Nonetheless, aspirations to theatricality were not entirely absent. Forder spoke of the need for a building that was 'economical, without luxury, yet to provide glamour and a sense of occasion'.[50] The audience would decorate it: an attempt was made to display, as the architect put it, 'happy customers perambulating within to hesitating onlookers' through the provision of large foyer windows.[51] Careful detailing elevated some areas beyond the mundane. One newspaper concluded that while 'some of the economies can be seen—or felt [...], the restaurant is a winner on both décor (Habitat bright-red, straw-seated chairs) and food—a limited, serve-yourself menu of really tasty, imaginative items'.[52] Amery, too,

42 ERO, D/Z 455/2/16, clippings: 'Colchester', *Plays and Players*, August 1969.

43 'The Mercury Theatre, Colchester', *Stage*, 11 May 1972.

44 ERO, D/Z 455/2/14, clippings: 'Two Fine Sites', *Essex County Standard*, 28 April 1967.

45 ERO, D/Z 455/2/18, clippings: 'The Repertory Revolution', *Essex County Standard*, 26 March 1971.

46 ERO, D/Z 455/2/14, clippings: 'Civic Theatre Job Goes to Local Architect', *Colchester Express*, 18 January 1968.

47 'The Recruiting Officer', *Financial Times*, 12 May 1972.

48 'Theatre at Colchester', *Architects' Journal* 156 (5 July 1972), pp. 19–34 (p. 34).

49 'Theatre at Colchester', p. 26.

50 ERO, C1310/21, clippings: 'Economy Glamour Revolution', *Essex County Standard*, 12 May 1972.

51 'Theatre at Colchester', p. 22.

52 ERO, C1310/21, clippings: 'Nearest New Theatre', *Harlow Citizen*, 19 May 1972.

Figure 7.4. 'Contemporary regional': the Mercury Theatre, Colchester, in 1972 (Architectural Press Archive/RIBA Collections)

praised the 'jazzy-Magistretti' restaurant, which he felt might overwhelm 'serious' visiting architects.[53] On the whole, he concluded that the Mercury 'stands as a modest monument to the determination of its director and architect to give the repertory company a new home at the relatively low cost of £200,000'.

The Mercury offered an attractive model in an inflationary era, and Downie was commissioned to provide a near-replica of it in Salisbury. Even then, an Arts Council committee concluded in November 1973 that it was a 'sad reflection on recent inflation' that Salisbury would cost more than twice as much as Colchester.[54] Salisbury Playhouse, which opened in 1976, was similarly intended for a booming repertory company whose premises were decrepit. During one performance in the old theatre, a member of the audience was asked 'to take down her umbrella'.[55] The management was also concerned that the old building compared unfavourably with new theatres elsewhere: 'we realise the difficult economic situation but, even so, more concrete progress has been made in other towns and cities where there are

[53] 'Theatre at Colchester', p. 28.

[54] V&A, ACGB/120/34, Salisbury Playhouse Special Committee, 15 November 1973. A brochure in the Playhouse's own archive states £500,000, amended to £650,000.

[55] John Bavin, *Heart of the City: The Story of Salisbury Playhouse* (Salisbury, 1976), p. 20.

similar out-dated theatres'.[56] Mention was made of the potential to attract residents, businesses, and tourists to Salisbury: 'a company of such good repute provides an added attraction'.[57]

The kind of frugal approach that shaped the conception and design of Downie's theatres in Colchester and Salisbury was, of course, not new. Previous chapters have included such examples as the Young Vic (1970) and Chichester Festival Theatre (1962). Amateur theatres, too, were often economically conceived. For example, the 350-seat Questors Theatre in Ealing was constructed in the early 1960s for £65,000.[58] Nonetheless, economy was to become a recurrent theme in 1970s theatre design, with the scale and scope of several projects being dictated by the need for frugality. Such projects include the Redgrave Theatre, Farnham (1974). Farnham's repertory company had begun in the mid-1960s to plan for a new building to replace the town's Castle Theatre.[59] The Yvonne Arnaud Theatre was about to open in nearby Guildford, and the Thorndike in Leatherhead was in the offing. It was reported that a site adjacent to a listed building in Farnham town centre, Brightwell House, had been earmarked for a 'civic or cultural building',[60] and it was allocated to the theatre. A rather stodgy design was produced by F. L. Pusey,[61] before Frank Rutter took over the project in June 1967.[62] Brightwell House was converted to accommodate front-of-house functions, with a 350-seat auditorium and extended foyers being built next to it. A large collection of drawings illustrates the development of Rutter's designs—in terms of their plan and elevations—between 1967 and 1972. Some have a relatively austere appearance while others are more allusive, with 'castle'-like detailing.[63] The development of the design was evidently shaped by economic circumstances: 'the many different plans [. . .] have reflected not only the changing attitude to repertory theatre and its special place in the community, but also an increasingly difficult financial climate', it was noted.[64] The executed design took a more modest course than some of the early proposals, having straightforward brick elevations crowned by exposed concrete beams. In its materials and in the combination of a new auditorium with a historic building, it anticipated the similar Brewhouse arts centre, Taunton, which opened in 1977 to the designs of the Somerset county architect and Norman Branson. Branson had previously designed the Questors, and the Brewhouse was similarly conceived in terms of economy after earlier proposals for a theatre in Taunton had failed to get off the ground.[65]

56 W&SA, G23/132/249, W. G. Vizard to G. Richardson, 20 January 1969.
57 'The New Playhouse Theatre', brochure in the archive at Salisbury Playhouse.
58 QTA, uncat., 'Proposed New Theatre in Mattock Lane: Instructions to Architect, Mr Norman Branson, A.R.I.B.A', n.d.; Frederick Bentham, *New Theatres in Britain* (London, 1970), p. 67.
59 SHC, 6894/7/1/3/12, Theatre Projects Consultants report, *c.*1970.
60 SHC, 6894/2/3, Directors' minutes, 25 October 1966.
61 SHC, 6894/7/1/3/7, 'The New Castle Theatre', F. L. Pusey drawing, 19 May 1967.
62 SHC, 6894/2/3, Directors' minutes, 27 June 1967.
63 SHC, 6894/7/1/3/1–12 comprises the drawings.
64 SHC, 6894/2/21, Commemorative Programme [1974].
65 V&A, ACGB/120/9, HTA minutes, 25 June 1975.

The new Dundee Repertory Theatre of 1982 was similarly shaped by the need for economy. The city's repertory company had been set up in 1939, but its theatre burnt down in 1963.[66] Proposals were made to convert part of the massive Caird Hall into a 500-seat theatre,[67] but in summer 1967 it was reported that the scheme had been postponed.[68] The university offered a site on Tay Square and considered building the theatre alongside a multipurpose hall,[69] but subsequently opted to construct only the hall, for which it had funding, to the designs of Gillespie Kidd and Coia.[70] By 1973, it had been decided that the theatre would have 650 seats,[71] and the local authority committed the product of a penny rate for two years.[72] Costs, however, began to rise. By January 1974 the likely cost was £750,000,[73] and by December 1974 it had reached £1.6 million.[74]

The project brief was reconsidered, with the aim now being 'the minimum necessary accommodation and standard of finish'.[75] In autumn 1975, two options were considered.[76] The first, a prefabricated building with a thirty-year life, was costed at £552,000. However, this sum was hardly less than the £556,000 price tag (plus fees) attached to the alternative, a permanent structure designed by local architects Andrew Nicoll and Ric Russell, which was accordingly selected.[77] Further economies followed as the design was detailed between 1976 and 1979.[78] By September 1976, the theatre had shrunk to 460 seats but came with a cost of £600,000,[79] and as of September 1977 a figure of £622,000 was being quoted for a building without a fly tower or workshop.[80] Russell later recalled the period as one in which parts of the design were repeatedly 'amputated',[81] though the fly tower (needed for visits from the likes of Scottish Opera) and workshop ultimately returned, with a £920,000 estimate by September 1978.[82] Funding came from local, national, and European sources. The case for support was made in various ways, including the contribution that a successful theatre would make to Dundee's cultural life and reputation, while an application was submitted to the European

66 STA, STA Bb 1/1, Lady Duncan of Jordanstone to Donors, 9 October 1978.

67 V&A, ACGB/120/41, 'Caird Hall Alterations, Dundee'.

68 V&A, ACGB/120/41, Housing the Arts—Fifth Progress Report, 28 August 1967; Ronald Mavor to Peter Longman, 27 February 1970.

69 UoDun, RU 162/1/1, Finance Committee, 19 February 1968; RU 162/1/3, University Court, 20 October 1969 and Building Committee, 19 January 1970.

70 UoDun, RU 162/1/5 (ii), minute of 17 January 1972.

71 V&A, ACGB/120/41, folder 2, Dundee Repertory Theatre—Architect's Brief, June 1973.

72 UoDun, MS 316/44/5 (ii), 'The Case for a New Theatre for the Rep', n.d. [late 1970s]. Further funding was committed after local government reorganization in 1975 by the new district and regional councils.

73 Quoted in V&A, ACGB/120/41, folder 3, Harry McCann to Peter Longman, 27 January 1975.

74 DA, Lord Provost's Committee, 30 January 1975.

75 STA, Bb Box 1/4, Maurice Cantley to Robert Robertson, 1 June 1978.

76 DA, Lord Provost's Committee, 20 October 1975.

77 The architects worked for Robbie and Wellwood before subsequently forming their own studio. They became involved in the theatre project during 1974.

78 STA, Bb Box 6, 'Schedule of Dates'.

79 DA, Lord Provost's Committee, 20 September 1976.

80 DA, Lord Provost's Committee, 19 September 1977.

81 Ric Russell, interviewed 8 November 2013.

82 DA, General Purposes Subcommittee, 6 September 1978.

Regional Development Fund (ERDF) in 1979: 'a modern theatre provides not only a focus for social and cultural activities within a city but also an important stimulus to economic development'.[83] It was noted that Dundee's industrial sector was declining, and that it was imperative to attract new employers to the city. This kind of argument was increasingly common during the 1970s and 1980s, not least as other sources of public funding for theatre-building became scarce. Such justifications also addressed the government's growing interest in the tangible 'economic value' of the arts, something that went hand-in-hand with its belief that the arts should operate in more obviously commercial ways.

Viewed from Tay Square, the dominant element is the auditorium, which is set diagonally on the site (see Figure 7.5). Below it are tucked two levels of foyers, conceived as a 'theatre beneath the theatre' and linked by a curved stair. Frameless glazing gives views into these spaces from Tay Square. Its intersecting planes and the views into and through the building create a sense of depth, as if the foyers have been carved from a solid block, while the unrelieved blockwork elsewhere imbues the theatre with a sense of mass. Although one reviewer saw echoes of Russian constructivism in the design, for Russell the guiding principle was one of

Figure 7.5. Contextual monumentality: Dundee Repertory Theatre from Tay Square, 2013 (Alistair Fair)

[83] DA, GD/DRT, Green Folder 15/5, 'Application for European Regional Development Fund Grant (Draft)'.

pragmatism.[84] The final cost in 1982 was £1.2 million, less than had been forecast in 1974. Nonetheless, the architects were resourceful, and the theatre is an accomplished work. *Building Design* concluded that 'despite what in some ways is minimal architecture, the building is full of clever and surprising details which revel in this approach to design, while interior spaces, pared to the bone as they often are, generate a sense of excitement and occasion'.[85] The theatre is also a contextual building, echoing the proportions and colours of the adjacent four-storey terrace, and in this respect it highlights a further significant theme in 1970s theatre design, to which we now turn.

'LIKE A SECOND-HAND WAREHOUSE': CONTEXTUALISM

In 1965, the trustees of Bristol's Theatre Royal decided to add new foyers, backstage areas, and a studio auditorium to their eighteenth-century playhouse.[86] Their aim was a 'theatre centre' which would cement Bristol's place as a leading regional rep, and it was concluded that 'a bold imaginative scheme is more likely to attract interest from Trusts, Foundations, Industry and the public than a modest scheme of mere improvements'.[87] The announcement of the 'Housing the Arts' programme similarly suggested that an ambitious approach might be successful,[88] and by November 1965, the projected cost of the proposals, some £470,000, was similar to that of a new theatre, as was the final cost in 1973 of some £650,000 (excluding fees).[89] Peter Moro was appointed because of his experience of theatre design; significantly, Bristol's director, Val May, was newly arrived from Nottingham Playhouse. Moro noted that he would 'love to design a brand new theatre', but that 'the issue is made difficult due to the existence of an exceptionally beautiful and historic theatre'.[90] He created new foyers within the adjacent Coopers' Hall, which was carefully restored, while an extension, which presented plain elevations of brown brick to the street, housed a flexible studio and new backstage facilities (see Figure 7.6). Demolished in 2016, its appearance excited a degree of debate. Moro sought to evoke the character of the nearby historic warehouses. There was much public discussion of whether the roofline ought to have a simple straight edge, as Moro wanted, or a more varied form with gable ends or curved 'pediments'; one councillor thought that the completed theatre 'looked more like a second-hand warehouse than it did

[84] Ric Russell, interviewed 8 November 2013.
[85] 'Curtain Call for Dundee Theatre', *Building Design* 621 (3 December 1982), pp. 14–15.
[86] RSA, BOV/MIN/000009, Bristol Old Vic Trust minutes, e.g. 17 September 1965.
[87] RSA, BOV/MIN/000009, Bristol Old Vic Trust minutes, e.g. 17 September 1965.
[88] RSA, BOV/MIN/000009, Bristol Old Vic Trust minutes, 17 September 1965 and 17 December 1965.
[89] RSA, BOV/MIN/000009, Bristol Old Vic Trust minutes, 19 November 1965. A letter from Nigel Abercrombie to Douglas Morris refers to the earlier £200,000 scheme (RSA, uncat. brown folder, 16 July 1965). For later costs, see RSA, uncat. Appeal Committee Update memo, July 1971.
[90] RSA, uncat. Theatre Royal material, Peter Moro to Douglas Morris, 15 November 1965.

Figure 7.6. Too reticent? Theatre Royal, Bristol, showing the Coopers' Hall (right) and Peter Moro's extension (left) (Architectural Press Archive/RIBA Collections)

before'.[91] Moro complained in 1970 that 'architects have frequently been accused of not paying sufficient respect to neighbouring buildings [...], but this must surely be the first time that a Planning Committee has criticised an architect for exercising self-restraint'.[92]

The contextual nature of the Theatre Royal's extension distinguished it from other theatres by Moro's office, which, as stand-alone buildings, were designed in a rather more abstracted manner. Its contextualism was, however, increasingly common in theatre architecture. Thus HKPA's theatre and arts centre at Christ's Hospital, Horsham (1974) took the octagonal forms of the same architects' earlier Young Vic and clothed them in red brick to echo the adjacent Edwardian buildings. Similarly, Roderick Ham's proposals of 1972–5 for a new theatre in Bedford eschewed the abstract, monolithic forms of his earlier work to draw instead on local precedent, with Ham writing that his design had 'something in common with the boathouses nearby' (see Figure 7.7).[93] The theatre was to have the same

[91] 'Theatre: bid to settle design row', *Bristol Evening Press*, 17 December 1970.
[92] RSA uncat. Theatre Royal material, Peter Moro to J. Bennett, 24 November 1970.
[93] BedA, Z900/4/4, Feasibility Study, 1973.

Figure 7.7. 'Something in common with the boathouses': model of the unbuilt Bedford theatre, *c.*1974, with the main auditorium at the top of the photograph (Architectural Press Archive/RIBA Collections)

yellow bricks as Ham's unbuilt Dove Arts Centre, but they were now to be coupled with pitched slate roofs rather than the Dove's concrete cornice. In addition, whereas the plan of the Dove was concentrated and largely symmetrical, the Bedford theatre was to be dispersed and asymmetric in the best picturesque fashion.[94] Dressing rooms and a workshop were to be located to one side of the auditorium, while foyers, a café, and a studio theatre were to be gathered around a courtyard. The proposed eight-sided, galleried auditorium was not unlike the Young Vic, which was popular with the theatre's promoters,[95] and it was hoped that the Bedford theatre would be similarly inexpensive. Indeed, the initial cost estimate was just £200,000, but by April 1974 had reached £760,000, and there were predictions that the final bill would be more than £1 million.[96] As was discussed in Chapter 2, the failure of the theatre's fundraising appeal meant that the project was soon postponed indefinitely.

[94] 'Theatre, Bedford', *Architectural Review* 159 (January 1976), p. 54; BedA, Z900/4/3, 'Bedford Theatre Project Design Report'.

[95] V&A, ACGB/84/18, Iain Mackintosh note, 18 September 1973.

[96] V&A, ACGB/84/18, Peter Longman memo, 22 April 1974.

Aspects of the Bedford design reappeared in Ham's subsequent work. The Sackville Theatre at Sevenoaks School (1982) reprised its pitched roofs and brick elevations, as did Ham's contemporaneous unexecuted proposals for an arts centre in Harrow.[97] There are also clear echoes of Bedford in Ham's design for the Wolsey Theatre, Ipswich, a project which he inherited from the local firm of Vine and Vine. As in Dundee a few years later, initial proposals dating from the 1960s were followed in the early 1970s by what was described as a 'minimum theatre brief' in the face of rising costs, with a simple end-stage auditorium and small foyers.[98] The management argued that with a final building cost of £489,000 in 1979,[99] the Wolsey Theatre was:

> not an extravagant building. No doubt a cheaper building could have been built—the 1977 Design Report referred to a scheme built using porta-cabins [sic]—but it occupies what the planning authority has always regarded as a prime site.[100]

Vine and Vine's 1974 scheme comprised a simple rectilinear building, while Ham's executed design suggests a well-resolved domesticity, with brick walls, a low-slung pitched roof, and even a large bay window. Although its horizontality suggests Frank Lloyd Wright's Prairie Style, Ham argued that he had drawn on the East Anglian domestic vernacular and had sought a 'human scale' in deliberate contrast with the adjacent municipal buildings.[101] Yet the theatre did not entirely reject the idea that a public building—distinct from a house—might demand a certain architectural register. Entering via its large, chunkily detailed wooden doors was likened by Colin Amery to 'that glorious moment of anticipation when you try the door of a country church that you have never been inside before'.[102] The doors needed 'a good pull to open them' such that they 'provide a pause to consider the nature of the rituals that are to be observed'.[103] In this respect, Ham's design can be understood as a contribution to an ongoing debate about the nature of public architecture. Amery reported that:

> the architect has decided to employ for a public building a kind of enlarged domestic style. This is a growing tendency and an interesting one: police stations look like cosy, brick houses [...]. The reasons behind the architectural arguments for this curious new camouflaged style are hard to fathom. Is it fear of monumentalism? Or is a reaction to the 'let it all hang out' boys a wish to hide all that functionalism under a tea-cosy of vernacular respectability?[104]

Describing it as 'a house with a theatre in it', he concluded that 'it is the "playhouse" again, the return of an informal approach to the theatre as a relaxed public building'.[105] There are similarities in intention with the civic centre designed by

[97] TTT, Roderick Ham archive, for material relating to both.
[98] SRO, A1/3/2/4060/486, Management Committee report, 20 November 1974.
[99] 'Wolsey Theatre', *Architects' Journal* 171 (6 February 1980), pp. 277–92 (p. 288).
[100] SRO, A1/3/2/4060/676, David Heckels to C. Stephenson, 30 August 1979.
[101] 'Wolsey Theatre', p. 282.
[102] 'Wolsey Theatre', pp. 282–3.
[103] 'Wolsey Theatre', p. 280.
[104] 'Wolsey Theatre', p. 282.
[105] 'Wolsey Theatre', p. 282.

RMJM at Uxbridge in west London (1978), where, at the insistence of Hillingdon Borough Council, the architects turned for inspiration to sources including the interwar suburban housing of west London in place of the prefabricated systems for which they were then well known.[106] With faceted elevations of brick and tiles and a picturesque pile-up of roofs, their design served to domesticate the image of the local authority, and one might similarly conclude that the Wolsey Theatre domesticated the image of the civic playhouse.

Similar contextualism and domesticity are evident in two projects in Scotland by Graham Law and James Dunbar-Nasmith. The first, Eden Court, Inverness, was the biggest theatre of the post-war boom to be built north of the border (see Figure 7.8). Completed in 1976 at a cost of £2 million, it enjoyed a larger budget than most of the examples discussed in this chapter, although the sum paled beside such projects as the £16 million National Theatre, opened during the same year.[107] The project's origins date from the mid-1960s, when a riverside site became

Figure 7.8. Eden Court, Inverness, in 1976, with the Bishop's Palace to the right (Architectural Press Archive/RIBA Collections)

[106] 'How Hillingdon Happened', *Architectural Review* 165 (February 1979), pp. 85–92 (p. 85).

[107] For comparison, Theatr Clwyd, which also opened in 1976, cost £2.6 million but included two auditoria and a television studio.

available.[108] The Central Hall had long since become a Methodist church, and the Empire Theatre was being sold for development. With an eye on the potential for a major theatre to cement the status of Inverness as the capital of the Highlands, the Provost later summarized his intentions in expansive terms:

> One of the things that the Highlands has most sadly lacked has been a theatre [...] adaptable enough to cater for the widest spectrum of cultural activities [...] or as a conference centre. We shall now offer first-class entertainment to people who live in the Highlands and to the thousands who visit Inverness every year. Establishing such a centre in Inverness is an ambitious undertaking but one that is as commercially necessary as it is socially desirable.[109]

The discovery of North Sea oil added further impetus, as it became apparent that north-east Scotland would undergo an economic boom. An application to the Highlands and Islands Development Board discussed the employment to be offered by the new theatre, its likely contribution to the region's economic development, and its regional (rather than local) significance.[110] Representatives from Inverness toured English theatres during 1967, including the Belgrade and Nottingham Playhouse, while the Arts Council encouraged councillors to build a dedicated theatre rather than a multipurpose hall.[111] By the start of 1970, the project had been defined as an 800-seat theatre-cum-concert hall, and the Highlands and Islands Development Board agreed to contribute.[112] A loan offer in 1973 from the Northern Meeting (a long-established group that organizes social activities) came with the condition that Eden Court also be able to host piping competitions and an annual dance.

A theatre consultant, John Wyckham, had been appointed to develop the brief in 1967, while the architects were selected in January 1972.[113] Law and Dunbar-Nasmith were by this date working on proposals for a new theatre in Pitlochry, which will be discussed shortly. In the *Architectural Review*, Colin Amery suggested that their designs for Eden Court offered 'a curious mixture of domestic and monumental architecture which is never quite resolved' on account of the 'piling up of a series of pitched slate roofs against the large fly tower'.[114] At the centre of the building is the lead-clad auditorium, around three sides of which are clustered the foyers. The lower foyer occupies a connected series of vaulted spaces at ground level, each of which is hexagonal in plan. At this level, there is a spacious bar and restaurant, planned to open from 10 a.m., while the kitchen could cater for 800 people. The scale of the facilities responded to the 'regional' nature of the theatre

[108] HA, HCA/D628/1/2, Derek C. Bigg, 'The Pre-history of Eden Court Theatre, Inverness' [MS].

[109] 'Eden Court', *Stage*, 15 April 1976, pp. 8–9 (p. 9).

[110] HA, HCA/D628/1/2, Bigg, 'Pre-history', p. 1.

[111] HA, BI/1/1/101, Inverness Town Council Planning and Development Committee, 5 May, 14 June, and 12 July 1967.

[112] V&A, ACGB/120/41, Ronald Mavor to Peter Longman 27 February 1970.

[113] HA, BI/1/1/105, Inverness Town Council Planning and Development Committee, 5 January 1972.

[114] 'Theatre, Inverness; Theatre, Dundee', *Architectural Review* 160 (October 1976), p. 208.

as a centre for the Highlands: audiences and visitors would potentially have travelled some distance, and might want to eat on arrival, or before leaving for home. Above, the upper foyers are tucked below a delicately folded roof of slate tiles. The foyers' glazed gable ends echo the pointy skyline of the adjacent former Bishop's Palace, which was converted for the theatre administration and to house the actors' green room.

When they took on Eden Court, Law and Dunbar-Nasmith had already been commissioned to design a new Pitlochry Festival Theatre, but the theatre was not completed until 1981, by which time Eden Court had been open for five years. The architects were first approached during 1965, apparently after Kenneth Ireland, the director, had been impressed by Dunbar-Nasmith's contributions to a discussion about the Edinburgh 'opera house'.[115] An initial proposal sought to recreate the spirit of the tented theatre which had been in use since 1951. It featured a 700-seat auditorium below a dramatic aluminium-clad sweeping roof, and was estimated to cost £550,000.[116] Nothing came of it, but, with the 'temporary' theatre becoming functionally unsuitable—at one stage it was deemed a significant fire risk—it was clear that doing nothing was not an option. By 1971, nine locations for a new theatre had been evaluated, with a site on the north bank of the River Tummel winning out.[117] Drawings of *c.*1973 show a building whose octagonal geometries and monolithic elevations suggest the influence of the Crucible Theatre; one might also see a family resemblance with the hexagons at Eden Court (see Figure 7.9). The theatre was expansively planned, with spacious foyers, an art gallery, and restaurant, and would have enjoyed good views of the river. Again, however, nothing came of this £3 million proposal, and in March 1976 it was decided to proceed on more economical lines with a £1.5 million target price.[118] As in Inverness and Dundee, the case for the theatre was partly made in terms of its role in economic development. An approach to the ERDF netted £475,000, a quarter of the theatre's total cost in 1981.[119]

A new site was selected, adjacent to the projected Pitlochry bypass. The requirement was now 'the cheapest theatre which would be acceptable to the Governors and which would enable the theatre company to continue the operation which they have carried on for the last 25 years'.[120] Accordingly, the design was considerably simplified, although its geometries echo the mid-1970s designs. It comprises a compact structure with an elevated glass-fronted foyer and restaurant located above the actors' dressing rooms. A yet more economical arrangement in which the auditorium rake would have followed the contours of the sloping site was rejected because the front-of-house areas would then have faced away from the river.

115 James Dunbar-Nasmith, interviewed 18 December 2013.

116 PFT, uncat., 'Pitlochry Festival Theatre: Feasibility Study', Law and Dunbar-Nasmith, 1967.

117 PFT, uncat., 'Proposed New Pitlochry Festival Theatre' [purple covered booklet, *c.*1973].

118 PFT, uncat., 'Stage D Report', 1977. The final cost in 1981 was £2 million: see the gazetteer in *Making Space for Theatre: British Architecture and Theatre Since 1958*, edited by Ronnie Mulryne and Margaret Shewring (Stratford-upon-Avon, 1995), p. 140.

119 PFT, uncat., Gala Performance Programme, 1981.

120 PFT, uncat., 'Stage D Report', 1977.

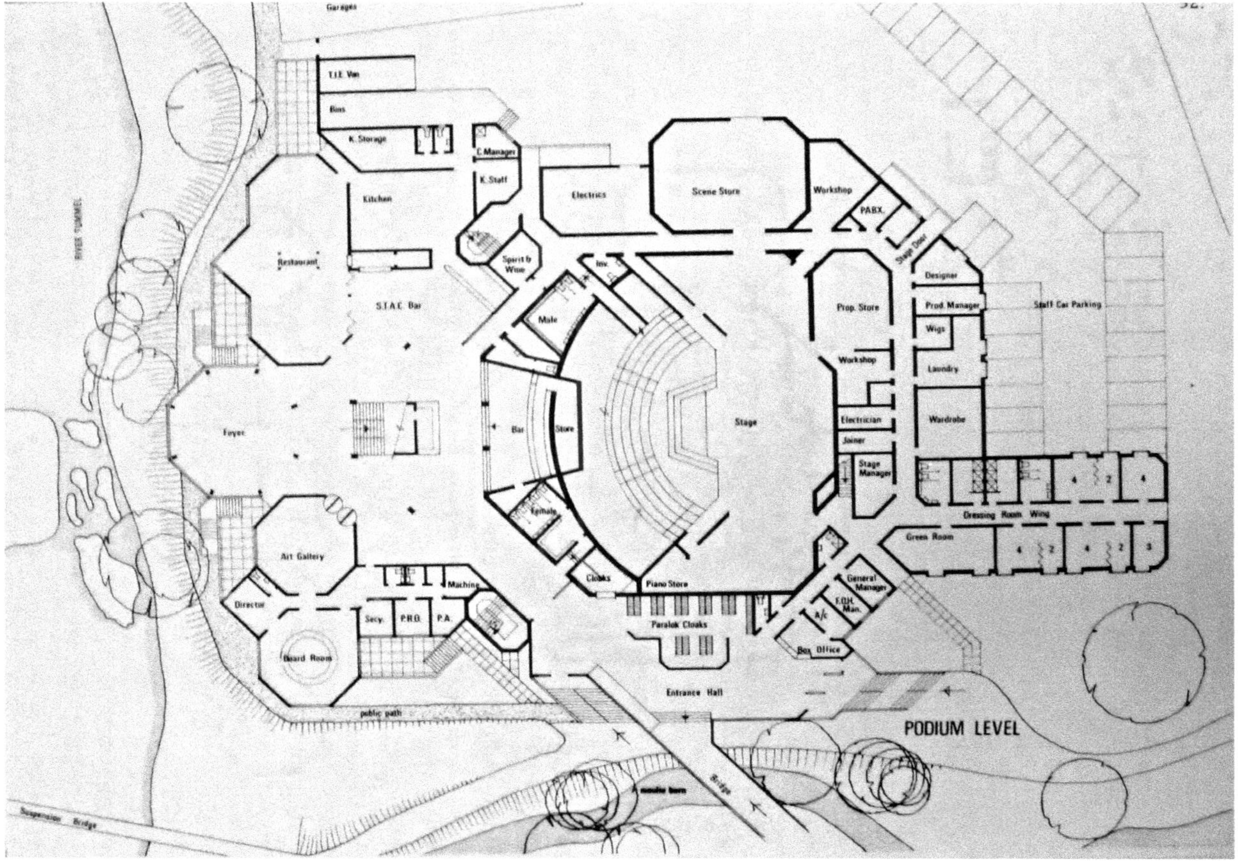

Figure 7.9. Pitlochry Festival Theatre, unbuilt design by Law and Dunbar-Nasmith for a theatre on the north bank of the River Tummel, *c.*1974 (Pitlochry Festival Theatre Archive)

Overall, the impression is one of pragmatism, tempered by a few witty touches such as 'tent-pole'-like roof supports within the foyer. In this respect, the governors were keen to keep the 'quaintly fussy appearance and atmosphere' of the old tented theatre, which they preferred to the 'chilling effects' they perceived in much recent architecture.[121] They argued that:

> within the Pitlochry concept [...] there is this intangible matter of 'atmosphere' [...]. The retention of this atmosphere is of paramount importance to the theatre's patrons, and the client will not be able to imbue an austere building with it; to clothe concrete with congeniality, steel with style, and so on, must be the responsibility of the architect. [...] Another key-word is 'plush' to counteract austerity. With a few notable exceptions, most of the new city theatres chill and silence by their severe formality and gloomily lit auditoria.[122]

The new theatre was thus conceived in opposition to a notional image of uniform civic monumentality:

> an orderly functional theatre that nevertheless recalls the warmth and elegance of the red-plush of a more leisured age, that avoids the scaffolding and down-draughts of the new 'civics', and comes up with a different 'Scottish/away from it all/remember the tent/all in good taste' type of congruous 'Showcase' in which to display our present and future wares.[123]

In suggesting that modern architecture had failed theatre, it was proposed that Pitlochry might be at the forefront of something new:

> Reaction to austerity is bound to increase as people tire of new hotels, airports, multi-stores and theatres becoming so atmospherically uniform. Pitlochry's new theatre can lead the reactionary vanguard with impunity and certainty of public acceptance.[124]

And yet, the new Festival Theatre was, conceptually at least, still very much in the mould of the modern playhouses of the previous two decades in making provision for food, art, and social activity. Its architecture, too, was hardly revivalist, but rather represented the kind of mainstream modern approach that had been established in theatre design since the 1950s. Furthermore, how novel was the emphasis on warmth? As was discussed in Chapter 4, festivity was often prized in theatres of the 1960s. Where Pitlochry differed, perhaps, was in the terms used to evoke these qualities, and the slightly reactionary way in which they were emphasized.

Two years after the Festival Theatre was completed, and with the 'Housing the Arts' fund being wound down, the Arts Council reported that Leeds was, like Stoke-on-Trent, one of the last remaining places where it anticipated that a new theatre would be built with its help.[125] In 1984, a competition was launched to find an architect for the city's new Playhouse, replacing a temporary sports hall conversion

[121] PFT, uncat., 'Brief and Schedule of Accommodation' [1972], p. 24.
[122] PFT, 'Brief and Schedule of Accommodation', p. 2.
[123] PFT, 'Brief and Schedule of Accommodation', p. 3.
[124] PFT, 'Brief and Schedule of Accommodation', p. 3.
[125] V&A, ACGB/120/3, 'New Victoria Theatre, Stoke-on-Trent', 27 April 1983.

of 1970 by William Houghton-Evans. The design competition was a condition of Arts Council support,[126] but was not welcomed by all of the theatre's administration: there were fears of an expensive, impractical scheme.[127] Peter Moro, chairing the judges, asked how useful a competition was likely to be given that the theatre's requirements seemed to be well defined.[128] There was also discussion of whether the proposed budget was sufficient, prompting an increase from £4.5 million to £5.4 million, a figure still thought too small by some of the competing teams.[129] More than a hundred entries were received,[130] with twelve competitors proceeding to a second round at the end of October 1984.[131]

The plan was to create a park around the theatre,[132] and it was hoped that the theatre and park would together prompt private-sector development at Quarry Hill. Mention was made of a possible £60 million leisure and shopping development.[133] Several competitors proposed new external spaces, including public squares by its entrances (Tim Foster/Burrell Foley, Levitt Bernstein), stepped terraces (Barry Gasson), and space for external performances (Roderick Ham, Edward Cullinan). Some also suggested how the theatre could form part of a larger development. Cullinan proposed a *cour d'honneur* of trees stepping up the hill, while Derek Walker illustrated an open-plan structure for shopping and exhibitions adjacent to the Playhouse, as well as a concert hall. As far as the theatre building itself was concerned, the competing designs demonstrate a range of architectural positions. Derek Walker, for example, offered an exercise in high tech which developed the approach of his earlier shopping centre at Milton Keynes, while others were deliberately contextual; the so-called 'Leeds look' was then favoured by local planners. The gabled elevations of Roderick Ham's proposal bring to mind Victorian warehouses, while Law and Dunbar-Nasmith referred to the local tradition of brick architecture. Some of the competitors presented their approach in slightly reactionary terms. Levitt Bernstein, for example, suggested that some recent theatres had failed to capture the imagination of audiences, in part because of their 'overbearing' modernism.[134] Instead, they proposed something on the lines of their recently completed Wilde Theatre, Bracknell, a modest composition in brick and tile. HKPA and Edward Cullinan opted for a more overt theatricality,

[126] UoL, BC MS 20c Theatre LP Arc/2, Box 4, File A, 1 of 2, 'Administrator's Report on Investigations into the Proposed Competition', 7 December 1983.

[127] UoL, BC MS 20c Theatre LP Arc/2, Box 4, File A, 1 of 2, copy of letter from Alec Baron.

[128] UoL, BC MS 20c Theatre LP Arc/2, Box 4, File A, 1 of 2, Peter Moro to William Weston, 17 July 1984.

[129] UoL, BC MS 20c Theatre LP Arc/2, Box 4, File A, 1 of 2, correspondence with competing architects and Northcroft, November 1984.

[130] 'Successful Stage-Call at Leeds', *Architects' Journal* 180 (24 October 1984), p. 30.

[131] 'Leading Lights', *Architects' Journal* 181 (20 March 1985), pp. 28–31; 'Curtain Call', *Architects' Journal* 181 (3 April 1985), pp. 16–23. For the drawings and accompanying information, see UoL, BC MS 20c Theatre LP Arc/2, Box 9, 'LP Buildings'.

[132] UoL, BC MS 20c Theatre LP Arc/2, Box 4, File A 1, Report of the Chief Officer and Director of Administration, to Policy and Resources Committee, 12 April 1983.

[133] 'Leading Lights', p. 29.

[134] UoL, BC MS 20c Theatre LP Arc/2, Box 9, initial application by Levitt Bernstein.

the former disguising the fly tower in such a way as to make the building look like a circus 'big top':

> the theatre should have an important and exhuberant [sic] entrance visible from all the main approaches. One which reaches out invitingly to the city and entices people in to the real and partly unreal world that theatre can portray.[135]

However, while HKPA thus evoked dramatic fantasy, the winning design by Ian and Marjorie Appleton suggested, apparently unintentionally, a more prosaic parallel, namely the 'vernacular' supermarket buildings then being built across Britain (see Figure 7.10). Their design features polychromatic brickwork and pitched slate roofs, which clothe a compact, efficient building of essentially hexagonal plan. Ian Appleton had earlier worked for Peter Moro, and the theatre's tight, geometric planning recalls Moro's approach. The critic Kenneth Powell was less than impressed with the Playhouse's supermarket-like overtones, but the director Jude Kelly, who opened the theatre in 1990, was more positive, suggesting that the theatre's familiar appearance made it seem more approachable to potential patrons.[136] In this respect, her interpretation reprised the concern for accessibility articulated by the likes of Jennie Lee some twenty-five years before, while the

Figure 7.10. 'The Leeds Look': West Yorkshire Playhouse, 1990 (Alastair Hunter/RIBA Collections)

[135] UoL, BC MS 20c Theatre LP Arc/2, Box 9, Scheme 9 (HKPA), n.p.

[136] Jude Kelly, 'The West Yorkshire Playhouse', in *Making Space for Theatre: British Architecture and Theatre Since 1958*, edited by Ronnie Mulryne and Margaret Shewring (Stratford-upon-Avon, 1995), pp. 74–9 (p. 76).

building itself could be understood as a statement of mainstream modernism, which, as was the case two decades before in such places as Billingham and Coventry, could be applied with varying inflections to a range of building types.

CONCLUSIONS: 'AN EVOLVING PROJECT'

Writing about the continued interest of central government in inner-city reconstruction after 1979, the historian Otto Saumarez Smith has argued that the aims of the welfare state were hardly a spent force by the end of the 1970s.[137] Rather, he suggests, these ambitions were developed in new ways in an 'evolving, self-critical and robust project' which lasted into the 1980s. Much the same might be concluded of theatre-building—something which, after all, had previously been framed in terms of the broader social-democratic ambitions of the 1950s and 1960s. Economic factors were increasingly present in justifications of new theatres, but so too were such established themes as civic identity, the place of theatres in the urban landscape, and the role of culture in modern Britain. The architecture of these buildings also suggests an 'evolving, self-critical and robust project' which responded to a range of agendas, from a need for value in challenging economic circumstances, to the wish for a more 'domestic' civic architecture amid debates about the nature of modernism itself. As this chapter has shown, the modern playhouses of the 1970s and early 1980s were diverse in form, ranging from the volumetric massing and concrete blocks of Plymouth Theatre Royal and Dundee Rep, to the frugal contextualism of the Wolsey in Ipswich, or the calculated warmth of Pitlochry Festival Theatre. These buildings nonetheless all reveal an ongoing search for an appropriate modern theatre architecture, as well as a degree of continuity in terms of their civic, social, and artistic ambitions. As HKPA pointed out in their submission to the Leeds Playhouse competition in 1984, 'the theatre should be fun as well as serious, and should express outwardly the aspirations, the culture and the collective spirit of the city', while Ian and Marjorie Appleton's winning entry neatly summarized the entire underlying rationale of the post-war subsidized theatre boom in referring to the 'theatre complex as a place of entertainment, education and excitement'.[138]

[137] Otto Saumarez Smith, 'The Inner City Crisis and the End of Urban Modernism in 1970s Britain', *Twentieth Century British History* 27, no. 4 (2016), pp. 578–98.

[138] UoL, BC MS 20c Theatre LP Arc/2, Box 9, Schemes 9 and 8, n.p.

8

'Theatre of the Future'

Rethinking the Auditorium

In 1963, the Ballet Rambert and the Royal Shakespeare Company appointed Basil Spence to design the New Mercury Theatre, Notting Hill, which they planned to share. Spence's approach was collaborative:

> Peter [Hall, the RSC director,] and Basil [Spence] used to get together and talk about the design, after which Basil, because he was so mad keen, used to rush off and produce a lot of drawings and preliminary sketches. And when they next met, it was usually not what Peter wanted at all![1]

Spence also acknowledged the input of the directors Michel Saint-Denis and Peter Brook,[2] while Hall worked with the designer John Bury to 'stage' productions using scale models.[3] The first designs that emerged from these discussions were conventional, with the auditorium having a steep gallery as well as boxes which stepped down its side walls.[4] However, later proposals were more radical. Notably, they lacked the traditional kind of proscenium arch stage, in which the stage and auditorium are separated by a wall containing a large opening that serves to 'frame' the audience's view of the stage, while the auditorium seating blocks were laid out asymmetrically (see Figure 8.1).[5] Hall emphasized the informality of this arrangement and suggested that it was fundamentally contemporary: 'an uneven pile-up of seats would really be of our time'.[6]

The New Mercury was never built, for the reasons discussed in Chapter 4. Nonetheless, it raises some significant themes. The first is the increasingly collaborative nature of auditorium and stage design. The second is the extent to which auditorium and stage design could be understood in 'modern' terms. The third is the way in which the relationship between the stage and the auditorium was often the subject of debate. In this respect, the director Tyrone Guthrie suggested in 1960 that the proscenium arch stage could no longer be considered as 'the only

[1] SBTA, DR1108/2/4/2, Fordham Flower to John Fletcher, 9 April 1965.
[2] HES, MS 2329/X/19/7/64–66, Basil Spence to J. M. Richards, 7 February 1964.
[3] HES, MS 2329/ENG/56/4/53, Peter Hall to Basil Spence, 17 February 1964.
[4] HES, SPE ENG/56/2/8/2, sightline diagram, September 1963.
[5] HES, SPE ENG/56/2/8/6, stalls plan, January 1964.
[6] HES, MS 2329/ENG/56/4/53, Peter Hall to Basil Spence, 17 February 1964; MS 2329/ENG/56/4/33, Basil Spence to Peter Hall, 27 May 1964; MS 2329/ENG/56/4/34, Peter Hall to Basil Spence, 23 May 1964.

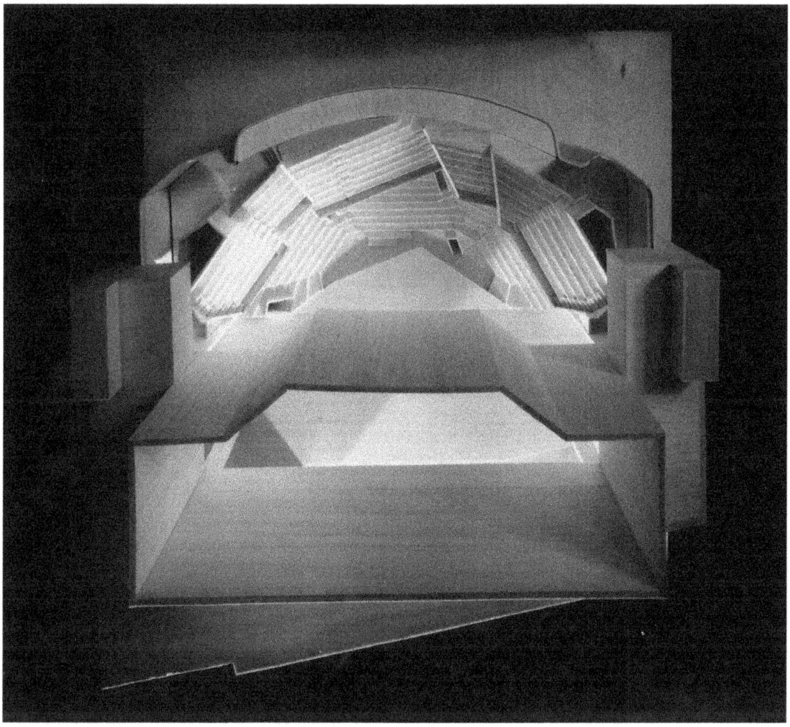

Figure 8.1. 'An uneven pile-up': the proposed New Mercury Theatre, London, 1963 (©HES. Sir Basil Spence Archive)

kind of stage on which a progressive production can be satisfactorily performed'.[7] In its place, Guthrie advocated the 'thrust' stage, with the audience sitting around three sides of the acting area. He was one of a growing number who favoured such so-called 'open' stage arrangements as an alternative to the long-dominant proscenium arch stage. In addition to the thrust stage, these alternatives included 'in-the-round' or 'arena' staging (in which the stage is encircled by the audience), 'transverse' stages (in which the audience sit on two sides of the stage), and open 'end' stages (which feature a single block of seating facing the stage).

This chapter begins with a discussion of the collaborative nature of stage and auditorium design before examining the arguments made in favour of open staging, not least by the director Stephen Joseph, who edited several books on the subject. It then considers the impact of these debates on the design of key examples. As we will see, the rejection of the proscenium arch stage could be understood as evidence of a fundamentally modern attitude, with the theatre technician Frederick Bentham arguing in 1951 that 'one can hardly mention theatre design or lighting

[7] Tyrone Guthrie, *A Life in the Theatre* (London, 1960), p. 181.

without being called reactionary unless one scorns the proscenium arch'.[8] Similarly in 1970, the thrust stage which was then under construction in Sheffield at the Crucible Theatre was described as 'the stage of the future',[9] while Antony Hampton, the chairman of the theatre's trustees, noted that 'the injection of new life and thought into the presentation of the drama is the concern of many people today, especially amongst the young'; the article in which he was quoted was similarly titled 'Sheffield's theatre of the future'.[10] In this respect, innovations in stage and auditorium design were not only significant in themselves but also formed part of broader debates about the nature of the modern playhouse.

THE CONTEXT: PROFESSIONAL ROLES

Post-war British theatre design was shaped by professionals from a range of backgrounds, including architects, actors, directors, and technical specialists, especially where the stage and auditorium were concerned. Not least among the growing band of professionals was the 'theatre consultant'. This role emerged during the 1950s, initially in West Germany, in response to the growing complexity of stage equipment.[11] Although technical advice and the specification of equipment often formed a significant part of the consultant's work, the role could extend to architectural matters, especially when an architect was new to theatre design, or when a theatre was being designed without a defined user, as might be the case for a civic venue. It is, therefore, worth briefly outlining the early history of theatre consultancy, and of the Association of British Theatre Technicians (ABTT). Many of the figures whose ideas are discussed in this chapter were among the ABTT's early members, and the topic of open staging loomed large in its initial meetings.[12]

One of the first people in Britain to be described as a 'theatre consultant' was the designer and historian Richard Southern, in 1960.[13] He was then working with Peter Moro on the designs for Nottingham Playhouse, it being reported in 1959 that the functional brief had been prepared 'in consultation with many theatre people' to avoid 'the defects in such buildings as the Stratford-upon-Avon theatre and the Belgrade'.[14] In March 1962, the term seems to have been sufficiently well understood for the architect George Grenfell-Baines to ask Southern, with reference to the proposed University Theatre at Manchester, 'would you be willing to work

[8] 'The Royal Festival Hall; the Arena Stage', *Tabs* 9, no. 3 (December 1951), pp. 18–23.

[9] CTA, uncat., typescript with information about the new theatre, May 1970.

[10] 'Sheffield's Theatre of the Future', *Sheffield Spectator* 7, no. 51 (June 1969), n.p.

[11] Iain Mackintosh, *Architecture, Actor and Audience* (London, 1993), p. 118.

[12] 'there was a strong bias towards some form of open staging, and a feeling that the future of the theatre lay in that direction': RSA, Box labelled 'RS Papers', copy of *ABTT Bulletin* 3 (October 1961).

[13] 'Civic Theatre, Nottingham', *Architectural Review* 127 (January 1960), p. 26; RSA, 28/22/01, copy of letter to Sir William Haley (*The Times*) concerning the Nuffield Theatre, 13 May 1960. (When *The Times* published an account of the Nuffield, Southern was described as a 'theatrical advisor': '£130,000 Gift to Southampton University for a Theatre', *The Times*, 24 May 1960.)

[14] NA, DD/NP/1/2/1/1, letter to Bertrand Hallward, 11 May 1959.

with us as Theatre Consultant?'[15] Southern, who had trained at Goldsmith's and the Royal Academy of Art, was a specialist in the history of stage equipment. He became theatre planning adviser to the Arts Council in 1947, and two years later designed the University of Bristol's flexible drama studio.[16] Several consultancy projects followed, along with an academic post at Bristol. From 1964, he was also the director of the Nuffield Theatre, Southampton, having previously served as consultant when the theatre was being designed.

Southern was not alone in working as a theatre consultant. Several directors and technicians offered similar advice, while the firm of Theatre Projects Consultants grew out of a lighting design/hire service which had been founded in 1957 by Richard Pilbrow.[17] By the 1970s, it was involved in a significant number of projects (see Appendix). Other prominent consultants included John Wyckham, whose work frequently took him to Scotland, and, by the end of the 1970s, Peter Angier and Martin Carr (who had been assistant stage director at Covent Garden). Some consultants were engaged primarily to deal with technical matters. At the Northcott Theatre, Exeter, it was noted in 1963 that the involvement of the actor and designer Michael Warre would reduce the architects' workload by allowing the formulation of a 'generally agreed plan for the stage, its equipment and the seating'.[18] Other consultants also engaged with more conceptual questions, working on feasibility studies, business plans, or the design of the auditorium. In the case of the Barbican Arts Centre, London, Southern was described in 1959 by the architects as having 'collaborated' in the design of the theatre and concert hall.[19] Similarly, the stage designer Sean Kenny worked closely with Peter Hall in 1961 on unexecuted proposals for alterations to the Shakespeare Memorial Theatre at Stratford-upon-Avon,[20] and was involved at the Gardner Arts Centre at Sussex University, where, as will be discussed shortly, he had a significant influence. Yet the Gardner's architect, Basil Spence, was reluctant to surrender all control, firing off a robust response when Kenny criticized his approach to interior decoration: '[Kenny] was certainly not called in to advise on architectural finishes or the building as a whole—I would never have agreed to that arrangement.'[21]

The establishment of the ABTT in early 1961 came in response to a proposal by the recently created International Association of Theatre Technicians (AITT) to hold its next congress in London.[22] The ABTT was to oversee the congress, but it also set out to offer a forum for the discussion of theatre architecture more generally.

[15] RSA, uncat., Box labelled 'Nuffield Theatre and Manchester University Theatre—Plans and Correspondence', G. Grenfell-Baines to Richard Southern, 5 March 1962.

[16] Richard Southern biography, <http://www.bristol.ac.uk/theatre-collection/explore/theatre/richard-southern-collection/> (accessed 20 June 2017); 'At Bristol', *Stage*, 15 February 1951, p. 12.

[17] Richard Pilbrow, *A Theatre Project* (New York, 2011), p. 21.

[18] UoLiv, D147/C74/1, ink draft letter, William Holford to Vice Chancellor, December 1963.

[19] GLL, QL 55.4 BAR, Chamberlin Powell and Bon, 'Barbican Redevelopment, 1959' [printed report, 1959], p. 12.

[20] SBTA, DR1108/2/3/4, Peter Hall to Fordham Flower, 20 January 1961.

[21] HES, MS 2329/ENG/52/5/6-7, Basil Spence to Walter Eysselinck, 16 July 1969.

[22] RSA, Box labelled 'RS Papers', ABTT minutes, 3 March 1961. The ABTT also maintains an archive, and there is further material at JRL, SJ/1/37.

In this respect, members had in mind the Belgrade Theatre's poor backstage planning, which was blamed on a lack of theatrical expertise.[23] A committee, chaired by the director Norman Marshall, was elected, including Frederick Bentham, Stephen Joseph, Sean Kenny, Richard Pilbrow, Victoria Pilbrow, Peter Moro, and Richard Southern. It proposed that the ABTT should encourage high standards in design and theatre technology, and that it could act as a conduit for information.[24] The multidisciplinary design teams that carried out research for government ministries and published their work in technical bulletins were cited as a possible model.[25] Thus, for example, the ABTT's Theatre Architecture and Planning Committee, which was chaired initially by Peter Moro and later by Roderick Ham, contributed articles on technical subjects to the architectural press, leading in 1972 to Ham's book, *Theatre Planning*. The committee, whose initial members included architects, consultants, and directors,[26] also met regularly to comment on the design of proposed theatres. By the end of the 1960s, schemes seeking 'Housing the Arts' funding were routinely referred to it for an assessment of their technical competence. Some designers and their clients found these discussions undeniably helpful,[27] and much good advice was evidently dispensed. However, experiences were mixed. Geoffrey Axworthy of University College Cardiff emerged somewhat bruised by the ABTT's assessment of the proposed Sherman Theatre:

> I hope you have recovered from ABTT's breathtaking session of 'instant criticism'. A little shocking to see how these things are actually handled—in view of the importance of the issues. No-one there seemed to have seen the plans in advance; nor indeed, in such cramped quarters could they really take in the whole plan [...][28]

He concluded: 'Moro and the chap with the beard were good value, and one would have been happier to have talked to them alone.' A certain amount of alcohol was apparently consumed during meetings and coloured the nature of the assessment given to designs considered later on the agenda.[29] On occasion, it also seems that professional rivalries may have shaped some judgements. Norman Branson's designs for the Brewhouse, Taunton, for example, received a sceptical response in the mid-1970s, perhaps because Branson appeared to have a difficult relationship with some members of the ABTT.[30] Unorthodox schemes, too, were sometimes singled out for criticism. In 1981, the committee considered Florian Beigel's designs for the Half Moon Theatre in London. Conceived as a flexible space, the proposed auditorium attempted to distil the essence of an outdoor performance area surrounded by the varied 'facades' of different 'buildings'. These 'facades'

[23] Norman Marshall, 'Planning Adaptable Theatres', *Drama* 62 (1961), pp. 38–41 (p. 39).

[24] RSA, Box labelled 'RS Papers', ABTT minutes, 3 March 1961.

[25] RSA, Box labelled 'RS Papers', ABTT minutes, 3 March 1961.

[26] The initial members were Norman Branson, Elidir Davies, George Devine, John English, Roger Furse, Peter Hall, Stephen Joseph, Sean Kenny, and R. C. E. Shields, with Peter Moro in the chair. See RSA, Box labelled 'RS Papers', *ABTT Bulletin* 3 (October 1961).

[27] John Brownrigg, 'For a New Theatre', *Tabs* 23, no. 3 (September 1965), pp. 8–13.

[28] CUA, UCC/R/F/71, Geoffrey Axworthy to David Hughes, 27 October 1969.

[29] Peter Longman, email to author, 11 July 2017.

[30] Peter Longman, email to author, 11 July 2017.

could be inhabited by audiences or used by actors as part of a production. The committee was seemingly baffled: 'all the normal practical considerations in theatre design had been rejected or ignored'.[31] Yet members understood that their views might be problematic if too strongly expressed. Of the New Lincolnshire Theatre in 1973, they concluded that 'the Committee is aware of the danger that its views on such things as adaptability may thwart experiment and therefore hesitates to be too doctrinaire in its comments'.[32]

'PEEP-SHOW MENTALITY': REJECTING THE PROSCENIUM ARCH

In February 1961, *The Times* welcomed the news that Nottingham City Council was to proceed with the construction of the new Playhouse. Indeed, the article took a positive tone as far as new theatre architecture was concerned, outlining the apparent artistic and technical deficiencies of older proscenium arch theatres:

> In their time they catered for visual effects and a peep-show mentality now better served by cinema and television or, in the theatre, by technical appliances they were never designed to accommodate. The case against this type of playhouse is reinforced by reference to classical drama [...], never meant to be projected across an orchestra pit [...]. Few architects [...] would any longer choose to plan along these lines except in a spirit of antiquarian piety.[33]

In criticizing the proscenium arch stage, the article reflected a debate whose intensity was increasing. For example, *Essentials of Stage-Planning*, co-written by Norman Marshall and Richard Southern with Stanley Bell, noted in 1949 that theatre design was in a transitional phase.[34] In 1962, Southern's *The Seven Ages of the Theatre* argued that the most recent 'seventh age' comprised 'anti-illusionism', a reaction against 'composed' scenes observed by the audience as detached spectators rather than participants.[35] Southern welcomed this development: in 1953 he had called for a 'stage *in* an audience' rather than a 'stage *before* an audience'.[36]

A prominent advocate of open staging was the director Stephen Joseph, whose writing and practice drew together several arguments in favour of change. One was the apparent economy of the open stage theatre. In 1961, it was reported that Joseph's proposed 400-seat in-the-round theatre at Newcastle-under-Lyme 'could

[31] ABTT Archives, uncat., Report on the proposed Half Moon Theatre, 2 July 1981.
[32] ABTT Archives, uncat., Report on the proposed Lincolnshire Theatre, 19 November 1973.
[33] 'Should We Build New Theatres?', *The Times*, 3 February 1961.
[34] Stanley Bell, Norman Marshall, and Richard Southern, *Essentials of Stage-Planning* (London, 1949), p. 1.
[35] Richard Southern, *The Seven Ages of the Theatre* (London, 1964), pp. 268–83.
[36] Richard Southern, *The Open Stage and the Modern Theatre in Research and Practice* (London, 1953), p. 42.

be erected for a tenth of the cost of a conventional building'.[37] Designed by Stephen Garrett, the theatre was estimated to cost £60,000. Its low price resulted from the lack of a fly tower and the equipment needed for elaborate scene changes. Another motive for rethinking stage and auditorium lay in the opportunity to escape the apparent social inequalities of many older proscenium arch theatres. Joseph criticized the shabby side entrances and barren staircases that typically led to the cheaper seats in older venues.[38] By contrast, at the Mermaid Theatre in London, the former warehouse converted in 1959 for the director Bernard Miles by Elidir Davies, all of the audience entered via the same doors at the back of the auditorium. A further refinement involved wrapping the audience around three or four sides of the stage, giving within only a few rows the same seating capacity that in an end-on arrangement would need a longer seating rake, and so meaning that all patrons would enjoy a close view of the action.

There were, therefore, practical arguments for open staging, but, at the same time, Joseph suggested that 'open stages have their own artistic and aesthetic attractions'.[39] It would, he thought, be stimulating to present works originally written for the proscenium arch stage in new ways.[40] Open staging seemed to offer novel possibilities, especially for the kinds of abstract stage settings being designed by the likes of Tanya Moiseiwitsch. Such designs were far removed from the illusionistic sets for which the proscenium arch stage had evolved. Sean Kenny, an architect and designer who was well known for his work on the 1960 stage production of *Oliver!*, suggested in 1964 that the proscenium arch itself was limiting: 'if you wanted a Picasso, and you said, "Look, Picasso, here is a frame, paint me a picture," he would throw you out'.[41] In addition, it was frequently argued that open stages offered a clear way for theatre to distinguish itself from film and television, which both presented a 'framed' picture akin to the view of the stage as seen through a proscenium arch. Open staging offered something different, especially in auditoria where the audience encircled the stage. Such theatres provided their audiences with a range of views of the action in place of the single focus of the proscenium arch stage (or the camera lens). Actors might be seen from behind or sideways on, prompting Joseph to observe that 'to present the audience with a three-dimensional image is the unique privilege of the theatre'.[42] Furthermore, open stage layouts were often thought to encourage a close relationship between actors and audience. Colin George, the director at Sheffield Playhouse and then the Crucible Theatre, contrasted proscenium arch productions (which he felt encouraged passive spectatorship) with pop concerts, which he felt were more interactive.[43]

[37] 'Man in the Centre', *Guardian*, 6 January 1961. See also Stephen Joseph, 'Newcastle-under-Lyme Civic Theatre', in *Adaptable Theatres*, edited by Stephen Joseph (London, 1962), pp. 67–70. For drawings, see 'Building Theatres: Congress of Theatre Technicians', *Architects' Journal* 134 (12 July 1961), pp. 49–50.

[38] Stephen Joseph, *New Theatre Forms* (London, 1968), p. 114.

[39] Joseph, *New Theatre Forms*, p. 16.

[40] Joseph, *New Theatre Forms*, pp. 18–19.

[41] Sean Kenny, 'The Shape of the Theatre', in *Actor and Audience*, edited by Stephen Joseph (Manchester, 1964), pp. 57–66 (p. 60).

[42] Joseph, *New Theatre Forms*, p. 19.

[43] 'Suicide or Salvation?', *Yorkshire Architect*, March 1971, pp. 386–8 (p. 388).

There are parallels here with the calls for more participatory approaches to worship by liturgical and architectural reformers which transformed church design in this period.[44]

FROM JOSEPH AND GUTHRIE TO CHICHESTER

In 1955, the director of Scarborough Library received a letter asking to use part of the building as a theatre. Its author was Stephen Joseph, who had studied English at Cambridge in the late 1940s before undertaking a drama degree in Iowa, where he experienced in-the-round theatre at first hand. Paul Elsam's biography casts Joseph as a radical, at odds with the theatrical establishment.[45] Joseph, who died at an early age in 1967, was certainly a strong character. He sought to popularize theatre not only through the performance of new work but also by stripping away the traditional trappings of theatre buildings. He underlined the human basis of performance, seeing drama as 'a ritual' to which 'there can be no better background [. . .] than other human beings'.[46] Joseph's request to perform in Scarborough was accepted, and by 1956 his company was also touring the Midlands. However, his proposed theatre at Newcastle-under-Lyme, a location suggested by the Arts Council, remained unbuilt after an application by the Borough Council to the Ministry of Housing and Local Government to borrow the money required to build it was turned down. In what was intended as an interim measure, a former cinema in Stoke-on-Trent became the Victoria Theatre, which was run initially by Joseph with Peter Cheeseman, and then by Cheeseman alone. Only in 1986 was an all-new building, the New Vic, finally opened in Newcastle-under-Lyme as the country's first major purpose-built in-the-round theatre.[47]

One of the directors whose ideas figured large in early ABTT discussions and Joseph's books was John English, founder of the Arena Theatre in Birmingham in 1949.[48] Although the term 'arena' theatre was often synonymous with in-the-round staging, for English it meant a fusion of the thrust stage and the Greek amphitheatre. English claimed to have arrived at this hybrid form following an examination of 'the needs of a twentieth-century playhouse'.[49] His target audience was the young, among whom he hoped to inculcate a love of live drama and 'a climate of cultural literacy'.[50] Parents would be encouraged to bring their children; a network of

[44] Peter Hammond, 'A Radical Approach to Church Architecture', in his *Towards a Church Architecture* (London, 1962), pp. 15–37.

[45] Paul Elsam, *Stephen Joseph: Theatre Pioneer and Provocateur* (London, 2013), pp. ix–xiv.

[46] 'Stephen Joseph Writes on His Theatre in the Round at Newcastle-under-Lyme', *Plays and Players*, March 1962.

[47] V&A, ACGB/120/3, 'New Victoria Theatre, Stoke-on-Trent', 27 April 1983.

[48] John English, 'The Cannon Hill Theatre', in *Adaptable Theatres*, edited by Stephen Joseph (London, 1962), pp. 41–7.

[49] English, 'Cannon Hill Theatre', pp. 42–3.

[50] 'John English in Conversation with Iain Ball', *English in Education* 1, no. 3 (September 1967), pp. 46–56 (p. 50).

'cultural fosterparents' (i.e. schoolteachers) would bring children whose parents were uninterested. From 1960, a permanent organization began to form at the Midlands Arts Centre, which was intended to have a flexible auditorium that could be used in thrust, 'in-the-round', and proscenium arch formats, and in a looser arrangement that English termed the 'space stage'.[51] The proposals, the work of Herbert Jackson, were discussed in the *Architects' Journal* in July 1961, which called them 'a shot in the arm' for British theatre architecture.[52]

The principal advocate of the thrust stage theatre was Tyrone Guthrie, who was influenced by the open stage of the short-lived Cambridge Festival Theatre of the late 1920s.[53] After Cambridge, Guthrie moved to the Old Vic, where he sought to abandon scenic realism while still working on a proscenium arch stage, but the real breakthrough came in 1936 when an outdoor performance of *Hamlet* at Elsinore was rained off at short notice. Guthrie moved the play to a local ballroom, arranging the audience around an improvised acting area. The idea was developed in his 1948 production of David Lyndsay's *Satire of the Three Estates* in the Church of Scotland's Assembly Hall, Edinburgh, in which the Moderator's dais became a stage surrounded by the audience. Scenery was minimized, with meaning instead being conveyed through costumes and props. Guthrie went on to create successful theatres on these lines in Stratford, Ontario (1953 and 1957) and Minneapolis (1963).

On 4 January 1959, Guthrie was the subject of BBC television's *Monitor* programme. Among those who saw the broadcast was Leslie Evershed-Martin, a Chichester optician who had been an amateur actor in the 1930s and was twice mayor of the town.[54] He realized that Stratford, Ontario, was the same size as his home town: if a thrust stage theatre worked there, why not in Sussex?[55] He also was aware that nearby Glyndebourne was successful as a privately run opera house.[56] Evershed-Martin met Guthrie and secured his support; Guthrie thought Evershed-Martin 'a very driving energetic fellow' who would be able to realize this 'crackpot scheme'.[57] It proceeded with considerable pace: the building opened just a year after the construction contract had been signed.[58] During the first season, *The Chances* was staged in the minimal Guthrie manner, while a similarly bare set was devised by Sean Kenny for *Uncle Vanya*.[59]

The venture was described in 1962 as a fusion of old and new:

> Of late there has been an increasing need for some new stimulus to be given to the living theatre, and when the Chichester Festival Theatre opens [...] we shall see the realisation of a new conception of theatre. The building, which combines the classical

[51] English, 'Cannon Hill Theatre', pp. 43–7.
[52] 'Building Theatres', *Architects' Journal* 134 (12 July 1961), pp. 49–50.
[53] Iain Mackintosh, 'Guthrie's Genesis', *Architectural Review* 151 (February 1972), pp. 93–4; *The Guthrie Thrust Stage: A Living Legacy*, edited by Iain Mackintosh (London, 2011).
[54] 'Obituary: Leslie Evershed-Martin', *Independent*, 28 January 1994.
[55] Daniel Rosenthal, *The National Theatre Story* (London, 2013), p. 44.
[56] 'Plans Are Announced for £70,000 Festival Theatre at Chichester', *Stage*, 11 February 1960.
[57] Rosenthal, *National Theatre*, p. 44.
[58] WSRO, CFT Box 44, building contract, 10 May 1961. The contract sum was £95,064.
[59] Rosenthal, *National Theatre*, p. 55.

> lines of the old Greek and Elizabethan playhouses with those laid down by contemporary requirements, is hexagonal in shape, with the stage surrounded by the audience on three sides. This is a deliberate departure from the conventional proscenium arch and has been designed so that all may see and hear perfectly from every part of the auditorium, the furthest seat being only sixty feet from the stage.[60]

The live qualities of theatre would be emphasized in 'a real alternative to the attractions of cinema and television; the kind which by dispensing with the proscenium arch, exploits to the full the unobstructed, three-dimensional presentations whose dramatic impact on audiences can be so electrifying'.[61] The project architect for Powell and Moya, Christopher Stevens, recalls that there was never a formal briefing document as such.[62] Evershed-Martin simply outlined his interest in creating something like the theatre at Stratford, Ontario, as well as the need for economy. Mention was made of 'thumbnail sketches' by Guthrie,[63] and there was apparently at least one occasion on which Guthrie visited the architects to comment on their work, but the impact of these sessions might be questioned, because the final design diverged somewhat from the Guthrie model. Guthrie's preference was for the audience to be distributed fairly equally around the stage, but some 70 per cent of the seats at Chichester face the end of the stage (see Figure 8.2).[64] In addition, the size of the stage is such that a much smaller proportion of the audience is behind the centre line compared with other Guthrie auditoria, and the seating rake is shallower.[65] Stephen Joseph later suggested that none of the key personnel 'knew very well what he was doing',[66] and others made similar comments.[67]

If the Festival Theatre is thus an incomplete expression of Guthrie's ideas, it was nonetheless a remarkable piece of design. The roof structure, according to a 1962 report, aroused 'interest and excitement amongst technical experts' for the way in which it created a column-free, wide-span interior.[68] The interior design similarly generated 'much controversy and discussion'.[69] The *Sunday Telegraph* described the journey into the auditorium, a space which it characterized in almost scientific or industrial terms as the location of a 'process':

> The transition from factual parkland to fictional playland is subtle and momentous. You go through the big glass foyer walls, up gradually enclosed stairs, progressively darkening as daylight is filtered through blue glass slips and finally step into the dark blue, grey and black auditorium where you can see and experience the whole theatrical process.[70]

60 WSRO, CFT Box 59, 'Festival' [programme], 1962.
61 WSRO, CFT Box 59, 'Festival', 1962.
62 Christopher Stevens, email to author, 18 May 2015.
63 RSA, Box labelled 'RS Papers', *ABTT Bulletin*, June 1963, n.p.
64 WSRO, CFT Box 126, 'Thirty Years On' [report, 1992], p. 11.
65 WSRO, CFT Box 126, 'Thirty Years On', p. 6; *Guthrie Thrust Stage*, ed. Mackintosh, p. 12.
66 Quoted in Elsam, *Stephen Joseph*, p. 34.
67 GLL, S L 50.01, Anthony Besch, 'Report to the Corporation of the City of London [...]', 1964, pp. 60–1.
68 WSRO, CFT Box 54, Draft Report, 1962, p. 2.
69 WSRO, CFT Box 54, Draft Report, 1962, p. 2.
70 *Sunday Telegraph*, 6 May 1962, quoted in WSRO, CFT Box 59, 'Festival' [programme], 1962.

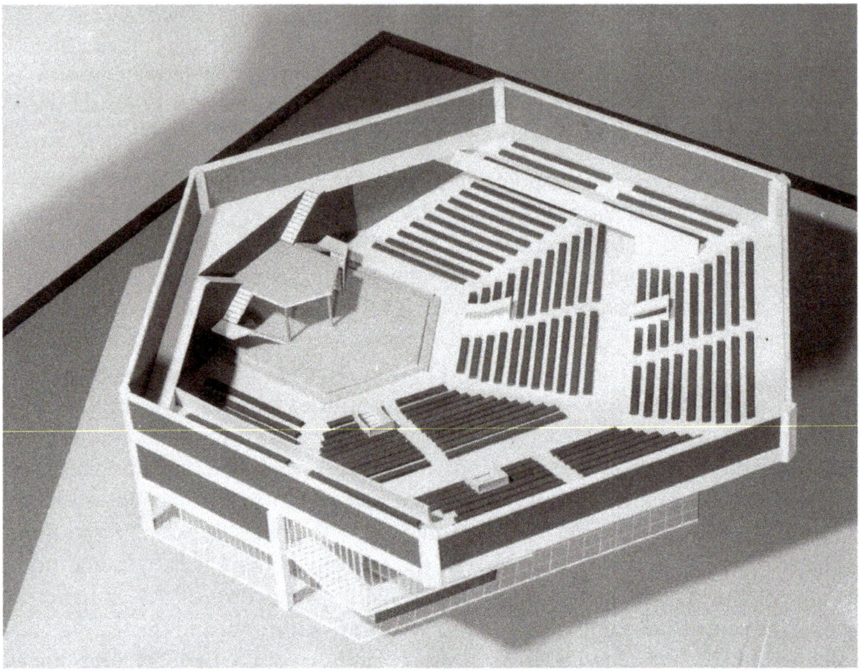

Figure 8.2. Chichester Festival Theatre, model, *c.*1961 (Architectural Press Archive/ RIBA Collections)

The colour scheme was selected on the basis that Chichester was 'essentially a summer theatre' and thus 'the colours should be cool and also subdued in order to lend emphasis to what was happening on the stage'.[71] This discussion touched on a broader principle. In contrast to proscenium arch theatres, in which the audience and actors occupy distinct areas which can therefore be differently decorated, the location of the stage in the centre of a thrust stage auditorium often suggested a more recessive treatment. In essence, the dark colours that on the proscenium arch stage would be hidden backstage were brought out into the auditorium as a neutral backdrop for performances.

The prices charged at Chichester also differed from multi-tiered theatres. An initial proposal to charge 25 shillings for most of the 1358 seats met with a cool response from Evershed-Martin, who commented that 'there should be enough seats at reasonable prices for those people who were unable to afford higher priced seats'.[72] Nonetheless, the idea of a truly popular theatre seems not to have been wholly embraced. In 1963, it was reported of the theatre restaurant that:

> Those people who are used to dining out were delighted with it. Those who expect to eat in ordinary restaurants with the usual idea of three courses for under 10/- were

[71] WSRO, CFT Box 62, minutes, 6 December 1961.
[72] WSRO, CFT Box 62, minutes, 19 February 1962.

> sometimes resentful of the type of food provided. [...] The style of management and fare provided upheld the Board's hopes of always making this Festival different and better than the usual Theatre organisation.[73]

One might see this discussion not so much as an attempt to expand audiences' horizons, as was the case in many of the examples considered in previous chapters, but rather as a desire to appeal to a certain class of patron. In the same vein, there was discussion of the results that might be obtained by advertising in the *Sunday Times* (described in a note as 'the most widely read Sunday paper amongst the professional classes') rather than the local press.[74]

When it came to running the theatre, Evershed-Martin wrote in 1962 that 'we envisaged a director of the calibre of Dr Guthrie, but knew it was very improbable that he would be able to be with us'.[75] Guthrie's advice was nonetheless sought.[76] Stuart Burge, who was then increasingly well known as an accomplished director, was mentioned, as was Peter Ustinov, the actor and writer. However, it was 'decided to try Olivier, Peter Brook'.[77] Three days later, Evershed-Martin 'sent off details to New York asking Sir Laurence [Olivier] whether he would be director'.[78] The pair met in June 1961 and a deal was struck.[79] For Evershed-Martin, the result was instant credibility, with Olivier able to cast his famous friends at what otherwise might simply be seen as an untried new theatre with an unusual stage.[80] Why did Olivier accept? He seems to have felt no great sympathy with the intended non-scenic approach, later recording that he had been concerned by the lack of facilities for scenic production.[81] Nonetheless, Olivier was increasingly an advocate for the new. Having in 1956 seen John Osborne's *Look Back in Anger*, he asked the author to write a play for him.[82] By approaching Osborne, Olivier recognized that the kind of grand acting with which he had long been associated was increasingly unfashionable, as well as the extent to which the Royal Court under George Devine had emerged as a centre for cutting-edge drama.[83] The resulting play, *The Entertainer*, came at a moment of renewal for Olivier, both professionally and personally.[84] He divorced Vivien Leigh and married Joan Plowright, who had co-starred with him in *The Entertainer*, and moved to Brighton. He surrounded himself with innovators, including the ever-provocative critic Kenneth Tynan, who

73 WSRO, CFT Box 54, Draft Report, 1962, p. 5.

74 WSRO, CFT Box 54, Promotional and Advertising Campaign. Report by Barry C. Dimeck, 1962.

75 WSRO, CFT Box 52, Leslie Evershed-Martin memo, n.d [late 1962?].

76 WSRO, CFT Box 62, 'Dates Continued', 8 January 1961.

77 WSRO, CFT Box 62, 'Dates Continued', 8 January 1961.

78 WSRO, CFT Box 62, 'Dates Continued', 11 January 1961.

79 Philip Ziegler, *Olivier* (London, 2013), p. 234.

80 Ziegler, *Olivier*, p. 238.

81 Laurence Olivier, Introduction to Leslie Evershed-Martin, *The Impossible Theatre: The Chichester Festival Theatre Adventure* (London, 1971), p. ix.

82 Michael Billington, *State of the Nation: British Theatre Since 1945* (London, 2007), pp. 105–8.

83 Barnabas Calder, 'Committees and Concrete: the genesis and architecture of Denys Lasdun's National Theatre' (PhD diss., University of Cambridge, 2007), p. 67.

84 Calder, 'Committees and Concrete', p. 67.

reported in 1964 that 'L[aurence] O[livier]'s preoccupation with change [in theatre trends] is really that he wants to keep in line with "les jeunes" '.[85]

In addition, Evershed-Martin's timing was opportune.[86] Olivier's tenure at the St James' Theatre in London had proved expensive, he had failed to raise money for a film of *Macbeth*, and his recent screen career had excited few. Opening Chichester and experimenting with an open stage offered Olivier a dry run for the post to which it seemed increasingly likely that he would be appointed, namely director of the National Theatre. With the LCC having committed to part-fund the National in 1961, it seemed only a matter of time before the theatre might actually come into being, and indeed on 3 July 1962, the first night at Chichester, it was reported that the final hurdles seemed to have been overcome.[87] In early August, Olivier confirmed to Evershed-Martin that he would continue working in Chichester, but that he had taken the National job. There he was to oversee the design of a larger and more complex open stage auditorium.

OPEN STAGING AT THE NATIONAL

The decision to build three different kinds of auditoria for live spoken-word drama at the National Theatre, rather than an adaptable compromise between proscenium arch and open stage formats, made it unique in international terms.[88] The 1949 Act of Parliament that set in train the establishment of the theatre called for a building with two auditoria, one large and one small, which Sadler's Wells Opera would share with the theatre company. In Brian O'Rorke's initial designs, the larger auditorium has a proscenium arch stage; later drawings show an open stage amphitheatre.[89] After O'Rorke had been replaced by Denys Lasdun in 1963, Olivier asked for a single, adaptable auditorium, feeling that two spaces might lead to confusion.[90] Lasdun, however, soon concluded that true adaptability was impossible. In spring 1964, the National's Building Committee—representing the notional 'users' of the theatre—informed the South Bank Theatre and Opera House Board (SBTOHB), the formal client, that it now preferred a single auditorium. The SBTOHB insisted on the provision of a 700-seat proscenium arch theatre alongside a larger open stage auditorium, an idea that elicited little enthusiasm from the Building Committee.[91] Nonetheless, by October 1964, it had been established that the National Theatre would have two auditoria, as well as a separate opera house and, potentially, an experimental studio.[92]

[85] Calder, 'Committees and Concrete', p. 67.
[86] Rosenthal, *National Theatre*, p. 45.
[87] Rosenthal, *National Theatre*, pp. 47–56.
[88] Calder, 'Committees and Concrete', p. 16.
[89] RIBA, PA823/14/1–29 for earlier proposals; PA 824/1/2 and PA 824/1/5, drawings of December 1960.
[90] Calder, 'Committees and Concrete', pp. 78–89.
[91] Calder, 'Committees and Concrete', p. 115.
[92] Calder, 'Committees and Concrete', p. 90.

The larger theatre—later known as the Olivier Theatre—was conceived as an open stage auditorium with 'scenic possibilities'.[93] Although it might seem simply to be a classical amphitheatre in modern dress, Lasdun's office developed the design iteratively. Intensive model-making sessions followed often tempestuous discussions with the National's Building Committee, which proved to be keen on argument and was divided in its views.[94] A sequence of five formal design proposals emerged.[95] The first, later known as 'Scheme A', comprised a wide fan-shaped auditorium with a vestigial proscenium arch. It was quickly followed by the so-called 'Scheme B', which was more radical in locating actor and audience within a single 'room' of essentially square plan, in one corner of which was to be the stage. A balcony encircling both stage and seating added to the sense of a single space shared by actor and audience, an idea to which Lasdun attached particular significance. Scheme B was accepted in principle by the Building Committee in May 1964, and Lasdun turned to the design of the theatre complex as a whole. Doubts soon started to emerge on the part of some of the members of the Building Committee, however, and were exacerbated by an enforced pause in their meetings during 1965 and early 1966 as the SBTOHB worked to ensure that the National would, in fact, be built. In the absence of continued consultation, some members of the Building Committee concluded that they were being conspired against, and by April 1966 they had decided that Scheme B had been foisted upon them. Lasdun responded with Scheme C, which revisited the ideas of Scheme A; it was thought dull. To break the impasse, it was suggested that a subcommittee should undertake focused work with Lasdun. The director John Dexter and the designer Jocelyn Herbert, in particular, made significant contributions, cutting up models and experimenting with different options in a practical manner which recalled the *modus operandi* of the Lasdun office. The resulting Schemes D and E of 1966 refined the principles of Scheme B. Although Olivier himself seemed to prefer the single-tier Scheme D, Scheme E was popular with Dexter, Herbert, and Richard Pilbrow, and served as the basis of the Olivier Theatre as built.

Just as Lasdun's unsuccessful competition design for Liverpool Metropolitan Cathedral had in 1959 sought to reimagine the cathedral in modern terms, having a centralized layout which brought the clergy close to the congregation, Lasdun argued that the Olivier Theatre was contemporary yet rooted in precedent, and that it encouraged contact between actor and audience:

> We searched for a single room [...] whose spatial configuration, above all else, would promote a dynamic and emotional relationship between audience and actor—between a fixed architectonic geometry of vision, acoustics and concentration and the chance irregular demands of dramatic performance. We searched for an open relationship that looked back to the Greeks and Elizabethans and, at the same time, looked forward to a contemporary view of society in which all could have a fair chance to see, hear and share the collective experience of exploring human truths.[96]

[93] Pilbrow, *A Theatre Project*, p. 118.
[94] Calder, 'Committees and Concrete', pp. 66–85.
[95] This summary is based on Calder, 'Committees and Concrete', pp. 91–111.
[96] 'Olivier Theatre', *Architectural Review* 161 (January 1977), pp. 36–7 (p. 37).

The audience occupies a fan-shaped arc of seating. The idea was that an actor would be able to stand at the midpoint of the stage (the 'point of command') and address the whole audience with a single gesture or glance. Unlike Chichester, where the auditorium surfaces are highly recessive, the parts of the Olivier occupied by the audience feature precisely detailed board-marked concrete, the silver colour of which is complemented by pale purple seating. The use of concrete brings into the auditorium the material of the National's exterior and foyers, but also resulted from John Bury's suggestion that light should reflect onto the audience in order to allow actors to see the people to whom they were playing.[97] The stage itself is large, with extensive flying facilities and a huge revolve (lift) which allows complete sets to be brought up to the stage from three floors below. Richard Pilbrow played a significant role in the technical specification of the stage, something that was not entirely welcomed by Lasdun, who deemed Pilbrow's interventions 'an impertinence verging on the unprofessional' for the way in which they added 'ears' to the fly tower.[98]

YORKSHIRE THRUST: LEEDS AND SHEFFIELD

While the National Theatre was being designed, open stage theatres were being discussed and built in Sheffield and Leeds. Leeds Playhouse was planned as a temporary structure and opened first, in 1970.[99] Designed by William Houghton-Evans and built for £150,000, the theatre was housed within a building that had been constructed as a sports hall for the university. A 'Greek shape of theatre' was requested, with a projecting stage and a steep rake of seating. A tower at each side of the stage provided balconies for use during performance and also served to house ductwork and plant; together, these towers suggested a vestigial proscenium arch. Dark colours predominated, with purple drapes hiding the auditorium's concrete-block walls and the seats being upholstered in deep blue fabric. The theatre was replaced in 1990 by the West Yorkshire Playhouse, designed by Ian and Marjorie Appleton, the form of whose main auditorium recalls its 1970 predecessor.

More substantial, however, was the purpose-built Crucible Theatre, Sheffield (1971), which, as was discussed in Chapter 4, replaced the Playhouse. The Crucible's stage was informed by the ideas of Tyrone Guthrie, whose associate Tanya Moiseiwitsch collaborated with the theatre's director, Colin George, and architect, Nick Thompson of Renton Howard Wood (RHW).[100] Colin George's interest in open staging reflected his wish to encourage a two-way relationship between actor and audience.[101] His starting point was the recently opened Nottingham Playhouse on account of its adaptable forestage, which provided a large acting area in front

[97] Calder, 'Committees and Concrete', p. 97.
[98] Calder, 'Committees and Concrete', p. 109.
[99] 'Description of the Leeds Playhouse', *Tabs* 28, no. 4 (December 1970), pp. 138–43.
[100] *Guthrie Thrust Stage*, ed. Mackintosh, p. 15.
[101] 'Suicide or Salvation?', p. 388.

of the proscenium arch.[102] By early 1967, it was proposed to build a 900-seat theatre in Sheffield with a similar 'thrust forward' stage, along with a studio 'of spartan simplicity'.[103] In the main auditorium, two stage layouts were required. In one, a small forestage would be coupled with a proscenium arch of between 30 and 36 feet, and in the other a bigger thrust stage would be projected into the auditorium. However, in October 1967, Tyrone Guthrie lectured in Sheffield,[104] and recommended the construction of a true thrust stage.[105] George, together with the Playhouse's administrator, David Brayshaw, arranged an impromptu trip to North America, and returned convinced of the Guthrie approach.[106] A new Schedule of Accommodation, dated March 1968, called for 'an open stage theatre in which will be presented classical and modern plays by a resident company of the highest professional standard'.[107] Notably, Chichester was not used as a model, with both George and Thompson being critical of it.[108] The stage at Sheffield was to be narrower, while the seating rake was to be steeper. A 'moat' around the stage would differentiate it from the front row of seating, but would not form a visual barrier; this was described as 'important'.

The new approach was lent credence by Guthrie's involvement, which George later recalled as having been crucial in securing the Board's approval.[109] Others, however, were less sure, and a letter of January 1970 suggests that the theatre's assistant director, Wilfred Harrison, felt that a thrust stage was being imposed upon him.[110] In this respect, the highly personal nature of the vision becomes apparent, with contemporary accounts noting George's ability to 'sell refrigerators to Eskimos'.[111] Certain members of the City Council were also unenthusiastic. One councillor apparently suggested that, if the Crucible failed, it would become 'the best-known bingo hall in the north of England'.[112] Many in the press were critical, too, apparently encouraged by disparaging remarks made by Bernard Miles.[113]

Moiseiwitsch specified the height, width, and length of the Crucible's stage (see Figure 8.3).[114] Whereas for George the thrust stage was fundamentally a way to achieve a close actor–audience relationship, Moiseiwitsch as a designer thought more in terms of production style, seeing the thrust stage as a platform for abstract, non-scenic work, with a permanent architectural backdrop, movable *periaktoi* (scenic towers), and a stepped edge.[115] Once the stage concept had been established,

[102] V&A, ACGB/84/246, 'Sheffield New Theatre', September 1966.

[103] V&A, ACGB/84/246, Schedule of Accommodation, February 1967.

[104] V&A, ACGB/84/246, Antony Hampton to Nigel Abercrombie, 31 October 1967.

[105] V&A, ACGB/84/246, D. B. Harrison to Nigel Abercrombie, 2 January 1968.

[106] V&A, ACGB/84/246, D. B. Harrison to Nigel Abercrombie, 2 January 1968; V&A, ACGB/84/246, Reports by Colin George and David Brayshaw on their American visit, 1967.

[107] V&A, ACGB/84/246, Schedule of Accommodation, 6 March 1968.

[108] Nick Thompson, interviewed 20 June 2006; Colin George, interviewed 26 June 2006.

[109] Colin George, interviewed 26 June 2006.

[110] SCA, LD2287, letter [not signed] of 5 January 1970.

[111] Quoted in a special supplement published by the *Morning Telegraph* in 1982 to celebrate the theatre's tenth anniversary, filed in the Crucible's archive.

[112] Colin George, interviewed 26 June 2006.

[113] E.g. clippings in RSA, RS/0080/1/59.

[114] Nick Thompson, interviewed 20 June 2006.

[115] Billington, *State of the Nation*, p. 51.

Figure 8.3. 'Stage of the future': Crucible Theatre, Sheffield, 1971 (John Donat/RIBA Collections)

the design was developed outwards to generate the form of the rest of the building.[116] An octagonal geometry emerged, with the audience being seated in five banks around the stage and the furthest seat being 58 feet from the edge of the stage. This degree of concentration was intended to generate the kind of active participation that George sought. Equality was important, too. Initially, seats were priced according to their distance from the stage, in order to avoid any sense that the central block was somehow the best.[117] The auditorium ambiance was muted, with Thompson later suggesting that it was a 'technical space'.[118] The one poetic gesture came in the galaxy of twinkling lights above the seating, which suggested the open-air theatres of classical antiquity. Otherwise, the auditorium was straightforward in appearance. Seating was (and remains) orange-brown, the walls were finished in painted render with cork panels, while the space above the stage was left open, exposing the lighting and services.

[116] Nick Thompson, interviewed 20 June 2006.
[117] SCA, LD2317, Kevan Scholes, 'The Crucible Theatre, Sheffield' [unpublished typescript, 1976], p. 9.
[118] Nick Thompson, interviewed 20 June 2006.

For Colin George, the Crucible's stage embodied theatrical modernity.[119] It was to be used for 'all contemporary forms of expression'; as 'an exciting stage form', it was hoped that it would tempt audiences, actors, and directors away from television. George noted that 'the theatre's influence and popularity can only grow if it is presented [...] in a way that corresponds to the vitality of other modern art and "pop" '.[120] But the Crucible was not simply a modern playhouse on account of its stage design, nor, indeed, its contemporary foyers. Rather, its modernity also stemmed from the circumstances of its conception. As a subsidized repertory theatre with a resident company of actors and directors, it did not matter that the Crucible's thrust stage was distinctive. It was not intended to take touring shows, which were typically designed for proscenium arch auditoria, although the suggestion was made that visiting companies interested in working on this kind of stage would be welcome. Arts Council subsidies plus support from the local authority thus allowed an imaginative client team and their designers to rethink the forms and practice of theatre. The result was, perhaps, the very model of a modern playhouse.

FLEXIBLE SOLUTIONS

Reflecting on his American visit at the end of the 1960s, Colin George argued that 'you cannot have a theatre which is adaptable from proscenium to promontory stage'.[121] Those who had tried it had, he said, concluded that 'adaptability is costly and in practice uneconomic'.[122] In Britain, the difficulties inherent in designing a fully adaptable theatre which worked well in all formats were repeatedly pointed out by architects,[123] consultants,[124] and practitioners alike.[125] Peter Moro's views were typical:

> it is doubtful whether [a fully flexible 'laboratory'] would in itself be acceptable as a permanent method of housing theatrical performances as, after the first excitement of 'seeing the works' the aesthetics of a technical lab are not lasting or, in the long run, likely to create the right atmosphere for a theatrical occasion. Also, to have unlimited possibilities would put a great strain on the writer and producer. Most artists welcome some limitations, provided they are of the right kind, and would feel lost if all these were removed.[126]

A few large flexible auditoria were nonetheless constructed. These auditoria could be thought to be especially modern, not only because they avoided the use of a proscenium arch but also on account of the technology used in some of them to effect the transformation from one layout to another.[127]

[119] 'Suicide or Salvation?', p. 388.
[120] 'Suicide or Salvation?', p. 388.
[121] 'Suicide or Salvation?', p. 386.
[122] 'Suicide or Salvation?', p. 386.
[123] Roderick Ham, *Theatre Planning* (London, 1972), p. 8.
[124] Frederick Bentham, *New Theatres in Britain* (London, 1970), pp. 6–7.
[125] Joseph, *New Theatre Forms*, p. 104.
[126] RSA, Box labelled 'RS Papers', Peter Moro, 'Is the Proscenium Obsolete?', *ABTT Bulletin*, June 1963.
[127] E.g. the press release of 1972 for the New London Theatre, quoted in Ronald Bergan, *The Great Theatres of London: An Illustrated Companion* (London, 1987), p. 108.

North American theatres often had flexible auditoria suitable for a range of kinds of event in order to maximize income in a context where public subsidy for the arts was minimal.[128] The same concern occasionally surfaced in Britain. The New London Theatre in the West End, for example, was not subsidized, and so needed 'to be sufficiently adaptable to attract different kinds of production and ensure maximum use'.[129] Completed in 1971 to the designs of Michael Percival and Paul Tvrtkovic, the auditorium was designed in collaboration with Sean Kenny. By rotating part of the seating and the stage, it could be used in either end-stage or in-the-round layouts. The Hexagon, Reading (RMJM, 1977) was similarly conceived in flexible terms in order to maximize income, although unlike the New London it was supported by the local authority. Early proposals for a new arts complex in Reading had included two auditoria, one a civic hall with 1500 seats and the other a 500-seat theatre.[130] However, rising costs and the replacement of a Labour-run council with a Conservative-led administration saw this plan abandoned in favour of a single flexible 1500-seat hall in which 'different styles of theatre could be achieved by rearranging the seating and equipment'.[131] Although it was perhaps the building's appearance which prompted a proposal to name it the 'Futurist Hall',[132] the modernity of the venture was also suggested by its adaptability as well as the technologies used to achieve that adaptability. One review suggested that the Hexagon was an 'architectural appliance'.[133] The stalls seating could be retracted to create a flat floor, platform lifts allowed the stage height and size to be altered, while screens created a 'proscenium arch' of variable width when needed.[134] The acoustic requirements of different uses were accommodated by a system of electronic 'Assisted Resonance', as had been used in the Festival Hall. However, not everyone was convinced, including Francis Reid, the lighting designer who reviewed the building for the *Architects' Journal*. His criticism covered not only the technical installation, which he thought inadequate, but also extended to the way in which flexibility was implemented.[135] For example, the use of the proscenium 'arch' meant that large areas of seating lost their view of the stage and so were taken out of use simply by turning out the lights, a move which, Reid suggested, meant that the auditorium felt half full. The management protested. They had already suggested that the Hexagon was a wholly new type of building,[136] and now they argued that it could hardly be assessed in the conventional terms of a theatre specialist.[137]

[128] Thomas DeGaetani, 'The Adaptable Theatre in the American University; and the Loeb Drama Centre', in *Adaptable Theatres*, edited by Stephen Joseph (London, 1962), pp. 17–21.

[129] M. J. Percival, 'New Winter Garden Theatre', *Tabs* 28, no. 2 (June 1970), pp. 53–7.

[130] RCL, Hexagon file, clipping: Tony Knott, 'No Business Like a Proper Theatre', *Evening Post*, 17 October 2007.

[131] RCL, Hexagon file, untitled clipping from the *Evening Post*, 28 February 1973.

[132] RCL, Hexagon file, clipping: 'Name Game', *Evening Post*, 12 April 1976.

[133] 'The Hexagon, Reading', *Architects' Journal* 169 (28 February 1979), pp. 415–30 (p. 424).

[134] 'The Hexagon, Reading', p. 419. [135] 'The Hexagon, Reading', p. 426.

[136] RCL, Hexagon file, clipping: 'A New Heart for Reading?', *Evening Post*, 28 September 1977.

[137] 'The Hexagon, Reading', p. 428.

Similarly intended for a range of uses was the hall designed in 1958–9 by Chamberlin Powell and Bon for the Barbican Arts Centre in London. Drawings by the theatre consultant, Richard Southern, show a two-tier auditorium of polygonal plan.[138] Thrust and in-the-round arrangements were possible, the transformation being achieved not with technological wizardry but rather with curtains and rostra. For the architects, the imperative was to maximize the use of the hall, but for Southern the justification was artistic. He produced sketches to explain that different kinds of play needed different kinds of staging.[139] However, the design presented serious challenges. Would curtains really have generated a satisfactory environment, visually and acoustically? The concert hall (and theatre) eventually constructed at the Barbican had a much more conventional, fixed layout.

The challenges of flexibility meant that most flexible auditoria were small. They were frequently found in amateur and university theatres, where volunteer or student labour could be relied upon. A prominent amateur example was the Crescent Theatre, Birmingham, the first—and ultimately only—phase of which was completed to Graham Winteringham's designs in 1964 (and which was replaced by a new building in 1998). Winteringham was inspired by the illustration of Walter Gropius's unbuilt, flexible *Totaltheater* proposal of 1927 in J. B. Priestley's *The Story of Theatre*,[140] and sought to achieve something similar by mounting the front part of the Crescent's stalls and its stage on a turntable which could be reversed to create an in-the-round auditorium (see Figure 8.4). Another key amateur example was the Questors Theatre, Ealing (1964), Norman Branson's design for which was widely publicized.[141] The director, Alfred Emmet, saw stage flexibility as a fundamentally modern quality: 'no one can be sure today what kind of playhouse really best meets contemporary needs and therefore adaptable theatres must be built to find out'.[142] In his view, 'every out-of-date new theatre that is built puts the clock back on development, not only because it creates another vested interest in the status quo, not only because it is another missed opportunity, but also because it will appear to hundreds and thousands of young people that the theatre will always be old-fashioned and therefore a bore'.[143] He sought 'a theatre for actors', which would be 'specifically designed for experiment [...] with actor-audience relationships'.[144] To shape the design of this space, Emmet assembled an 'Advisory Panel' in 1953.[145] It included Frederick Bentham, Muriel St Clare Byrne, George Devine, Bernard Miles, Tyrone Guthrie, and Norman Marshall. They were asked, for example, how and why modern

[138] RSA, TCP/T/000094 nos. 4–10, 'RS CPB 59' and no. 26, '10.9.58'. See also TCP/T/000094/22-24 of *c.*1961, in which the space has become hexagonal.

[139] 'Theatre and Concert Hall in Barbican Scheme', *Interbuild* 6 (July 1959), pp. 40–2.

[140] Graham Winteringham, interviewed 13 December 2013.

[141] E.g. 'Questors Theatre', *Architects' Journal* 140 (29 July 1964), pp. 291–7.

[142] Alfred Emmet, 'Adaptable Theatre', *New Theatre Magazine* 4, no. 1 (October–December 1962), pp. 15–21 (p. 18). The theatre was funded by the company itself, plus donations from organizations including the Calouste Gulbenkian Foundation, the Pilgrim Trust, and the John Lewis Partnership. Ealing Borough Council also made a small grant.

[143] Emmet, 'Adaptable Theatre', p. 19.

[144] QTA, uncat., Alfred Emmet, 'The Theatre, 1964–1989 and Beyond', memo of 1989.

[145] QTA, uncat., 'Towards the New Theatre: memorandum to Advisory Panel', memo, n.d., and 'Memorandum No. 2'.

Figure 8.4. Midland *Totaltheater*: the Crescent Theatre, Birmingham, *c.*1965 (Architectural Press Archive/RIBA Collections)

theatres 'fail to be contemporary'. Their responses do not survive, although reports summarizing their views were prepared. Emmet's conclusion was that the new theatre 'must be flexible in a contemporary way' but with 'theatre atmosphere'.[146]

Early designs for the Questors aroused scepticism when presented to the Royal Society of Arts, for reasons ranging from the practicality of the stage arrangements to the whole idea of an open stage auditorium.[147] Although initial proposals included two tiers of seating,[148] the theatre as built has around 400 seats arranged on one level around a thrust stage, behind which is a wider platform with a permanent cyclorama.[149] Seating can be arranged on the rear stage to create an in-the-round theatre, while a proscenium arch layout is also possible. Branson subsequently worked on further theatres including a successful studio auditorium at St Mary's College at Twickenham (1963), which has a fully modular stage,[150] and an efficient

[146] QTA, uncat., 'Memorandum to Advisory Panel—No. 3', n.d.

[147] 'A New Concept in Theatre Design', *Journal of the Royal Society of Arts* 104 (17 August 1956), pp. 756–74.

[148] Norman Branson, 'The Questors Theatre', in *Adaptable Theatres*, edited by Stephen Joseph (London, 1962), pp. 25–9.

[149] Bentham, *New Theatres in Britain*, p. 67.

[150] Bentham, *New Theatres in Britain*, p. 129; Branson was 'consultant' to architect Sir Albert Richardson, Houfe and Partners. See also p. 133 for Wennington School.

open stage auditorium at the Brewhouse, Taunton (1977). At Taunton, a single tier of seating is gathered around three sides of a projecting stage, which has a limited degree of flexibility. The design, as has been noted, was reportedly not well received by the ABTT's Theatre Architecture and Planning Committee, whose advice was overruled by Peter Longman and Hugh Willatt.[151] Subsequently, however, one of the key antagonists admitted that the design was in fact rather well conceived,[152] and, largely staffed by volunteers in the same spirit of economy in which the theatre was conceived, the Brewhouse proved a successful venue.[153]

The Questors formed a model for Bolton's (professional) Octagon Theatre, which was completed in 1967.[154] Although it was thought that an open stage auditorium would be slightly cheaper than one with a proscenium arch,[155] the director Robin Pemberton-Billing, also believed that open staging would attract young patrons and create an informal atmosphere.[156] He consciously sought to innovate: it was noted that 'it is sad to reflect that most of the new theatres built since the war, in spite of their modern design, are really little more than Victorian'.[157] In this respect, the Octagon was presented as achieving a more thoroughgoing modernity than many of its contemporaries, because its modernity extended beyond its appearance to the actor–audience relationship. The design was shown to the ABTT in June 1966.[158] As built, the basic arrangement was in-the-round, with a central stage measuring some 26 feet by 17 feet 6 inches. Of the 422 seats, 195 were fixed.[159] By rearranging and removing some of the seating tiers, it was possible to create an end stage arrangement with 356 seats or a thrust layout with 322 seats.[160] Of the first sixty-two productions, twenty-three took the thrust form and twenty-six were end-on.[161]

Flexibility also appealed to those teaching Drama as a way to stage plays in something like the spatial conditions for which they had originally been written. Nonetheless, the first example of this kind, Frederick Gibberd's 1940s proposal for the University of Oxford, was relatively conventional, with only a limited degree of adaptability in the stage area.[162] The *Manchester Guardian* was sceptical: 'Mr Gibberd seems to have tried to cater for a variety of different bright ideas, without having any strong views of his own.'[163] By contrast, Richard Southern's studio at the University of Bristol (1949–51) had fewer limitations. A disused squash court was

[151] Peter Longman, email to author, 11 July 2017.
[152] Peter Longman, email to author, 11 July 2017.
[153] 'Brewhouse, Taunton's First Year', *Stage*, 18 May 1978.
[154] Robin Pemberton-Billing, *The Octagon Theatre: Concept to Reality* (Bolton, 2011), pp. 9, 14, 53.
[155] BA, ABZ/45, Box 1/2, 'Draft Report on Civic Theatre', [1964].
[156] Pemberton-Billing, *Octagon Theatre*, pp. 14, 81–8.
[157] BA, 711 BOL, 'Octagon Theatre, Bolton' (booklet, n.d.).
[158] V&A, ACGB/84/37, copy of ABTT report, 3 June 1966.
[159] Bentham, *New Theatres in Britain*, p. 43.
[160] Pemberton-Billing, *Octagon Theatre*, p. 72.
[161] Pemberton-Billing, *Octagon Theatre*, p. 123.
[162] [Oxford University Drama Commission], *Report of the Oxford University Drama Commission* (Oxford, 1948), esp. pp. 15–23 for report by Gibberd.
[163] 'Experimental Theatre', *Manchester Guardian*, 28 October 1948.

reworked as 'a tiny theatre where almost any form of production can be reproduced' for £5600.[164] With a balcony at each end and provision for galleries at each side, it could reportedly be transformed from a proscenium arch theatre into an 'Elizabethan' auditorium in eight minutes. The same philosophy informed Hull's Gulbenkian Centre (1969), which was the first completely new building specifically for the teaching of Drama at a British university.[165] The university was inspired by the example of Bristol to build a studio for its new Drama department in 1963. The brief grew to include facilities for the production of audiovisual teaching aids, an enthusiasm of the vice chancellor, Brynmor Jones.[166] Jones had chaired a UGC committee on this subject between 1963 and 1965, and the centre at Hull was to be involved in 'the propagation of the gospel'.[167] Peter Moro was appointed on the recommendation of the university's consultant architect, Leslie Martin, with whom he had worked on the execution of the Festival Hall. Given the emphasis on audiovisual aids, his experience of television studio design as well as theatre stood in his favour. The building was conceived in quasi-civic terms, with its architecture being intended to suggest its status on campus.[168] In plan, it is an elongated octagon, with elevations of brick and concrete which have a varied pattern of window openings. Its centrepiece is the studio theatre, which has a single fixed rake of seating forming the rear part of the stalls when used in an end stage or proscenium arch arrangement; thrust and transverse layouts are also possible (see Figure 8.5). The idea was very much a 'laboratory', with provision being made for 'only so much audience as is required to give to the actors the vital sense of audience response'.[169]

In contrast to the Gulbenkian Centre, the University of Sussex's Gardner Arts Centre was primarily intended for professional performances. The initial 'specification' of December 1963 took an innovative view of what this kind of centre might contain.[170] It called for a pair of buildings, one for the arts and the other, to be constructed later, including studios for film, television, and radio. For experimental drama there was to be a 200-seat 'theatre workshop', a term surely derived from Joan Littlewood's work in London; there would also be space for painting, crafts, and music. An 800-seat hall would accommodate performances, meetings, and lectures. As completed in 1969, however, the Gardner had a circular auditorium seating up to 500, with a wedge-shaped main stage and two smaller, similarly shaped subsidiary stages (see Figure 8.6). This unusual layout may largely have been Spence's work, as some of its features are evident on the drawings that illustrate his initial proposals

164 'At Bristol', *Stage*, 15 February 1951, p. 12.

165 Gulbenkian Centre list description, <www.historicengland.org.uk/listing/the-list/list-entry/1427682> (accessed 14 December 2015).

166 HHC, University Archives, Parcel 118, 17/4, Buildings Committee, 2 July 1964.

167 Trevor A. Scott, 'Audio-Visual Aids in Higher Scientific Education: 25 years on', *Studies in Higher Education* 16, no. 2 (1991), pp. 225–7 (p. 225).

168 For an early design with less robust elevations, see 'Drama Studio, Hull University', *Architectural Review* 137 (January 1965), p. 25.

169 HHC, Registrar Uncat. Box 14, File 33/3, D. Campbell to F. Harris-Jones, 26 October 1965.

170 HES, MS 2329/ENG/52/5/54–56, 'Users' Specification for an Arts Centre', first draft, 3 December 1963.

Figure 8.5. Gulbenkian Centre, Hull, with the auditorium set up 'in-the-round' (Colin Westwood/RIBA Collections)

for the university as a whole. An early campus plan, for example, shows an external amphitheatre whose curved form anticipates that of the eventual Gardner Centre,[171] while an undated but seemingly early design for the arts centre itself has a drum-like auditorium intersecting with a cubic stage block.[172] Furthermore, the centre's appearance as a collection of largely windowless brick cylinders seems to have been important to Spence. As was noted in Chapter 4, in November 1965 he defended this aspect of the design in the face of criticism from Walter Eysselinck, the Gardner's director. Its bold massing also parallels the approach adopted by Spence's office at the Nuffield, Southampton, and in the design of the unbuilt New Mercury Theatre.

Assuming, therefore, that Spence came up with the basic concept for the Gardner Arts Centre as a collection of cylinders housing a flexible auditorium, might he nonetheless have taken advice from others in developing his ideas?

[171] Spence's designs for the university more generally consciously echoed antique precedents: see 'Influences of Greek and Roman Architecture in the Proposed Sussex University', *Architect and Building News* 217 (13 April 1960). An early drawing of the campus at Southampton University describes the Nuffield Theatre as an 'amphitheatre': see HES, SPE ENG/35/1/1, photograph of site layout, 1957.

[172] HES, SPE ENG/52/2/12/1, undated early plan of the Gardner Arts Centre.

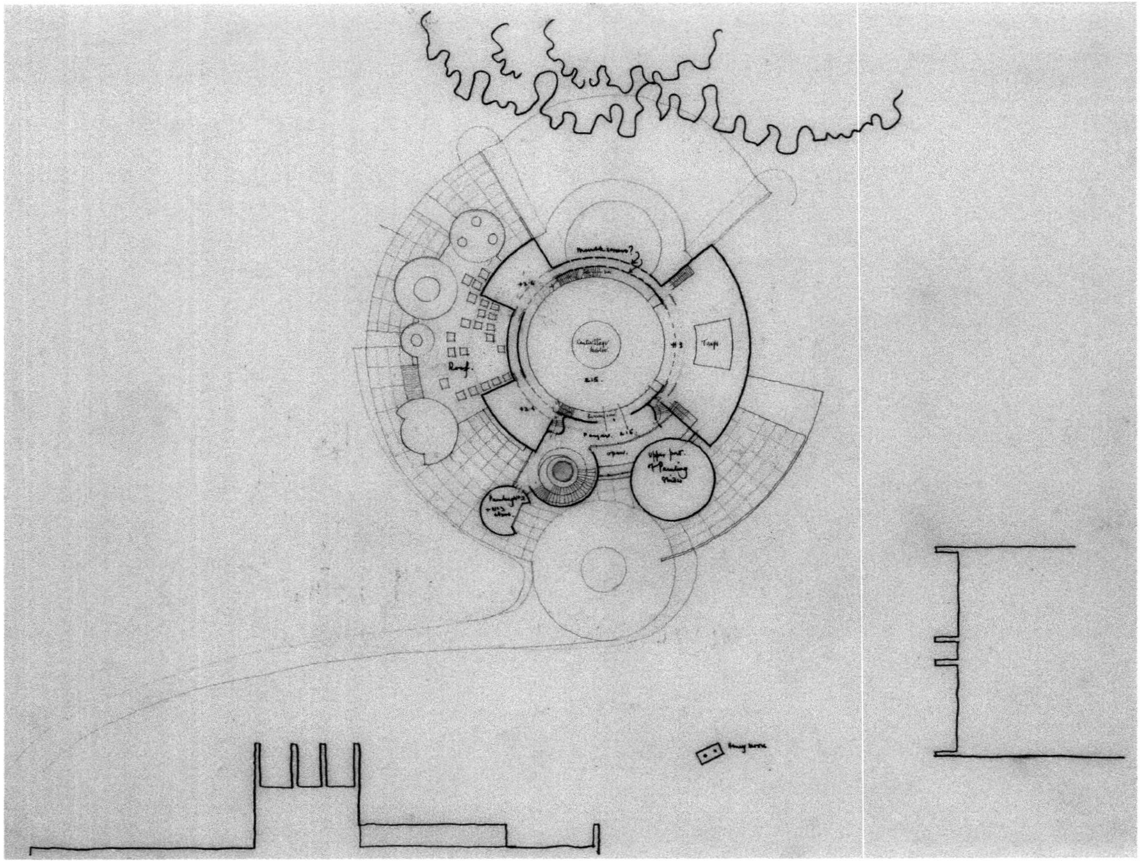

Figure 8.6. Gardner Arts Centre, University of Sussex: an early version of the design though with the circular auditorium and three stages of the executed scheme (©HES. Sir Basil Spence Archive)

The design could have been shaped by Eysselinck prior to his arrival at Sussex in September 1965, as he had been appointed in April that year,[173] and was evidently involved in discussions of the project by June.[174] That said, the contrast between the 'light and simple building' he requested and the monolithic brick elevations of the Gardner as built throws doubt on his influence at this stage.[175] The other key figure in the design process was Sean Kenny. He had joined the design team by May 1966,[176] and while one contemporary report suggested that Kenny's input was sought by Eysselinck in 1965,[177] Kenny would already have been known to Spence. He designed part of the interior of the British Pavilion at Expo 67, which was the work of Spence and was being designed during summer 1965.[178] It is not impossible that Spence and Kenny discussed the project at this early stage, especially in view of Kenny's international prominence as a theatre designer.

Whoever it was that came up with the Gardner's basic layout, its technical specification was certainly developed by Eysselinck and Kenny during 1966–7.[179] Kenny's involvement was seen at the time as having been crucial,[180] and, as completed, the auditorium certainly embodied the interests in flexibility and technology which characterized much of his work.[181] In 1963, he had designed a mechanized stage set for the Dunes Hotel, Las Vegas, whose disc-shaped platforms were swung into position using hydraulic arms,[182] and his staging of *The Flying Dutchman* at Covent Garden in 1966 had a similar quality.[183] Kenny conceived the Gardner's auditorium not as a conventional theatre but rather as an infinitely adaptable 'room' for performance in which performers and audiences were to feel 'free and happy'.[184] The seating, which was designed to swivel so that any or all of the stages could be used in a single performance, was located on movable blocks.[185] In practice, however, the layout was never thought to be entirely successful.[186] In particular, inadequate thought appeared to have been given to the way that actors

[173] UoSx, SxUOS1/1/5/13/1, 'Director of the Arts Centre', 21 April 1965.
[174] E.g. UoSx, SxUOS1/1/5/13/1, Walter Eysselinck, 'Toward an Arts Centre', 3 June 1965, which notes a visit to Sussex, 'discussions with the architects', and a meeting in May 1965.
[175] UoSx, SxUOS1/1/5/13/1, Walter Eysselinck, 'Toward an Arts Centre', 3 June 1965.
[176] UoSx, SxUOS1/1/5/13/1, Buildings Committee, 27 May 1966.
[177] 'Making Art a Part of People's Lives', *Focus: The News Magazine of the University of Surrey*, November 1969, p. 12, <http://www.sussex.ac.uk/internal/bulletin/downloads/1960–1969/1969/November/196911.pdf> (accessed 24 June 2017).
[178] Project meetings had begun before June 1965: HES, MS 2329/CA/1/1/48, Gordon Collins to Sean Kenny, 14 June 1965.
[179] UoSx, SxUOS1/1/5/22/11, Gardner Arts Centre drawings.
[180] NRS, ED61/87, Martin Carr to Brian Annable, 10 July 1973 refers to Kenny as Spence's 'wayward adviser'.
[181] Alistair Fair, 'Rethinking the Post-war British Theatre: monumentality, Sean Kenny, and the state, *c.*1966–73', in *Architecture, Institutions and Change*, edited by Paul Hogben and Judith O'Callaghan (Sydney, 2015), pp. 146–56.
[182] 'A Mechanical Stage', *The Times*, 19 November 1963.
[183] 'The Stage Designer Who Makes One Sit Up', *The Times*, 24 January 1966.
[184] 'Making Art a Part of People's Lives', p. 12.
[185] 'Gardner Centre for the Arts', *Building Specification* 2, no. 11 (November 1971), pp. 41–6.
[186] 'Gardner Centre for the Arts', *Tabs* 28, no. 2 (June 1970), pp. 58–61.

would actually get onto the stage. (As altered in 2011–15, the auditorium remains flexible but has been significantly reconfigured.[187])

Many of the major regional theatres of the 1960s and 1970s included small flexible studios alongside their larger, typically more 'fixed' main auditoria, offering adaptable space for innovation which aped the ad hoc experimental theatres being created elsewhere. In addition, their small size meant that there was no need to draw a large audience. Some theatres' studios were created by repurposing a rehearsal room or workshop, but others were purpose-built: the Crucible's intended 'spartan' studio has already been noted. In Bristol, for example, Peter Moro's initial proposals of 1966 for the historic Theatre Royal included what was described as a room for rehearsals 'but capable of use also by a public audience'.[188] By 1970—and as built—this space had become more clearly defined as a second auditorium which contrasted with the fixed arrangement and historic detailing of the restored main theatre in its flexibility, achieved by the use of movable rostra, and in its dark colours.

Not all were convinced by such architectural negativity. When the architect Bill Howell proposed at the end of the 1960s that the Young Vic should be 'a non-building in which you can do anything',[189] his client, Frank Dunlop, was not keen. While Dunlop certainly wanted 'a kind of theatre factory in a utilitarian building', he nonetheless felt that theatre always comprised 'acting in architecture'.[190] Accordingly, the Young Vic's octagonal auditorium combined flexibility and fixity, with a reconfigurable Guthrie-like thrust stage, fixed tiers of seating, and a narrow encircling gallery that in one drawing has almost Elizabethan-style balustrades.[191] Early schemes were yet more 'structured', with two galleries.[192] The aim was immediacy, and there was little provision for scenery. Dunlop argued that 'The Elizabethans must have acted with speed and vulgarity and flamboyance [...] young people want fireworks, and they are right.'[193]

The Young Vic's auditorium influenced the theatre designed by Roderick Ham for Bedford in 1973, which was to have an auditorium adaptable to thrust or in-the-round forms, with 450–500 seats arranged in the stalls and two shallow encircling galleries.[194] It also formed the natural starting point for Howell Killick Partridge and Amis's theatre at Christ's Hospital school, near Horsham.[195]

[187] Richard York, 'Attenborough Centre for the Creative Arts', *Sightline* 39, no. 2 (Summer 2016), pp. 7–17.

[188] UoB, RA/422 Box 2, folder entitled 'Theatre Royal Development', Philip Morris to Peter Moro, 28 July 1966.

[189] W. G. R. Howell, 'The Young Vic: theatre on a budget', *RIBA Journal* 78 (1971), pp. 287–9 (p. 288).

[190] Frank Dunlop to Malcolm Potter, 28 August 1968; Howell, 'Young Vic', p. 288. Letter in the collection of the late John Partridge.

[191] Bill Howell to Frank Dunlop, 13 August 1968: 'what do you think of the gallery front idea? Very Elizabethan, we think'. Letter in the collection of the late John Partridge.

[192] Geraint Franklin, *HKPA* (London, 2017), p. 134.

[193] Cited in 'Casual Approach for Young Vic', *Daily Telegraph*, 4 August 1969.

[194] BedA, Z900/4/4, 'Feasibility Study', 1973.

[195] Christ's Hospital Archive, 867.2, Bill Howell to A. W. Robinson, 19 February 1971; Franklin, *HKPA*, pp. 137–40.

In August 1970, HKPA was approached by Christ's Hospital, which had been presented with designs for a theatre by a former pupil, the famous wartime engineer Barnes Wallis.[196] It was suggested that HKPA might develop the scheme; Christ's Hospital's new headmaster, David Newsome, may have been familiar with HKPA's many Cambridge buildings of the 1960s as he had previously been a fellow of Emmanuel College (1959–70). Wallis's rather traditional designs, which included a fan-shaped auditorium, were unlikely ever to appeal to the arch-modernists at HKPA, who by March 1971 had managed to have them jettisoned in favour of their own proposals.[197] Howell developed the scheme in close collaboration with Duncan Noel-Paton, the director of Drama at nearby Cranleigh School, who served as the client representative and who subsequently moved to Christ's Hospital. The theatre—along with a classroom block and extension to the music school—opened in 1974. Its auditorium is in plan an elongated octagon (like the Young Vic), enclosed on three sides by galleries with timber balustrades (see Figure 8.7). The railings are stained red and festooned with lightbulbs in an even more strident statement of architectural presence than was the case at the Young Vic. The primary stage arrangement is end-on, in which form the theatre originally seated 580.

Figure 8.7. Cheerful courtyard: Christ's Hospital Arts Centre, the theatre arranged 'in-the-round' in 2014 (Toby Phillips/Christ's Hospital)

[196] Christ's Hospital Clerk to HKPA, 21 August 1970. Wallis had recently retired as Treasurer of Christ's Hospital. Letter in the collection of the late John Partridge.

[197] Christ's Hospital Archive, 867.1 and 867.2, drawings of early 1971.

Yet the auditorium was also intended to be flexible. Noel-Paton later recalled that he had asked Howell for 'a full opera house, an arena like a small version of Earls Court, a thrust stage like Stratford, Ontario, and a real theatre in the round like nobody really has yet at all'.[198] Four three-storey 'towers' were provided, each equivalent in size to a single bay of the galleries. Described as 'boy-movable but boy-proof',[199] these towers could be moved using their integral large-diameter wheels. When positioned at the rear of the stage, the towers complete the encirclement of the auditorium and permit in-the-round performances; they can also be used to make a proscenium 'arch'. They were detailed by Theatre Projects Consultants, who also explored the idea of movable blocks of seating in designs for the unbuilt New Lincolnshire Theatre.

Echoes of Christ's Hospital are found in the National Theatre's third auditorium, the Cottesloe.[200] A studio theatre had been included in Lasdun's initial proposals but was postponed during 1968 to save money. As the studio's walls carried structural loads, the space could not be deleted, and in 1974 money was found to complete it. The work was considered 'fitting out' rather than 'architecture', and so was delegated to Theatre Projects Consultants' recent recruit, Iain Mackintosh. An enthusiast for the closely packed tiers of eighteenth-century auditoria, Mackintosh proposed the construction of shallow balconies around three sides of the space. The backs of these galleries were pulled away from the studio's walls, with stairs being inserted into the resulting gap. As a result, the perceived width of the studio is significantly narrower than would have been the case for Lasdun's design, a 250-seat auditorium with banks of seating on all sides. As installed, the columns that support the galleries were orange, although Peter Hall and John Bury demanded that they be painted in a darker colour. The stage could be located at the end of the space or in its middle, or removed altogether for promenade performances. Consistently popular with actors, the Cottesloe was modernized in 2014 and reopened as the Dorfman Theatre.

In 1984, Iain Mackintosh described the likes of Christ's Hospital and the Cottesloe as 'courtyard theatres'.[201] Although the term evokes the inn-yard theatres of Elizabethan England, Mackintosh played down its period specificity, seeing it as a reference to the spatial characteristics of these spaces. In its simple adaptability and its prominent galleries, some with less-than-perfect sightlines, the courtyard was a conscious reaction against the functional purity of the straight-rake, fan-shaped auditorium, as well as high-technology adaptability and architectural indeterminacy.[202] Mackintosh argued for its contemporary value as a form

[198] Franklin, *HKPA*, p. 137.

[199] Bill Howell to David Newsome, 12 March 1971. Letter in the collection of the late John Partridge.

[200] Calder, 'Committees and Concrete', pp. 121–2.

[201] Iain Mackintosh, 'Rediscovering the Courtyard', *Architectural Review* 175 (April 1984), pp. 64–71.

[202] Francis Reid, 'Theatre of Change', *Architects' Journal* 179 (6 June 1984), pp. 24–7.

which promoted audience–actor interaction, allowed for 'conventional end-stage scenic production' and 'free-stage experiment', and afforded scope for architectural invention. It was, he concluded, no 'avant-garde appendage' but was relevant to the mainstream; it put 'the fun back into functionalism'. By 1984, the courtyard approach was increasingly popular. A similar enclosing framework can be seen at the Wolsey, Ipswich (Roderick Ham, 1979), where a continuous gallery encircles the stage and audience seating, with a second lower gallery around the stage joining the seating rake halfway up.[203] The encircling timber-fronted galleries of the Swan Theatre, Stratford-upon-Avon (Michael Reardon, 1986), were clearly inspired by Christ's Hospital.[204] At a smaller scale, Cottesloe-like (and Christ's Hospital-like) studios were proposed by several competitors in the Leeds Playhouse competition of 1984, while the Tricycle Theatre, Kilburn (Tim Foster, 1980), featured an economical courtyard made from orange-painted scaffolding which applied the proportions of the Georgian Theatre Royal at Richmond, North Yorkshire (1788) to striking and successful effect.

The main auditorium in the Derngate Centre, Northampton (RHWL, 1983), represents a variation on these ideas.[205] Conceived in 1979 and combining a new 1500-seat multipurpose hall with the refurbished Theatre Royal, the Derngate was financed by the local authority but was to be run as a commercial venture, hence the need to maximize income through a range of uses.[206] The multipurpose hall had to look complete in each of its arrangements; the improvised ambiance and bouncy floors of many flexible auditoria were to be avoided. RHWL's solution has two fixed galleries at one end of the auditorium, flanked by four boxes stepping down towards the floor. As at Christ's Hospital, movable three-storey 'towers' were provided, though shifted not by 'boy power' but on hovercraft-like air cushions (see Figure 8.8). In concert and arena formats, the towers are positioned to encircle the stage; in the proscenium arch arrangement, two are angled inwards to frame the stage opening. The stalls, meanwhile, are made up of raked seating on movable wagons. However, it was not only technology that made this type of auditorium seem modern but also its courtyard format. In this respect, Francis Reid, reviewing the smaller Wilde Theatre, Bracknell (Levitt Bernstein, 1984), concluded that the courtyard was 'the form that seems likely to characterise late twentieth-century theatre building'.[207] He praised its strong architectural framework; he especially enjoyed the Wilde's bright colours (in contrast to what he termed the 'municipal bland' of Derngate). 'This theatre,' Reid concluded, 'is a pointer to the twenty-first century.'[208]

[203] The auditorium concept was developed by the theatre consultant, Martin Carr, before Ham's appointment: V&A, ACGB/84/147, D. G. Heckels to Peter Longman, 27 August 1975.

[204] *Guthrie Thrust Stage*, ed. Mackintosh, p. 18.

[205] 'Municipal Multi-form', *Architects' Journal* 179 (7 March 1984), pp. 49–64.

[206] V&A, ACGB/107/294, Derngate Centre Brief, 6 September 1979.

[207] Reid, 'Theatre of Change', pp. 24–7.

[208] Reid, 'Theatre of Change', p. 27.

Figure 8.8. 'Pointer to the twenty-first century': one of the 'towers' at Derngate, Northampton, 1983 (Architectural Press Archive/RIBA Collections)

CONCLUSIONS

On 6 January 1970, it was reported that Sheffield Playhouse was to receive a visit from Harold Wilson.[209] The Prime Minister was to attend a performance of *The Golden Fleece*, but the real reason for his visit was apparently 'Mr Wilson's interest in the New Sheffield Theatre', i.e. the Crucible, then under construction. Just as Chichester Festival Theatre had been described by the critic Diana Rowntree as a theatre for 'poets and scientists',[210] the Crucible embodied the kind of technocratic modernity prized by Wilson's government. Market research carried out in 1974 suggests the Crucible was seen thus, with almost a quarter identifying it as 'a modern theatre' and the same number knowing it had a 'thrust stage'.[211] Over half of those who had been to a performance either strongly agreed or agreed with the statement 'I prefer the thrust stage to the traditional proscenium arch', and of those who strongly agreed a higher proportion was from the C2DE social group,

[209] 'PM at Sheffield Playhouse', *The Times*, 6 January 1970.
[210] 'Chichester's New Theatre', *Guardian*, 4 May 1962.
[211] SCA, SY/43/Z1/6, 'Analysis of Audiences, July 1974'.

the working population that Colin George was so keen to attract.[212] Similarly, the Crucible's auditorium was seen as more equitable in its functionality than other theatres with which respondents were familiar, with more than half thinking that it was possible to hear and see well anywhere in the auditorium.

The rejection of the proscenium arch stage and galleried auditorium was not, therefore, simply an exercise in neophilia. Rather, it also represented a belief in at least some circles that theatre might only be saved by abandoning the proscenium arch for more participatory forms of actor–audience relationship. It also reflected a sense on the part of some designers that the framing effect of the arch itself limited their horizons, as well as a belief that traditional auditoria were socially divisive. Yet not everyone was convinced. One in ten of those interviewed by the Crucible in 1974 thought that the theatre was 'avant-garde'. Of course, the theatre's programming may have informed this response, but the design of the building was also implicated. Some stated that the theatre's modernity was exactly the reason that they had not yet visited it.

[212] SCA, SY/43/Z1/8, Market Research Report, August 1974.

9

'The Most Revolutionary Thing'

Modern Proscenium Arch and End Stage Auditoria

On 25 August 1962, an article in the *Surrey Advertiser* discussed the design of the Yvonne Arnaud Theatre in Guildford, which was then three years from being opened. Of its proscenium arch stage and two-tiered auditorium, a member of the theatre profession was reported as saying that the Yvonne Arnaud, 'is out of date before it is started. Theatres are now being built with the open stage'.[1]

As was discussed in Chapter 8, open staging was by the 1960s routinely presented as being 'modern' on account of its rejection of the long-established proscenium arch stage. In 1960, the director Norman Marshall reported of a conference at which 'the proscenium theatre, contemptuously referred to as "the peep-show theatre", was hardly dealt with and there were the usual happy prophecies of its imminent demise'.[2] And yet, as Marshall pointed out with reference to recent theatres in other European countries, and as the construction of the Yvonne Arnaud Theatre also demonstrates, the proscenium arch theatre did not disappear. Indeed, a significant number of Britain's new civic and repertory theatres of the 1960s and 1970s had, if not a full proscenium arch stage, then an open end stage which could be equipped with a proscenium arch for particular productions.

To what extent was the design of this kind of auditorium and stage an opportunity for creativity? The National Theatre's Building Committee apparently regarded the proscenium arch theatre which had been foisted upon them—the eventual Lyttelton Theatre—as the 'any other business' theatre.[3] Unlike the National's open stage (Olivier) auditorium, they afforded it relatively little discussion, and in this respect Barnabas Calder has suggested that 'the widespread assumption appears to have been that the proscenium was a formulaic theatre, and that the formula had now been perfected, [...] leaving in essence only decorative variables to the architect'.[4] Some architects certainly adopted what might seem to be a 'formulaic' approach. For example, the unexecuted theatres that Frederick Gibberd designed in the late 1940s for the University of Oxford and Harlow town centre both feature

[1] SHC, 7018/2/4/143, clippings: *Surrey Advertiser*, 25 August 1962.

[2] Norman Marshall, 'Theatre Design', *Drama* 59 (1960), pp. 25–7 (p. 26).

[3] Barnabas Calder, 'Committees and Concrete: the genesis and design of Denys Lasdun's National Theatre' (PhD diss., University of Cambridge, 2007), p. 120.

[4] Calder, 'Committees and Concrete', p. 113.

wedge-shaped auditoria with serrated sides.[5] Peter Moro's designs of *c.*1975 for Plymouth Theatre Royal and the unbuilt Brentford Arts Centre have almost identical auditoria, while Norman Downie's Salisbury Playhouse (1976) was a near copy of his Mercury Theatre, Colchester (1972). The architect Leslie Martin justified this kind of replication by likening functional types of building to biological species, each having an underlying set of formal and planning principles which then were varied in practice.[6] He came up with very similar auditoria at West Road Concert Hall, Cambridge (1975), and the Royal Scottish Academy of Music and Drama, Glasgow (1987), both of which are based on his Middleton Hall at Hull (1965–7). For other designers, however, emulation was a matter of pragmatism rather than architectural theory. For example, when the initial designs for Poole Arts Centre were criticized by the Association of British Theatre Technicians (ABTT), the project was reworked with a Thorndike-alike theatre.[7] This move was perhaps an astute one, given that the Thorndike's architect, Roderick Ham, sat on the ABTT's Theatre Architecture and Planning Committee.

Yet these examples notwithstanding, exact copies were few and far between. Furthermore, proscenium arch theatre design was rarely an exercise in antiquarian revivalism, but was thought by some to offer real scope for experiment and innovation. For example, the designers of the Northcott Theatre, Exeter, were indignant when questioned about its proscenium arch auditorium: 'it is not in the least like a Victorian theatre proscenium', they spluttered.[8] While the likes of the Northcott were hardly avant-garde in their design, this type of theatre could nonetheless be understood in 'modern' terms. The ever-provocative Kenneth Tynan told the National Theatre's Building Committee in October 1964 that 'the most revolutionary thing [...] could be a perfectly designed proscenium theatre',[9] while in December 1966 a meeting between the National's architect, Denys Lasdun, and the Arts Council Drama Panel concluded that the Lyttelton Theatre should represent 'in twentieth-century terms, the quintessence of what was meant by a "proscenium" theatre'.[10] This chapter considers what that idea could mean in practice. It explores the post-war survival of the proscenium arch stage and the ways in which it could be presented in terms of the 'modern playhouse'. The discussion begins with the arguments that were made in favour of this kind of stage before examining how it was rethought in practice, focusing first on the proscenium arch itself before turning to the auditorium.

5 'Harlow New Town', *Architects' Journal* 107 (5 February 1948), pp. 127–31 (p. 130).

6 Roger Stonehouse, 'Theme and Variation', in *Architecture, Education and Research: The Work of Leslie Martin*, edited by Peter Carolin and Trevor Dannatt (London, 1996), pp. 84–93.

7 V&A, ACGB/120/16, ABTT reports, 22 June 1972 and 20 February 1973. The earlier proposals were likened to the Wyvern, Swindon.

8 UoLiv, D147/C73/3, Transcript of interview, n.d.

9 Quoted in Calder, 'Committees and Concrete', p. 119.

10 RIBA, LaD/207/1, 'Detailed Design Proposals for the National Theatre', 8 November 1967, Appendix C, p. 13.

'NOT AVANT-GARDE': JUSTIFYING THE PROSCENIUM ARCH

In 1958, the *Architects' Journal* came to the same conclusion about Coventry's newly opened Belgrade Theatre as the *Surrey Advertiser* was to do of the Yvonne Arnaud four years later, namely that it was retrograde. With a proscenium arch stage and two-tiered auditorium which—unlike most theatres of the 1920s and 1930s—also had boxes stepping down the walls, the Belgrade seemed to be 'basically a Victorian or Edwardian theatre', in spite of its contemporary appearance.[11] In seeking to explain the form of its auditorium and stage, one might point to the theatre's local authority origins—rather than with a repertory company—and its conception in *c.*1954, i.e. before the debates about open staging really gained traction. For the *Architects' Journal*, however, the reason was the conservatism of the theatre world:

> People in the theatre are like most other clients: they want what they have seen already [...] done a little bit better and if possible a little cheaper and quicker [...]. Any fundamental rethinking of the playhouse and the method of presenting plays is out of the question.[12]

There were, in fact, plenty of people in theatre who did want a 'fundamental rethinking of the playhouse', as Chapter 8 showed. Nonetheless, there were many others who were less keen to reject the basic principles of the proscenium arch stage. Of the Yvonne Arnaud, for example, the *Guardian* commented that the architects 'deliberately did not design an avant-garde theatre', lest the building go out of date.[13]

The survival of the proscenium arch was not simply the product of conservative thinking. There were sound reasons favouring the essential principles of this kind of stage, as distinct from the socially segregated auditoria typically found in conjunction with it in older theatres. Practically speaking, open staging posed challenges with respect to safety regulations, which usually assumed that a safety curtain would isolate the auditorium in case of fire,[14] but there were also artistic arguments in favour of this kind of stage. For example, in October 1964, Tynan told the National Theatre's Building Committee that:

> there are certain staging and atmospheric effects that you can only get on a straight-edged stage. Many people have confirmed this when comparing the productions of OTHELLO at Chichester and the Old Vic.[15]

Another director, Bill Gaskill, took up the argument:

> I must admit I was greatly relieved to get back to the Old Vic [from Chichester] with THE DUTCH COURTESAN. Setting aside all romantic considerations, I believe

[11] 'Theatre in Corporation Street, Coventry', *Architects' Journal* 128 (7 August 1958), pp. 201–14 (p. 202).

[12] 'Theatre in Corporation Street, Coventry', p. 202.

[13] 'Memorial in the Round', *Guardian*, 2 June 1965.

[14] Roderick Ham, *Theatre Planning* (London, 1972), pp. 43, 262.

[15] Quoted in Calder, 'Committees and Concrete', p. 118.

> that any kind of intellectual or didactic theatre is better in a proscenium. A theatre like Chichester works for the highly-introvert or spectacular kind of play. If someone can see an entirely new vision of theatre, the best [of] luck to them, but I am not sure that I could make the same impact where some plays are concerned.[16]

It was not only the National that was affected by this kind of thinking. The architect J. A. Brownrigg commented of the Yvonne Arnaud Theatre that an experimental layout would 'preclude productions designed for more formal buildings'.[17] Richard Southern, too, noted that 'many plays produced on well-loved traditional lines will still need the picture-frame stage; for them, we must continue to build such theatres'.[18] (In this respect, many of the new West German theatres which were visited by British architects and directors retained this arrangement because they were often used for traditional operatic performances, and they therefore demonstrated how this kind of stage could form part of a modern theatre.)

Another line of argument stressed the value of the proscenium arch stage not so much as the setting for naturalistic designs and illusion but rather as a stage suitable for a wide range of work. Although in 1960 the management of Birmingham Repertory Theatre concluded that 'some plays (e.g. ancient Greek plays, pageants, medieval plays such as *The Three Estates*) are virtually impossible to present in a picture frame', they nonetheless thought that 'the conventional picture-frame stage cannot be beaten as an all-purpose platform from which an author is to speak through the actors'.[19] Brownrigg thought similarly in Guildford:

> The case seemed overwhelmingly to be in favour of a theatre basically traditional. Only thus could a theatre be produced which would do everything that might be required of it.[20]

This idea was particularly important in repertory theatre. Although some repertory companies, such as Sheffield, made non-proscenium staging an integral part of their identity, it was possible to turn the argument around by suggesting that flexibility was essential in this kind of theatre. Many of them staged plays from different periods, in a variety of styles, and so the design brief in Nottingham called for 'a stage and auditorium suitable (or flexible) enough for the performance of plays of many periods and countries'.[21] Such flexibility did not necessarily mean full adaptability, if one concluded that the proscenium arch stage was itself suitable for a wide spectrum of work and especially if new technologies—such as the highly mechanized stage of Bromley's Churchill Theatre (1977)—were deployed.

In addition, abstract questions of actor–audience relationships were of little interest to some directors and administrators. Braham Murray, who co-founded

[16] Calder, 'Committees and Concrete', p. 118.

[17] J. A. Brownrigg, 'Every Kind of Show: designer's dilemma', *Stage*, 3 June 1965.

[18] V&A TC, Belgrade file, uncat., Richard Southern, 'Shape of Theatres to Come', undated document.

[19] LoB, MS 978/1/6/1/1, 'The Birmingham Repertory Theatre: its present and future', November 1960, p. 3.

[20] Brownrigg, 'Designer's Dilemma', *Stage*, 3 June 1965.

[21] NA, DD/NP/1/2/1/1, Nottingham Playhouse architects' brief.

Manchester's Royal Exchange Theatre in the 1970s, later reflected on the flexibility of the city's University Theatre:

> None of this interested me very much. A stage was a stage was a stage; give me one and I'll put a play on it.[22]

In 1967, Hazel Vincent Wallace made much the same point after a visit to the International Theatre Colloquium in Montreal:

> They were talking about the relationship between theatre and life in general. It was all a bit high falutin and rather too abstract for my taste. They were fully concerned with the theatre of tomorrow, but I am fully occupied with the theatre of today![23]

She was similarly dismissive of attempts to achieve dematerialized theatre space:

> [The delegates] talked about [...] the theatre of empty space not bound by walls or ceilings. This could not be done.[24]

Indeed, it was sometimes felt that radical experiment was not the main purpose of repertory theatre,[25] nor, indeed, in some cases, of university venues. In Cardiff, Geoffrey Axworthy noted that doing 'away with theatres' in favour of 'environments for drama' posed considerable technical challenges, and that his aim was to construct a university theatre rather than to make Cardiff a leading centre in experimental drama.[26] However, even when innovative work was done, the proscenium arch stage was not inimical to it. The Belgrade Theatre, for example, staged early performances of the 'kitchen-sink' realism of Shelagh Delaney and Arnold Wesker,[27] while Peter Brook's abstract production of *A Midsummer Night's Dream* was successfully staged at Stratford-upon-Avon in 1970.

A proscenium arch stage was essential if a venue was to take touring shows of any scale, simply because the majority of theatres visited by the major touring companies had this kind of stage. Although commercial touring declined during the 1950s and 1960s, the national drama, opera, and ballet companies continued to travel, as did groups like the Prospect Theatre Company. Thus when Theatr Clwyd was on the drawing board it was recorded that:

> as a result of recent discussions with visiting companies it appears that a proscenium opening is desirable for classical plays. It is also desirable for musicals. Therefore, the majority of performances will involve the use of proscenium, proscenium with apron stage, or open end stage.[28]

[22] Braham Murray, *The Worst It Can Be Is a Disaster: The Life Story of Braham Murray and the Royal Exchange Theatre* (London, 2007), p. 53.

[23] SHC, 6368/10/6, clippings: *Surrey Comet*, 26 July 1967. See also similar comments about Expo 67 in Percy Corry, 'Montreal—EXPOsure 67', *Tabs* 25, no. 3 (September 1967), pp. 3–5.

[24] SHC, 6368/10/6, clippings: *Surrey Advertiser*, 22 July 1967.

[25] Hazel Vincent Wallace, interviewed 26 October 2006.

[26] CUA, UCC/R/F/72, Geoffrey Axworthy to Mike Pearson, 7 May 1970 (draft).

[27] Arthur Marwick, *The Sixties: Cultural Revolution in Britain, France, Italy, and the United States, c.1958–1974* (Oxford, 1998), p. 348.

[28] FRO, CC/TC/1/164, 'Proposed Arts Centre, Mold', 18 April 1969, p. 21.

By the late 1970s, the Arts Council had formulated guidance relating to the design of major touring theatres, the aim being that the companies they supported would easily be able to transfer their work.[29] Its recommendations included a proscenium arch 12 metres (40 feet) wide, as well as provision for an orchestra of seventy-five players. This size of stage would typically be coupled to an auditorium of up to 1400 seats rather than the 500–700 seats typical of repertory, where shows were not dependent on achieving a maximum return during a residency of one or two nights. What emerged, therefore, was a two-fold model of proscenium arch (or end stage) theatre: a larger version which catered to touring shows, and a smaller version suitable for repertory. How this kind of stage and auditorium might be designed, and the terms in which they were discussed, are the subjects of the rest of the chapter.

'ELIMINATE THE DIVISION': THE ACTOR/AUDIENCE THRESHOLD

In 1959, Richard Southern noted that he had been discussing the design of an 'experimental theatre' at Southampton University with the architect Basil Spence.[30] In 1961, Southern apparently referred to the theatre, which opened in 1964 as the Nuffield, as 'the first twentieth-century theatre—except for one in Ontario—to be specifically designed for the open stage', much to the irritation of Chichester Festival Theatre's Leslie Evershed-Martin, who claimed otherwise.[31] It provided for both proscenium arch and thrust stage productions, with the former arrangement also being intended to serve for lectures.[32] Since altered, the auditorium as built had long rows of stalls seating, the front rows of which curved around three sides of a projecting stage. This stage could be lowered and replaced by additional forward-facing seating when a pure proscenium arch arrangement was required.[33] The proscenium arch itself comprised a large rectangular opening punched through the brick wall of the auditorium, like a large window.

The kind of obvious 'frame' around the Nuffield's stage was not always thought desirable. In 1982, Peter Moro suggested that 'the problem facing the architect [...] is [...] to eliminate the division between auditorium and stage [...] and to shape the stage so that it interlocks with the geometry of the auditorium'.[34] To this end, two strategies were often deployed. First, the visual prominence of the proscenium arch could be played down, and second, the stage could be connected physically with the auditorium. An 'invisible' proscenium arch became common during the 1960s, being, in effect, the opposite of the Nuffield's very visible

[29] Michael Forsyth, *Auditoria: Designing for the Performing Arts* (London, 1987), p. 119.
[30] UoB, RSA, 28/22/01, Richard Southern to D. G. James, 13 May 1959.
[31] UoB, RSA, 28/22/01, Leslie Evershed-Martin to Richard Southern, 1 February 1961.
[32] UoB, RSA, 28/22/01, Richard Southern to D. G. James, 13 May 1959.
[33] Frederick Bentham, *New Theatres in Britain* (London, 1972), pp. 122–3.
[34] Peter Moro, 'Modern Proscenium Theatre', 23 August 1982 [copy supplied by Andrzej Blonski].

frame.[35] Typically it was formed by pulling in the auditorium walls so that they terminated at the sides of the stage opening, with the auditorium ceiling then sloping down to form the top of the 'arch'. It was also possible to blur the stage/auditorium boundary by projecting the stage into the auditorium. Traditionally, the proscenium arch stage has a 'setting line', parallel with but behind the proscenium arch, which marks the limit of the 'designed' stage set. A 'forestage' offered the opportunity for closer contact between actors and audiences and was commonly provided during the 1960s and 1970s. Typically in this kind of auditorium, the forestage could be lowered to create an orchestra pit, while sometimes it could also be enlarged or removed entirely. An early example was Nottingham Playhouse (see Figure 9.1). In March 1956, Richard Southern recorded his discussions with Peter Moro regarding an 'adaptable forestage theatre'.[36] As completed in 1963, the theatre seated 756 in two tiers. The front rows of the stalls could be removed to allow the construction of a substantial forestage in front of the proscenium arch. In this arrangement, stage and audience would both be contained within the auditorium drum, the form of which was conceived by Moro as a 'neutral' shape that would also work well when the forestage was removed and the proscenium arch was used.[37]

Leicester's Haymarket Theatre (designed by the city architect, opened in 1973, and closed in 2007) coupled a large forestage with an invisible proscenium arch (see Figure 9.2). The design brief, prepared in 1967, called for 'a fairly traditional

Figure 9.1. Nottingham Playhouse: the auditorium in 1963 with the orchestra pit in use (RIBA Collections)

[35] Percy Corry, 'Billingham Forum', *Tabs* 25, no. 4 (December 1967), pp. 18–24 (p. 22: 'as is now usual').

[36] UoB, 2.8/23/A5, Richard Southern to Hugh Willatt, 19 March 1956.

[37] Michael Mellish, interviewed 22 August 2006.

Figure 9.2. Haymarket Theatre, Leicester: the auditorium (Architectural Press Archive/ RIBA Collections)

relationship' between actor and audience, 'with no provision for flexibility of seating arrangements, since it was felt that this often tended to produce poor conditions for some of the audience'.[38] The stage formed a half hexagon in plan; around it, the audience was seated in a wide, angled fan, in two tiers. Generous wing space was provided at either side of the stage opening, while provision was made to fly scenery over the entire stage, with a cranked safety curtain following the line of the stage's front edge. In this respect, although fundamentally an end stage theatre (like its predecessor, the Phoenix), the Haymarket retained many of the principles of the proscenium arch stage, prompting Colin Amery to describe it as 'a traditional theatre without a proscenium'.[39] Dundee Repertory Theatre (Nicoll Russell, 1982) is similar. The design brief stressed 'the need for intimacy' between actor and audience and that, while there was to be a proscenium arch, there should be no 'apparent visual demarcation'; the Haymarket was cited as a successful precedent.[40] Thus the walls and ceiling of the auditorium, which seats 450, are simply brought in to make the sides of the stage opening, while there is a

[38] 'Haymarket Theatre', *Architects' Journal* 159 (20 March 1974), pp. 607–22 (p. 608).
[39] 'Haymarket Theatre', p. 615.
[40] V&A, ACGB/120/41, Dundee Repertory Theatre: Architects' Brief, June 1973.

projecting forestage which can be further extended into the auditorium by removing the first three rows of seating.[41] *Periaktoid* towers and a 'header' allowed the narrowing of the proscenium opening.[42] Within the auditorium itself, a low wall, originally marked out by neon tubes, divides the tenth row from the rear four rows of seats and creates an auditorium in two parts. The intention was that the audience for smaller shows might be seated entirely in the front ten rows.

Invisible proscenia and the provision of projecting forestages thus offered ways of breaking down the apparent barrier between actor and audience while retaining the scenic possibilities of the proscenium arch stage. In a related strategy, open end stage auditoria were often equipped with a removable proscenium arch and facilities for scenic production. For example, at Theatr-y-Werin, Aberystwyth (Alex Gordon and Partners, 1972), the straight side walls of the 400-seat auditorium continue into the stage area, defining its width, but panels or curtains could be placed at right angles to these side walls, creating a narrowed stage opening and forming a proscenium arch of sorts.[43] The arrangement of the auditorium and stage at Farnham's Redgrave Theatre (1974) was similar. Frank Rutter's design evolved through several phases after 1967.[44] As of 1968, the auditorium was to have gently curving rows and a wide stage opening, but as built the geometries were more angular and the proscenium arch was less overt.[45] Nonetheless, panels at either side of the stage implied the possibility of a proscenium arch approach, even if the theatre lacked a fly tower.

Some of the designs for the Redgrave Theatre locate the stage and auditorium within a single space with a hexagonal plan, a shape which suggests the influence of Norman Downie's well-received Colchester Mercury Theatre (1972) and Salisbury Playhouse (1976), both of which had a six-sided auditorium. The Mercury was described, not entirely accurately, as 'the first theatre in the country with an auditorium that can actually change shape' and 'easily adaptable for every type of production except theatre-in-the-round'.[46] As of 1966, the brief comprised a 500-seat end stage auditorium: 'a simple building' was wanted, and an end stage layout was thought to be cheaper than a proscenium arch auditorium.[47] There was, however, a requirement that the stage should also accommodate proscenium arch productions, and 'the director of the Repertory Company provided a specific brief including a preliminary model to show the relationship of stage to auditorium'.[48] This 'relationship' was the work of the Royal Shakespeare Company's Christopher Morley, who acted as consultant, with the technical detail being worked out by the

[41] Derek Blackwood, Charles Moodie, Eddie O'Donnell, and John Holt, 'Two Theatres in Scotland at Pitlochry and Dundee', *Arup Journal* 18, no. 1 (April 1983), pp. 12–17 (p. 15).

[42] Blackwood et al., 'Two Theatres in Scotland', p. 16.

[43] 'Sherman Theatre; Theatr-y-Werin', *Architects' Journal* 160 (24 July 1974), pp. 207–23.

[44] The scheme can be traced through the drawings in SHC, 6894/7/1/3 (twelve folders).

[45] The earlier scheme recalls the nearby Thorndike Theatre: see 'Redgrave Theatre', *Architects' Journal* 152 (25 November 1970), pp. 1240–1, which reproduces a plan.

[46] ERO, C1371/21, clippings: 'Economy Glamour Revolution', *Essex County Standard*, 12 May 1972.

[47] ERO, D/Z 455/2/13, clippings: 'The Theatre Plan Takes More Shape', *Colchester Gazette*, 11 January 1966.

[48] 'Theatre at Colchester', *Architects' Journal* 156 (5 July 1972), pp. 19–34 (p. 20).

equipment supplier, Mole Richardson, and by Theatre Projects Consultants. The design was published in 1969.[49] There is a projecting semi-thrust stage, the rear part of which has a fly tower. Although one local report played up the open stage arrangement as an alternative to the 'crippling' picture frame,[50] Colin Amery noted that 'the stage is basically a proscenium with a forestage extension.'[51] However, a yet more definite proscenium arch arrangement was possible. The panels which formed the auditorium's side walls could be moved along special tracks towards the centre of the space in order to reduce the width of the auditorium as well as the size of the stage opening. In so doing, the stage gained, in effect, an 'invisible' proscenium opening.

A proscenium arch stage could also form the basis for a flexible approach, as was the case at the Northcott, Exeter (1967). In early drawings, the auditorium and stage are hexagonal in plan, but as built the auditorium is fan-shaped, with a single fixed rake of seating.[52] The stage was intended to work in three ways.[53] The first deployed a proscenium arch, 36 feet wide and 33 feet tall. A lift in front of the arch could either be raised to form a platform which extended the stage or could be dropped to make an orchestra pit. Second, an open end stage arrangement was possible by removing the sides of the proscenium arch and by placing blocks of seating against the side walls of the stage; this was thought to be suitable for Greek and Elizabethan drama as well as some modern plays. Finally, a 569-seat 'in-the-round' theatre could be formed by placing further blocks of seating on stage so as to surround completely the acting area. Such adaptability was thought to be original: 'no other theatre of its size in the country provides for so large a range of possibilities', remarked the management in 1966.[54] (There was, in fact, a slightly smaller precedent, namely the theatre at LAMDA on which the Northcott's theatre consultant, Michael Warre, had previously worked, and which had 'greatly impressed' the university authorities in Exeter 'by what seemed to them a wholly successful experiment and a complete refutation of the argument that a "multi-purpose theatre ends up by being a no-purpose theatre"'.[55])

A similar kind of flexibility was attempted in Manchester's University Theatre, whose architect, George Grenfell-Baines, was assisted by Richard Southern. Neither Southern nor the Drama department's Hugh Hunt was keen on the idea of a large adaptable auditorium: the university's small studio could be used as a 'laboratory' and in any case the theatre was also intended as a replacement for the Worthington Hall, which was used for student drama productions.[56] Although drawings of

[49] 'Polygonal Playhouses: proposed theatres at Sheffield and Colchester', *Architects' Journal* 150 (6 August 1969), pp. 274–6 (p. 275).

[50] ERO, C1371/21, clippings: 'Mechanics of the Mercury', *Essex County Standard*, 12 May 1972.

[51] 'Theatre at Colchester', p. 28.

[52] UoLiv, D147/C73/3, Holford's 'Queries and Comments on Latest Drawings and Perspectives for the Northcott Theatre: EXETER: 20/8/64'; also (undated) drawings in D147/C74/6.

[53] UoEx, 26/1d/3c, 'Northcott Devon Theatre Management Committee 28th February 1966: Agendum Number 3'.

[54] UoEx, 26/1d/3c, 'Northcott Devon Theatre Management Committee 28th February 1966: Agendum Number 3'.

[55] UoEx, 26/1d/3c, Notes on visit to LAMDA, 1963.

[56] UoB, RSA, uncat., Southern's notes of a meeting on 31 March 1962.

summer 1962 show hexagonal and fan-shaped layouts, by November 1962 the design had been rationalized, with the auditorium gaining straight sides and prompting Southern to worry that it now had an 'orthodox' quality.[57] Stephen Joseph, who had recently joined the university, similarly thought that the design was unhelpfully conventional and that a theatre of this size offered the ideal opportunity to try a more innovative approach:

> I think it is a waste of time, space and money to have so small a theatre designed along the lines of a Moss Empire building—there are simply not the seats nor the potential paying public to justify it; besides, I think the convention is both economically and aesthetically out of date.[58]

He was similarly unconvinced by its claimed flexibility:

> The building is the wrong shape for an adaptable theatre, and it may be worth starting afresh if this is considered a requirement, as I believe it must essentially be.[59]

As built, the auditorium had a single rake of seating, broken into two sections with a flat-floored area at the front. Flexibility was achieved by removing the proscenium arch and raising the floor in front of the stage.[60] Some of the seating could be placed around this raised area to make an open stage, or for in-the-round staging. Joseph, however, remained sceptical:

> I am still depressed by all the wings and borders and drapes. If they could be stowed away until required—fine. But if they are once put up I fear they will stay up and condemn us to a permanent Women's Institute type of staging which everyone is familiar with, everyone therefore feels safe with, and no-one will have time to take the things down and explore the open stage. Am I being pessimistic?[61]

Given Joseph's well-known reluctance to embrace theatrical convention, his comments are not surprising. Nonetheless, although he correctly recognized that the auditorium was something of a compromise, its flexibility—even if it was not unlimited—not only represented an attempt to rethink the auditorium in a pragmatic way, but was in fact put to productive use once the theatre opened.

Some of these attempts to reshape the design of the traditional stage were received positively. For example, Colin Amery thought that 'Colchester has neatly solved its stage problem by opting for clear alternatives[,] either an open stage or a proscenium', although there was evident regret in his observation that the management had not 'been brave enough to abandon the proscenium completely'.[62] The theatre's adaptability was reported in the Essex press with evident pride, with the Mercury being compared to the Crucible at Sheffield, also then under construction.

[57] UoB, RSA, uncat., letters from Southern to BDP and Hugh Hunt, both 26 November 1962.
[58] JRL, SJ/1/43, 'Theatre: notes from SJ to HH [Hugh Hunt], October' 62' [typescript].
[59] JRL, SJ/1/43, 'Theatre: notes from SJ to HH, October' 62'.
[60] UoB, RSA, uncat. box entitled 'Theatres, Printed Information, M–Z', brochure entitled 'Manchester University Theatre'.
[61] JRL, SJ/1/43, document entitled 'University Theatre: Marek's letters of 20 and 27 May'.
[62] 'Theatre at Colchester', p. 28.

It was pointed out that, unlike the Mercury, the Crucible was a thrust stage theatre alone.[63] Indeed, the opening productions at the Mercury demonstrated both possible layouts. Farquhar's *The Recruiting Officer* was staged on an open stage and was followed by Noel Coward's *Present Laughter* in order to demonstrate the proscenium arch format.[64] For the *Stage*, the result was an 'enchanting modern playhouse'.[65] For one local newspaper, however, the Mercury was more than modern, being almost a harbinger of the future.[66] The proscenium arch would surely soon come back into fashion, and, when it did, Colchester would be ready.

RETHINKING THE AUDITORIUM: FUNCTION AND APPEARANCE

Thus far, it has been suggested that it was possible to rethink the actor/audience interface while at the same time retaining the essentials of the proscenium arch stage. However, the proscenium arch auditorium itself could also be reimagined and presented in modern terms as 'functional' space rather than the unimaginative repetition of a tired typology. For example, on 18 March 1958, an invited audience gathered in the auditorium of the newly completed Belgrade Theatre to watch Arthur Ling fire a pistol on stage.[67] The occasion was one of a number of acoustic tests carried out under the aegis of the Building Research Station (BRS), whose advice shaped the design of the Belgrade as it had previously that of the Festival Hall. The public nature of the test presented the theatre as a rational, even scientifically functional space. In this respect, this period has subsequently been characterized, often negatively, as marking the apogee of 'functionalism' in theatre architecture to the detriment of more apparently 'theatrical' concerns.[68] But what did the 'functional' auditorium mean in practice, and did it really work against the idea of theatricality?

Although the idea that 'form follows function' in modern architecture is a simplification, the design of new theatres was frequently presented during the 1960s and 1970s as an exercise in meeting functional requirements. For example, the Yvonne Arnaud Theatre was described by its architect as a 'problem' to be solved.[69] The answer, it was suggested, was 'a functional building, all the parts of which stemmed logically from the design requirements'.[70] Thus within the auditorium 'every seat should have an excellent view of the stage and [...] the acoustics should

[63] ERO, D/Z 455/2/18, clippings: 'The Rep Looks to a Happy Future', *Colchester Express*, 14 January 1970.

[64] 'Colchester Launches Remarkable Theatre', *Daily Telegraph*, 11 May 1972.

[65] 'The Mercury Theatre, Colchester', *Stage*, 11 May 1972, p. 17.

[66] ERO, D/Z 455/2/18, clippings: 'The Rep Looks to a Happy Future', *Colchester Express*, 14 January 1970.

[67] CHC, PA2313/5/2/1, clippings: *Birmingham Mail*, 19 March 1958.

[68] E.g. Gay McAuley, *Space in Performance: Making Meaning in the Theatre* (Ann Arbor, 1999), p. 267.

[69] V&A TC, Guildford file, uncat., J. A. Brownrigg, 'Some Aspects of the Architectural Problem', n.p.

[70] SHC, 7350/2/52, J. A. Brownrigg [Typescript text for the [illegible] Faculty of Architects of Architects and Surveyors], n.d.

be as perfect as possible'.[71] Early designs of April 1960 show an almost circular auditorium that recalls Nottingham Playhouse, the proposals for which had been published the previous year, and locate the stalls and gallery seats in curved rows.[72] As constructed, the rows were straightened out, perhaps in order to give more patrons a clear view of the stage.

The emphasis on function in theatre design was not simply a matter of architectural fashion, nor was it solely the product of increasingly complex theatre systems, nor can it be related only to the legislation affecting auditorium design, important though that was. The idea of the functional auditorium had much deeper roots, being partly a response to the perceived inadequacies of Victorian theatres. As Roderick Ham pointed out, modern audiences would not put up with the same levels of discomfort that might have been acceptable when theatre lacked competition from cinema and television.[73] Given the limited nature of subsidy, audiences still needed to be attracted to theatre.

Both an auditorium's planning and appearance could be conceived and discussed in functional terms. Thus in the case of the Belgrade Theatre, the artist Martin Froy noted in November 1954 the city architect's view 'that [...] the auditorium should be regarded as an accommodation for 910 people who can see and hear in warmth and comfort everything which is going on there'.[74] Although sightlines at the rear of the Belgrade's gallery are actually slightly problematic, they are nonetheless an improvement on those in many older theatres, because all seats basically face forwards and, with a single gallery, the vertiginous 'gods' of the Victorian theatre are absent. The design of the auditorium boxes, meanwhile, contrasts with that of many late-Victorian theatres, where the boxes typically faced backwards into the auditorium. At the Belgrade, they are 'pulled out' of the wall and angled towards the stage in echo of those at the Festival Hall; the *Daily Mail* commented on their good design.[75] As far as the appearance of the auditorium was concerned, Froy proposed a rich decorative scheme,[76] but his proposals were soon judged claustrophobic as well as inimical to the auditorium's 'clear line and functional appearance'.[77] Instead, the BRS's advice informed the choice of panelling material (dark makore hardwood), the design of the ceiling reflectors (similar to those in the Festival Hall), and such details as the saw-tooth profile of the balcony soffit.[78] The idea that the auditorium formed a space in which to see and hear a play was thus integral to its entire conception and design, with one report dubbing the Belgrade 'a functional building'.[79] Such functionality arguably took on new meaning with the advent of the 'democratic' subsidized theatre, with Tynan commenting that the

[71] V&A TC, Guildford file, uncat., Brownrigg, 'Some Aspects of the Architectural Problem', n.p.

[72] SHC, 4580/11, design of 1960. For photographs of the model, see SHC, 4580/21.

[73] Ham, *Theatre Planning*, p. 11.

[74] Martin Froy, 'Second Report to the Arts Council', 14 November 1954. Copy supplied by Martin Froy.

[75] CHC, PA2313/5/2/1, clippings: *Daily Mail*, 13 March 1958.

[76] Martin Froy, 'Report to the Arts Council' [February 1954], p. 2. Copy supplied by Martin Froy

[77] Froy, 'Report to the Arts Council', p. 2.

[78] 'The Belgrade Theatre', *Architect and Building News* 213 (18 June 1958), pp. 797–806.

[79] CHC, PA2313/5/2/1, clippings: *Birmingham Evening Dispatch*, 20 March 1958.

Belgrade treated its patrons like 'first-class citizens' on account of its good sightlines and acoustics.[80]

Summarizing the circumstances in which his proposals for the decoration of the Belgrade's auditorium were set aside, Froy reported that the architects felt that they had two choices. Either 'the "machine" interior [could] be left to speak for itself' or 'sacrifices [could] be made in the comfort, audibility and vision [...] for the sake of what might, inadequately, be called "atmosphere"'.[81] The implication is that 'atmosphere' and 'meaning' had no place in the functional auditorium. Some critics in the 1980s and 1990s certainly thought that the auditorium designers of the 1960s and 1970s had overlooked such subjective matters as 'mood, intimacy, magic and memory' and that they had instead prioritized apparently objective functional criteria.[82] The move towards a simpler auditorium aesthetic had begun in the 1920s. Applied ornament was, of course, treated with suspicion by many modernist designers, but within the specific context of theatre design it was often suggested that aesthetic simplicity would prevent audiences from being distracted during performances by the architecture that surrounded them. The avoidance of ornament and the use of muted colours made it easier to maintain a uniform darkness during performances by minimizing the number of surfaces that might reflect the stage lighting. In this respect, the increasing tendency to provide stage lighting positions within the auditorium rather than the stage alone was significant, as such lights could illuminate the auditorium to a greater degree than lights housed wholly within the stage area.[83] John Bury thus reported of the Barbican Theatre that:

> It was [RSC director] Trevor Nunn who must take the credit for the final décor. He put his foot down when he saw the proposed finishes and declared that no way was he going to have orange walls and the bright parquet floors and the fancy alternate colour seating they've got in the concert hall. The theatre as we've got it—and this was part of the original conception—concentrates everyone's attention on the stage, [and] what is in front of you, not what's behind or above you, the people in the galleries, and so on.[84]

Furthermore, a subdued aesthetic was sometimes linked to 'serious purpose' and to theatre's new status as a subsidized cultural amenity rather than a form of mass popular entertainment.[85] There was also a sense, related to the rise of the open stage, that a decorated auditorium might somehow distance actors from their audience by emphasizing that these two groups occupied different spaces. Peter Moro,

[80] CHC, PA2313/5/2/1, clippings: *Observer*, 30 March 1958.

[81] Froy, 'Second Report', p. 2.

[82] E.g. Forsyth, *Auditoria*, p. 125.

[83] Hazel Vincent Wallace, interviewed 26 October 2006.

[84] Anthony Masters, 'Doyen of a design revolution' [photocopied article from unknown publication in John Bury file, V&A TC].

[85] Francis Reid, 'Seeing, Hearing and Contact', in *Making Space for Theatre: British Architecture and Theatre Since 1958*, edited by Ronnie Mulryne and Margaret Shewring (Stratford-upon-Avon, 1995), pp. 28–33 (p. 29).

for example, reported that he had 'eliminated the usual clutter which so often tends to separate the actor from the audience' in the Nottingham Playhouse.[86]

There were, therefore, several motivations favouring a more subdued auditorium aesthetic, ranging from the practical to the essentially psychological. Yet theatricality was not entirely rejected. For example, Frederick Bentham called in 1969 for theatres to be 'works of art' rather than 'machines'.[87] The architect John Brownrigg similarly commented in the early 1960s that:

> A theatre, more than any other building except perhaps a church, is a physical enclosure for an almost entirely non-physical experience. For this reason the creation of atmosphere is even more important than the solution of a series of functional problems.[88]

Indeed, one might conclude that theatrical atmosphere was a functional necessity, rather than the antithesis of efficient function. It was certainly emphasized by some architects, and was integral to their work. How could it be created? At the end of the 1950s, Peter Moro wrote that 'atmosphere [...] is achieved by the handling of space, the choice of material, the use of colour and the quality of light'.[89] In terms of space, the approach to the auditorium was often dramatized, with a deliberate sense of compression and release as patrons passed from expansive foyers through narrow passages of sometimes complex form into the auditorium. Within the auditorium itself, compactness and the presence of galleries were often thought to encourage a festive atmosphere. The *Architects' Journal* suggested of the Leicester Haymarket that its two-tiered auditorium supplied a lively setting for audiences, who were, it thought, 'almost a part of the show',[90] in the manner of the humanized 'modern monuments' discussed in Chapter 4. Of the Belgrade Theatre, it was noted that 'an effect of richness was to be achieved by the use of functional materials, for example the acoustic panelling, carefully detailed by the architect and chosen for its colour'.[91] Several other theatres followed in the Belgrade's footsteps in deploying rich wood panelling, including the Ashcroft in Croydon, and Billingham Forum. Other materials could be similarly used. The concrete ribs in the Yvonne Arnaud Theatre's auditorium have a varied profile that creates a pleasing play of light and shade. They anticipate the precisely detailed and carefully illuminated board-marked concrete walls of the National Theatre's auditoria. In Leatherhead, Roderick Ham lined the Thorndike Theatre's auditorium with brick tiles, whose warm tones (when illuminated) echo the orange-coloured seating. Something similar is seen at Theatr Clwyd, where the auditorium walls have sculpted brick

[86] [Peter Moro], 'Playhouse Theatre, Nottingham', *Architectural Design* 34, no. 2 (February 1964), pp. 90–4 (p. 94).

[87] Frederick Bentham, 'A Tale of Two Theatres', *Tabs* 27, no. 4 (December 1969), pp. 10–21 (p. 11).

[88] Eric Longworth and John Brownrigg, 'The Yvonne Arnaud Theatre, Guildford', *New Theatre Magazine* 3, no. 1 (October 1961), pp. 14–18 (p. 16).

[89] 'Civic Theatre Nottingham' [Schedule of Accommodation, n.d., copy supplied by Andrzej Blonski], p. 15.

[90] 'Haymarket Theatre', *Architects' Journal* 159 (20 March 1974), pp. 607–22 (p. 617).

[91] Martin Froy, 'Belgrade Theatre, Coventry' [report, 1958, supplied by Martin Froy].

tiles of varying sizes, in shades of red and brown. Again, downlighters are deployed to good use, picking out the surface texture and colours. At Derby Playhouse, bands of unshaded lightbulbs run up the walls and across the ceiling at regular intervals (see Figure 9.3): 'a very attractive and sparkling idea that does linger on the retina', said the *Architectural Review*.[92]

Like Roderick Ham, Peter Moro's office was adept at using colour, materials, and lighting to suggest theatricality. At the end of the 1950s, Moro noted—with reference to the then-proposed Nottingham Playhouse—that:

> the auditorium should radiate a festive atmosphere which will be subdued as the curtain rises, and this can be done by lighting so that there is no danger of an exciting auditorium distracting from the action on stage.[93]

Moro would have understood how lighting and colour could generate atmosphere and meaning within essentially 'neutral' spaces on account of the exhibitions that

Figure 9.3. 'Very attractive and sparkling': the auditorium at Derby Playhouse in 1976, showing the 'invisible' proscenium arch and 'festive' lighting (Richard Einzig/Arcaid Images/RIBA Collections)

[92] 'Theatre, Derby; Theatre, Inverness', *Architectural Review* 160 (October 1976), pp. 212–15 (p. 215).
[93] 'Civic Theatre Nottingham' [Schedule of Accommodation, n.d., copy supplied by Andrzej Blonski], p. 7.

he had designed during the late 1940s, many in collaboration with Robin Day.[94] For example, in 1947 a travelling display for the Atomic Scientists' Association included a section on atomic weapons with black-painted walls and ceiling before, in the final area, the benefits of nuclear power were set out in a brighter environment where 'much light and warm colours are used to create an appropriate atmosphere'.[95] Moro's theatres applied similar principles. At Nottingham Playhouse—whose auditorium was likened by one reviewer in 1964 to 'the world of exhibition design'—colour and interest were introduced within the auditorium by peacock-blue seats (designed by Day), and a yellow stage curtain,[96] and by the colour and movement of the audience. Lighting was also important. The walls have a uniform surface of three-inch wide slats separated from each other by a one-inch gap. Behind these slats were placed the acoustic materials and lighting, which shines through and creates a pattern that recalls the theatre's fenestration (see Figure 9.1). The *Sunday Times*' drama critic described the result as 'the only modern theatre that I have seen which, spurning chandeliers and cherubs, gilt and plush, manages to be warm and glamorous and glowing'.[97]

Automatically to dub all theatres of this period sterile, then, is to miss the point and to judge at least some of them by criteria other than those used by their architects. That said, some were not entirely successful. Take, for example, the Northcott, Exeter. The architects were certainly aware of the need for colour and excitement:

> It is not like an examination hall, or a refectory. Theatre is an occasion, and therefore you want accentuated colour.[98]

Nonetheless, the extent to which colour should penetrate the auditorium was to be more limited:

> You need a dark auditorium with the stage providing the colour and the light; and then, to heighten the sense of occasion, when you come out into the foyer, you want something cheerful [...][99]

There was some consideration of a brightly coloured stage curtain:

> The character of the curtain should not [...] be too assertive or complicated: there is a lot of it and it is close to the tiers of seats when drawn. It could easily become boring and soon go out of date. [...] On the other hand, it would be dull if it were quite plain. An overall abstract pattern is suggested, which would not draw attention to itself at first sight but reveal a subtle composition when studied. It should also light up well, and echo the scale and proportions of the auditorium. It is suggested that five or six shades of the dark basic material should be used, at full material width, i.e. 23 lengths

[94] Lesley Jackson, *Robin and Lucienne Day: Pioneers of Contemporary Design* (London, 2011), pp. 17–21.

[95] 'Atom Train', *Architects' Journal* 106 (13 November 1947), pp. 434–5.

[96] GLL, S L 50.01, Anthony Besch, 'Report to the Corporation of the City of London on the Subject of the Concert Hall and Theatre to Be Built in the Barbican Area' [1964], p. 57.

[97] RIBA, MoP/10, Peter Moro, 'A Sense of Proportion: memoirs of an architect', unpublished MS., *c.*1989, p. 130.

[98] UoLiv, D147/C74/3, Transcript of interview, n.d.

[99] UoLiv, D147/C74/3, Transcript of interview, n.d.

in all, each 23 ft. high. The horizontal joints in the pattern would correspond with the levels of the tiers of seats in the auditorium. There would be thin insertions or 'slashes' of bright colour (copper, apricot, pale vermilion, deep yellow), which would gleam in the vertical folds of the curtain but which would be hidden when the curtain was folded back against the side walls of the stage.[100]

However, one visitor commented in December 1967 on his 'gloomy first impression' of the building.[101] Poor lighting had apparently prompted some more experienced patrons to bring torches with which to illuminate their programmes. Another customer complained that 'the more I see of the Northcott with its gloomy decoration and dull lighting, the more I am convinced that it was a mistake to allow the destruction of the Theatre Royal'.[102] The management offered a robust response:

> This is one of the features which the Architects and Theatrical Consultants found necessary in the auditorium to centre audience attention upon the stage. Theatre planning has moved a long way from the red velvet and gilded cherubs; not everyone may agree this is progress—but it is contemporary thinking.[103]

In this respect, the modern playhouse perhaps offered its patrons an education in architectural modernity (and a version of architectural taste) as well as an instruction in good drama.

'A LOGICAL TWENTIETH-CENTURY THEATRE': CONTINUITY AND CHANGE

In 1976, the theatre consultant Iain Mackintosh referred to the 'neat, efficient form of the new 500-seat single-tier theatres' which had emerged during the previous ten years.[104] Mackintosh presented this kind of auditorium as the embodiment of functionalism:

> the architects [. . .] resolved to rid themselves of all those bad seats where one can neither see nor hear properly and instead [sought] to provide throughout an equally good seat for everybody. Once in your seat in the darkened auditorium of one of these new proscenium arch theatres, you, the audience, would be focused on the stage in front of you to the exclusion of all else.[105]

Mackintosh had in mind the Macrobert Centre, Stirling (RMJM, 1971), but he could have named numerous examples, including, in addition to some of the examples discussed in this chapter so far, Warwick Arts Centre (Renton Howard Wood Levin, 1974), and Stevenage Arts and Leisure Centre (Vincent and

[100] UoLiv, D147/C74/1, William Holford to F. J. Llewelyn, 19 May 1967.
[101] UoEx, 26/1d/2d, Geoffrey Baker to Peter Cherington, 8 December 1967.
[102] UoEx, 26/1d/2d, Mr G. [?] Butt to Roderick Ross, 28 November 1967.
[103] UoEx, 26/1d/2d, Roderick Ross to Mr Butt, 6 December 1967.
[104] 'Introducing Eden Court' [1976 booklet, copy supplied by Eden Court].
[105] 'Introducing Eden Court'.

Gorbing, 1975). The designers of the Northcott Theatre, for example, summarized their intentions in this way:

> Concentration is on the actors. In spite of all the variations now proposed for the National Theatre and other projects, this is the essence of the problem. People are grouped around the action so that they can see everything and hear everything. This leads to a compact and geometrical shape of some kind, so that one's ideas have this sort of kernel, and this kernel creates its shell.[106]

Perhaps the best example of this type—and certainly more interesting than the banal spaces against which Mackintosh railed—is the Thorndike, Leatherhead, of 1969 (see Figure 9.4). The 530-seat auditorium, neatly designed by Roderick Ham to fit within the shell of the former Crescent Cinema, has an invisible proscenium arch and a single, compact tier of seating arranged in continuous curved rows with no intervening gangways. The aisles are pushed to the sides of the auditorium, a layout facilitated by a change in the Greater London Council's fire regulations (often then taken as the national standard) in 1965,[107] which permitted uninterrupted

Figure 9.4. Thorndike Theatre, Leatherhead, with 'invisible' proscenium arch, 'continental' seating, and brick-tiled walls (RIBA Collections)

[106] UoLiv, D147/C73/3, Transcript of interview, n.d.
[107] 'Open House at the Thorndike', *Design* 252 (1969), pp. 48–53 (p. 50).

rows of so-called 'continental seating' provided that they were sufficiently widely spaced to allow easy evacuation. Derby Playhouse is in plan and section very closely related to the Thorndike, while Ham's unbuilt design for the Dove Arts Centre, High Wycombe, broke up the 'continental seating' with aisles and added shallow galleries at the rear of the auditorium but was otherwise to be very similar.[108]

Other designers looked to the Thorndike. As well as the Towngate Theatre at Poole Arts Centre (1978), which has been mentioned already, the Thorndike's influence is seen in the main auditorium at Theatr Clwyd (1976), which is almost identical in terms of size, layout, and décor. At Pitlochry Festival Theatre (1981), a Thorndike-like single tier of seating and invisible proscenium arch stage proved an economical strategy after the abandonment of the architects' 1973 proposals for a Guthriesque thrust stage.[109] In addition, the designers of the Sherman Theatre, Cardiff, were encouraged to study the Thorndike by the ABTT's Theatre Architecture and Planning Committee. After the committee had discussed the initial proposals for the theatre in 1969, it was recorded that:

> as a body [the committee] reflected the orthodox professional allegiance to the proscenium theatre ('the most flexible of all forms' (!)). The ideal theatre of the moment seemed to be the newly opened Thorndike Theatre at Leatherhead.[110]

Sure enough, the Sherman emerged with a single-tier auditorium which was very much like the Thorndike in plan and appearance (see Figure 9.5), as well as an octagonal arena theatre. More original was the auditorium at Newcastle University Theatre, which opened to the designs of William Whitfield in 1971. Flexibility having been discounted as impractical, Whitfield presented his approach in terms of tradition rethought:

> The basic concept is that of an 'open air' theatre enclosed. There are no confining boxes and balconies, and the back wall of the stage functions much as the 'scena' at Sabratha without the architectural embellishments [...] It accepts lessons learned from the Großer Redoutensaal in Vienna, the Little Theatre at Drottningholm, and from many of those juicy baroque theatres all over Europe—needless to say, it looks like none of them.[111]

The theatre's single tier of seating was combined with elevated 'promenade' galleries—complete with a coffee bar—at either side of the seating rake (see Figure 9.6). The stage opening was framed on either side, although there was no 'header' above the stage, and so there were views from the auditorium to the rear of the stage.

The single-tier auditorium had its limits, however. At Birmingham Repertory Theatre (1971), all 900 seats were located in one tier, something which was presented

[108] Roderick Ham, 'Theatre Design in Britain', *Architectural Design* 40, no. 7 (July 1970), pp. 352–7 (p. 354).
[109] PFT, 'Pitlochry New Theatre Project' [*c.*1973], unnumbered pages with drawings entitled 'Simplified Diagrammatic View of a Thrust Stage' and 'The First Concept'.
[110] CUA, UCC/R/F/71, Notes on the ABTT Review, 27 October 1969.
[111] UoN, uncat., 'The University Theatre, Newcastle' [booklet, 1970], p. 13.

Figure 9.5. Sherman Theatre, Cardiff: the Thorndike-like auditorium (Architectural Press Archive/RIBA Collections)

as an essentially democratic, modern gesture.[112] However, a layout that worked well for 500 seats was more problematic at this larger scale. To fit 900 seats into a single tier without that tier becoming too long meant that the width of the auditorium at Birmingham was not inconsiderable. The result was described as an 'enormous' stage that had prompted many to try to 'fill it', even though budgets did not often allow for this.[113] Colin Amery noticed the problem, comparing the Rep with the thrust-stage Crucible Theatre of the same year, which accommodated a similar number of people:

> Alas at Birmingham, unlike Sheffield, magic sparks do not fly. The reason is a fairly simple one: the brief was for a proscenium theatre with 900 seats in a single tier. [...] As it stands, the Rep condemns the audience to an evening afloat in a vast (albeit democratic) void with no rapport with the stage.[114]

Amery wondered if a different approach might not have been better, with either a different form of stage or more than one tier of seating. Perhaps a better solution might have been the kind of layout used at the Wyvern, Swindon (1971).[115]

[112] LoB, MS 2339/4/9, 'The Birmingham Repertory Theatre Appeal' [leaflet, February 1969]: 'a truly one-class arrangement'.

[113] V&A, ACGB/84/28, 'Report on the New Rep to the Board of Directors', n.d.

[114] 'Repertory Theatre, Birmingham', *Architects' Journal* 154 (22 December 1971), pp. 1431–7 (p. 1435).

[115] 'Wyvern Theatre and Arts Centre, Swindon', *Architects' Journal* 154 (22 December 1971), pp. 1420–3.

Figure 9.6. 'An "open air" theatre enclosed': the auditorium at Newcastle University Theatre, 1971, with 'promenade' galleries and bars (Architectural Press Archive/RIBA Collections)

Within its 658-seat proscenium arch auditorium, the seating is deftly arranged in two sections, namely a tiered central block surrounded by a slightly raised horseshoe.

Most proscenium arch and end stage auditoria of the scale of Birmingham Rep in fact did have at least one balcony. The Festival Hall and Belgrade Theatre set the trend during the 1950s, as did the smaller Middlesbrough Little Theatre. These examples were followed in the early 1960s by the Nottingham Playhouse, the Yvonne Arnaud Theatre, and the Ashcroft Theatre in Croydon. One might also note the Congress Theatre, Eastbourne (1963), which has a broken rake of stalls seating, an almost straight-fronted balcony at the rear of the auditorium, and two narrow galleries at either side. Unusually, the auditorium has large windows screened by curtains, which can be opened when it is used for conferences. By the 1970s, more complex arrangements of galleries were increasingly evident. For example, the gallery at Leicester's Haymarket Theatre was broken into three sections, of which the central section was the largest with, in turn, three sub-blocks of seating (see Figure 9.2). Of these sub-blocks, the middle directly faced the stage while the other two were angled inwards. The outer sections of the gallery, meanwhile, were set very slightly below the central section, creating a link to the stalls below. The theatre was constructed with 710 seats after smaller capacities were discounted. Four hundred and fifty seats was liked by the director of productions on account of its potentially intimate character but was felt too small 'in view of growing leisure, literacy, affluence',[116] and likely to require a higher level of subsidy.[117] Reference was also made to the growth of Leicester, whose population was predicted to increase by 15 per cent by 1981.[118]

As is evident from the way in which the Belgrade was described as 'basically a Victorian or Edwardian theatre', a galleried auditorium could be interpreted in terms of tradition rather than modernity. For example, in 1966, the proposed inclusion of galleries in the theatre at Billingham Forum confused the North East Arts Association, which suggested that 'three separate tiers are not in accord with current thinking'.[119] Although, as has been noted, auditoria with balconies were built in Britain during the 1960s, to have so many levels—let alone boxes—was unusual. The Forum, which was completed in 1968, originally seated 675, or 600 when the full apron stage was used.[120] There are two shallow galleries at the rear of the auditorium, and these galleries then cascade towards the stage as a series of boxes (see Figure 9.7). The inspiration for this design is unclear. The theatre was

Figure 9.7. 'Opera-house manner': Billingham Forum, 1968 (RIBA Collections)

[116] V&A, ACGB/84/157, 'The New Civic Theatre, Leicester'.
[117] V&A, ACGB/84/157, Draft Report of the Town Clerk to the General Purposes Committee, Leicester City Council, 4 September 1967
[118] V&A, ACGB/84/57, 'Proposed Civic Theatre, Leicester', 8 June 1967.
[119] V&A, ACGB/84/21, letter from Clive Webster, NEAA, to Jo Hodgkinson, 28 March 1966.
[120] Percy Corry, 'Billingham Forum', *Tabs* 25, no. 4 (December 1967), pp. 18–24.

conceived without a defined user, and although the brief given to the theatre consultant Michael Warre, described an 'intimate theatre', Warre's primary responsibility was reportedly the design and specification of the stage rather than the auditorium.[121] In this context, the historian Paul Iles has suggested that the design was informed by the recent West German opera houses that had been studied by the architects,[122] and indeed a letter of October 1965 describes the design as being 'in the opers [sic] house manner'.[123] Such a source may well reflect the local council's aspirations to excellence and its international outlook. Just as the Forum was to contain an Olympic-sized swimming pool, perhaps the idea was also to have the 'best' type of theatre possible, with an opera house understood in this way, and contemporary West Germany thought to have the best modern examples.

In 1976, Colin Amery saw echoes of Billingham Forum in the newly completed Eden Court, Inverness (see Figure 9.8).[124] As was discussed in Chapter 7, Eden Court was conceived in the mid-1960s as a cultural focal point for the Highlands. The architects Graham Law and James Dunbar-Nasmith were appointed in January 1972, and the theatre consultant Iain Mackintosh joined the team two months later. Eden Court was intended for touring productions rather than a resident company with its own strong artistic vision, and so Mackintosh's enthusiasm for

Figure 9.8. 'Papering the walls with people': Eden Court, Inverness, 1976 (Eden Court)

[121] V&A, ACGB/84/21, F. M. Dawson to Nigel Abercrombie, 29 March 1966.

[122] Paul Iles, 'Towards the Prevention of a Theatre Demolition', text of 2002, <http://www.thelaughingaudience.co.uk/billingham_forum_theatre.html> (accessed 10 March 2017).

[123] V&A, ACGB/84/21, F. M. Dawson to Nigel Abercrombie, 7 October 1965.

[124] 'Theatre, Derby; Theatre, Inverness', p. 215.

the galleried auditoria of the eighteenth century was to have a fundamental effect on the design. The need to accommodate touring shows dictated a proscenium arch stage with a fly tower and orchestra pit. For grand opera, 830 seats were required, but it was felt that the theatre should not feel empty when not full.[125] It was also thought—not least by Mackintosh—that a multitiered, horseshoe-shaped plan in which the walls were 'papered with people' would generate a greater sense of theatrical intensity than 'the customary modern single tier fan shaped auditorium'.[126] To that end, there are around 500 seats in the central raked stalls area, with another 300 seats located in three curved galleries that step down towards the stage.

In 1976, Mackintosh argued that Eden Court was a deliberate response to the single-tier auditoria of recent years, which in his view aimed only to facilitate 'contact between performer and theatre-goer'.[127] Eden Court, he said, was intended to create a 'three-way relationship: performer, [...] theatre-goer, and [...] the other members of the audience'. The emphasis, as at Billingham, was the idea of the audience as a community whose presence decorated and enhanced the otherwise rather plain auditorium. In addition, while Eden Court's auditorium evoked the form of earlier galleried theatres, for Mackintosh this development was entirely appropriate. He wrote of the way in which pre-nineteenth-century theatres had made extensive use of the forestage and had been less reliant on the kind of scenic illusionism that had dominated subsequent proscenium arch productions. The twentieth-century rejection of stage illusionism was therefore presented as an opportunity to return to earlier values and forms. Thus for Mackintosh the design of Eden Court sprang not from 'antiquarian academicism' but rather 'a twentieth century re-evaluation of the nature of theatre'.[128] As a result, its auditorium could be understood as a fundamentally modern space, if one with a solid historical foundation. Accordingly, Mackintosh referred to Eden Court as 'at once a twentieth century synthesis of attitudes and a development of earlier well tried forms',[129] while for Graham Law, 'the design was thought out, as a major modern European theatre, from first principles, and if vestiges of the past appear it is because they have stood the test of time, and twentieth century scrutiny'.[130] Along with the courtyard auditoria which also emerged at this time, it was to influence the many galleried auditoria of the 1980s and 1990s.

A similar synthesis of contemporary thinking and historical influence seems to have shaped the design of the theatre in London's Barbican Arts Centre. Chamberlin Powell and Bon's initial scheme of 1956 included a straightforward two-tiered auditorium with a projecting forestage,[131] but, as was the case for the Barbican concert hall (discussed in Chapter 8), their approach changed after the engagement of the

[125] 'Theatre, Derby; Theatre, Inverness', p. 215.

[126] 'Eden Court Theatre', gazetteer entry in *Making Space for Theatre: British Architecture and Theatre Since 1958*, edited by Ronnie Mulryne and Margaret Shewring (Stratford-upon-Avon, 1995), p. 136.

[127] 'Introducing Eden Court' [1976 booklet, copy supplied by Eden Court].

[128] 'Introducing Eden Court'. [129] 'Introducing Eden Court'.

[130] 'Introducing Eden Court'.

[131] GLL, Fo pam 748, Chamberlin Powell and Bon, Report to the Court of Common Council, 1956, plates VII–IX.

theatre consultant, Richard Southern. Not only did the theatre's functionality improve, with a tall fly tower and generous wings, but the auditorium also now took on a quite different flavour. Drawings of 1958, credited to Southern and the architects, show a fan-shaped auditorium with two rear galleries.[132] Along the side walls are three levels of boxes divided by low screens, while at either side of a variable forestage were to be four stage boxes. A revised scheme of 1959 provides continuous rows of 'continental' seating in the stalls, doubles the number of rear galleries, and arranges these galleries so that they stepped forward from the back of the auditorium.[133] In addition, the side boxes are now set behind arched openings punched through the sides of the auditorium, not unlike Andrea Seghizzi's Teatro Formagliari, Bologna (1640).[134] Clearly Southern's knowledge of the history of theatre architecture was influential, but the architects' interest in architectural history may also have been significant. This interest informed their contemporaneous designs for New Hall, Cambridge, which drew on historically resonant architectural plan forms (such as the basilica, which was transformed to become New Hall's library) and structures (such as domes).

Although it was not built, the 1959 Barbican proposals set the course for the final scheme, which was published in 1968 and opened in 1982.[135] In 1963, it was decided that the Guildhall School of Music and Drama should have its own facilities instead of sharing the Barbican Arts Centre with other users, and there were also changes to the overall estate plan which affected the site of the Arts Centre.[136] In 1964, the Corporation of London's consultant, Anthony Besch, concluded that the Arts Centre should comprise a bespoke set of spaces for professional performers.[137] With the Arts Centre site having already been defined, the architects faced the challenging tasks of squeezing in additional facilities and redesigning the performance spaces in the light of these changed requirements. In the case of the theatre, which was allocated to the Royal Shakespeare Company (RSC), Peter Hall later claimed a fundamental role in the design process, along with John Bury,[138] and Hall's theory of the 'point of command'—the position on the stage where an actor might address the whole audience with a single gesture or glance—certainly shaped the form of the open end stage with removable proscenium arch that was provided. However, in other ways, the theatre, which had been designed by 1966,[139] represents a rationalized version of the 1959 scheme, enlarged to suit the RSC's needs. Key features of the earlier concept survived, including the forward-stepping galleries and the location of the aisles outside the main envelope of the auditorium. (As in the same architects' lecture theatre at Leeds University, each row of seating at the Barbican has its own access door, which closes automatically as the performance starts.)

132 RSA, TCP/T/000094/25, Barbican Theatre drawings, 1958.
133 RSA, TCP/T/000094/11, Barbican Theatre sketch, 1959.
134 'A Triumph of Theatre', *Architects' Journal* 176 (18 August 1982), pp. 31–9.
135 GLL, QL 55.4 BAR, Chamberlin Powell and Bon, 'Barbican Arts Centre, 1968'.
136 TNA, HLG/79/1454, Barbican documents of 1962–3.
137 GLL, S L 50.01, Besch, 'Report', p. 23.
138 Peter Hall, *Making an Exhibition of Myself: The Autobiography of Peter Hall* (London, 2000), p. 214.
139 SBTA, RL5/2/1023-31, photograph of auditorium model, 1966.

However, the arch-fronted auditorium boxes of the 1959 designs were now rendered more prosaically as forward-facing 'sledges' in the manner of such German theatres as Gelsenkirchen.[140] As built, therefore, the Barbican Theatre does not allude to history in quite such a deliberately romantic way as the earlier schemes, but rather suggests a nuanced accommodation of past and present. In this way, it mirrored the philosophy of the RSC, which was committed to the demonstration of Shakespeare's contemporary relevance while also touching on the eternal qualities of the Bard's work. For the *Daily Mail*, the result was 'a logical twentieth-century theatre'.[141]

CONCLUSIONS: A 'MODERN PROSCENIUM' THEATRE

In 1982, as Plymouth Theatre Royal neared completion to his practice's designs, Peter Moro suggested that it was a 'modern proscenium' theatre (see Figure 9.9).[142]

Figure 9.9. Plymouth Theatre Royal, auditorium in 1982. This view from the upper gallery shows the asymmetric lower gallery and the reflective safety curtain (RIBA Collections)

[140] Similar 'sledges' appeared in RMJM's 1974–5 proposals for the Edinburgh 'opera house': see Figure 7.3, Chapter 7, this volume, and e.g. 'Edinburgh's Opera House', *Architects' Journal* 160 (24 July 1974), pp. 200–1. Although the rear of the auditorium does not step forward in the same way as the Barbican, was it nonetheless the source? John Bury was involved in Edinburgh and at the Barbican. Given that one of the drawings in the Edinburgh file is labelled 'Gelsenkirchen', it could also be that Robert Matthew was looking to the same German examples as Chamberlin Powell and Bon.

[141] V&A TM, Barbican file, clipping from *Daily Mail*, 4 November 1966.

[142] Peter Moro, 'Modern Proscenium Theatre', 23 August 1982 [copy supplied by Andrzej Blonski].

The Theatre Royal's modernity was evident in several ways. Like many of the theatres discussed in this chapter, it maintained the principles of the proscenium arch stage but played down the presence of the arch itself and sought to bring actor and theatre goer into a close relationship through the provision of a projecting forestage. The shape of its safety curtain, too, may have suggested modernity. As at Leicester Haymarket, it is cranked to follow the line of the stage edge, and so the forestage is treated as part of the main stage area. Furthermore, the auditorium also presented a contemporary appearance, with an asymmetric middle gallery, plain green gallery fronts and side walls, and yellow seating. Members of the audience were reflected, in distorted form, in the mirrored safety curtain. In this way, just as their presence would have animated the theatre's elevations and foyers as they mingled before the performance, so now they took over from traditional ornament in completing the decoration of the auditorium. The most significant way in which the Theatre Royal could be understood to be 'modern', however, was surely the way in which its seating capacity could be reduced. The entire auditorium ceiling—complete with its lighting and ventilation installation—could be lowered. A three-tiered auditorium seating 1296 for touring shows can thus be reduced to a two-tiered auditorium with 768 seats for smaller productions, with the lowered ceiling hiding the upper gallery. In this way, Moro was able to satisfy the competing visions of different local factions, namely those who wanted a large theatre for touring shows, and those who favoured a smaller venue for less-commercial productions.

For Moro, theatre design was:

> based upon hard facts and is rarely a matter of inventing new forms. The architect works within a large number of constraints, and, if inventiveness comes into it at all, it is in the way that theory is put into practice.[143]

By 'hard facts', Moro seems to have meant practical requirements, such as the general concerns of sightlines, acoustics, and fire safety, as well as more specific demands relevant to an individual commission. Yet it is significant that Moro allowed for 'inventiveness'. For architects, consultants, engineers, and theatre staff, the design of open end stage and proscenium arch theatres represented, if not quite the 'revolutionary' act proposed by Tynan at the National, then at least an opportunity to innovate. If, as was suggested in Chapter 8, open staging offered a chance to restate the live, participatory nature of performance, then the kinds of theatre discussed in this chapter represent a different but no less valid kind of modern playhouse in which modernity and continuity were closely related.

[143] Quoted by Michael Barron, *Auditorium Acoustics and Architectural Design* (London, 1993), p. 1.

10

'Escaping From Boarded Concrete and Modern Finishes'

Impermanency, Mobility, Rehabilitation—and Emulation

In 1976, the director Michael Elliott suggested that the 'vast majority' of recent British theatres 'have proved partial or total failures'.[1] It was not the first time that Elliott had taken a critical view of the country's theatre architecture. In 1973, he used a radio talk to reflect on the scale and permanence of recent theatre buildings.[2] The modern theatre, Elliott began, was a 'hyper-sophisticated and very expensive architectural, mechanical, and electronic monument, all designed to conjure up a rainbow'. Yet, he went on, 'sometimes it seems ridiculous to hope that so heavy and inert a piece of real-estate can catch that rainbow as it moves rapidly over the landscape of society's changing dreams'. As he saw it, 'visiting the several grand new regional civic theatres, or as one leans on the parapet of Waterloo Bridge pondering the huge mushrooming concrete of the new National Theatre, all one's doubts centre round one question—was this the right theatre to build now?' In his view, many theatres seemed to be misconceived:

> Isn't it time we stopped lumbering our children with our mistakes—understandable mistakes, but mistakes nevertheless? Don't we need something different, some less expensive, less daunting, less expressive of civic or national pride, more reflective of changing taste [...]?

Elliott wanted to reimagine theatre as something more immediate, less time-consuming to build, and, perhaps, less costly. Even the whole idea of subsidized theatre was suspect:

> The great danger of subsidised theatre is institutionalisation which can lead directly to fossilisation. We are not only building huge, inflexible, hard-to-demolish buildings, but huge, inflexible, hard-to-demolish institutions.

The National Theatre, he went on, was akin to a 'battleship'. Elliott concluded by asking if theatre buildings might not more productively be 'less permanent':

[1] 'Exchange Experience', *Architectural Review* 160 (December 1976), pp. 361–2.

[2] Subsequently published as 'On Not Building for Posterity', *Tabs* 31, no. 2 (June 1973), pp. 41–4, and reprinted in *Making Space for Theatre: British Architecture and Theatre Since 1958*, edited by Ronnie Mulryne and Margaret Shewring (Stratford-upon-Avon, 1995), pp. 16–20.

> In future, shouldn't we try to retain a certain lightness and sense of improvisation, and sometimes build in materials that do not require a bomb to move them? In short, shouldn't we stop building for posterity?

Elliott's ideas were to have a significant influence on the conception and design of Manchester's Royal Exchange Theatre, which opened in 1976. The theatre trod a distinctive architectural course, with the *Architectural Review* deeming it 'an oddity in more senses than one' on account of its galleried, in-the-round arrangement, and because the auditorium was contained within what was described as a 'module' of steel and glass.[3] This 'module' was located within a redundant Victorian trading hall whose area had been halved in 1953 but which nonetheless still measured a substantial 52 metres by 40 metres. In view of Elliott's scepticism of contemporary theatre architecture, the reuse of this space could be read as a conservationist, even anti-modern gesture; indeed, the building had recently been 'listed' as a structure of architectural and historic importance. Elliott, however, suggested otherwise:

> Is using such a building a terrible vote of no confidence in our ability to create good new buildings this half century, apart from cost? Yes, partly. But also the fun and joy of escaping for once from boarded concrete and modern finishes. Nostalgia it is not, since the theatre itself is so modern.[4]

In other words, the Royal Exchange represented a different kind of modern playhouse.

Thus far, the present study has explored the emergence of 'modern' theatre architecture between the 1950s and the 1980s, understood in terms of the ways in which these buildings were conceived and described, their appearance, the spaces they contained, and the design of their auditoria and stages. This chapter now turns to examine how the idea of the modern playhouse as a substantial, purpose-built structure was challenged between the 1960s and the 1980s. It begins with theatres conceived in a spirit of impermanence and then continues, after brief discussion of more 'participatory' spaces, with mobile performance venues. The second half of the chapter considers a trend which became prominent during the 1970s, namely the restoration of Victorian and Edwardian theatres. Although in one sense the rehabilitation of these theatres represented a critique of modern architecture, the nature of the alterations made to these buildings in fact developed many of the same themes that also shaped the design of contemporaneous new theatres.

IMPERMANENCY AND PARTICIPATION: THEATRE MODULE, FUN PALACE, ARTS CENTRE

In June 1972, the critic Michael Billington reflected on the changing landscape of British theatre in terms that anticipated those which would be used the following

[3] 'Stage Exchange', *Architectural Review* 160 (December 1976), pp. 356–61 (p. 356).
[4] Elliott, 'Posterity', p. 19.

year by Michael Elliott.[5] 'New theatres are springing up like mushrooms,' he reported, but did they perhaps suggest an 'edifice complex'? Billington suggested that it would be more productive to 'learn from the past and build more theatres that are cheap, impermanent, and even portable'. The article ended with a call for a 'new-style theatre' which, though framed in terms which now seem rather dated (being a place 'in which people can smoke and drink while the entertainment is in progress'), challenged the architectural solidity of the recent generation of theatres as well as the broadly conventional ideas that had shaped them.

That a theatre could be impermanent and fleet-of-foot was not a new idea in the early 1970s. For example, the 'Pavilions in the Parks Advisory Service' was motivated by the idea that traditional galleries, concert halls, and theatres distanced artists from the public, and so used portable structures to present performances and exhibitions in public parks, supported partly by the Arts Council but largely by private sponsorship.[6] None of the structures used by the organization was found to be ideal in terms of capacity, weather-proofing, and vandal resistance, and so in 1970 a competition was held in which entrants were required to design a pavilion of at least 625 square feet, with the assessors including the acoustician Sandy Brown, the engineer Frank Newby, and the architect Cedric Price (of whom more shortly). The competition was won by a team of Peter Rice, Ann Meisen, Lennart Grut, and Monica Schmoller, who proposed a polygonal structure made from laminated components.[7] Less portable but no less temporary was the system promoted a few years later by the theatre consultant John Wyckham. Known as 'Theatrespace' and intended for theatre-less towns, so-called 'Theatrepods' with a twenty-year life would be grouped around a circular prefabricated auditorium seating 450 people.[8] The system was considered in Dundee in 1975 but was rejected when it was discovered that it would be unlikely to cost much less than a permanent building.

The Royal Exchange in Manchester was not to be quite so transient as the Pavilions in the Parks or the Theatrespace, but it was nonetheless a light touch alternative to the likes of the National Theatre. Its origins lie at the end of the 1950s in the short-lived 59 Theatre Company, a group led by the directors Casper Wrede and Michael Elliott. Elliott and Wrede continued to work together, and by 1967 were based at the University Theatre, Manchester. Supported by the Arts Council, they formed the 69 Theatre Company with the director Braham Murray and began planning for the construction of an 800-seat repertory theatre and 'real social centre' in Manchester.[9] In 1970, Elliott outlined the company's ambitions: 'from 1973 or 74 we shall be asking for a grant equivalent to the top level of subsidy for any major provincial theatre'.[10] A scheme was drawn up by Eric Jordan, the in-house architect at Theatre Projects Consultants, in collaboration with the

[5] 'Bricks and Mortifying', *Guardian*, 26 May 1972.
[6] 'Pavilions in the Parks', *Architects' Journal* 153 (17 February 1971), pp. 346–8.
[7] 'Competition Result: pavilions in the parks', *Architects' Journal* 152 (16 December 1970), p. 1415.
[8] DA, Lord Provost's Committee, 20 October 1975.
[9] V&A, ACGB/84/182, 'A New Theatre For Manchester', n.d.
[10] V&A, ACGB/84/182, Michael Elliott to Hugh Willatt, 10 March 1970.

production designer Richard Negri and Richard Pilbrow.[11] Within a galleried auditorium, the audience was to sit around the thrust stage in a 210-degree fan, being, as Elliott put it, 'wrapped around the actor like a scarf round your neck on a cold winter's day'.[12] The aims were compactness and intensity. The upper galleries overhung the lower ones, while there was also a degree of inbuilt flexibility, with it being intended that the lower gallery could be removed. Provision was also made for a second stage which could encircle the auditorium itself. In early March 1970, N. V. Linklater of the Arts Council recorded the existence of 'fairly advanced proposals' but noted that no firm architectural appointment had yet been made.[13] The scheme was then projected to cost £1 million, with the aim being that one-third of the total cost would be made available by the Arts Council and a similar sum by the city authorities.[14] Four days later, Elliott wrote that 'there is now a steady dialogue in progress between, informally, the Corporation, the developer of a large central site in Manchester and ourselves and our theatre consultants'.[15] However, by November 1970 plans had changed.[16] Robert Scott, the company's administrator, reported that the group's present finances and the view of Manchester City Council both seemed to weigh against a free-standing theatre on a central site. They now proposed to lease the Royal Exchange for the time being. Within the former trading hall, a tented auditorium seating 430 was to be constructed. It was likened to a 'cocoon'; without it, the long echo generated by the volume of the hall would make speech unintelligible.[17] By June 1971, a twenty-one year lease had been signed.[18]

The tented theatre was popular, reportedly achieving 86 per cent average attendance,[19] but was less than ideal in terms of comfort and practicality. Its replacement would not only address these problems, but was also to be larger. The design was developed iteratively by Negri and members of the company, not least Elliott, by means of intensive model-making and discussion sessions. Negri worked creatively, as Murray recalled:

> Sometimes [the models] were bizarrely incomprehensible. On one occasion we were confronted by a rubbish heap with two golden nails suspended above it.[20]

Only subsequently was an architectural appointment made. Axel Burrough of Levitt Bernstein was selected after more than thirty practices had been interviewed, being the only candidate felt by the team to understand their aims.[21] In a press

[11] V&A, ACGB/84/182, 'A New Theatre For Manchester', n.d.; David Burrows, *The Life and Work of Richard Negri*, online book at <www.richardnegri.co.uk> (accessed 6 July 2017), pp. 142–6.

[12] Burrows, *Negri*, p. 145.

[13] V&A, ACGB/84/182, N. V. Linklater memo, 6 March 1970.

[14] V&A, ACGB/84/182, N. V. Linklater memo, 6 March 1970.

[15] V&A, ACGB/84/182, Michael Elliott to Hugh Willatt, 10 March 1970.

[16] V&A, ACGB/84/182, Robert Scott to Peter Longman, 16 November 1970.

[17] 'Theatre May Have New Home', *Guardian*, 25 September 1970.

[18] V&A, ACGB/84/182, N. V. Linklater memo, 26 July 1971.

[19] V&A, ACGB/120/34, Arts Council review of 'Manchester 69 Theatre', 9 October 1974.

[20] Braham Murray, *The Worst It Can Be Is a Disaster: The Life Story of Braham Murray and the Royal Exchange Theatre* (London, 2007), p. 129.

[21] Burrows, *Negri*, <www.richardnegri.co.uk> (accessed 6 July 2017), p. 155.

Figure 10.1. 'Poised for take-off': Royal Exchange Theatre, Manchester, 1976 (RIBA Collections)

release of November 1972, the 'revolutionary' scheme was presented to the public (see Figure 10.1):[22]

> A multi-coloured steel-framed and highly intimate auditorium will sit clear of the walls, contrasting their ancient weight by the modern open-work light-weight design of the structure. The audience will be accommodated on five different levels, with every seat having a perfect view of the stage. The farthest member of the audience from the acting area will be closer than in any other theatre of this size in the world.[23]

The concept was described in transformative terms that recalled the language earlier used of such new theatres as Coventry's Belgrade: 'a Chinese lantern lighting up an old dark place—a symbol of the new life seething into the old personality of Manchester'.[24] Clustered around it on the Exchange's parquet floor would be tables, kiosks, 'life': all the essential attributes of a theatre conceived as a social centre. The auditorium itself would be compact, with a diameter of 26 feet.[25] By October, the cost of the scheme was estimated at £300,000.[26]

The proposals received a slightly sceptical response from the Arts Council.[27] The design was considered idiosyncratic on account of such things as the way in which

[22] For 'revolutionary' see '69 Theatre May Find Home', *Guardian*, 28 October 1972.
[23] V&A, ACGB/84/182, Press Release, 9 November 1972.
[24] V&A, ACGB/84/182, Press Release, 9 November 1972.
[25] 'Theatre Exchange', *Guardian*, 11 December 1976.
[26] V&A, ACGB/84/182, Michael Elliott to N. V. Linklater, 8 October 1971.
[27] V&A, ACGB/120/34, Arts Council review of 'Manchester 69 Theatre', 9 October 1974.

the balconies encircled the acting area and so would restrict scenic possibilities. More fundamentally, was the basic idea right? An Arts Council committee concluded in October 1974 that:

> Visually and symbolically the structure gives the appearance of being temporary and no particular attempt appears to have been made to relate it to the old building around it. The Committee wondered whether, as the novelty value wore off, the appearance of being temporary might not prove a disadvantage in future years.[28]

Furthermore, it had already been pointed out in October 1971 that the Mercury Theatre in Colchester was on course to cost rather less than the Royal Exchange and would be permanent, if with a smaller capacity.[29] With the anticipated cost of the project reaching £450,000 by October 1972, the 'Housing the Arts' officer, Peter Longman, recorded that 'I think that £450,000 for a conversion is getting a bit excessive'.[30] In an animated correspondence, members of the company defended their ideas. Their dedication to see the project succeed without compromise perhaps inspired Longman's description of the project as the 'Manchester 69 bulldozer'.[31] For example, in January 1974, Laurence Harbottle, the chairman, wrote to Longman:

> To debate whether a theatre can be erected more cheaply seems to me, in the context of schemes for other theatres, very remarkable. This must be the cheapest project for a permanent structure that can be imagined and to achieve a theatre with the proposed facilities in any other circumstance would presumably cost well over a million pounds.[32]

Later that year, Elliott pointed out that the auditorium would not be impracticably flexible: fewer seats were movable than had initially been intended, which would in fact make rearrangement easier and cheaper, and potentially more frequent.[33] He also rebuffed suggestions that there should be an 'off-stage' area within the module. Such an area would, he said, run entirely counter to the philosophy of the project. He wanted actors and audience to mix in the shared area around the module: it had worked for the temporary theatre. And so the project proceeded, in spite of rising costs and technical challenges. A redesign was necessary when it was discovered that the floor of the Royal Exchange could not support the weight of the module. Steel prices increased, too, and money was spent on restoring the Exchange itself.[34] By autumn 1975, it was expected that the theatre would cost nearly £1 million, in spite of cuts being made to such things as the backstage specification. Scott argued that Birmingham Rep and the Sheffield Crucible—both theatres with a similar capacity—had cost as much four years before, and would now

[28] V&A, ACGB/120/34, Arts Council review of 'Manchester 69 Theatre', 9 October 1974.
[29] V&A, ACGB/84/182, N. V. Linklater to Michael Elliott, 9 November 1971.
[30] V&A, ACGB/84/182, Hugh Willatt to Laurence Harbottle, 2 October 1972, with annotation by Peter Longman.
[31] V&A, ACGB/84/182, Peter Longman memo, 10 December 1975.
[32] V&A, ACGB/84/182, Laurence Harbottle to Peter Longman, 23 January 1974.
[33] V&A, ACGB/84/182, Michael Elliott to Peter Longman, 18 November 1974.
[34] V&A, ACGB/84/182, Robert Scott to Peter Longman, 30 August 1975.

cost at least £3 million.[35] The Arts Council—now contributing £250,000—sought to encourage a greater commitment by the local authorities.[36]

The theatre opened in September 1976 with Braham Murray's production of *The Rivals*, a play whose Georgian origins seemed at odds with the kind of in-the-round stage on which it was presented but which served to underline the universal claims of this stage form.[37] In *The Times*, Irving Wardle suggested that the Royal Exchange seemed to reject the kind of modern theatre architecture developed during the previous two decades:

> Besides the relatively small cost of building inside an existing installation, it is a masterstroke to have created Manchester's new theatre at the very heart of Mancunian tradition, rather than to have set up yet another boarded-concrete cultural supermarket with no link to the past.[38]

Irving thus interpreted the rejection of 'boarded-concrete' not as a matter of architectural fashion but rather as an attempt to address the city's heritage and to root the theatre in Manchester through the reuse of a prominent historic building. In particular, the preserved cotton price boards offer a tangible link to the city's industrial past of a kind that was increasingly prized by architects and designers. In this respect, the Royal Exchange can be aligned with the emergence since the 1960s of a growing number of performance venues housed in converted buildings, including the Roundhouse in London and the Everyman in Liverpool. Some of these 'found spaces' were born of pragmatism, in that redundant buildings could be acquired cheaply, but some theatre-makers deliberately embraced the aesthetic potential of these buildings. The director Jude Kelly has suggested that conversions possess 'human history in the[ir] very bones [...], a certain kind of authenticity',[39] and in this respect they contrast with the innate and deliberate 'new-ness' of purpose-built theatres. Nonetheless, in the case of the Royal Exchange the effect was not entirely nostalgic. The title of Wardle's review, 'Poised for Take-Off', implied a renewed modernity, as did his description of the theatre: 'a seven-sided structure in steel and glass, its metal struts running uncompromisingly between the Corinthian columns, it stands amid the parquet like a descended spaceship'.[40] Reporting to his colleagues at the Arts Council in July 1976, Peter Longman similarly suggested that it 'resembles one of the American moon landing craft and is probably just about as technically sophisticated, and nearly as expensive'.[41] For the *Stage*, meanwhile, it was a 'huge science-fiction spider'.[42]

[35] V&A, ACGB/84/182, Robert Scott to Peter Longman, 30 August 1975.

[36] V&A, ACGB/84/182, Roy Shaw to Robert Scott, 5 January 1976.

[37] 'Robin Thornber Reviews *The Rivals*', *Guardian*, 16 September 1976.

[38] 'Poised for Take-off', *The Times*, 16 September 1976.

[39] Jude Kelly, 'The West Yorkshire Playhouse', in *Making Space for Theatre: British Architecture and Theatre Since 1958*, edited by Ronnie Mulryne and Margaret Shewring (Stratford-upon-Avon, 1995), pp. 74–9 (p. 74).

[40] 'Poised for Take-off', *The Times*, 16 September 1976.

[41] V&A, ACGB/84/182, Peter Longman memo, 22 July 1976.

[42] 'The Royal Exchange, Manchester', *Stage*, 9 September 1976, p. 18.

Yet more expensive, potentially even more technically sophisticated, and quite consciously intended to have a finite existence was the Fun Palace, a proposal developed after 1961 by the architect Cedric Price and the radical theatre director Joan Littlewood.[43] Littlewood, whose Theatre Workshop had moved in 1953 to Stratford, east London, presented her ambitions in radical terms:

> Knowledge & skilled delight have been hoarded in the past [by] those who were arrogant & cunning enough to get the better of society. It is time now for each individual to extend their awareness, increase their knowledge & delight; they will also increase their pain or sense of inadequacy. [...] As a temporary measure a large scale expendable play-thing is suggested. A minimum of 20 acres in large urban areas where self-education & discovery may begin and time-wasting be enjoyed.[44]

The intention was to allow visitors to become engaged rather than passive citizens. There was to be space for political meetings, film showings, and a children's nursery, as well as car maintenance workshops, a television studio, and a live newsroom. These facilities would evolve: 'nothing is to last for more than ten years, some things not even ten days: no concrete stadia, stained and cracking; no legacy of noble contemporary architecture, quickly dating; no municipal geranium-beds or fixed teak benches'.[45] The Fun Palace would thus be an antidote to the theatre-as-civic-monument, even if Littlewood's belief in the transformative potential of leisure and the arts was not so far removed from the kind of argument being made at the Arts Council and in local government.

Price shared Littlewood's interest in architectural flexibility, and her distrust of convention. The Fun Palace was thus to be housed within a giant steel framework, likened by Price to a 'shipyard'. His choice of word and the form of the Fun Palace both recall Basil Spence's Sea and Ships Pavilion at the 1951 Festival of Britain, in which a similar framework accommodated exhibits.[46] In the case of the Fun Palace, facilities—housed in discrete volumes and enclosures—could theoretically be added to and removed from the framework at will. A cybernetics system would assess user priorities, removing the need for a human authority figure. Escalators, attached at ground level only, would swivel to connect the various parts of the centre, which would include an auditorium reconfigurable to accommodate between twenty-five and 1500 spectators. However, the Fun Palace was never built, not least because it would have been expensive. As of 1965, the estimate was between £4 million and £5 million for a structure intended to last only a decade. Nonetheless, the Fun Palace was an important influence on Renzo Piano and Richard Rogers's designs for the Pompidou Centre, Paris (1971–7), while Price himself reprised the concept in the Inter-Action Centre, Camden (1976). Like the Fun Palace, the Inter-Action Centre was conceived as a flexible structure with a

[43] For the following discussion, I am indebted to Barnabas Calder, 'The Limits of 1960s Radicalism: the Fun Palace versus the National Theatre', in *Setting the Scene: Perspectives on Twentieth-century Theatre Architecture*, edited by Alistair Fair (Farnham, 2015), pp. 164–78.

[44] Quoted in Calder, 'The Limits of 1960s Radicalism', p. 168.

[45] Calder, 'The Limits of 1960s Radicalism', p. 172.

[46] Price had visited the Festival of Britain, and later referred to the Sea and Ships Pavilion as 'the best thing [Spence] ever did' (Cedric Price, *Re: CP*, edited by Hans-Ulrich Obrist (Basel, 2003), p. 83).

finite lifespan, containing spaces including a hall, rehearsal rooms, workshops for print and film, a youth club, and a garage. In 1974, the Arts Council assessed the proposals, then anticipated to cost £350,000, and concluded that they represented 'a novel and exciting experiment in terms of catering for the flexible and organic growth of an organisation whose influence is felt throughout the community arts field'.[47]

Echoes of Price and Littlewood's participatory and accessible ideals are evident in the facilities provided at the Albany in Deptford, south-east London.[48] The Albany was a long-established welfare institution, which by the 1970s was threatened by a road scheme. Initial designs for a new building were prepared by Peter Moro but had been abandoned by 1976, when Howell Killick Partridge and Amis (HKPA) was appointed in Moro's place; the project architect, Tim Ronalds, subsequently designed several well-received theatre projects in his own right. In terms of its functional content, the Albany was very much in the mould of the Fun Palace and Inter-Action Centre. Indeed, the latter was a conscious reference point.[49] Alongside rooms for the welfare project, it was to include space for crafts and performance and would be accessible and welcoming: 'bright/cheerful/gaudy/inviting [...] not "in good taste"/echoing cabaret, burlesque, variety/with flashing lights which out-do the local bingo palace'.[50] HKPA responded to these ideas with a design that was rather more conventional than the Fun Palace. In its brick walls and pitched, tiled roof, it was contextual and, by implication, also accessible. For the *Architectural Review*, 'here the brutalism once associated with the genre has been tempered so that the effect is cosy rather than heroic, fun rather than exciting'.[51] It went on:

> Though the building does not seem visually inappropriate, its functional reciprocities and its porosity to the activities in its immediate surroundings are more important. Transparency and porosity, interaction and reciprocity between activities, are taken further inside a building which is an exceptionally relaxed and warm example of its genre.[52]

Large windows offered views into the building: 'the building should be as public as possible', stated the brief, despite concerns about vandalism. Views within the building were also emphasized. The auditorium, dubbed the New Albany Empire, developed the form of the same architects' earlier theatre at Christ's Hospital, comprising a centralized flexible auditorium with a fixed gallery. However, there was no obvious stage: performances could be set up anywhere. As with HKPA's other theatres, it was intended to have a strong character. Although the dark brick walls that form the auditorium's actual perimeter recede into the distance, the gallery's gilded columns provide a prominent framework. These columns rise from the floor, cross the gallery fronts, and continue up and across the ceiling to support a circular beam located above the centre of the space. Meanwhile the gallery fronts

[47] V&A, ACGB/120/35, 'Camden: Inter-Action Trust', 12 July 1974.
[48] Geraint Franklin, *HKPA* (London, 2017), pp. 142–5.
[49] Franklin, *HKPA*, p. 142. [50] Franklin, *HKPA*, p. 143.
[51] 'New Albany: Community Centre, Deptford, London', *Architectural Review* 172 (September 1982), pp. 61–70 (p. 65).
[52] 'New Albany', p. 64.

(since replaced) combined the red-painted timbers and cheerful lighting of Christ's Hospital with gold-painted steel lattice. Something similar was also proposed by HKPA in their Leeds Playhouse competition entry in 1984. The Albany 'is a space of striking and festive character', concluded the *Architectural Review*.[53] It offered 'a strong but suggestive framework that encourages and can absorb a wide range of different ways of using it and an accumulation of the inevitable tat, yet offers a loose but pervasive discipline'.[54]

If the Albany thus took the programme of the Fun Palace and clothed it in rather more solid and visually traditional form than Price and Littlewood had proposed, a more transient approach was evident elsewhere. In April 1970, the *Bracknell News* reported on proposals for the construction of an arts centre in the town, citing the views of Alan Fen-Taylor, a local classical musician and teacher, for whom the ideal centre would be anything but monumental:

> Because artists want to get away from the impersonal, we should talk rather in terms of creating an environment. I think the concept of making a building malleable should be a guiding principle. This nowadays could mean inflatible [sic], collapsible and movable structures.[55]

He suggested that there might be 'a sort of "public collage" space where anyone who wanted could stick on pictures, posters, colour supplements, etc.'. Art would, ultimately, be demystified. Fen-Taylor suggested that while it might not be desirable to have members of the public watching rehearsals, there could nonetheless be screens and 'listening points' so that visitors could unobtrusively see and hear work taking shape. Fen-Taylor's comments fitted into a wider local debate. As in Coventry in the 1950s, some local people thought that there was little to do in Bracknell, one of the post-war new towns begun in the late 1940s.[56] A pressure group had been formed in 1965 to call for the construction of an arts centre,[57] and it presented a report to the local authority in November 1969.[58] A key point made in this document was that the centre should not address itself to audiences who might already seek out cultural activities. Already, then, there was an emphasis on accessibility.

While Fen-Taylor's ideas—conceptually and architecturally—suggested the Fun Palace transplanted from east London to suburban Berkshire, the reality was a little more pragmatic. In 1970, it was decided to convert a mansion within Bracknell's South Hill Park into an arts centre. Such centres were then becoming increasingly common; by 1977, around 150 were reportedly in existence.[59] Some, such as the Wyvern in Swindon, were essentially conventional venues for professional performance, but others were framed in more diverse, participatory terms. For example,

[53] 'New Albany', p. 69. [54] 'New Albany', p. 69.

[55] BRO, NT/B/G23, clippings: 'Arts Centre Plan Takes Shape', *Bracknell News*, 16 April 1970.

[56] BRO, NT/B/G23, clippings: 'Newcomers Settle for Bracknell', *Evening Post*, 28 June 1971.

[57] Robert Hutchison, 'Three Arts Centres: a study of South Hill Park, the Gardner Arts Centre, and Chapter' [Arts Council report, 1977], p. 9.

[58] BRO, NT/B/S2/9, Society for the Promotion and Encouragement of the Arts and Recreation within the Rural District of Easthampstead, 'The Society's Report on Its Investigation into a Proposal for an Arts Centre in Bracknell', November 1969.

[59] Hutchison, 'Three Arts Centres', p. 5.

the Midlands Arts Centre in Birmingham included studios for artists and crafts people, while the Gardner Arts Centre at the University of Sussex hoped to stimulate creative work by members of the university and the local community.[60] Bracknell Development Corporation, the official body charged with the planning and construction of the town, laid particular stress on community participation:

> there will be room for everybody. The arts centre could really be called a 'multi-purpose centre with the emphasis on the arts', just as the Bracknell Sports Centre is far more than its simple title indicated. There's lots of space. Not just for the new theatre and auditorium, studios, the crèche, the basement—which could be anything—but for individuals and individual societies. For artistic eccentrics who want to make or do things which perhaps make sense only to themselves. Any activity which is constructive, is within the laws of the land, and can be linked with the arts in the broadest sense, is welcome. It is hardly to be expected that the arts centre will show a profit. That is hardly the intention. It is intended that as many people as possible get as much pleasure and artistic satisfaction as possible from this new centre for creativity.[61]

The extent to which this kind of facility might accommodate non-professional activity had been suggested by the Arts Council's 1945 arts centre prototype, which included provision for amateur performances as well as social activities and dancing. In this respect, the arts centre promised cultural transformation through 'doing' rather than 'seeing' alone, although seeing what other visitors were doing might in itself prove an invitation to join in.

Many arts centres were set up within redundant inner-city buildings. For example, Chapter, an arts centre in Cardiff, took over a semi-derelict school.[62] The building was intended to provide a low-cost home for individual artists and groups alike:

> When we moved into the old Canton High School at the end of 1971 our concerns were two-fold: to encourage artists from all disciplines to move into the building to produce art and to ensure that the local community was encouraged to use the building as much as possible.[63]

The centre's community ambitions were emphasized:

> Within this building we could provide a nucleus for creative activity in Cardiff. A nucleus that would be involved with, and play an active part in the community as a whole. Through co-operation and managerial policy, facilities, equipment and services would be made available to artists who, for financial reasons, would never previously have obtained them. This centre would bridge the gap between the 'established' as sponsored by art galleries, museums and theatres etc., and those active on the work-shop or 'grass-roots' level. We envisage a centre of creative/social interactivity

60 Hutchison, 'Three Arts Centres', p. 46.

61 BRO, NT/B/S2/14, 'South Hill Park Arts Centre and Theatre, Bracknell' ['produced by David Reade and the Bracknell Development Corporation'], n.d.

62 Chapter Arts, 'The Original Proposal for an Arts Centre in Cardiff' (c.1970), <http://www.chapter.org/original-proposal-arts-centre-cardiff-c1970> (accessed 6 July 2017).

63 Christine Kinsey (co-founder of Chapter), interviewed by Gilly Adams, 1999, <http://www.chapter.org/chapter-early-years> (accessed 6 July 2017).

> encompassing all aspects of the audio-visual arts. A centre that would not be introspective in attitude or ambition but would go out in the community—into schools, pubs, clubs, and hospitals.[64]

One might speculate that the reuse of the old school—a building with which many local people would have been familiar—suggested accessibility. Yet for some residents it might also have had undesirable connotations of authority. Was there an alternative, which perhaps developed the flexible, anti-monumental approach proposed by the likes of Cedric Price? One answer was to make theatre mobile.

THE MOBILE THEATRE

In 1982, Manchester Royal Exchange Theatre Company applied for support from the Arts Council's 'Housing the Arts' programme. Their intention was a transportable auditorium, 'designed to recreate the parent theatre within existing buildings'.[65] Made of aluminium tubing and fireproofed canvas panels, it was to be 20 metres in diameter and 6.6 metres in height, with 400 seats, and so would fit inside many community and sports halls. The cost was anticipated to be £60,000, of which the Exchange had by June 1982 already raised half from trusts and industry.[66] A contribution of £5000 was promised by the 'Housing the Arts' Committee in August.[67] In seeking to acquire its own portable theatre, the Royal Exchange followed in the footsteps of such groups as Caryl Jenner's Mobile Theatre, which during the 1950s travelled with a compact structure to towns and villages without a theatre. By the mid-1960s, the ideal of the mobile theatre was being increasingly discussed. For some, it was a way to bring theatre to theatre-less areas, but for others it represented a challenge to established ideas of performance space.

The role of mobile theatre in areas that lacked permanent facilities was noted in Jennie Lee's 1965 White Paper on the arts:

> It is to be hoped that one day fine permanent buildings for housing the arts will be universally available. But in the meantime enterprising localities might well investigate the possibility of mobile arts centres and travelling theatres. This means growing accustomed to some of the latest developments in building technology. Temporary inflatable structures are already in use by industry.[68]

The Arts Council, which had previously highlighted the need for new theatres in Scotland and Wales, now supported a study into the potential for a mobile theatre which would accommodate the Welsh Theatre Company until a future Welsh National Theatre was ready.[69] The structure was designed by Sean Kenny. It reflected

[64] Chapter Arts, 'Original Proposal'.

[65] V&A, ACGB/84/180, 'Draft—The Young Exchange'.

[66] V&A, ACGB/84/180, Linda Ridding to Judith Strong, 8 June 1982.

[67] V&A, ACGB/84/180, copy HTA minutes, 29 September 1982.

[68] 'A Policy for the Arts: the first steps', Cmnd. 2601 [1965], para. 54.

[69] This account reprises Alistair Fair, 'Rethinking the Post-war British Theatre: monumentality, Sean Kenny, and the state, *c.*1966–73', in *Architecture, Institutions and Change*, edited by Paul Hogben and Judith O'Callaghan (Sydney, 2015), pp. 146–56.

his interest in a dynamic, flexible architecture, and his wish to rethink theatre architecture. Revealed to the press in January 1967,[70] Kenny's mobile theatre was described as a shell made from aluminium panels that could be dismantled for transport by lorry. It also included a restaurant, which was to be served in high-tech fashion by vending machines, and a 350-seat auditorium, which could be used in three different formats: proscenium arch, thrust, and in-the-round.[71] A network of serviced sites would be created at which the theatre could be erected. Ultimately, however, the £120,000 cost of the mobile counted against it,[72] as did its likely running costs. There was reportedly also opposition from those who preferred a more conventional theatre architecture.[73] It nonetheless achieved a certain prominence. Lee was impressed, commenting 'I have always been eager to see the development of mobiles because I know of no other way in which we can reach through to the villages and smaller towns'.[74] The designer Patrick Ide was excited by Lee's enthusiasm:

> By golly, [Lee] makes the living theatre sound as if it was living and stimulating and interesting and not as if it was some remote plane to which we should approach with reverence rather than enjoyment. The Welsh Arts Council shows enormous initiative in commissioning Sean Kenny to design a new mobile theatre but it is Miss Lee's enthusiasm which will make it live.[75]

Ide was a member of the Council of Management of the Century Theatre, which he described as 'the only truly mobile theatre in the world', and with which Braham Murray—soon to co-found Manchester's 69 Theatre Company—was also involved. Lee visited Century later that same year.[76] It had been founded in 1945 by Hinckley-based engineer and theatre enthusiast, John Ridley.[77] A lightweight aluminium structure with 200 seats, the mobile theatre was pressed into service in 1952. It was transported on ex-military trailers; unpacking took a day and a half, and packing up a day. Pulled by a tractor, with the company's caravans following at a stately pace, Century toured Britain until 1974, when changing traffic regulations forced it off the road. It then took up permanent residence in Keswick, remaining there until the 1990s, when a new, purpose-built theatre was opened and Century moved again, to Coalville.

To some extent, both the Century Theatre and the Welsh Mobile Theatre were conceived to plug gaps. Yet there was also a sense, especially in the case of the latter,

[70] 'Mobile Theatre Could Be Ready Within a Year', *The Times*, 19 January 1967.

[71] V&A, THM/166, 'A Mobile Theatre for Wales: Feasibility Study', n.d.

[72] ACGB, 'The Theatre Today in England and Wales: the report of the Arts Council Theatre Enquiry' [1970], p. 44.

[73] V&A, THM/166, clipping: 'Cambria e Mobile', *Liverpool Daily Post*, 7 February 1967.

[74] V&A, THM/166, clipping: 'Backing for Mobile Theatre', *South Wales Echo and Evening Express*, 13 January 1967.

[75] 'Mobile Theatre', *The Times*, 23 January 1967.

[76] Jennifer Wilson, email to author, 22 December 2015.

[77] 'Century Theatre: history', <www.centurytheatre.co.uk/history> (accessed 6 July 2017).

that a mobile structure could form a new model for theatre. Kenny's description of the concept anticipated the terms used early in the next decade by Michael Elliott:

> I am still developing this scheme and trying to make everything in it as expendable as possible. Maybe one day the ideal theatre will be made of paper, so we can burn it down after each performance.[78]

The Welsh Mobile Theatre, he suggested, would offer 'an entirely new image' of performance space,[79] certainly less permanent and perhaps also less civic than many contemporaneous developments. The Welsh Arts Council seems to have thought on similarly universal lines. It saw itself 'at the moment actively promoting what we think may be the most important theatrical innovation of our day'.[80] Yet Kenny did not entirely reject the idea of the theatre as a special place. Like the writer Richard Hoggart, he distanced theatre from mass culture, arguing that 'if you're able to drop into the theatre like a drug store, it'll be too readily available'.[81] Instead, he thought, 'there must be a certain amount of struggle involved, a certain sense of pilgrimage'. In this respect, one might conclude that, as much as the Mobile might have offered a new image of theatre, it nonetheless was framed in relatively conventional terms.

Discussions of mobile and prefabricated theatre lasted into the 1970s. In 1974, the Arts Council proposed the establishment of two study groups, one looking at temporary and short-life theatres, the other at portable venues.[82] A 'Research Bulletin' subsequently reported on portable structures, including the Bubble Theatre in London, which had been founded in 1972 and was using 'two Barracuda tensi domes'.[83] In June 1976, the architect Roderick Ham sent Peter Longman details of his 'Theatrebase 300 and 550', a system devised for a client in the Middle East who had wanted a theatre quickly.[84] Ham pointed out that the system was not intended as a universal solution but might nonetheless find more widespread application. Using a steel frame and standard components, it provided an auditorium based on that of the Thorndike Theatre and was projected to cost between £250,000 and £500,000. During the same year, the Arts Council hosted a seminar on short-life and mobile theatres, which, it was now reported, would be eligible for its support.[85]

Ultimately, these examples demonstrate that mobility was not only embraced by theatre-makers. Rather, the state (in the person of Jennie Lee) and the Arts Council could also promote innovation. To some extent, the interest in these alternatives reflected the economic difficulties that undid many other ambitious public schemes after the mid-1960s, and which, indeed, eventually forced the abandonment of the

78 V&A, THM/166, Sean Kenny to Tyrone Guthrie, 7 February 1968.

79 V&A, THM/166, clipping: 'Theatre on Wheels', *Western Mail*, 11 August 1967.

80 V&A, THM/166, clipping: 'Cambria e Mobile', *Liverpool Daily Post*, 7 February 1967.

81 'The Stage Designer Who Makes One Sit Up', *The Times*, 24 January 1966.

82 V&A, ACGB/120/12, Meeting about Portable Theatres, 1 April 1974. Anthony Field noted on his copy of the note that this sort of project was then ineligible for capital funding.

83 V&A, ACGB/120/12, 'Research Bulletin No. 2. Portable Structures for the Arts'.

84 V&A, ACGB/120/12, Roderick Ham to Peter Longman, 11 June 1976.

85 V&A, ACGB/120/3, 'Housing the Arts Seminar', 8 July 1976.

Welsh scheme. However, the shift also reflected Lee's interest in the 'ends' rather than the 'means', and her view of the 'Housing the Arts' programme not as an attempt to create new architecture for its own sake but rather as a way to build new audiences through better and more comfortable provision.[86] Much the same might be said of another emerging trend, namely the restoration of older theatres.

RESTORATION—AND EMULATION

In 1972, Bradford City Council commissioned John Wyckham to report on the steps that would be necessary to complete the city's Prince's Theatre, which was then an empty shell within a Richard Seifert-designed office development.[87] To seat 1000, the theatre had been intended to replace the previous Prince's Theatre, which had been demolished in 1961. The city's other main theatre, the Alhambra, was also scheduled for redevelopment. However, Wyckham's report was critical of the half-finished theatre, suggesting that major alterations would be needed for it ever to be functionally satisfactory, and the City Council eventually concluded that a refurbished and extended Alhambra might therefore prove the better option. In 1980 the abandoned space was finally fitted out as the home of the National Museum of Photography, Film and Television.

This story demonstrates an important theme in theatre design since the 1970s, namely the restoration and reconfiguration of pre-1914 theatres. The trend was recognized in the second edition of Roderick Ham's *Theatre Planning*, which was published in 1987 under the revised title *Theatres: Planning Guidance for Design and Adaptation*, with a new chapter on restoration. This trend represented not only a remarkable transformation of attitudes to historic theatre architecture but also the fortunes of the commercial touring theatre.[88] During the 1950s, increasing production costs contributed to the decreasing number and quality of shows touring the country. Furthermore, the support during the 1950s and 1960s of the Arts Council for repertory companies over commercial touring skewed provision in favour of the former. When a programme of funding for touring groups was subsequently introduced (as is discussed later in this chapter), it distorted matters yet more in that it allowed subsidized companies to accept lower guarantees and other fees from theatre managements, thus driving down the overall level of these payments for all. In addition, a growing amount of lucrative work in television reduced the number of actors willing to tour for long periods.[89] The declining fortunes of touring theatre then created a vicious circle in which the improvement of older touring theatre buildings was still less likely to be viable. Finally, we might also note the very size of older theatres' auditoria, designed to maximize the return on their valuable town-centre sites through the provision of a large seating capacity,

86 Patricia Hollis, *Jennie Lee: A Life* (Oxford, 1997), p. 268.

87 Judith Strong, *Encore: Strategies for Theatre Renewal* (London, 1999), p. 89.

88 For the following, see Paul Iles, 'Issues in Theatrical Management: Howard and Wyndham and the evolution of the British touring circuit' (MPhil diss., University of Glasgow, 1997), pp. 90–4.

89 'Act Now to Save Provincial Theatres', *Architectural Review* 160 (October 1976), pp. 216–20 (p. 216).

often above 1500 seats. Of some 130 commercial venues which had been open in 1939, only thirty-three remained in use as theatres by 1976.[90]

However, change was in the air. In 1958, following the threatened demolition of the St James' Theatre in London, the Council for Theatre Preservation was founded under the auspices of the Society for Theatre Research,[91] while in 1959 one writer suggested that a few historic theatres of architectural merit might be taken on by a 'National Trust for Theatres'.[92] The Arts Council's 'Housing the Arts' reports of 1959 and 1961 similarly suggested that some older theatres might be brought into public ownership.[93] The Theatres Advisory Council was founded in the early 1960s on the initiative of the MP Hugh Jenkins and others, with a broad remit that included preservation. An early draft of its possible role suggested that 'its job will be to stop the destruction of existing viable buildings, and encourage and advise on the construction of new ones'.[94] The Save London's Theatres Campaign followed in 1972, while the designation of 1975 as European Architectural Heritage Year further promoted consideration of historic theatres.[95] Attention was also drawn to the issue by writers such as Christopher Brereton, who discussed significant regional theatres in an important *Architectural Review* article in 1976.[96] A major survey of pre-1914 British theatres followed, entitled *Curtains!!! Or, a New Life for Old Theatres*, edited by Iain Mackintosh and Michael Sell, and published in 1982.[97]

An inquiry in 1969 into the proposed demolition of Frank Matcham's Lyric Theatre, Hammersmith, proposed that its auditorium plasterwork be dismantled and stored for possible reuse, while the destruction in 1971 of the Granville, Fulham, prompted a major survey of the capital's theatres by the Greater London Council and a recommendation that twenty-four should be 'listed'. However, the most significant moment in the growing tide of theatre conservation came with the establishment in England and Wales of The Theatres Trust by Act of Parliament in 1976.[98] A further Act in 1978 extended the Trust's work to Scotland. The creation of the Trust was the work of individuals and groups including the Theatres Advisory Council. David Crouch, a Member of Parliament sympathetic to the theatre, secured the opportunity to propose a Private Member's Bill in the ballot for the 1975–6 parliamentary session, and agreed to support the idea. With cross-party support, the legislation received royal assent on 22 July 1976.[99] The Trust came

[90] 'Act Now to Save Provincial Theatres', p. 216.

[91] Elspeth Cox and Peter Longman, 'History of The Theatres Trust', 2008 typescript, copy supplied by The Theatres Trust.

[92] Richard Findlater, *The Future of the Theatre* (London, 1959), pp. 16–18.

[93] ACGB, 'Housing the Arts in Great Britain', 2 vols [1959 and 1961], II, pp. 4, 41.

[94] V&A, THM/351/5/66, 'Theatre Preservation and Encouragement of New Theatre Building', 14 July 1961.

[95] Peter Longman, interviewed 9 August 2006.

[96] 'Act Now to Save Provincial Theatres', p. 216.

[97] Iain Mackintosh and Michael Sell (eds.), *Curtains!!! Or, a New Life for Old Theatres* (Eastbourne, 1982).

[98] Hansard, HC Deb 17 December 1975, vol. 902 c.1399.

[99] Cox and Longman, 'History', p. 3.

into being at the end of 1976, with its first chairman being Lord Goodman. By 1979, Hugh Jenkins was part-time director.

The Theatres Trust's 'objects' were formally defined as 'to promote the better protection of theatres for the benefit of the nation'.[100] Lord Harmar-Nicholls reported that the Trust would 'make it more difficult for anyone to add to the demise of existing live theatres by demolishing them or by radically changing their nature and making them unusable as live theatres'.[101] However, the 1976 Act made no provision for the Trust within the planning process. Although such provision had been intended, it was deleted from the final legislation, and it was therefore through an amendment to English and Welsh planning policy in March 1977 that the Trust secured a position as a statutory consultee in cases where planning proposals affected theatres.[102] Its existence was touch-and-go in the early years. Parliamentary convention is that Private Members' Bills make no demands on the public purse, and so the Trust was initially denied public funding for its work, making it unlikely that it would 'acquire', 'contribute', or 'assist' in any way other than through the provision of advice and lobbying. Only in 1980 were government grants made to the Trust for the first time,[103] and it was not until the 1990s that the Trust was able to take on full-time staff.

Somewhat poetic arguments were often made in favour of the conservation of pre-1914 theatres, arguments which at times turned modernist wisdom on its head by, for example, suggesting that these theatres were inherently popular, even democratic spaces.[104] However, their survival can also be explained by the fact that touring began to revive during the 1970s, because older theatres' proscenium arch stages and large capacities made them ideally suited to the new breed of touring show. In 1970, an Arts Council report painted a bleak picture of regional commercial theatre,[105] prompting the council to take over the hitherto-independent Dramatic and Lyric Theatres Association (DALTA).[106] DALTA was a consortium of regional managements, founded by John Tooley and operated by Jack Phipps, which coordinated touring activities. Reconstituted as the Arts Council's Touring Committee and later a department in its own right, it oversaw the touring activities of the national companies while also funding its own clients.[107] Purely commercial productions also prospered during the 1970s and 1980s, with the advent of the blockbuster musical being especially notable. The boundaries between the subsidized and commercial sectors were sometimes blurred. For example, the Arts Council and the impresario Cameron Mackintosh jointly financed national tours of the Leicester Haymarket Theatre's productions of *My Fair Lady* and *Oklahoma!* in

[100] Cox and Longman, 'History', p. 4.

[101] Hansard, HL Deb 27 May 1976, vol. 371 cc. 445–56.

[102] '"Betrayal" of the Theatres', *Guardian*, 11 May 1976. In Scotland, it was only in 1992 that the Trust became a statutory consultee; the Trust's role was extended informally to Northern Ireland in 1993.

[103] Cox and Longman, 'History', p. 6.

[104] E.g. Victor Glasstone, *Victorian and Edwardian Theatres: An Architectural and Social Survey* (London, 1975), p. 7: 'suitably stimulating environment for all levels of society'.

[105] ACGB, 'Theatre Today', p. 11.

[106] Jack Phipps, interviewed 14 August 2006.

[107] Iles, 'Issues', p. 94.

1978 and 1979.[108] In these circumstances, although many pre-1914 theatre buildings had come into civic ownership, the revival of touring also promoted the growth of new commercial owner-operators such as Apollo Leisure.

RHWL's £4.6 million reworking of the Theatre Royal, Nottingham, between 1976 and 1978 set a new standard for the rehabilitation of older theatre buildings, combining sympathetic restoration with the reconstruction and expansion of the front-of-house, stage, and backstage areas.[109] This model was reprised by RHWL at Northampton Theatre Royal (which became part of the Derngate complex in 1983), Newcastle Theatre Royal (1986–8), and the Lyceum, Sheffield (1990–1). Similar in scale was Law and Dunbar-Nasmith's transformation of the Empire Palace Theatre in Edinburgh to make the Festival Theatre (1994), which finally provided the city with many of the facilities that twenty years before had been intended for its unbuilt 'opera house'. By restoring and reworking highly ornamented, historic buildings, such projects might be understood to represent the ultimate 'escape from boarded concrete'. They were certainly popular. It was suggested in 1995 that 'reconstructed theatres by Frank Matcham [...] could turn out to be the most successful "new" theatres of the last forty years'.[110] Yet, in conclusion, it is worth examining two cases of restoration and refurbishment from the 1960s which demonstrate that this kind of project was not always a negative reaction to the idea of architectural modernity, and which show how the new breed of modern playhouse supplied a model for emulation.

In March 1964, Donald Bodley, director of York Theatre Royal, described the poor state of the building.[111] Two of its bars apparently had no running water, while 'the face of the building is dirty and singularly unattractive'.[112] After a local architect's apparently uninspired designs were rejected, Bodley sought out Patrick Gwynne:

> Some six or eight weeks ago I was in London and lunched at the Hyde Park [Serpentine] Restaurant you designed [...] and very much admired your creation. I would welcome the opportunity to discuss the important scheme and 'new image' we plan for this theatre.[113]

The modernization of the theatre's appearance and its transformation into a 'social amenity' were deemed critical if it was to survive.[114] The Theatre Royal's cramped landings, for example, were thought to deny 'any form of foyer or social meeting area which is now customary and expected by most patrons'.[115] In response, Gwynne described his four-storey foyer extension as a 'dramatic and forthright

[108] Jack Phipps, interviewed 14 August 2006.
[109] Iain Mackintosh, 'A Royal Return', *Tabs* 36, no. 2 (June 1978), pp. 3–6.
[110] Ronnie Mulryne and Margaret Shewring, 'Introduction', in *Making Space for Theatre: British Architecture and Theatre Since 1958*, edited by Ronnie Mulryne and Margaret Shewring (Stratford-upon-Avon, 1995), pp. 11–14 (p. 13).
[111] YSJU, Theatre Royal archive, Donald Bodley to Town Clerk, 12 March 1964.
[112] YSJU, Theatre Royal archive, Donald Bodley to Town Clerk, 12 March 1964.
[113] YSJU, Theatre Royal archive, Donald Bodley to Patrick Gwynne, 16 July 1965.
[114] YSJU, Theatre Royal archive, 'Proposed Improvements to the Theatre Royal, York, March 1965'.
[115] YSJU, Theatre Royal archive, 'Proposed Improvements to the Theatre Royal, York, March 1965'.

structure' whose architecture would be explicitly contemporary: 'a glass-walled structure is envisaged with the interior space broken up as little as possible by changes of level so that the function of the building is understood from outside and made inviting'.[116] Much like the Serpentine Restaurant, hexagonal grit-blasted concrete 'mushrooms' sprout from slim columns to form the foyer ceilings, while the walls are glazed in order to offer views into and from the theatre (see Figure 10.2). The extension originally contained a coffee bar, restaurant, and bar, finished stylishly with slate, mosaic, and green vinyl, while a curving staircase was inserted to connect all the levels of the theatre. The theatre's previously segregated circulation was removed; the new foyer was shared by all in what Gwynne described as the 'modern trend'.[117] Essentially, therefore, the extended Theatre Royal took the architectural themes, principles, and content of the modern playhouse and applied these ideas in an extension to an existing building. The result was a dramatic change in its image, as the *Architects' Journal* recognized: 'the formidable quality previously presented to the world at large—through which the converted battled at the appropriate times to enjoy the play within—has given way to a friendly meeting place offering the life

Figure 10.2. 'Dramatic and forthright': Theatre Royal, York, 1968 (Henk Snoek/RIBA Collections)

[116] YSJU, Theatre Royal archive, Patrick Gwynne, 'Strategy Documents'.
[117] YSJU, Theatre Royal archive, Patrick Gwynne, 'Strategy Documents'.

of restaurant and coffee bar for many hours each day'.[118] 'Fashion parades', concerts, and late night shows amplified the impression of a relaxed, contemporary space.

The contemporaneous alterations made to Liverpool Playhouse dealt not only with its public areas but also the theatre's backstage facilities. The project, which was completed in 1968, was inaugurated in early 1964 when the lease on workshops adjacent to the theatre expired. The theatre's architects were soon invited to make a study of the entire building and its potential for improvement. By 1965, several ambitions had been defined, including an enlarged stage, new workshop, more and better-equipped dressing rooms, a rehearsal room, and expanded foyers in which meals could be served.[119] Underpinning these developments were several motivations: a wish to improve working conditions; a desire to save money by making and storing scenery on site; and the idea that modernized facilities would appeal to new audiences. As in York, the proposals were conceived in the light of developments elsewhere. The chairman concluded in 1965 that 'frankly we are trying and hoping to get the best of both worlds, we are leaving untouched the charming auditorium and basement coffee lounge but adding to them new technical and additional audience facilities in line with the design of modern theatre'.[120] Thus to one side of the original Playhouse, the workshops were swept away and a cul-de-sac was closed. In their place came an extension housing galleried foyers as well as a substantial quantity of backstage accommodation. As of 1965, the project was estimated to cost at least £180,000, with £125,000 having been promised collectively by the city authorities, the Arts Council, the Gulbenkian Foundation, and the Pilgrim Trust.[121]

Designed by Ken Martin of Hall, O'Donahue and Wilson, the extension was intended to make a very definite statement of the Playhouse's presence in Williamson Square, which was then the site of a major commercial development (see Figure 10.3). As the *Liverpool Daily Post* noted, 'the first problem was to make the new section dominant, unmistakeably the main entrance to the whole building'.[122] Accordingly, it was boldly modelled, presenting interlocking glass and board-marked concrete cylinders, each supported by a single central column. Cantilevered above the pavement and projecting beyond the building line, the result is a dynamic grouping that seems almost too big for its site. The foyers actually occupy a relatively small part of the extension, but the views into and between the various levels makes these spaces seem bigger than they are, while the curved plan means that they seem constantly to disappear around corners. For the *Architects' Journal*, 'the complex interpenetration of geometric volumes is appreciated only by active involvement and movement'.[123] In other words, here was yet another humanized 'modern monument'.

[118] 'Theatre Royal at York', *Architects' Journal* 148 (4 December 1968), pp. 1335–42 (p. 1335).

[119] LCL, Q792.1 PLA, Box marked 'James Rushworth, Chairman, 1965–72', 'Statement made by the Chairman at the Annual General Meeting on Friday 17 December 1965', pp. 12–13.

[120] LCL, Q792.1 PLA, Box marked 'James Rushworth, Chairman, 1965–72', 'Statement', pp. 12–13.

[121] LCL, Q792.1 PLA, Box marked 'James Rushworth, Chairman, 1965–72', 'Statement', pp. 12–13.

[122] LCL, Q792.1 PLA, clippings: 'Playhouse 68', *Liverpool Daily Post*, 12 September 1968.

[123] 'Playhouse', *Architects' Journal* 148 (4 December 1968), pp. 1327–34 (p. 1330).

Figure 10.3. 'Conventionally futuristic': Liverpool Playhouse in 1978 (Architectural Press Archive/RIBA Collections)

The extension was seen as a fundamentally modern structure. A brochure suggested that the Playhouse was 'moving into the future extensively modernised and redeveloped to cater for the space age',[124] while a photograph of the theatre illustrated a newspaper advertisement for 'Liverpool—city of challenge and change'.[125] In June 1966, the *Weekly News* concluded that 'Liverpool's theatreland will soon be moving into the jet age, in common with other aspects of Merseyside's commercial and artistic life'.[126] The Playhouse's extension, it went on, was an 'arrestingly modern block' which embodied 'the "new look" theatre'. This choice of words not only evoked the world of fashion but also suggested the extent to which the rethinking of theatre architecture in this period had delivered a coherent and recognizably modern approach. In this respect, Kay Gardner, the Playhouse's administrator, reported that the remodelled building 'obviously catches the eye and is in step with new and renovated theatres [...] throughout the country'.[127] Certainly the steady, mainstream modernism of many of those 'new and renovated

[124] LCL, Q792.1 PLA, Box marked 'James Rushworth, Chairman, 1965–72', leaflet entitled 'Liverpool Playhouse Redevelopment Appeal'.

[125] LCL, Q792.1 PLA, clipping from *Merseyside Industrial News*, January 1969.

[126] LCL, Q792.1 PLA, clippings: 'The Playhouse Goes "Mod"', *Weekly News*, 9 June 1966.

[127] LCL, Q792.1 PLA, clippings: 'The Playhouse Goes "Mod"', *Weekly News*, 9 June 1966.

theatres' was very much in evidence. Just as York's Theatre Royal extension reprised the slick glamour of the Serpentine Restaurant in its exquisitely detailed concrete and sinuous staircase, so did the Liverpool Playhouse extension offer a considered if nonetheless bold sense of the contemporary. As the local press put it, in a telling turn of phrase, 'this exciting new construction [...] of glass and steel' was at once 'refreshingly modern' and (my emphasis) '*conventionally* futuristic in design'.[128]

[128] LCL, Q792.1 PLA, clippings: 'The Playhouse Goes "Mod"', *Weekly News*, 9 June 1966.

Conclusions

'Out of Its Sick-bed'

At the end of 1977, Michael Billington reflected on the previous twelve months in theatre.[1] It had been, he said, a 'remarkably good year'. As he saw it, 'the British theatre [...] is out of its sick-bed and indeed capering nimbly up and down the wards'. Notably, 'the subsidised repertory companies are far more exciting than the West End of London'. As a drama critic, Billington's interest was naturally what he had seen on stage. Nonetheless, his assessment could just as well have been applied to theatre architecture. During the previous two decades, new theatres had opened across Britain, and more were in the pipeline. The existence and operation of many of these buildings owed much to the introduction of a system of public subsidy in the 1940s. Though it was rarely generous, subsidy stabilized the operation of non-profit regional repertory theatre companies. Improved standards and rising audiences in turn led these companies to extend or rebuild, and here public subsidy again had a key role to play. Subsidy also supported the creation of a new breed of civic theatre, while universities, too, were now frequently patrons of the arts.

Theatre—hitherto apparently endangered by new forms of leisure activity—survived not only as an activity but also as a distinct type of building. In 1952, an engineer suggested that cinema and theatre auditoria were one and the same thing, with only minor technical differences.[2] Few would have made the same argument even ten years later. That the new theatres of this period represented something of a rediscovery of the type was recognized by *The Times* as early as August 1955, when it reported of the then-proposed Belgrade Theatre, Coventry, that it would 'have the look of a theatre' on account of its auditorium boxes, and that it would in this respect be 'unlike many theatres built in the 1930s', which had often borrowed from cinema.[3] From the 1950s onwards, a modern theatre architecture emerged in response to debates about the location of these buildings within the urban environment, the kinds of facilities that they might contain, and the optimum actor–audience relationship. These debates often transcended artistic concerns, with theatres being intended as demonstrations of civic pride, agents for the cultural enlightenment of Britain, or weapons in the fight against the commercialized temptations of the

[1] '"For once let's recognise that British theatre is out of its sick-bed" [...]', *Guardian*, 30 December 1977.

[2] Clifford Worthington, *The Influence of the Cinema on Contemporary Auditorium Design* (London, 1952).

[3] 'Coventry Civic Theatre', *The Times*, 18 August 1955.

affluent society. Modern architecture supplied the material, formal and spatial vocabularies with which to explore and embody these ideas. The result was a new image of theatre that drew on international sources but adapted these precedents to the realities of the British context.

The distinctiveness of the new theatres is evident in their reception. Certainly not everyone welcomed them. For example, the extent to which the extension added to Bristol Old Vic by Peter Moro in 1970 contrasted in its brown brick elevations with the ornate Coopers' Hall next door was the subject of contention. One correspondent was not being complimentary when she dubbed the result 'so completely modern'; she went on to note that 'the materials used were so ugly'.[4] Patrons in Leatherhead, meanwhile, wondered if the decorators had forgotten to plaster and paint the Thorndike Theatre's board-marked concrete.[5] In Newcastle, as already noted, the University Theatre's administrator wrote in 1971 that 'the theatre building itself, while being often criticised for the enigmatic face it presents to the passer-by, generally delights those who enter it'.[6] Nor were architectural writers immune from criticism. In 1971, Colin Amery thought that Birmingham Repertory Theatre's foyers lacked appeal.[7] He suggested that architects needed to learn that theatres 'are not designed solely for cement and concrete engineers'.

For those organizations that moved to a new theatre, the experience could be transformative, and sometimes challenging. Audience numbers often increased, and patrons typically spent more money. In 1970, it was noted that 'although the average attendance in 1969 for provincial theatres was 56%, that for new theatres, i.e. those built in the last decade, was 68%'.[8] Leatherhead's repertory company reported in 1971 that its income had doubled since the opening of the Thorndike Theatre two years before, with seat prices having increased by only 40 per cent.[9] Increased audiences were welcome, as these buildings—typically substantially larger and better appointed than their predecessors—were often expensive to run. The management of Derby Playhouse commented in 1978 that 'we have still perhaps not fully grasped the implications of the substantial cost of running an operation such as the new Playhouse'.[10]

Yet, for all that new theatres represented new ideas, they also demonstrated important continuities, both in conception and form. Britain's new post-war theatres were substantial and frequently expensive buildings, and were often described in traditional 'civic' terms. Many were relatively fixed in their auditorium and stage layouts, while the traditional proscenium arch stage and confrontational type of auditorium proved remarkably resilient. Their architecture represented productively mainstream forms of modernism, rather than avant-garde, theory-inflected approaches, and in this respect, the very act of theatre-going was often framed in a relatively

[4] RSA, RA/422, Box 2, Winifred Legg to Theatre Royal, 15 April 1972.
[5] Hazel Vincent Wallace, interviewed 26 October 2006.
[6] UoN, 00-1196, 'The University Theatre, 1970–71'.
[7] 'Repertory Theatre, Birmingham', *Architects' Journal* 154 (22 December 1971), pp. 1431–7 (p. 1437).
[8] DRO, D738/4/1, Forward Budget Planning Officer to Acting County Treasurer, 22 June 1970.
[9] 'Pattern of Theatre Changed by Growth of Subsidy', *Stage*, 29 April 1971, pp. 11, 24.
[10] DRO, D738/5/2, Derby Playhouse Report and Accounts, 1977–78.

conventional way. At the start of the 1970s, the manager of the Mercury Theatre, Colchester, suggested that audiences 'may want to dress up a little and enjoy a sense of occasion that they cannot get from watching the telly in their own homes',[11] while the *Los Angeles Times* told its readers in 1977 that Colchester 'is a market town with no airs about culture' in which 'you go to the theater to have a night out [...], not to take an exam or to show that you are "with it"'.[12]

A similarly balanced attitude to innovation is also evident in the kinds of plays staged in many of these theatres. In Colchester, the artistic director, David Forder, suggested that repertory was by nature not avant-garde.[13] As he saw it:

> Our plays are mainly entertainment. We don't want to educate people, we don't want to instruct people. We want them to be completely absorbed by the play so they can forget about their present troubles.[14]

In 1961, there had been some discussion in Colchester of the extent to which the theatre should try to appeal to the students of the newly founded University of Essex. Its then managing director concluded that 'we shall cater for them, but at the same time we shall remember that we have a duty to parties who come to the theatre for an evening's entertainment and for people—like myself—who do not think it a sin to laugh in the theatre'.[15] Similarly, of the then-proposed Thorndike Theatre, the *Surrey Comet* punningly suggested in 1966 that 'after the Theatre of the Absurd and the Theatre of Cruelty comes the new Leatherhead Theatre, which will be very much a Theatre of Enjoyment'.[16]

Farnham's Redgrave Theatre reportedly aimed to present 'a vigorous choice of plays, trying always to achieve a balance between sponsorship of modern and minority plays with popular and revenue-producing certainties, so that the one may assist to subsidise the more adventurous'.[17] Of Derby Playhouse at the end of the 1950s, the director, Peter Cheeseman, later recalled:

> [the] play programme seemed to be 'West End Comedy—week 1'. 'West End thriller—week 2'. 'West End comedy again—Week 3'. And week 4—'one for the Arts Council'.[18]

Audience tastes had to be borne in mind, and might vary from theatre to theatre. When attendances at Derby Playhouse fell slightly in 1977, the question was asked: was the programme in accordance with the taste of the audience?[19] In 1975–6,

[11] ERO, D/Z 455/2/16, clippings: 'Go-Ahead Repertory Theatre Manager', *East Anglian Daily Telegraph*, 21 October 1969.
[12] ERO, C1371/10, 'The Bright Lights Beyond London', *Los Angeles Times*, 1 June 1977.
[13] ERO, D/Z 455/2/18, clippings: 'The Rep Looks to a Happy Future', *Colchester Express*, 14 January 1970.
[14] ERO, D/Z 455/2/18, clippings: 'The Rep Looks to a Happy Future', *Colchester Express*, 14 January 1970.
[15] ERO, D/Z 455/2/11, clippings: 'Rep. Plays to Run Fortnightly', *Essex County Standard*, 26 May 1961.
[16] SHC, 6368/10/6, clippings: *Surrey Comet*, 24 October 1966.
[17] SHC, 6894/2/21, 'Report of Panel Assessment on the Redgrave Theatre, Farnham', n.d.
[18] Paul Elsam, *Stephen Joseph: Theatre Pioneer and Provocateur* (London, 2013), p. 45.
[19] DA, D738/4/1, Finance meeting, 11 July 1977.

My Fair Lady and *Hamlet* had both been popular, but *Lloyd George Knew My Father* was rather less so, suggesting to the management that '"traditional" theatre did not bring in the regional audience'.[20] Anthony Shaffer's *Sleuth* achieved average attendances of 76 per cent (perhaps because it had been filmed in 1972) and *Macbeth*, 81 per cent, but Shelagh Delaney's kitchen-sink drama *A Taste of Honey* managed only 40 per cent.[21] Audience research suggested that the Derby public wanted more classics, 'West End' plays, comedies, musicals, family shows, star names, and thrillers.[22] In Birmingham, it was noted at the end of the 1960s that the plays attracting the largest audiences were consistently those that were well-known.[23] Liverpool Playhouse, too, demonstrated the same trend in 1965: 'our audiences seem to be resisting modern trends in writing and presentation'.[24]

In this respect, it was sometimes suggested that regional audiences differed from those in London. In Salisbury, the Playhouse's management noted that 'Salisbury is not the area for an avant-garde policy'.[25] Nonetheless, they went on, 'the public have been broken in gently to the more modern kind of playwright so that few are offended by plays such as [Joe Orton's] *What the Butler Saw* and [Mart Crowley's] *The Boys in the Band*'. In Dundee, too, the management of the Repertory Theatre suggested that audiences should not be underestimated. In 1979, for example, the local press criticized a production of Tom Stoppard's *Travesties*, suggesting that it:

> projected at such a level as to cut itself off from the majority of the public. Good for art and thought stimulation. Not so good for Box Office. [...] If you've time before you go, look up Dada-ism in the dictionary, read 'Ulysses', and have a quick glance through the events leading up to the Russian Revolution.[26]

Later in the season, the management countered:

> Sometimes we do make errors of judgement, but what we try not to do is pander to the lowest common denominator. The interesting thing about Dundee audiences is that they may not have had the chance to see a lot of theatre, but they are 'nae mugs'.[27]

University theatres were no less affected by discussions of their policy. Students might feel shut out, as at Stirling: 'by providing a middle-class culture-oriented programme, the Centre is catering for the "Bridge of Allan fur coat mob"—who have even complained about the "dirty" students spoiling their smart nights out'.[28] Equally, the wider community could be sceptical of a university theatre. In Exeter,

[20] DA, D738/5/2, Derby Playhouse Report and Accounts, 1975–76.
[21] DA, D738/5/2, Derby Playhouse Report and Accounts, 1976–77; D738/4/2, Audience Survey, 1979.
[22] DA, D738/5/2, Derby Playhouse Report and Accounts, 1976–77; D738/4/2, Audience Survey, 1979.
[23] LoB, MS 2339/4/4, Minutes of Evidence Taken Before the Estimates Committee, 13 May 1968.
[24] LCL, Q792.1 PLA, clippings: 'Four-Point Development Plan for Liverpool Playhouse', *Liverpool Echo*, 17 December 1965.
[25] W&SA, G23/132/249, 'Salisbury Playhouse' [information sheet].
[26] DA, GD/DRT, 'Travesty of a History Lesson', *People's Journal*, 20 October 1979.
[27] DA, GD/DRT, 'Super Rep—And a Little Bit More', *Courier and Advertiser*, 22 December 1979.
[28] 'University of Stirling', *Architectural Design* 43, no. 3 (March 1973), pp. 154–75 (p. 170).

the local arts group feared that 'the plays that the students are interested in will be modern, unusual and experimental [...] what of the taste of the city playgoer?'[29]

Certainly the 'city playgoer' could make their disgruntlement clear. In September 1961, audiences in Colchester 'booed and walked out' of Harold Pinter's *The Birthday Party*.[30] On another occasion, an audience member complained about the language used in a play, and, on being told that the matter was 'a question of idiom', the unimpressed complainant retorted, 'what you call idiom, I call filth!'[31] In such circumstances, the increasingly frequent provision of an experimental studio alongside the main auditorium offered space for experiment. In Colchester, 'most of the four-letter words spoken in the Mercury Theatre for art's sake are confined to the Jenny Bone studio'.[32] Such examples reveal that regional theatres did, in fact, present challenging and demanding work, and in 1966 the *Guardian* noted that the increasing numbers of young people attending performances in some regional theatres allowed for greater experiment.[33] In Colchester, it was suggested in 1971 that changing patterns of attendance also allowed an increasingly diverse programme, because audience members no longer tended to see every show, as had often been the case in the 1950s.[34] Nonetheless, it is important to recognize the essentially 'mainstream' nature of many repertory productions, not in order to be critical of this kind of theatre or its audiences but rather to highlight the value of a history of architecture—and theatre—that looks beyond the avant-garde to a more representative range of practices.

One of the dangers of not attracting patrons was the risk that local councillors might attempt to become more involved in running an apparently poorly performing theatre. In Bromley in 1972, one elected member of the council suggested that the involvement of the authorities in the running of the theatre would be the only way to protect ratepayers' investment in the face of avant-garde tendencies: 'if [audiences] want to watch all-in wrestling or even a stage version of *Dixon of Dock Green*, instead of some of the trendy rubbish financed by the Arts Council, that's up to them'.[35] In Sheffield, heavy losses during the Crucible's first year prompted the local authority to attempt to intervene in the programming.[36] (Nonetheless, one report records that the Crucible's production of Aeschylus' *The Persians* gained higher audiences than a show featuring the television star Wilfrid Brambell.[37]) In addition, the extent to which new audiences were actually gained is also debatable. Market research at the Crucible demonstrated that a significant share of the theatre's

[29] UoEx, Box 4165 (2) aka 26/1d/2d, clipping from *Express and Echo* letters page, credited as both 16 and 17 February 1963.

[30] ERO, D/Z 455/2/11, 'Rep. Fans Booed and Walked Out!', *Essex County Standard*, 15 September 1961.

[31] ERO, D/Z 455/2/19, clippings: 'In Praise of Colchester Rep', *Essex County Standard*, n.d.

[32] ERO, C1371/10, clippings: 'A Year of Varied Drama at the Mercury', *Evening Gazette*, n.d. [1975].

[33] 'The Under-Rated Theatre', *Guardian*, 24 March 1966.

[34] ERO, D/Z 455/2/18, 'The Repertory Revolution', *Essex County Standard*, 26 March 1971.

[35] 'Lord Willis in Theatre Row', *Bromley Times*, 10 March 1972.

[36] SCA, LD2317, Kevan Scholes, 'The Crucible Theatre, Sheffield' [unpublished typescript, 1976].

[37] V&A TC, Crucible file, uncat., untitled and undated clipping; also SCA, LD2310, Box Office Returns.

audiences came from the city's affluent south-western suburbs, much as had been the case in the old Playhouse.[38] In 1979, Derby Playhouse's audience survey revealed a similar pattern, with 32 per cent of the audience having professional and clerical backgrounds, 16 per cent being in 'blue-collar' occupations, 14 per cent housewives, 12 per cent students, 12 per cent teachers, 6 per cent doctors, 3 per cent retired, and 5 per cent from 'other' backgrounds.[39] Over half were nonetheless aged between twenty and forty. Much the same picture was evident on Tyneside, where a comparative study was carried out in 1973 of Newcastle University Theatre and Sunderland's Empire (which by then was a civic theatre).[40] The University Theatre tended to have a larger catchment than the Empire, and it attracted larger group bookings. Its audiences were typically judged to be middle class (75 per cent) and young (43 per cent under twenty-five, 69 per cent under thirty-five), with 'relatively high educational standards'. Twenty-three per cent of the region's 'ABC1' population—that is, those in skilled and professional occupations—had visited. The Empire's audience was described as more typical of the 'population at large' but nonetheless was typically middle class.

Not every theatre discussed in this study has survived. Changes in the distribution of subsidy since the 1980s have hit some hard, and some have closed after having had financial problems.[41] Changing attitudes to theatre architecture, too, have made their mark, and some, such as the Haymarket in Leicester, have been replaced by new buildings intended better to appeal to contemporary audiences. The critical trough into which much modern architecture fell during the 1980s and early 1990s also affected perceptions of some post-war theatres for a time. Most infamously, the National was dubbed 'a clever way of building a nuclear power station in the middle of London without anyone objecting' by the Prince of Wales.[42] In 1988, Richard Eyre, then director of the National, pondered alterations:

> Bill [Dudley] and John [Gunter] and I have been talking about how to improve the Olivier and the Lyttelton, or, as Bill says, 'how to turn it into a theatre'. John's made a model [...] but we don't show it to Lasdun. He tells us that we are 'custodians of the building'; we can change the 'fittings' but not the 'room'.[43]

The likes of the National can seem like a lumbering dinosaur to those twenty-first-century theatre-makers who prefer 'site-specific' approaches. Yet the post-war model has proved remarkably resilient. The Lottery-funded buildings of the late 1990s and early 2000s have been followed by further new theatres which continue to

[38] SCA, SY/43/Z1/6, 'Analysis of Audiences, July 1974'.

[39] DA, D738/4/2, Audience Survey, p. 7.

[40] UoN, 00-0181, Report: 'Audiences to Specific Productions at the University Theatre and the Sunderland Empire' [1973].

[41] Olivia Turnbull, *Bringing Down the House: The Crisis in Britain's Regional Theatres* (Bristol, 2008), and see also Kate Dorney and Ros Merkin, 'Introduction', in *The Glory of the Garden: English Regional Theatre and the Arts Council, 1984–2009*, edited by Kate Dorney and Ros Merkin (Newcastle-upon-Tyne, 2010), pp. 1–14.

[42] See e.g. the obituary of Lasdun: 'National Theatre Architect Dies', BBC News, 12 January 2001, <http://news.bbc.co.uk/1/hi/uk/1113298.stm> (accessed 7 July 2017).

[43] Richard Eyre, *National Service: Diary of a Decade* (London, 2003), p. 53 (8 November 1988).

engage with such ideas as the place of theatres in the city, the role of cultural buildings in articulating narratives of civic identity and pride, and the transformative potential of culture. In parallel with these developments, the heritage value of post-war theatre buildings is increasingly being recognized. At the time of writing, thirteen theatres in England, one in Wales, and one in Scotland are 'listed' for their special architectural or historical value.[44]

Writing in 1980, Hugh Willatt concluded that the previous thirty years could be considered a 'golden age' in British theatre.[45] Architecture supported and reflected that 'golden age'. As *Country Life* noted in 1965, the new theatres were 'monuments to a theatrical revival'.[46] Representative of an evolving modern architecture, these buildings are rarely dull. They embody the optimism, the belief in modernity, and the drive to improve life for the many that characterized much architecture and planning—and public policy—in post-war Britain. In 1963, Hazel Vincent Wallace looked forward to 'the day when every town has its own individual and attractive theatre, with well-run bars and restaurants and with a strong company presenting a wide variety of well-produced plays'.[47] 'Faith and imagination could bring this about,' she concluded, while 'pessimism and prejudice could destroy the hope of a wonderful future.'[48]

[44] National Heritage List for England, <http://historicengland.org.uk/listing/the-list> (accessed 7 July 2017): Chichester Festival Theatre (Grade II*); Christ's Hospital Arts Centre (II*); Congress, Eastbourne (II*); Gardner Arts Centre, Brighton (II*); National Theatre (II*); Nottingham Playhouse (II*); Barbican Arts Centre, London (II); Belgrade, Coventry (II); Billingham Forum (II); Crucible, Sheffield (II); Gulbenkian Centre, Hull (II); Thorndike Theatre, Leatherhead (II); and the Yvonne Arnaud Theatre, Guildford (II). The listing of York Theatre Royal (II*) includes the 1967 foyer extensions; Liverpool Playhouse is also listed (II*). In Wales, Theatr Ardudwy/Harlech is listed (II*); in Scotland, Eden Court is a Category 'A' listed building.

[45] Hugh Willatt, 'How the Arts are Promoted', in *The State and the Arts*, edited by John Pick, (Eastbourne, 1980), pp. 21–46 (p. 45).

[46] 'Monuments to a Theatrical Revival', *Country Life*, 2 September 1965, pp. 563–5.

[47] 'Let's Be Constructive', *Stage*, 2 May 1963, p. 16.

[48] 'Let's Be Constructive', *Stage*, 2 May 1963, p. 16.

APPENDIX

Summary of Principal Theatres Discussed

Key

Architects' names are indicated in parentheses
Theatre consultants (where given) are indicated in square brackets

- * unbuilt
- *a* amateur use
- *c* civic project
- *R* mainly a repertory/'producing' theatre (as built)
- *t* mainly a touring theatre
- *u* university/college/school venue

The number at the end of each entry indicates the capacity, usually as built.
Sources: *Architects' Journal*; *Stage*; Bentham, *New Theatres in Britain*; Mulryne and Shewring, *Making Space for Theatre*.

Theatre List

1945 Arts Council Arts Centre prototype* (based on a design by Geoffrey Jellicoe) 600
1948 Oxford, University theatre* (Frederick Gibberd) *u* 687
1949 Bristol, University drama studio (Richard Southern) *u* flexible
1951 Pitlochry, Festival Theatre (John Stewart and Kenneth Ireland [tent]) *R* 502
1957 Middlesbrough, Little Theatre (Elder and de Pierro) *a* 512
1958 Coventry, Belgrade Theatre (Coventry City Architect's Department [Donald Gibson/Arthur Ling, with Douglas Beaton and Kenneth King]) *c R* 910
1958 London, Barbican Arts Centre [early schemes]* (Chamberlin Powell and Bon) *c* [Richard Southern]
1959 London, Mermaid Theatre (Elidir Davies) *R* 498
1961 London, Fun Palace* (Cedric Price)
1962 Chichester, Festival Theatre (Powell and Moya) *R* 1360
1962 Croydon, Fairfield Halls (Robert Atkinson and Partners) *c* 1950 (hall) 750 (theatre)
1963 Eastbourne, Congress Theatre (Bryan and Norman Westwood) *c* 1678
1963 Leicester, Phoenix Theatre (City Architect, Stephen George) *c R* 274
1963 Nottingham, Playhouse (Peter Moro) *c R* [Richard Southern (stage)] 756
1964 Birmingham, Crescent (Graham Winteringham of S. T. Walker and Partners) *a* 288
1964 London (Ealing), Questors Theatre (Norman Branson) *a* 330–478
1964 London (Notting Hill), New Mercury* (Sir Basil Spence) *R* approx. 1100
1964 Southampton, Nuffield Theatre (Sir Basil Spence) *u* [Richard Southern] 420–500
1965 Dumbarton, Denny (Alan Reiach) *c a* 340
1965 Glasgow, Cultural Centre* (City Architect's office) *c*

1965 Guildford, Yvonne Arnaud (Scott Brownrigg and Turner) *R* 568
1965 Manchester, University Theatre (G. Grenfell-Baines) *u* [Richard Southern] 300
1967 Bolton, Octagon (Geoffrey Brooks) *R* [Robin Pemberton-Billing] 422
1967 Exeter, Northcott (William Holford and Partners) *u* [Michael Warre] 433
1967 York, Theatre Royal extension (Patrick Gwynne), *c R*
1968 Billingham, Forum (Elder and Lester) *c t* [Michael Warre] 593–675
1968 Chester, Gateway (Michael Lyell Associates), *c R* 500
1968 Edinburgh, Castle Terrace Theatre* (Rowand Anderson, Kininmonth and Paul) *c* 1400–1700
1968 Liverpool, Playhouse extension (Hall, O'Donahue and Wilson) *R*
1969 Brighton, Gardner Arts Centre (Sir Basil Spence, Bonnington and Collins) *u* [Sean Kenny] variable capacity
1969 Hull, Gulbenkian Centre (Peter Moro and Partners) *u* [Theatre Projects Consultants] 200
1969 Leatherhead, Thorndike (Roderick Ham and Partners) *R* [Theatre Projects Consultants] 530
1970 High Wycombe, Dove* (Roderick Ham and Partners) 550
1970 London, Young Vic (HKPA) *R* [Patrick Robertson (design)/Theatre Projects Lighting (equipment)] 400–480
1971 Birmingham, Repertory Theatre (Graham Winteringham of S. T. Walker and Partners) *R* [Theatre Projects Consultants] 901
1971 Newcastle-upon-Tyne, University Theatre (William Whitfield) *u R* 449 + studio
1971 Sheffield, Crucible (Renton Howard Wood Associates) *R* [Tanya Moiseiwitsch (stage and auditorium)/Theatre Projects Consultants (equipment)] 1013 + studio
1971 Stirling, Macrobert Arts Centre (RMJM) *u t* [John Wyckham] 500
1971 Swindon, Wyvern (Casson and Conder) *c t* [Theatre Projects Consultants] 658
1972 Aberystwyth, Theatr-y-Werin (Alex Gordon and Partners) *u t* 400
1972 Colchester, Mercury Theatre (Norman Downie Associates) *R* [Christopher Morley/Theatre Projects Consultants] 500
1972 Lincoln, New Lincolnshire Theatre* (Denis Clarke Hall and Sam Scorer) *R* [Theatre Projects Consultants] 443–570
1973 Bristol, Theatre Royal studio (Peter Moro and Partners) *R* 212 (max.)
1973 Cardiff, Sherman Theatre (Alex Gordon and Partners) *u t* 475 (proscenium arch) + 200 (arena)
1973 Glasgow, Cultural Centre* (Leslie Martin and Associates) *c* [Theatre Projects Consultants, Ian Albery] 600 (theatre) 200 (studio)
1973 Harlech, Theatr Ardudwy (Colwyn Foulkes) *u* 256
1973 Leicester, Haymarket (Leicester City Architect) *R* 710
1974 Bedford, new theatre* (Roderick Ham) *R* [Theatre Projects Consultants] 450–500
1974 Edinburgh, Castle Terrace Theatre* (RMJM) *c R* [Martin Carr/John Bury] 1400–1700
1974 Farnham, Redgrave (Frank Rutter) *R* [Theatre Projects Consultants] 350
1974 Horsham, Christ's Hospital (HKPA) *u t* [Theatre Projects Consultants] 450–580
1974 Warwick, Arts Centre (Renton Howard Wood Levin Partnership) *u t* [John Bury/Theatre Projects Consultants] 529 (theatre)
1975 Bangor (Wales), Theatr Gwynedd (Percy Thomas Partnership) *u* [John Wyckham Associates] 343

1975 Coleraine, Riverside Theatre (Peter Moro and Partners) *u* [Carr and Angier] 305–385
1975 Derby, Playhouse (Roderick Ham and Partners) *R* [Theatre Projects Consultants] 546
1975 Hornchurch, Queen's (Borough Architect) *c* 500
1975 Stevenage, Arts and Leisure Centre (Leonard Vincent, Raymond Gorbing and Partners) *c t* 501
1976 Brentford, Arts Centre* [Peter Moro and Partners] *c* [Carr and Angier] 420 (theatre)
1976 Inverness, Eden Court (Law and Dunbar-Nasmith) *c t* [John Wyckham Associates, with Iain Mackintosh] 814
1976 London, National Theatre (Denys Lasdun and Partners) [*R*] [Theatre Projects Consultants] 1160 (Olivier), 890 (Lyttelton), 200–400 (Cottesloe)
1976 Manchester, Royal Exchange (Levitt Bernstein) *R* [Richard Negri (design)/Theatre Projects Consultants (equipment)] 740
1976 Mold, Theatr Clwyd (Clwyd County Architects) *c R t* [Carr and Angier] 550 (+250 studio)
1976 Salisbury Playhouse (Norman Downie Associates) *R* [Theatre Projects Consultants] 500
1977 Bromley, Churchill Theatre (Borough Architect's department) *c* 780
1977 Reading, Hexagon (RMJM) *c t* [John Wyckham] 575–1500
1977 Taunton, Brewhouse (Somerset County Architect/Norman Branson) *t* 330
1978 Solihull, Library Theatre (Stanley Sellers) *c t* 336
1978 Poole, Arts Centre (Borough Architect's office) *c t* 600 (theatre)
1979 Ipswich, Wolsey (Roderick Ham and Partners) *R* [Carr and Angier] 436
1980 London (Kilburn), Tricycle Theatre (Tim Foster Architects) *R* [Theatre Projects Consultants] 225
1981 Pitlochry, Festival Theatre (Law and Dunbar-Nasmith) *R* [John Wyckham] 544
1982 Dundee, Repertory Theatre (Nicoll Russell) *R* [Andre Tammes] 455
1982 London, Barbican Arts Centre (Chamberlin Powell and Bon) *R* [John Bury (design)/Theatre Projects Consultants (equipment)] 1162
1982 London (Deptford), Albany (HKPA), flexible capacity
1982 Plymouth, Theatre Royal (Peter Moro Partnership) *c t R* [Carr and Angier] 768–1296 + studio
1983 Derngate, Northampton (Renton Howard Wood Levin Partnership) *c t* [Theatre Projects Consultants] 1088–1550
1984 Bracknell, Wilde Theatre (Levitt Bernstein) *t*/*R* [Theatre Projects Consultants] approx. 400
1984 Swansea, Taliesin Arts Centre (Peter Moro Partnership) *u* [Carr and Angier] 330–375
1990 Leeds, West Yorkshire Playhouse (The Appleton Partnership) *R* [Carr and Angier (stage machinery)]

Bibliography

1. MANUSCRIPT SOURCES IN PUBLIC ARCHIVES

Bedford

Bedfordshire and Luton Archives Service

Z 900, Bedford Theatre project

Belfast

Public Record Office of Northern Ireland

CAB/9/D/87/1, papers relating to a second university in Northern Ireland

D4327/2/1/31–38, NUU Council minutes, 1971–3

NUU/3/2/1/1–7, NUU Reports to University Court

NUU/3/2/2/1A, 'The New University of Ulster: Interim Report on Development Plan, August 1967'

Birmingham

Library of Birmingham

MS 978, Sir Barry Jackson/Repertory Theatre papers

MS 2339, Repertory Theatre papers

Bolton

Bolton Archives

ABZ/45, Octagon Theatre

ABZ/89, Octagon Theatre

711 BOL, J. B. McLoughlin, 'Report to the Chamber of Commerce of a General Survey of the Final Report of the Shankland Plan' [1965]

711 BOL, Graeme Shankland Associates, 'Bolton: Draft Town Centre Map' [November 1964]

711 BOL, Shankland Cox and Associates, 'Bolton: Town Centre Map. Planning Consultant's Final Report' [July 1965]

Brighton

The Keep [University of Sussex Archives]

SxUOS1/1/5/13, Gardner Arts Centre

SxUOS1/1/5/22/11, Gardner Arts Centre drawings

The Keep [East Sussex Record Office]

DE/A/5/15, Eastbourne Borough Council minutes

DE/A/5/16, Eastbourne Borough Council minutes

DE/A/18/6, Eastbourne Borough Council minutes

DE/A/43/52, Eastbourne Borough Council minutes

DE/C/1/2, Eastbourne Development Plan Written Analysis, 1951

Bristol

University of Bristol Theatre Collections/Richard Southern Archive

Box 28/22/01, Manchester University Theatre/Nuffield Theatre, Southampton

BOV/MIN/000009, Bristol Old Vic Trust minutes
RA/422 Box 2 (uncat.), Theatre Royal Development
TCP/T/000094, Barbican Arts Centre
Uncatalogued Richard Southern papers, including lectures, miscellaneous papers, documents relating to the ABTT, and files relating to the Bristol Old Vic/Theatre Royal, Nuffield Theatre (Southampton), Laurel Bank School (Glasgow), Mary Erskine School (Edinburgh), Reading University, and Bristol Drama Studio

Bromley
Bromley Archives and Local Studies
792.094223, W. S. Gage et al., 'Churchill Theatre, Bromley' [ACGB Case Study]
792.0942178, Churchill Theatre brochures

Cardiff
Cardiff University Archives
UCC/R/F/71–74, Sherman Theatre
UCC Misc/Pub/1, 'The Sherman Theatre is Five'
Reports of the University Council

Chelmsford
Essex Record Office
C1371/10 and /21, press clippings
D/Z 455/2/11–18, press clippings

Chichester
West Sussex Record Office
Chichester Festival Theatre archive, boxes 43, 44, 52, 54, 58, 59, 60, 62, 126
Add Mss 45575, Festival Theatre Society

Coventry
1. Coventry History Centre
AP/PL/38/1458/160–63, Drawings of alternate Belgrade Theatre design, April 1955
CCA/3/1/11161, Planning and Redevelopment files, 1947–51
CCA/TC/1/1/23–29, Press clippings, 1948–57
CCA/TC/5/4/2, Belgrade Theatre Annual Reports
PA282, Belgrade Theatre Opening Ceremony programme
PA2313, Belgrade Theatre press clippings
Policy Advisory Committee minutes

2. University of Warwick, Modern Records Centre
UWA/NAD/AC/ARC/2/1, Design and construction of Warwick Arts Centre
UWA/NAD/AC/2/1, University of Warwick Arts Centre: Annual Report 1974/75
UWA/M/B/1/1–3, University of Warwick, Building Committee
UWA/M/B/3/1, University of Warwick, Building Committee
UWA/R/5/1, 'Colonel Robert Hornsby's Development File', 1972–5

Croydon
Museum of Croydon
FS70 (711) RED, Fairfield Halls
Pf570 (792) FAI, Fairfield Halls

Dundee

1. Dundee City Archives

GD/DRT, Dundee Repertory Theatre

Dundee Corporation/District Council minutes, including Lord Provost's Committee

2. University of Dundee Archive Services

MS 316/44/5, Repertory Theatre

RU 162/1/1–10, University administration

Edinburgh

1. Historic Environment Scotland Archives

MS 2329/CA/1/1, Expo 67, designers

MS 2329/ENG/35/1, Nuffield, Southampton

MS 2329/ENG/35/3, Nuffield, Southampton

MS 2329/ENG/52/2, University of Sussex

MS 2329/ENG/52/5, Gardner Arts Centre

MS 2329/ENG/56/1–5, New Mercury Theatre

MS 2329/X/19/7, publicity material

SPE ENG/35/1/68, Nuffield Theatre, Southampton (drawings)

SPE ENG/52/2/12/1–10, Gardner Arts Centre

SPE ENG/56/2/5/1–11, New Mercury Theatre

SPE ENG/56/2/6/1–10, New Mercury Theatre

SPE ENG/56/2/8/1–11, New Mercury Theatre

SPE ENG/56/2/9/1–6, New Mercury Theatre

Uncatalogued RMJM archive, boxes 197, 198, and 446

2. National Library of Scotland

GEB.57 [1], 'Eden Court Theatre: Report and Decision Letter on the Public Local Inquiry' [1975]

3. National Records of Scotland

ED61/59, Edinburgh Cultural Centre

ED61/71, Edinburgh Cultural Centre, 1966–8

ED61/72, Edinburgh Cultural Centre, 1966–8

ED61/82, Edinburgh Cultural Centre, 1968–70

ED61/84, Edinburgh Cultural Centre, 1970–1

ED61/85, Edinburgh Cultural Centre, 1971–2

ED61/87, Edinburgh Cultural Centre, 1973

ED61/88, Edinburgh Cultural Centre, 1974

ED61/89, Edinburgh Cultural Centre, 1974–5

4. University of Edinburgh, Centre for Research Collections

GB 0237/PJM/CCC/A/1/1, Percy Johnson-Marshall, papers relating to the replanning of Coventry, 1940–5

RHM 29, Drawings of Castle Terrace Theatre by Robert Matthew

Exeter

University of Exeter Archives

26/1d/2d, Northcott Theatre

26/1d/3c, Northcott Theatre

Glasgow

1. Glasgow Archives

Glasgow Corporation minutes

2. Royal Conservatoire of Scotland
IA/3/6/1–2, RSAMD reconstruction

3. Scottish Theatre Archive, University of Glasgow
STA Bb Boxes 1–2 Dundee Repertory Theatre

Hawarden
Flintshire Archives
CC/3/9, 'The Official Opening of Theatr Clywd and Educational Technology Centre, Mold' [1976]
CC/TC/1/163, Theatr Clwyd programmes and brochures
CC/TC/1/164, Theatr Clwyd brochures and information
FC/1/68–73, Flintshire County Council minutes
FC/13/20, 'Flintshire: A County With a Future'
FC/A/9/2, 'New Shirehall—Flintshire County Council, Llwynegrin'

Hull
Hull History Centre
University Archives, Registrar Uncat. Box 14, File 33/3, Drama Studio
University Archives, Parcel 99, 17/4, Buildings Committee (temporary reference)
University Archives, Parcel 118, 17/4, Drama Studio (temporary reference)

Inverness
Highland Archives
Bl/1/1/101–8, Inverness Town Council minutes
HCA/D628/1/2, Derek C. Bigg, 'The Pre-History of Eden Court Theatre, Inverness', unpublished MS

Ipswich
Suffolk Record Office
A1/3/2/4060/486, Ipswich Arts Theatre Trust minutes
A1/3/2/4060/676, Ipswich Arts Theatre Trust

Leeds
University of Leeds, Brotherton Library
BC MS 20c Theatre LP Arc/2, West Yorkshire Playhouse design competition

Leicester
Leicester Archives
49/35, Haymarket Comprehensive Development Area
DE 3277/214–215, Leicester Town Planning Committee minutes

Liverpool
1. Liverpool Central Library
Q792.1 PLA, Playhouse archive

2. University of Liverpool, Special Collections
D147/C73 and/C74, William Holford archive, University of Exeter

London
1. British Library
Architects' Lives tapes, C467/07, Peter Moro interviewed by Louise Brodie, 1996

2. Guildhall Library
CoCoRep 1968/48, Report of the Rates, Finance, Barbican and Music Committees, 1968
Fo pam 748, Chamberlin Powell and Bon, Report to the Court of Common Council, 1956
QL 55.4 BAR, Chamberlin Powell and Bon, 'Barbican Redevelopment, 1959' [printed report, 1959]
QL 55.4 BAR, Chamberlin Powell and Bon, 'Barbican Arts Centre, 1968' [printed report, 1969]
S L 50.01, Anthony Besch, 'Report to the Corporation of the City of London [...]' [1964]

3. The National Archives
HLG/71/1287, Coventry redevelopment, 1949–56
HLG/79/1454, Barbican redevelopment, 1956–71

4. Rambert Dance Company Archives
Uncatalogued New Mercury Theatre papers, *c.*1960–75

5. Royal Institute of British Architects, Drawings, and Archives
LaD/164/2, Denys Lasdun archive, minutes, and notes
LaD/167/1, Denys Lasdun archive, 'telling extracts', and notes on the National Theatre design
LaD/167/4, Denys Lasdun archive, National Theatre Building Committee
LaD/170/4, National Theatre briefing documents
LaD/207/1–2, National Theatre (1967 report)
MoP/1–13, Archive of Peter Moro
PA823/13/1–6, National Theatre drawings by Brian O'Rorke
PA823/14/1–29, National Theatre drawings by Brian O'Rorke
PA824/1/2–5, National Theatre drawings by Brian O'Rorke
PA824/2/1–10, National Theatre drawings by Brian O'Rorke
Uncatalogued Leslie Martin archive, Glasgow Cultural Centre

6. The Theatres Trust
Roderick Ham archive

7. Victoria and Albert Museum, Theatre Collections
Barbican Arts Centre Building file
Belgrade Theatre Building file
Crucible Theatre Building file
Guildford (Yvonne Arnaud) Theatre Building file
Leatherhead (Thorndike) Theatre Building file
John Bury file
Peter Hall file
ABTT filmed interview with Roderick Ham, 1999
ACGB/84/18, Bedford, theatre project
ACGB/84/21, Billingham, Forum
ACGB/84/28, Birmingham, New Repertory
ACGB/84/37, Bolton, Octagon
ACGB/84/78, Chester, Gateway
ACGB/84/85, Coventry, Belgrade
ACGB/84/91, Derby, Playhouse
ACGB/84/147, Ipswich, Wolsey
ACGB/84/149, Leatherhead, Thorndike
ACGB/84/157, Leicester, Haymarket
ACGB/84/163, Lincoln, 'New' Theatre
ACGB/84/180, Royal Exchange Theatre mobile
ACGB/84/182, Royal Exchange Theatre mobile

ACGB/84/206, Nottingham, Playhouse
ACGB/84/246, Sheffield, Crucible
ACGB/84/260, Stevenage, Arts and Leisure Centre
ACGB/107/294, Northampton, Derngate
ACGB/107/443, Sheffield, Crucible
ACGB/120/1, Building studies
ACGB/120/3, HTA Committee papers
ACGB/120/4, HTA minutes, 1983–4
ACGB/120/6, Fundraising conference, 1976
ACGB/120/9, HTA Committee papers
ACGB/120/12, Temporary and Portable theatres
ACGB/120/16, HTA Committee papers
ACGB/120/20, Fundraising files
ACGB/120/22, HTA papers
ACGB/120/23, Fundraising files
ACGB/120/33, HTA correspondence with the ABTT
ACGB/120/34, HTA Committee papers
ACGB/120/35, HTA Committee papers
ACGB/120/40, HTA Committee papers, 1983–4
ACGB/120/41, Scottish Arts Council
ACGB/120/43, 'Fifteen years of achievements', MS. typescript, 1973
ACGB/120/47, HTA papers
THM/166, Sean Kenny archive
THM/351, Theatres Advisory Council archive

Manchester
1. John Rylands Library
Hugh Hunt uncatalogued papers, Box 12
SJ/1/37, Stephen Joseph archive (ABTT)
SJ/1/43, Stephen Joseph archive (Manchester University Theatre)

2. University of Manchester Archives
VCA/7/573, Vice Chancellor's Papers

Matlock
Derbyshire Record Office
D738/4/1, Derby Playhouse administrative papers
D738/5/2, Derby Playhouse accounts and reports
D4538/4/21–22, Derby Estates and Development Committee minutes

Middlesbrough
Teesside Archives
U/S/706, Billingham Town Centre development
U/S/1143, 'Billingham—Planned for People' [*c.*1965]
U/S/2409, Billingham Town Centre and Urban District Council brochures
Billingham Urban District Council minutes

Newcastle-upon-Tyne
Newcastle University Archives and Special Collections, Robinson Library
Team Valley 00-0053, 'Opening of Gulbenkian Theatre, 28th November 1970'

Team Valley 00-0181, Theatre Users Committee (minutes) 1970–5
Team Valley 00-1110, Committee of Management of University Theatre 1978–84
Team Valley 00-1196, Theatre Users Committee (minutes) 1969–84
King's College Council minutes
University Council minutes (including Site Development Committee)
Uncatalogued booklet, 'The University Theatre, Newcastle' [1970]

Nottingham
Nottinghamshire Archives
DD/NP/1/2/1/1, Nottingham Playhouse papers

Oxford
Bodleian Library
MSS. Eng. misc. c. 1017–18, Papers of Neville Coghill, Oxford University Drama Commission, 1944–50

Plymouth
Plymouth Central Library
Uncatalogued Theatre Royal clippings file

Reading
1. Berkshire Records Office
NT/B/G23, Bracknell press cuttings
NT/B/S2/9, Arts Centre
NT/B/S2/14, Arts Centre

2. Reading Central Library
Uncatalogued Hexagon file

Sheffield
1. Sheffield City Archives
This collection has been renumbered since it was consulted. The new numbers are given in brackets here but the footnotes have not been changed.
LD2287 (LD1549/1/6), Sheffield Playhouse and Crucible Theatre
LD2310 (LD1549/12/9a), Box Office Returns
LD2317 (LD1549/12/15), Kevan Scholes, 'The Crucible Theatre' [report]
LD2341 (LD1549/1/3/7), Playhouse Board minutes
SY/43/Z1/6 and/8 (SY43/1), Crucible Theatre market research study, 1974

2. Sheffield Local Studies Library
Pamphlets box, Crucible Theatre

Solihull
Central Library
R.027.4, 'Solihull Library and Arts Centre' [recollections by Stanley Sellers], 2008

Stirling
University of Stirling Archives and Special Collections
Uncatalogued Development Plan material, *c.*1966–71
UA/File/1, Development Committee papers

Stratford-upon-Avon
Shakespeare's Birthplace Trust Archive
DR1103/2/5/3, Brian O'Rorke's National Theatre scheme, 1950s
DR1108/2/4, Fordham Flower's papers relating to the New Mercury Theatre proposal, *c.*1963–5
RL5/2/1023-31, Photographs of Barbican Theatre model, dated 1966

Swindon
Wiltshire and Swindon Archives
G24/100/71–74, Borough of Swindon signed minutes
G23/132/249, Salisbury Arts Theatre/Playhouse
G24/132/996, Wyvern Theatre
G24/894/5, Arts Centre Project, 1968–9

Woking
Surrey History Centre
4580/8-14, Yvonne Arnaud Theatre, drawings
4580/21, Yvonne Arnaud Theatre, exhibition board
6368/3/3, Leatherhead/Thorndike Theatre Appeal Committee minutes
6368/3/9, Leatherhead/Thorndike Theatre
6368/4/1, Leatherhead/Thorndike Theatre Club minutes
6368/10/6, press clippings (Leatherhead)
6368/10/8, press clippings (Leatherhead)
6894/2/3, Farnham Repertory Company minutes
6894/2/21, Redgrave Theatre, Farnham, papers
6894/7/1/2, Redgrave Theatre, Farnham, publicity and press
6894/7/1/3, Redgrave Theatre, Farnham, drawings
7018/2/2, Yvonne Arnaud Theatre administrative files
7018/2/4/142, press clippings (Guildford)
7018/2/4/143, press clippings (Guildford)
7018/2/4/147, press clippings (Guildford)
7350/2/52, Scott Brownrigg and Turner papers (Yvonne Arnaud Theatre)
7432/1/1, Yvonne Arnaud Theatre Trust minutes

York
York St John University
York Theatre Royal archive

2. MANUSCRIPT SOURCES IN PRIVATE COLLECTIONS

Coleraine
Riverside Theatre, University of Ulster
Plans and reports by Peter Moro

Horsham
Christ's Hospital
867.1 and 867.2, Arts Centre correspondence/drawings

London
1. ABTT Archives
Folders of reports on schemes reviewed by the Theatre Planning Committee

2. Andrzej Blonski Architects
Papers relating to theatres by the Peter Moro Partnership

3. Questors Theatre, Ealing
Uncatalogued papers relating to the design of the theatre, *c.*1950–65

Pitlochry
Festival Theatre
Uncatalogued archive

Reading
Papers relating to the Belgrade Theatre, Coventry, in the possession of the late Martin Froy, artist

Salisbury
Playhouse Archive
Papers and drawings relating to the construction of the theatre

Sevenoaks
Papers relating to the work of Howell Killick Partridge and Amis, in the possession of the late John Partridge

Sheffield
Crucible Theatre
Archive, including press clippings

3. PRINTED SOURCES

Official papers
Arts Council of Great Britain, Annual Reports
[Arts Council of Great Britain], 'Plans for an Arts Centre' [1945]
Arts Council of Great Britain, 'Housing the Arts in Great Britain', 2 vols [1959–61]
Arts Council of Great Britain, 'The Theatre Today in England and Wales: the report of the Arts Council Theatre Enquiry' [1970]
Arts Council of Great Britain, 'The Arts Council of Great Britain: the first twenty-five years' [1972]
Arts Council of Great Britain, 'The Glory of the Garden: the development of the arts in England. A strategy for a decade' [1984]
Conservative Political Centre, 'The Challenge of Leisure' (1959)
Hansard
Hutchison, Robert, 'Three Arts Centres: a study of South Hill Park, the Gardner Arts Centre, and Chapter' [Arts Council report, 1977]
'A Policy for the Arts: the first steps', Cmnd. 2601 (1965)
[Wolfenden Committee], *Sport and the Community: the Report of the Wolfenden Committee on Sport* (London: Central Council for Physical Recreation, 1960)

Frequently cited periodicals
Architect and Building News
Architects' Journal
Architectural Design
Architectural Review

Builder
Concrete Quarterly
Country Life
Guardian
[Glasgow] Herald
New Theatre Magazine
Observer
The Stage (incl. *The Stage and Television Today*)
Sunday Telegraph
Tabs
The Times

4. BOOKS AND ARTICLES

'A New Concept in Theatre Design', *Journal of the Royal Society of Arts* 104 (17 August 1956), pp. 756–74

'Curtain Call for Dundee Theatre', *Building Design* 621 (3 December 1982), pp. 14–15

'Gardner Centre for the Arts', *Building Specification* 2, no. 11 (November 1971), pp. 41–6

'John English in Conversation with Iain Ball', *English in Education* 1, no. 3 (September 1967), pp. 46–56

'Open House at the Thorndike', *Design* 252 (1969), pp. 48–53

'Sheffield's Theatre of the Future', *Sheffield Spectator* 7, no. 51 (June 1969), n.p.

'Stephen Joseph Writes on His Theatre in the Round at Newcastle-under-Lyme', *Plays and Players*, March 1962

'Suicide or Salvation?', *Yorkshire Architect*, March 1971, pp. 386–8

'Theatre and Concert Hall in Barbican Scheme', *Interbuild* 6 (July 1959), pp. 40–2

Abercrombie, Patrick and Derek Plumstead, *A Civic Survey and Plan for the City and Royal Burgh of Edinburgh* (Edinburgh: Oliver and Boyd, 1949)

Allen, John, *Berthold Lubetkin: Architecture and the Tradition of Progress* (London: Black Dog, 2012)

Banham, Reyner, *The New Brutalism: Ethic or Aesthetic?* (London: Architectural Press, 1966)

Banham, Reyner, 'The Style: "flimsy…effeminate"?', in *A Tonic to the Nation: the Festival of Britain, 1951*, edited by Mary Banham and Bevis Hillier (London: Thames and Hudson, 1976), pp. 190–8

Barron, Michael, *Auditorium Acoustics and Architectural Design* (London: Spon, 1993)

Bavin, John, *Heart of the City: the Story of Salisbury Playhouse* (Salisbury: [Salisbury Playhouse], 1976)

Bell, S., N. Marshall, and R. Southern, *Essentials of Stage-planning* (London: Muller, 1949)

Bentham, Frederick, *New Theatres in Britain* (London: Rank Strand Electric, 1970)

Bergan, Ronald, *The Great Theatres of London: an Illustrated Companion* (London: Admiral, 1987)

Billington, Michael, *State of the Nation: British Theatre Since 1945* (London: Faber and Faber, 2007)

Black, Lawrence, *The Political Culture of the Left in Affluent Britain, 1951–64: Old Labour, New Britain?* (Basingstoke: Palgrave Macmillan, 2003)

Black, Lawrence, '"Making Britain a Gayer and More Cultivated Country". Jennie Lee, the creative economy, and the 1960s "Cultural Revolution"', *Contemporary British History* 20, no. 3 (2006), pp. 323–42

Black, Lawrence, 'An Enlightening Decade? New histories of 1970s Britain', *International Labor and Working-class History* 82 (2012), pp. 174–86

Black, Lawrence and Hugh Pemberton, 'The Benighted Decade? Reassessing the seventies', in *Reassessing 1970s Britain*, edited by Lawrence Black, Hugh Pemberton, and Pat Thane (Manchester: Manchester University Press, 2013), pp. 1–24

Blackwood, Derek, Charles Moodie, Eddie O'Donnell, and John Holt, 'Two Theatres in Scotland at Pitlochry and Dundee', *Arup Journal* 18, no. 1 (April 1983), pp. 12–17

Branson, Norman, 'The Questors Theatre', in *Adaptable Theatres*, edited by Stephen Joseph (London: ABTT, 1962), pp. 25–9

Bullock, Nicholas, *Building the Post-war World: Modern Architecture and Reconstruction in Britain* (London: Routledge, 2002)

Burns, J. H. and D. Sutherland Graeme, *Scottish University* (Edinburgh: Darien, 1944)

Calder, Barnabas, 'The Limits of 1960s Radicalism: the Fun Palace versus the National Theatre', in *Setting the Scene: Perspectives on Twentieth-century Theatre Architecture*, edited by Alistair Fair (Farnham: Ashgate, 2015), pp. 164–78

Calder, Barnabas, *Raw Concrete: the Beauty of Brutalism* (London: Heinemann, 2016)

Campbell, Louise, *Coventry Cathedral: Art and Architecture in Post-war Britain* (Oxford: Clarendon Press, 1996)

Campbell, Louise, Miles Glendinning, and Jane Thomas, *Basil Spence: Buildings and Projects* (London: RIBA, 2012)

Chamberlin, E. R., *Guildford* (Chichester: Phillimore, 1982)

Chapman, Don, *Oxford Playhouse: High and Low Drama in a University City* (Hatfield: University of Hertfordshire Press, 2008)

Cherry, Gordon E., *Birmingham: a Study in Geography, History and Planning* (Chichester: Wiley, 1994)

Cochrane, Claire, *The Birmingham Rep: a City's Theatre, 1962–2002* (Birmingham: Sir Barry Jackson Trust, 2003)

Cochrane, Claire, *Twentieth-century British Theatre: Industry, Art and Empire* (Cambridge: Cambridge University Press, 2011)

Conekin, Becky, '"Here Is the Modern World Itself" The Festival of Britain's representations of the future', in *Moments of Modernity: Reconstructing Britain, 1945–1964*, edited by Becky Conekin, Frank Mort, and Chris Waters (London; Rivers Oram, 1999), pp. 228–46

Conrads, Ulrich and Werner Marschall, *Modern Architecture in Germany* (London: Architectural Press, 1962)

Crook, Joseph Mordaunt, *The Dilemma of Style: Architectural Ideas from the Picturesque to the Postmodern* (London: Murray, 1987)

Crosland, C. A. R., *The Future of Socialism* (London: Jonathan Cape, 1956)

Cupers, Kenny, 'The Cultural Center: architecture as cultural policy in post-war Europe', *Journal of the Society of Architectural Historians* 74, no. 4 (2015), pp. 464–84

Curtis, William J. R., *Denys Lasdun: Architecture, City, Landscape* (London: Phaidon, 1994)

Darling, Elizabeth, *Re-forming Britain: Narratives of Modernity Before Reconstruction* (London: Routledge, 2007)

DeGaetani, Thomas, 'The Adaptable Theatre in the American University; and the Loeb Drama Centre', in *Adaptable Theatres*, edited by Stephen Joseph (London: ABTT, 1962), pp. 17–21

Dorney, Kate and Ros Merkin, 'Introduction', in *The Glory of the Garden: English Regional Theatre and the Arts Council 1984–2009*, edited by Kate Dorney and Ros Merkin (Newcastle-upon-Tyne: Cambridge Scholars Publishing, 2010), pp. 1–14

Dunn, Sheila, *The Theatres of Bromley* (Greenwich: Lanthorn, 1984)

Dunster, David, 'Introduction', to Alison Smithson and Peter Smithson, *The Shift* (London: Academy Editions, 1982)

Elliott, Michael, 'On Not Building for Posterity', in *Making Space for Theatre: British Architecture and Theatre Since 1958*, edited by Ronnie Mulryne and Margaret Shewring (Stratford-upon-Avon: Mulryne and Shewring, 1995), pp. 16–20

Elsam, Paul, *Stephen Joseph: Theatre Pioneer and Provocateur* (London: Bloomsbury, 2013)

Elsom, John, *Theatre Outside London* (London: Macmillan, 1971)

English, John, 'The Cannon Hill Theatre', in *Adaptable Theatres*, edited by Stephen Joseph (London: ABTT, 1962), pp. 41–7

English, John, 'Leisure and the Performing Arts', in *Actor and Architect*, edited by Stephen Joseph (Manchester: Manchester University Press, 1964), pp. 75–86

Esher, Lionel, *A Broken Wave: the Rebuilding of England, 1940–1980* (Harmondsworth: Penguin, 1983)

Evershed-Martin, Leslie, *The Impossible Theatre: the Chichester Festival Theatre Adventure* (London: Phillimore, 1971)

Eyre, Richard, *National Service: Diary of a Decade* (London: Bloomsbury, 2003)

Eyre, Richard and Nicholas Wright, *Changing Stages: a View of British Theatre in the Twentieth Century* (London: Bloomsbury, 2000)

Fair, Alistair, '"A New Image of the Living Theatre": the genesis and design of the Belgrade Theatre, Coventry, 1948–58', *Architectural History* 54 (2011), pp. 347–82

Fair, Alistair, 'The End of "Optimism and Expansiveness"? Designing for drama in the 1970s', *Twentieth Century Architecture* 10 (2012), pp. 75–87

Fair, Alistair, '"The Ideal Campus": the Sidgwick Site, Cambridge', *Twentieth Century Architecture* 11 (2013) pp. 103–21

Fair, Alistair, '"Brutalism Among the Ladies": modern architecture at Somerville College, Oxford, 1947–67', *Architectural History* 57 (2014), pp. 357–92

Fair, Alistair, '"A London Architect Who Has Specialised: Peter Moro and festivity in theatre design, *c.*1955–82', in *Setting the Scene: Perspectives on Twentieth-century Theatre Architecture*, edited by Alistair Fair (Farnham: Ashgate, 2015), pp. 133–62

Fair, Alistair, 'Rethinking the Post-war British Theatre: monumentality, Sean Kenny, and the state, *c.*1966–73', in *Architecture, Institutions and Change*, edited by Paul Hogben and Judith O'Callaghan (Sydney: SAHANZ, 2015), pp. 146–56

Fair, Alistair, '"An Object Lesson in How Not To Get Things Done": Edinburgh's unbuilt "opera house", 1960–1975', *Architectural Heritage* 27 (2017), pp. 91–117

Findlater, Richard, *The Future of the Theatre* (London: Fabian Society, 1959)

Fischer, P., 'Doing Princely Sums: structure and subsidy', in *The German Theatre: a Symposium*, edited by Ronald Hayman (London: Wolff, 1975), pp. 215–34

Forster, W. L., *The Universities, the Arts and the Public* (London: Arts Council of Great Britain, 1979)

Forsyth, Michael, *Auditoria: Designing for the Performing Arts* (London: Mitchell, 1987)

Franklin, Geraint, *HKPA* (London: Historic England, 2017)

Gavin, Brian, 'New Life for an Old GAG!', *Theatres* 11 (Spring 2007), pp. 6–9

Giedion, Sigfried, 'The Need for a New Monumentality' [1944], in his *Architecture, You and Me: the Diary of a Development* (Cambridge, MA: Harvard, 1957), pp. 25–39

Giedion, Sigfried, 'Social Imagination', in his *Architecture, You and Me: the Diary of a Development* (Cambridge, MA: Harvard, 1957), pp. 157–77

Glasstone, Victor, *Victorian and Edwardian Theatres: an Architectural and Social Survey* (London: Thames and Hudson, 1975)

Glendinning, Miles, *Modern Architect: the Life and Times of Robert Matthew* (London: RIBA, 2008)
Glendinning, Miles and Stefan Muthesius, *Tower Block: Modern Public Housing in England, Scotland, Wales and Northern Ireland* (New Haven/London: Yale University Press, 1994)
Goad, Philip, 'Post-war and Polygonal: special plans for Australian architecture, 1950–70', *Architectural Theory Review* 15, no. 2 (2010), pp. 166–86
Gold, John R., *The Practice of Modernism: Modern Architects and Urban Transformation* (Abingdon: Routledge, 2007)
Gunn, Simon, 'Ring Road: Birmingham and the collapse of the motor city ideal in 1970s Britain', *Historical Journal*, online publication 2017
Guthrie, Tyrone, *A Life in the Theatre* (London: Hamish Hamilton, 1960)
Hall, Peter, *Peter Hall's Diaries: the Story of a Dramatic Battle*, edited by John Goodwin (London: Hamilton, 1983)
Hall, Peter, *Making an Exhibition of Myself: the Autobiography of Peter Hall* (London: Oberon, 2000)
Ham, Roderick, *Theatre Planning* (London: Architectural Press, 1972)
Hammond, Peter, 'A Radical Approach to Church Architecture', in *Towards a Church Architecture*, edited by Peter Hammond (London: Architectural Press, 1962), pp. 15–37
Hampton, Anthony, 'Most Forward-looking Theatre in Europe Emerges in City', *Quality of Sheffield* 18, no. 2 (1971), pp. 22–3
Harwood, Elain, *Chamberlin Powell and Bon* (London: RIBA, 2011)
Harwood, Elain, *Space, Hope and Brutalism: English Architecture 1945–1975* (New Haven/London: Yale University Press, 2015)
Harwood, Elain, 'Theatres in West Germany, 1945–70', in *Setting the Scene: Perspectives on Twentieth-century Theatre Architecture*, edited by Alistair Fair (Farnham: Ashgate, 2015), pp. 103–32
Harwood, Elain and James O. Davies, *England's Post-war Listed Buildings* (London: Batsford, 3rd ed., 2015)
Harwood, Elain and Alan Powers, 'From Downtown to Diversity: revisiting the 1970s', *Twentieth Century Architecture* 10 (2012), pp. 9–36
Hayes, Nick, *Consensus and Controversy: City Politics in Nottingham, 1945–1966* (Liverpool: Liverpool University Press, 1996)
Hewison, Robert, *Culture and Consensus: England, Art and Politics Since 1940* (London: Methuen, 1995)
Hillier, Bevis, 'Introduction', in *A Tonic to the Nation: the Festival of Britain, 1951*, edited by Mary Banham and Bevis Hillier (London: Thames and Hudson, 1976), pp. 10–19
Hillier, John and Martin Blythe, *Poole's Pride Regained, 1964–1974* (Poole: Poole Historical Trust, 1996)
Hilton, Matthew, Chris Moores, and Florence Sutcliffe-Braithwaite, 'New Times Revisited: Britain in the 1980s', *Contemporary British History* 31, no. 2 (2017), pp. 145–65
Hodgkinson, G., *Sent to Coventry* (London: Maxwell, 1970)
Hollis, Patricia, *Jennie Lee: a Life* (Oxford: Oxford University Press, 1997)
Howell, W. G. R., 'The Young Vic: theatre on a budget', *RIBA Journal* 78 (1971), pp. 287–9
Hulme, Tom, '"A Nation Dependent on Its Children": school buildings and citizenship in England and Wales, 1900–1939', *Journal of British Studies* 54, no. 2 (2015), pp. 406–32
Jackson, Iain and Jessica Holland, *The Architecture of Edwin Maxwell Fry and Jane Drew* (Farnham: Ashgate, 2014)
Jackson, Lesley, *Robin and Lucienne Day: Pioneers of Contemporary Design* (London: Mitchell Beazley, 2011)

Joseph, Stephen, 'Newcastle-under-Lyme Civic Theatre', in *Adaptable Theatres*, edited by Stephen Joseph (London: ABTT, 1962), pp. 67–70
Joseph, Stephen, 'Introduction', in *Actor and Architect*, edited by Stephen Joseph (Manchester: Manchester University Press, 1964), pp. 1–29
Joseph, Stephen, *New Theatre Forms* (London: Pitman, 1968)
Kelly, Jessica, 'Vulgar Modernism: J. M. Richards, modernism and the vernacular', *Architectural History* 58 (2015), pp. 229–60
Kelly, Jude, 'The West Yorkshire Playhouse', in *Making Space for Theatre: British Architecture and Theatre Since 1958*, edited by Ronnie Mulryne and Margaret Shewring (Stratford-upon-Avon: Mulryne and Shewring, 1995), pp. 74–9
Kenny, Sean, 'The Shape of the Theatre', in *Actor and Audience*, edited by Stephen Joseph (Manchester: Manchester University Press, 1964), pp. 57–66
Kidson, Peter, Peter Murray, and Paul Thompson, *A History of English Architecture* (Harmondsworth: Pelican, 1965)
Landstone, Charles, *Off-Stage: a Personal Record of the First Twelve Years of State Sponsored Drama in Great Britain* (London: Elek, 1953)
Leventhal, Fred, '"The Best for the Most": CEMA and state sponsorship of the arts in wartime, 1939–1945', *Twentieth Century British History* 1, no. 3 (1990), pp. 289–317
Ling, Arthur, 'Satisfying Human Needs at the Core', in *Heart of the City*, edited by Jacqueline Tyrwhitt, J. L. Sert, and Ernesto Rogers (London: Lund Humphries, 1952), pp. 94–6
Linklater, N. V., 'The Achievement in Drama', in *The State and the Arts*, edited by John Pick (Eastbourne: John Offord, 1980), pp. 77–94
McArthur, Euan, *Scotland, CEMA and the Arts Council: Background, Politics and Visual Arts Policy* (Farnham: Ashgate, 2013)
McAuley, Gay, *Space in Performance: Making Meaning in the Theatre* (Ann Arbor, MI: University of Michigan Press, 1999)
Macewen, Malcolm, *Crisis in Architecture* (London: RIBA, 1974)
Mackintosh, Iain, *Architecture, Actor and Audience* (London: Routledge, 1993)
Mackintosh, Iain (ed.), *The Guthrie Thrust Stage: a Living Legacy* (London: ABTT, 2011)
Mackintosh, Iain and Michael Sell (eds), *Curtains!!! Or, a New Life for Old Theatres* (Eastbourne: John Offord, 1982)
McNeill, Alistair, 'Civic Theatre—or White Elephant?', *Scottish Theatre*, September 1969, pp. 19–20
Manley, Christine Hui Lan, *Frederick Gibberd* (London: Historic England, 2017)
Marshall, Norman, 'Theatre Design', *Drama* 59 (1960), pp. 25–7
Marshall, Norman, 'Planning Adaptable Theatres', *Drama* 62 (1961), pp. 38–41
Marwick, Arthur, *Culture in Britain Since 1945* (Oxford: Wiley-Blackwell, 1991)
Marwick, Arthur, *The Sixties: Cultural Revolution in Britain, France, Italy, and the United States, c.1958–c.1974* (Oxford: Oxford University Press, 1998)
Minihan, Janet, *The Nationalization of Culture: the Development of State Subsidies to the Arts in Great Britain* (London: Hamilton, 1977)
Moro, Peter, 'Is the Proscenium Obsolete?', *ABTT Bulletin* 2nd Year, No. 2 (June 1963), n.p.
Murray, Braham, *The Worst It Can Be Is a Disaster: the Life Story of Braham Murray and the Royal Exchange Theatre* (London: Methuen, 2007)
Muthesius, Stefan, *The Postwar University: Utopianist Campus and College* (New Haven/London: Yale University Press, 2000)
[Oxford University Drama Commission], *Report of the Oxford University Drama Commission* (Oxford: Oxford University Press, 1948)

Pemberton-Billing, Robin, *The Octagon Theatre: Concept to Reality* (Bolton: [Octagon Theatre], 2011)

Pentreath, B. T., 'Classical Modernism in Fifties Edinburgh: Adam House, by William Kininmonth', *Architectural Heritage* 5 (1995), pp. 97–111

Pick, John, 'Introduction: the best for the most', in *The State and the Arts*, edited by John Pick (Eastbourne: John Offord, 1980), pp. 9–19

Pilbrow, Richard, *A Theatre Project* (New York: PLASA Media, 2011)

Price, Cedric, *Re: CP*, edited by Hans-Ulrich Obrist (Basel: Birkhäuser, 2003)

Pringle, Marian, *The Theatres of Stratford-upon-Avon, 1875–1992: an Architectural History* (Stratford-upon-Avon: Stratford-upon-Avon Society, 1993)

Proctor, Robert, 'Social Structures: Gillespie Kidd and Coia's halls of residence for the University of Hull', *Journal of the Society of Architectural Historians* 67, no. 1 (2008), pp. 106–29

Proctor, Robert, *Building the Modern Church: Roman Catholic Church Architecture in Britain, 1955 to 1975* (Farnham: Ashgate, 2014)

Reid, Francis, 'Seeing, Hearing and Contact', in *Making Space for Theatre: British Architecture and Theatre Since 1958*, edited by Ronnie Mulryne and Margaret Shewring (Stratford-upon-Avon: Mulryne and Shewring, 1995), pp. 28–33

Richards, J. M., *An Introduction to Modern Architecture* (Harmondsworth: Penguin, 1940)

Roots, William, et al., *The Local Government Act, 1948* (London: Knight, 1948)

Rosenthal, Daniel, *The National Theatre Story* (London: Oberon, 2013)

Rowell, George and Anthony Jackson, *The Repertory Movement: a History of Regional Theatre in Britain* (Cambridge: Cambridge University Press, 1984)

Ruhnau, Werner, 'Das neue Stadttheater in Gelsenkirchen', *Bauwelt* 51 (1960), pp. 407–11

Saint, Andrew, *Towards a Social Architecture: the Role of School-building in Post-war England* (New Haven/London: Yale University Press, 1987)

Sandbrook, Dominic, *Never Had It So Good: a History of Britain from Suez to the Beatles* (London: Abacus, 2005)

Sandbrook, Dominic, *White Heat: a History of Britain in the Swinging Sixties* (London: Abacus, 2009)

Saumarez Smith, Otto, 'A Strange Brutalist "Primitive Hut": Howell Killick Partridge and Amis's Senior Common Room at Downing College, Cambridge', *Twentieth Century Architecture* 11 (2013), pp. 149–65

Saumarez Smith, Otto, 'Graeme Shankland: a sixties architect-planner and the political culture of the British left', *Architectural History* 54 (2014), pp. 393–422

Saumarez Smith, Otto, 'Central Government and Town-centre Redevelopment in Britain, 1959–1966', *Historical Journal* 58, no. 1 (2015), pp. 217–44

Saumarez Smith, Otto, 'The Inner City Crisis and the End of Urban Modernism in 1970s Britain', *Twentieth Century British History* 27, no. 4 (2016), pp. 578–98

Scott, Trevor A., 'Audio-Visual Aids in Higher Scientific Education: 25 years on', *Studies in Higher Education* 16, no. 2 (1991), pp. 225–7

Shapely, Peter, 'Civic Pride and Redevelopment in the Post-war British City', *Urban History* 39, no. 2 (2012), pp. 310–28

Shellard, Dominic, *British Theatre Since the War* (New Haven/London: Yale University Press, 2000)

Shellard, Dominic, 'Introduction: the Arts and Humanities Research Council (AHRC) British Library Theatre Archive Project, and the Golden Generation', in *The Golden Generation: New Light on Post-war British Theatre*, edited by Dominic Shellard (London: British Library, 2008), pp. 7–18

Shellard, Dominic, 'Stability, Renewal and Change: Gielgud and Olivier in 1957', in *The Golden Generation: New Light on Post-war British Theatre*, edited by Dominic Shellard (London: British Library, 2008), pp. 67–91

Short, C. Alan, Peter Barrett, and Alistair Fair, *Geometry and Atmosphere: Theatre Buildings from Vision to Reality* (Farnham: Ashgate, 2011)

Sinclair, Andrew, *Arts and Cultures: the History of the Fifty Years of the Arts Council of Great Britain* (London: Sinclair Stevenson, 1995)

Sinfield, Alan, 'Culture, Consensus and Difference: Angus Wilson to Alan Hollinghurst', in *British Culture of the Postwar: an Introduction to Literature and Society, 1945–1999*, edited by Alistair Davies and Alan Sinfield (London: Routledge, 2000), pp. 83–102

Southern, Richard, *The Open Stage and the Modern Theatre in Research and Practice* (London: Faber and Faber, 1953)

Southern, Richard, *The Seven Ages of the Theatre* (London: Faber and Faber, 1964)

Spence, Basil, *Phoenix at Coventry: the Building of a Cathedral* (London: Bles, 1962)

Stonehouse, Roger, 'Theme and Variation', in *Architecture, Education and Research: the Work of Leslie Martin*, edited by Peter Carolin and Trevor Dannatt (London: Academy Editions, 1996), pp. 84–93

Stonehouse, Roger, *Trevor Dannatt, Works and Words* (London: Black Dog, 2008)

Strong, Judith, *Encore: Strategies for Theatre Renewal* (London: Theatres Trust, 1999)

Summerson, John, 'The Mischievous Analogy', in his *Heavenly Mansions and Other Essays on Architecture* (London: Cresset Press, 1949), pp. 195–218

Summerson, John, 'The Case for a Theory of Modern Architecture', *RIBA Journal* 64 (June 1957), pp. 307–13

Summerson, John, 'Introduction', in Trevor Dannatt, *Modern Architecture in Britain* (London: Batsford, 1959), pp. 11–29

Swenarton, Mark, 'Politics Versus Architecture: the Alexandra Road Public Enquiry, 1978–81', *Planning Perspectives* 29, no. 4 (2014), pp. 423–46

Swenarton, Mark, Tom Avermaete, and Dirk van den Heuvel, 'Introduction', in *Architecture and the Welfare State*, edited by Mark Swenarton, Tom Avermaete, and Dirk van den Heuvel (Abingdon: Routledge, 2014), pp. 1–23

Tiratsoo, Nick, *Reconstruction, Affluence and Labour Politics: Coventry, 1945–60* (London: Routledge, 1990)

Todd, Selina, 'Phoenix Rising: working-class life and urban reconstruction, *c.*1945–1967', *Journal of British Studies* 54, no. 3 (2015), pp. 679–702

Todd, Susan, 'Strength Lies in Ideas Not Expertise', *Times Higher Education Supplement*, 4 May 1973

Tomlinson, Jim, 'De-industrialization Not Decline: a new meta-narrative for post-war British history', *Twentieth Century British History* 27, no. 1 (2016), pp. 76–99

Tubbs, Ralph, *Living in Cities* (Harmondsworth: Penguin, 1942)

Turnbull, Olivia, *Bringing Down the House: the Crisis in Britain's Regional Theatres* (Bristol: Intellect, 2008)

Urban, Florian, 'Glasgow's Royal Concert Hall and the Invention of the Post-modern City', *Journal of Architecture* 18, no. 2 (2013), pp. 254–96

University of Manchester Department of Town and Country Planning, *Regional Shopping Centres in North West England* (Manchester: [University of Manchester], 1964)

Welland, Dennis, John Prudhoe, and Donald Roy, 'American Literature: Drama: university courses', *Critical Survey* 3, no. 2 (1967), pp. 114–24

Whyte, William, *Redbrick: a Social and Architectural History of Britain's Civic Universities* (Oxford: Oxford University Press, 2015)

Wickham, Glynne, 'Conclusion: retrospect and prospect', in *The Universities and the Theatre*, edited by D. G. James (London: Colston Research Society, 1952), pp. 102–15

Wiles, David, *A Short History of Western Performance Space* (Cambridge: Cambridge University Press, 2003)

Willatt, Hugh, 'How the Arts Are Promoted', in *The State and the Arts*, edited by John Pick (Eastbourne: John Offord, 1980), pp. 21–46

Williams Goldhagen, Sarah, 'Something to Talk About: modernism, discourse, style', *Journal of the Society of Architectural Historians* 64, no. 2 (June 2005), pp. 144–67

Witts, Richard, *Artist Unknown: an Alternative History of the Arts Council* (London: Warner, 1998)

Worthington, Clifford, *The Influence of the Cinema on Contemporary Auditorium Design* (London: Isaac Pitman, 1952)

York, Richard, 'Attenborough Centre for the Creative Arts', *Sightline* 39, no. 2 (Summer 2016), pp. 7–17

Ziegler, Philip, *Olivier* (London: Maclehose, 2013)

5. UNPUBLISHED PAPERS AND THESES

Calder, Barnabas, 'Committees and Concrete: the genesis and architecture of Denys Lasdun's National Theatre', PhD diss., University of Cambridge, 2007

Cox, Elspeth and Peter Longman, 'History of The Theatres Trust', 2008 typescript, copy supplied by The Theatres Trust

Darling, Elizabeth, 'Spaces of Citizenship in Inter-war England', paper presented to the 'Architecture, Citizenship, Space' conference, Oxford, 15 June 2017

Fair, Alistair, 'British Theatres, 1926–1991: an architectural history', PhD diss., University of Cambridge, 2008

Fenton, Clive, 'Appleton's Architects: Building the University of Edinburgh (1949–65)', PhD diss., University of Edinburgh, 2002

Harwood, Elain, '"Reviving a great sector of London to the benefit of the community": the London County Council's rebuilding of the South Bank as a cultural quarter, 1945–76', PhD diss., University of Bristol, 2009

Iles, Paul, 'Issues in Theatrical Management: Howard and Wyndham and the evolution of the British touring circuit', MPhil diss., University of Glasgow, 1997

6. WEBSITES

Archives Hub catalogue of the papers of Sir Philip Robert Morris, <http://archiveshub.ac.uk/data/gb3-dm588> (accessed 14 December 2015)

BBC News, 'National Theatre Architect Dies', 12 January 2001, <http://news.bbc.co.uk/1/hi/uk/1113298.stm> (accessed 7 July 2017)

Brandt, George, 'Glynne Wickham', *Guardian*, 25 February 2004, <http://www.theguardian.com/news/2004/feb/25/guardianobituaries.highereducation> (accessed 14 December 2015)

Burrows, David, *The Life and Work of Richard Negri*, online book at <www.richardnegri.co.uk> (accessed 6 July 2017)

Century Theatre, <www.centurytheatre.co.uk/history> (accessed 6 July 2017)

Chapter Arts, <http://www.chapter.org> (accessed 6 July 2017)

Cinema Treasures, 'Hornchurch Theatre', <http://cinematreasures.org/theaters/30243> (accessed 20 June 2017)

Focus: the News Magazine of the University of Surrey, November 1969, <http://www.sussex.ac.uk/internal/bulletin/downloads/1960-1969/1969/November/196911.pdf> (accessed 24 June 2017)

Iles, Paul, 'Towards the Prevention of a Theatre Demolition', text of 2002, <http://www.laughingaudience.co.uk/billingham_forum_theatre.html> (accessed 10 March 2017)

Linklater, N. V., 'Obituary: Hugh Willatt', *Independent*, 18 November 1996, <http://www.independent.co.uk/incoming/obituary-sir-hugh-willatt-1353029.html> (accessed 27 January 2017)

National Heritage List for England, <http://historicengland.org.uk/listing/the-list> (accessed 7 July 2017)

North Lanarkshire Council, history of Motherwell Theatre, <http://www.northlanarkshire.gov.uk/entertainment/index.aspx?articleid=22412> (accessed 5 June 2015)

Richard Southern archive information, <http://www.bristol.ac.uk/theatre-collection/explore/theatre/richard-southern-collection/> (accessed 24 June 2017)

Theatres Trust database, <http://www.database.theatrestrust.org.uk/> (accessed 17 October 2017)

White, Martin, 'Professor Glynne Wickham', *Independent*, 11 February 2004, <http://www.independent.co.uk/news/obituaries/professor-glynne-wickham-37973.html> (accessed 14 December 2015)

Index